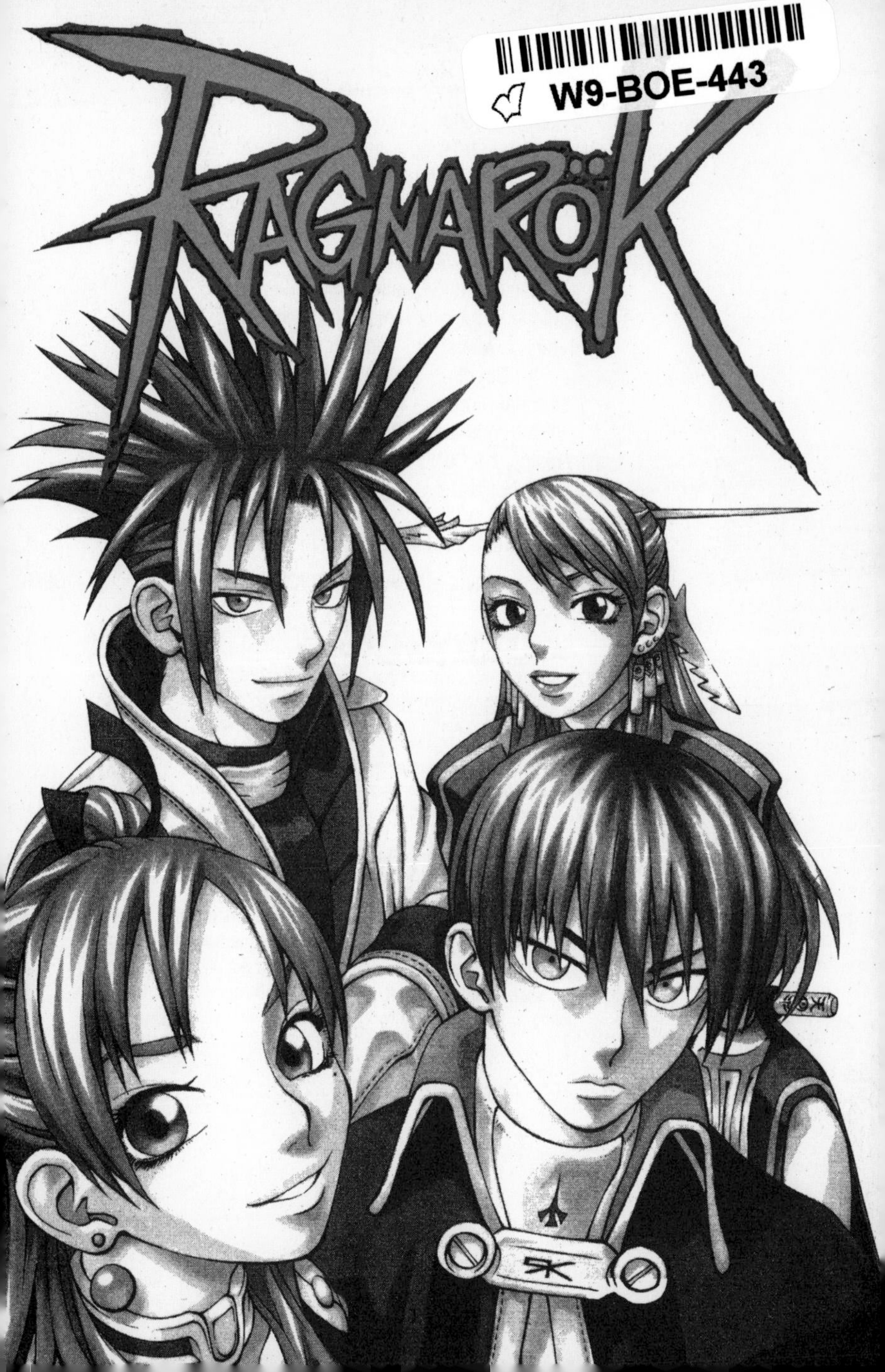
RAGNARÖK

Translator - Lauren Na
Copy Editor - Carol Fox
Retouch and Lettering - Jennifer Nunn
Cover Layout - Anna Kernbaum

Editor - Jake Forbes
Managing Editor - Jill Freshney
Production Coordinator - Antonio DePietro
Production Manager - Jennifer Miller
Art Director - Matt Alford
Editorial Director - Jeremy Ross
VP of Production - Ron Klamert
President & C.O.O. - John Parker
Publisher & C.E.O. - Stuart Levy

Email: editor@TOKYOPOP.com

Come visit us online at www.TOKYOPOP.com

A **TOKYOPOP** Manga
TOKYOPOP® is an imprint of Mixx Entertainment, Inc.
5900 Wilshire Blvd. Suite 2000, Los Angeles, CA 90036

ISBN: 1-59182-208-4

First TOKYOPOP® printing: January 2004

10 9 8 7 6 5 4 3 2 1
Printed in the USA

Volume 9:
Legacy of the Vanar

By
Myung-Jin Lee

English Version
by

Richard A. Knaak

Los Angeles • Tokyo • London

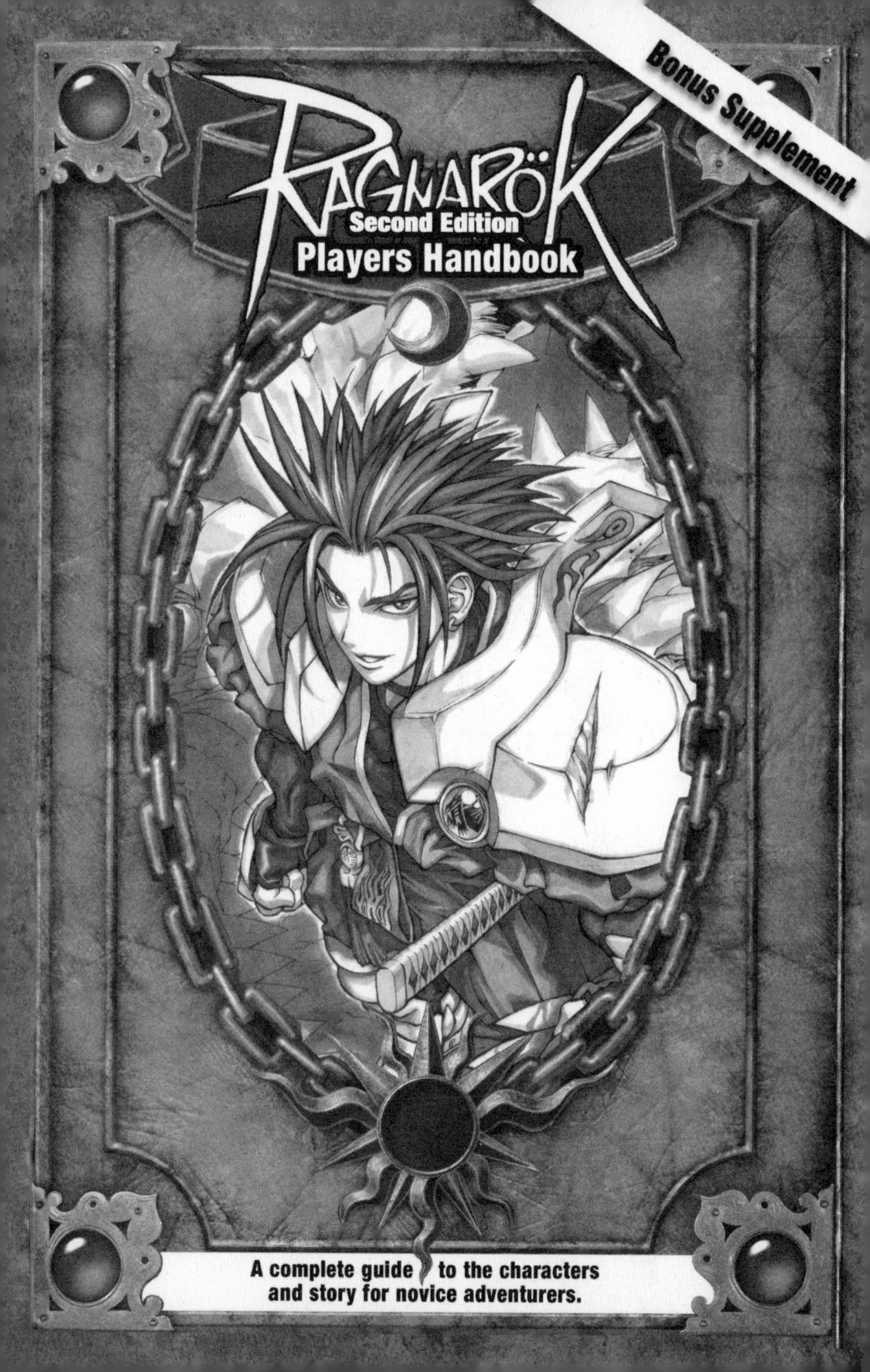
Bonus Supplement
RAGNARÖK
Second Edition
Players Handbook
A complete guide to the characters
and story for novice adventurers.

HEROES

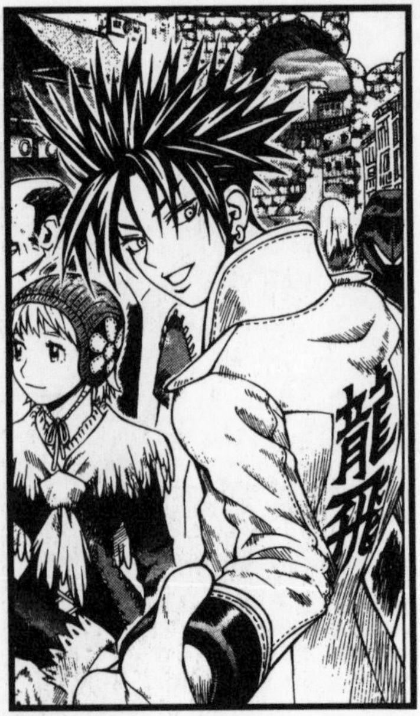
龍飛

NAME: Chaos
Class: Rune Knight (Dragon Knight?)
Level: 10
Alignment: Chaotic Good
STR: 17
DEX: 10
CON: 15
INT: 12
WIS: 14
CHR: 16

Equipment:
Vision- Enchanted sword- STR +2

Rune Armor- AC -4, 20% bonus saving throw vs. magical attacks.

Notes:
The reincarnation of the fallen god Balder, Chaos has been told by his divine mother, Frigg, that the fate of the world rests in his hands. He may also be tied to the legendary "Dragon Knights."

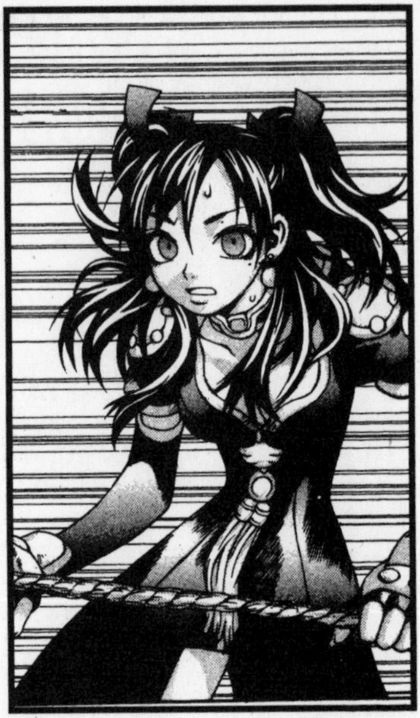

NAME: Iris Irine
Class: Cleric
Level: 6
Alignment: Lawful Good
STR: 7
DEX: 12
CON: 9
INT: 13
WIS: 16
CHR: 16

Equipment:
Chernryongdo- Enchanted dagger- STR +1, DEX +1, 1D4 damage if anyone but she touches it.

Pronteran Leather Armor- AC -3, DEX +1

Notes:
Iris would have become the new leader of the city of Fayon... that is, if it weren't destroyed by her sister, the Valkyrie Sara Irine. She now follows her close friend Chaos.

HEROES

NAME: Fenris Fenrir
Class: Warlock
Level: 10
Alignment: Neutral Good
STR: 14
DEX: 15
CON: 13
INT: 16
WIS: 12
CHR: 14

Equipment:
Psychic Medallion- Magic compass
which leads its bearer to whatever
his or her heart most desires.

Laevatein, Rod of Destruction- STR+1, extends
to staff on command.

Warrior's Hanbok- AC -4.
Notes:
The reincarnation of the Wolf God, Fenris
helped Chaos to realize his identity. She now
follows him on his quest.

NAME: Loki
Class: Assassin
Level: 10
Alignment: Lawful Neutral
STR:14
DEX: 18
CON: 12
INT: 12
WIS: 14
CHR: 10

Equipment:
Sword of Shadows- + 4 to hit, damage +2

Bone Armor- AC -5, STR +2

Notes:
Greatest of the Assassins, Loki's anonym-
ity is a testament to his skill at going
unseen. An enigma himself, his curiosity
and respect for the even more mysterious
Chaos caused him to join the Rune Knight
for as long as they follow the same road.

HEROES

ENEMIES

NAME: Lidia
Class: Thief
Level: 3
Alignment: Neutral Good
STR: 8
DEX: 15
INT: 13
WIS: 10
CHR: 15

Equipment:
Treasure Hunter's Bible- 50% chance of identifying magical items

Follower; Sessy, Cat o' Two Tails- +50% saving throw to pick pockets

Notes:
An "expert treasure hunter" by trade, Lidia "borrows" whatever she can get her hands on while she looks for bigger hauls. She was last seen leaving the city of Prontera. She's currently en route to Geffen in search of the treasures of Alfheim.

NAME: Skurai
Class: Cursed Prosecutor
Level: 12
Alignment: Chaotic Evil
STR: 17
DEX: 16
CON: 19
INT: 15
WIS: 8
CHR: 12

Equipment:
Talatsu- Cursed sword- STR+2, HP +12- cannot be discarded unless it tastes the blood it is looking for.

Notes:
Skurai follows the will of his sword, Talatsu, that seeks the one blood that will quench its thirst. He has an enormous bounty on his head.

The Story so far...

The Heart of Ymir, taken by the rogue Valkyrie Sara Irine from the city of Prontera, was just one shard of many. The second shard is said to be located in Shwarzwaard, far to the north.

After a quick respite and a change of costume, Chaos, Iris and the rest of the team booked passage to Shwarzwaard via a Sky Ship. Their journey was running smoothly until Wyverns, sent by the Valkyrie Zenobia, destroyed the ship half way along its course. Now our heroes are stranded in Geffen, City of Magic, during the annual Festival of Magic. In order to win transport out of the city, Fenris has enrolled to compete in the arcane arena while the others look on anxiously. Let the games begin!

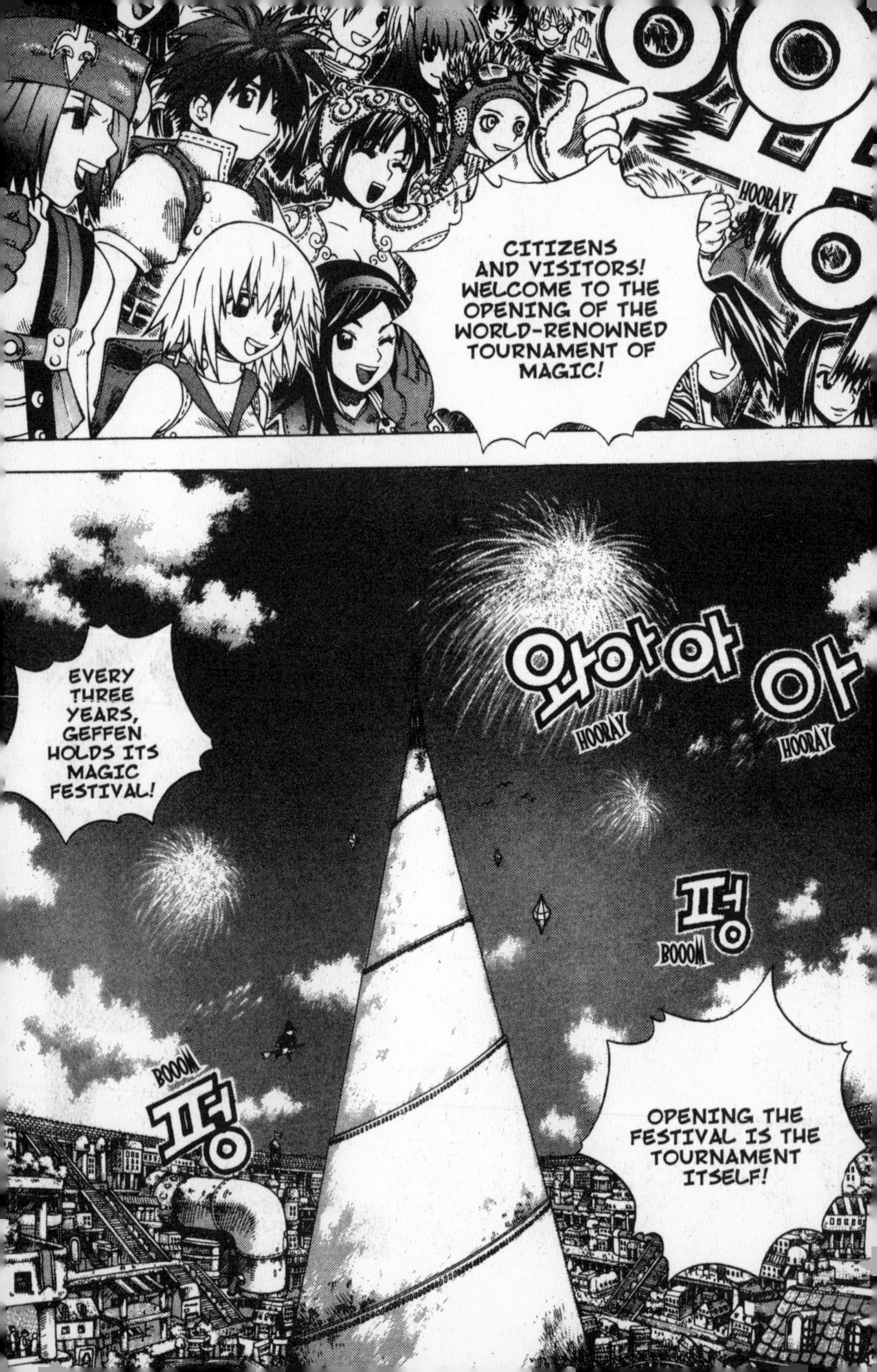

HOORAY!
CITIZENS AND VISITORS! WELCOME TO THE OPENING OF THE WORLD-RENOWNED TOURNAMENT OF MAGIC!
EVERY THREE YEARS, GEFFEN HOLDS ITS MAGIC FESTIVAL!
와아아 아
HOORAY
HOORAY
펑
BOOOM
BOOOM
펑
OPENING THE FESTIVAL IS THE TOURNAMENT ITSELF!

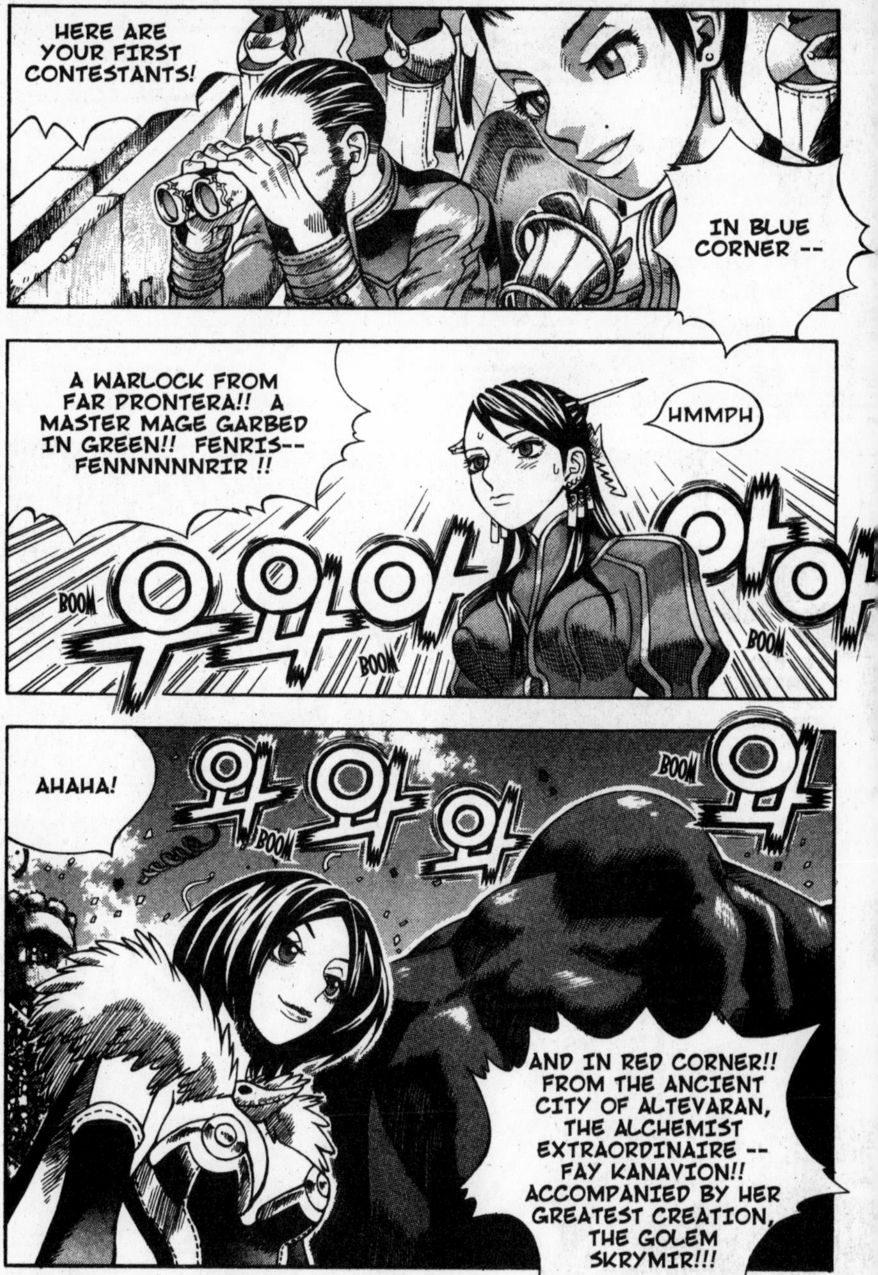
HERE ARE YOUR FIRST CONTESTANTS!
IN BLUE CORNER --
A WARLOCK FROM FAR PRONTERA!! A MASTER MAGE GARBED IN GREEN!! FENRIS-- FENNNNNNNRIR !!
HMMPH
우와아
BOOM
BOOM
BOOM
AHAHA!
와와와와
BOOM
BOOM
AND IN RED CORNER!! FROM THE ANCIENT CITY OF ALTEVARAN, THE ALCHEMIST EXTRAORDINAIRE -- FAY KANAVION!! ACCOMPANIED BY HER GREATEST CREATION, THE GOLEM SKRYMIR!!!

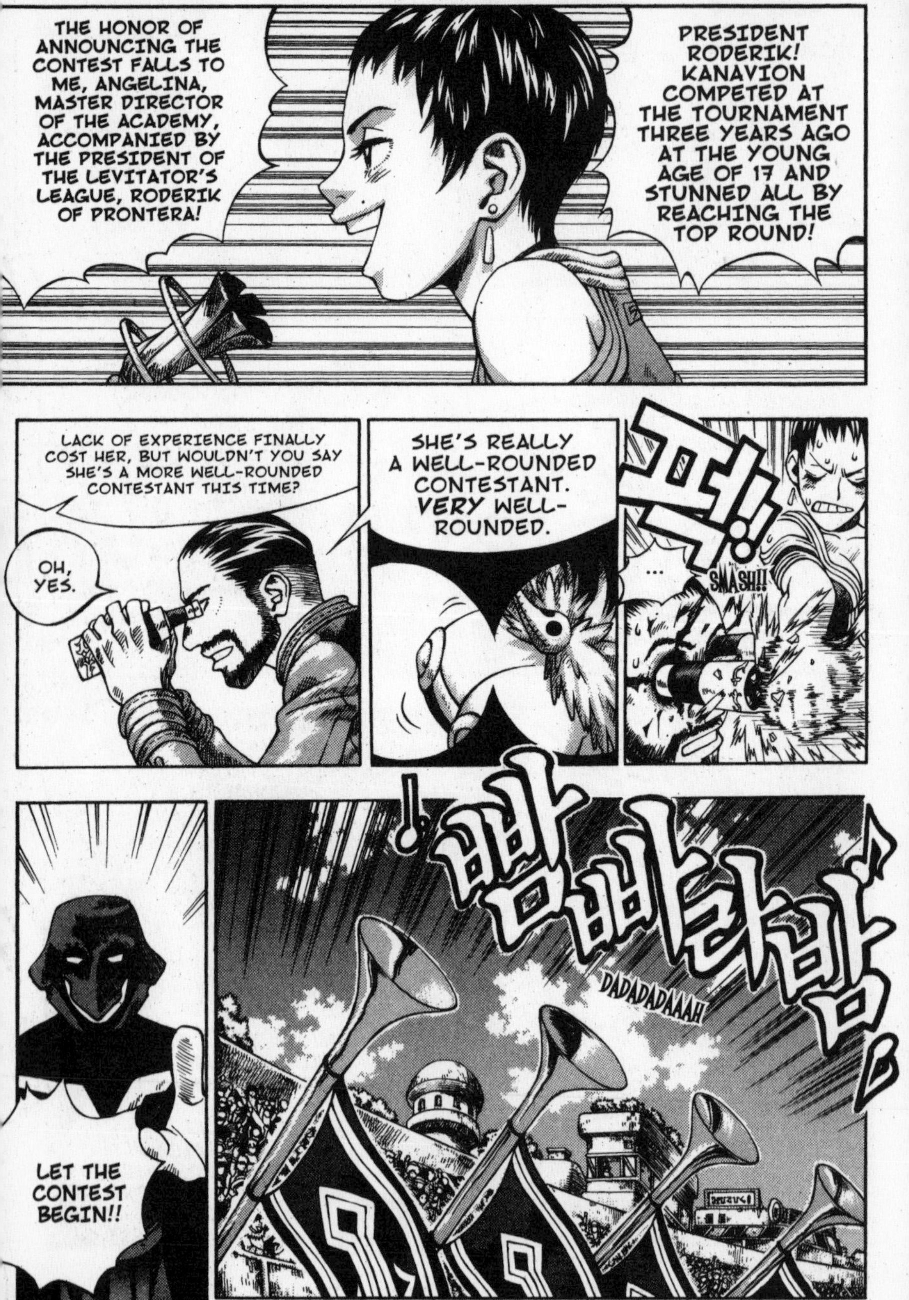

THE HONOR OF ANNOUNCING THE CONTEST FALLS TO ME, ANGELINA, MASTER DIRECTOR OF THE ACADEMY, ACCOMPANIED BY THE PRESIDENT OF THE LEVITATOR'S LEAGUE, RODERIK OF PRONTERA!
PRESIDENT RODERIK! KANAVION COMPETED AT THE TOURNAMENT THREE YEARS AGO AT THE YOUNG AGE OF 17 AND STUNNED ALL BY REACHING THE TOP ROUND!
LACK OF EXPERIENCE FINALLY COST HER, BUT WOULDN'T YOU SAY SHE'S A MORE WELL-ROUNDED CONTESTANT THIS TIME?
OH, YES.
SHE'S REALLY A WELL-ROUNDED CONTESTANT. *VERY* WELL-ROUNDED.
퍽!!
...
SMASH!!
LET THE CONTEST BEGIN!!
DADADADAAAH

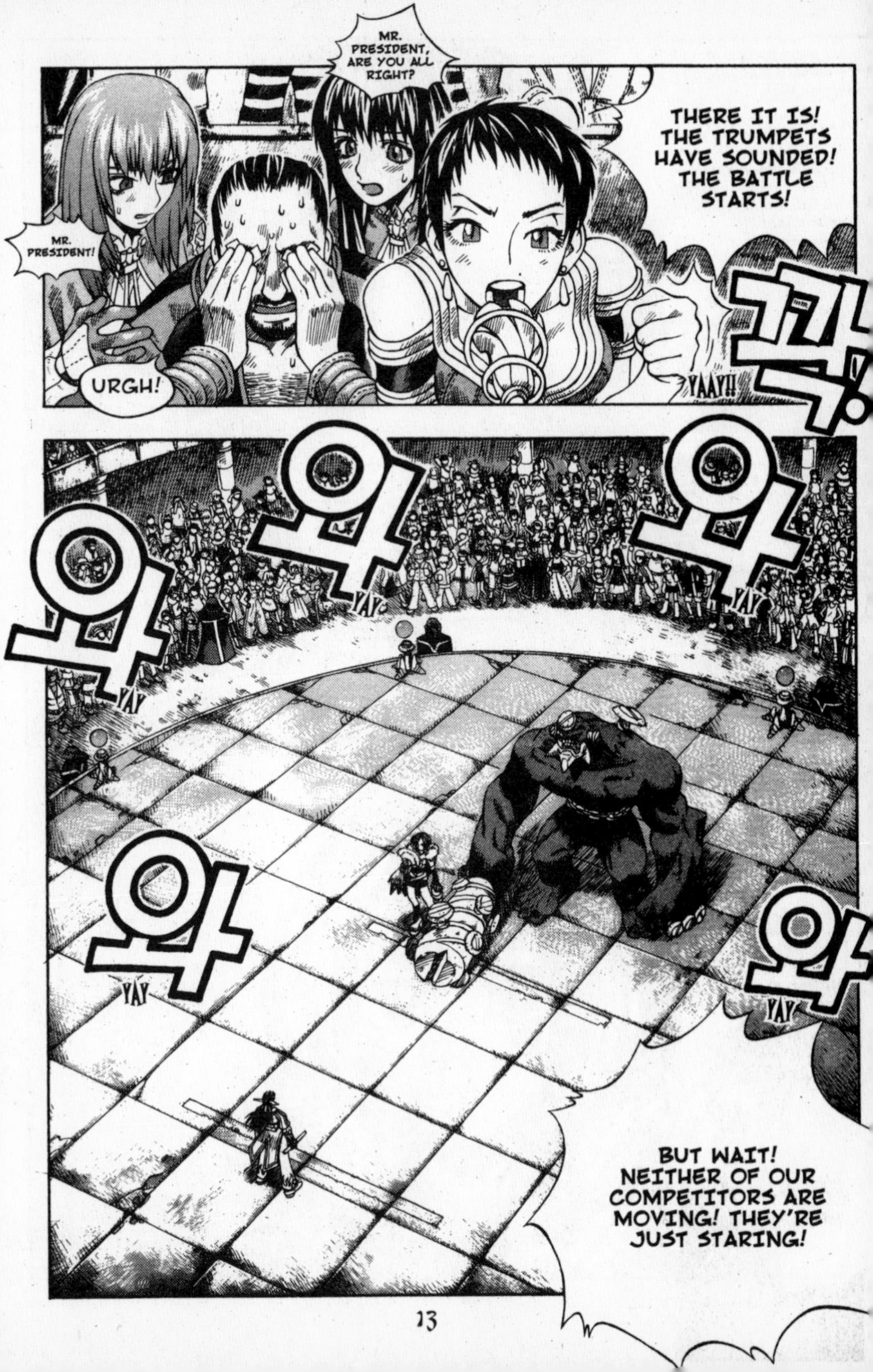
MR. PRESIDENT, ARE YOU ALL RIGHT?
THERE IT IS! THE TRUMPETS HAVE SOUNDED! THE BATTLE STARTS!
MR. PRESIDENT!
URGH!
YAAY!!
와
와
와
YAY
YAY
YAY
와
와
YAY
YAY
BUT WAIT! NEITHER OF OUR COMPETITORS ARE MOVING! THEY'RE JUST STARING!

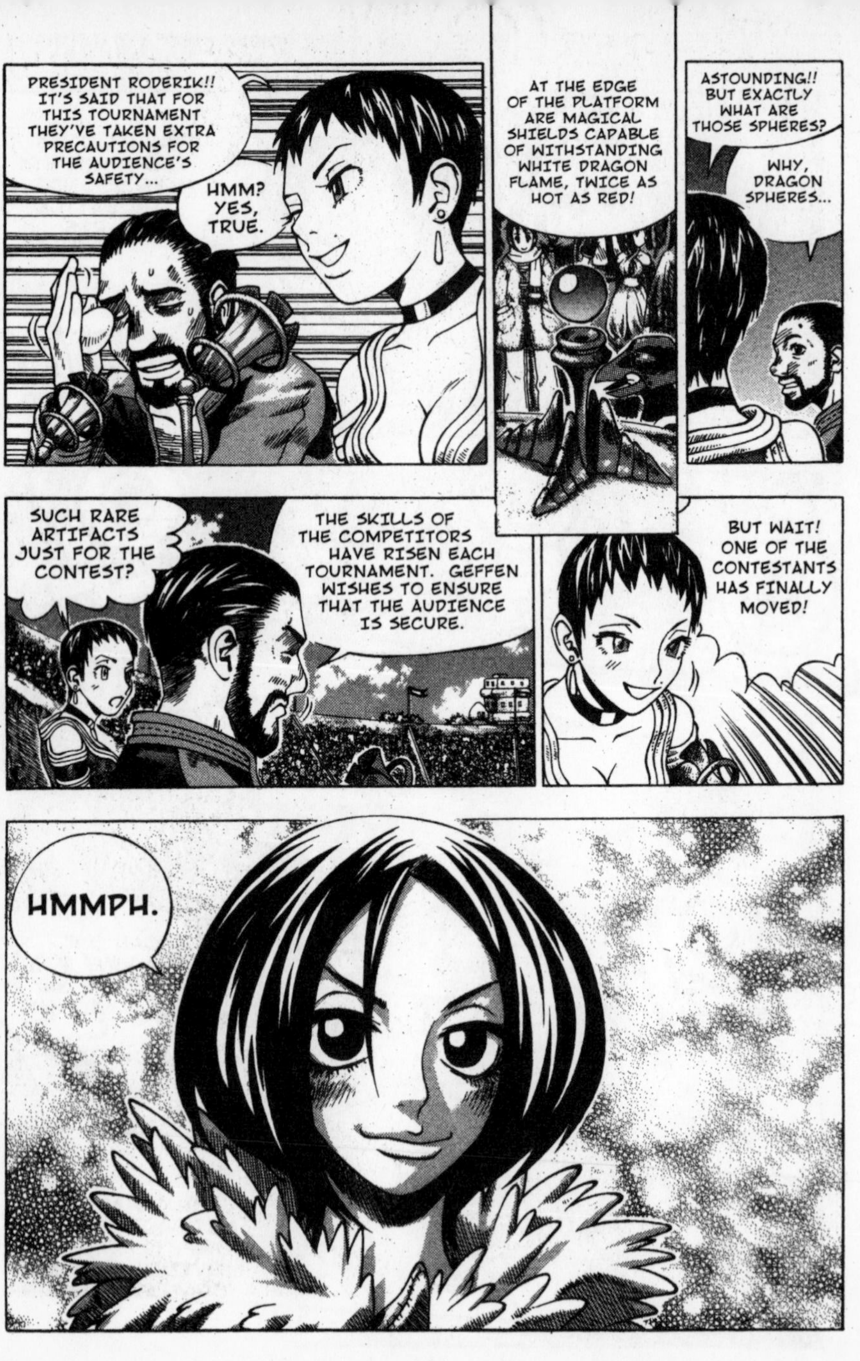
PRESIDENT RODERIK!! IT'S SAID THAT FOR THIS TOURNAMENT THEY'VE TAKEN EXTRA PRECAUTIONS FOR THE AUDIENCE'S SAFETY...
HMM? YES, TRUE.
AT THE EDGE OF THE PLATFORM ARE MAGICAL SHIELDS CAPABLE OF WITHSTANDING WHITE DRAGON FLAME, TWICE AS HOT AS RED!
ASTOUNDING!! BUT EXACTLY WHAT ARE THOSE SPHERES?
WHY, DRAGON SPHERES...
SUCH RARE ARTIFACTS JUST FOR THE CONTEST?
THE SKILLS OF THE COMPETITORS HAVE RISEN EACH TOURNAMENT. GEFFEN WISHES TO ENSURE THAT THE AUDIENCE IS SECURE.
BUT WAIT! ONE OF THE CONTESTANTS HAS FINALLY MOVED!
HMMPH.

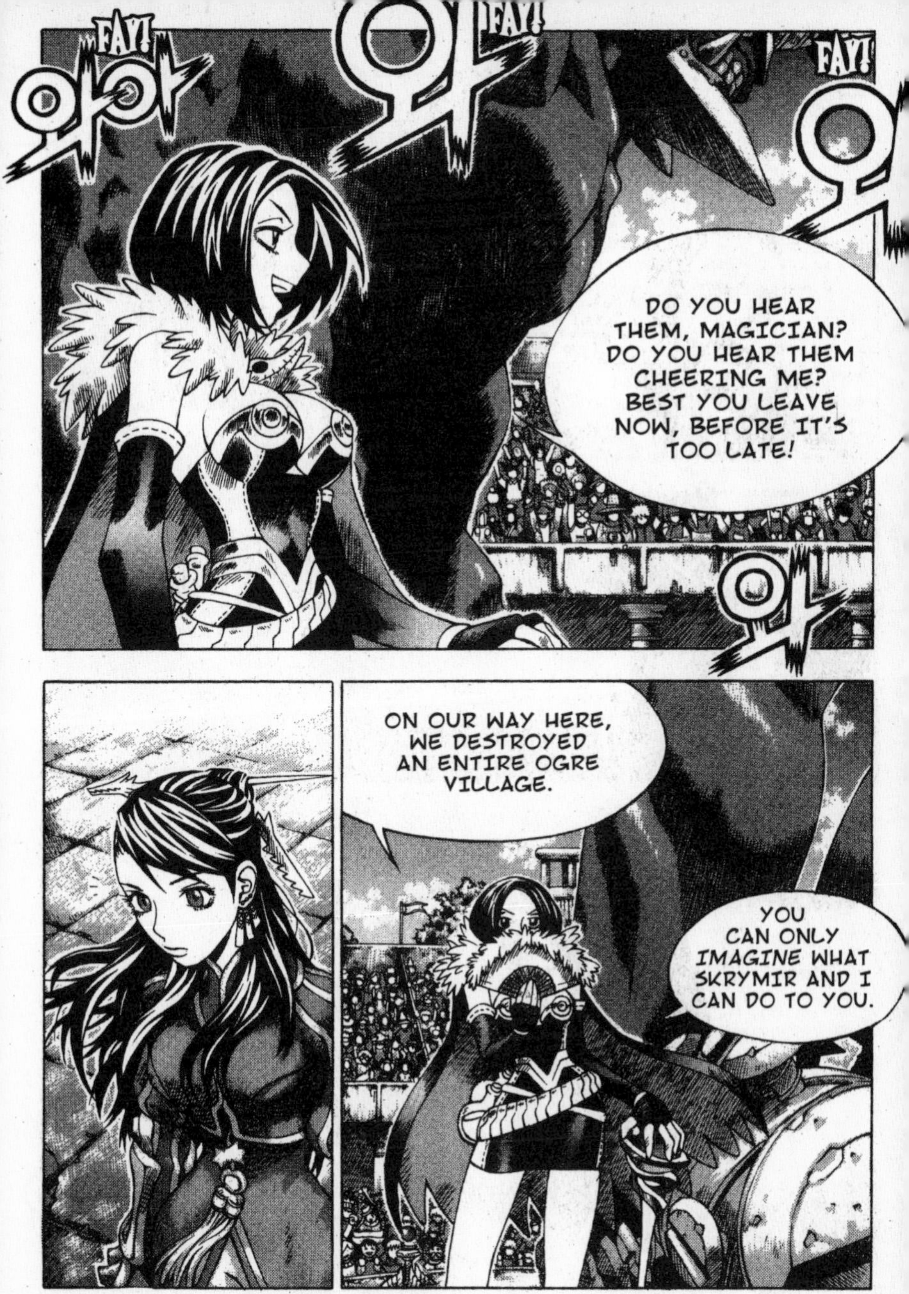
FAY!
FAY!
FAY!
DO YOU HEAR THEM, MAGICIAN? DO YOU HEAR THEM CHEERING ME? BEST YOU LEAVE NOW, BEFORE IT'S TOO LATE!
ON OUR WAY HERE, WE DESTROYED AN ENTIRE OGRE VILLAGE.
YOU CAN ONLY IMAGINE WHAT SKRYMIR AND I CAN DO TO YOU.

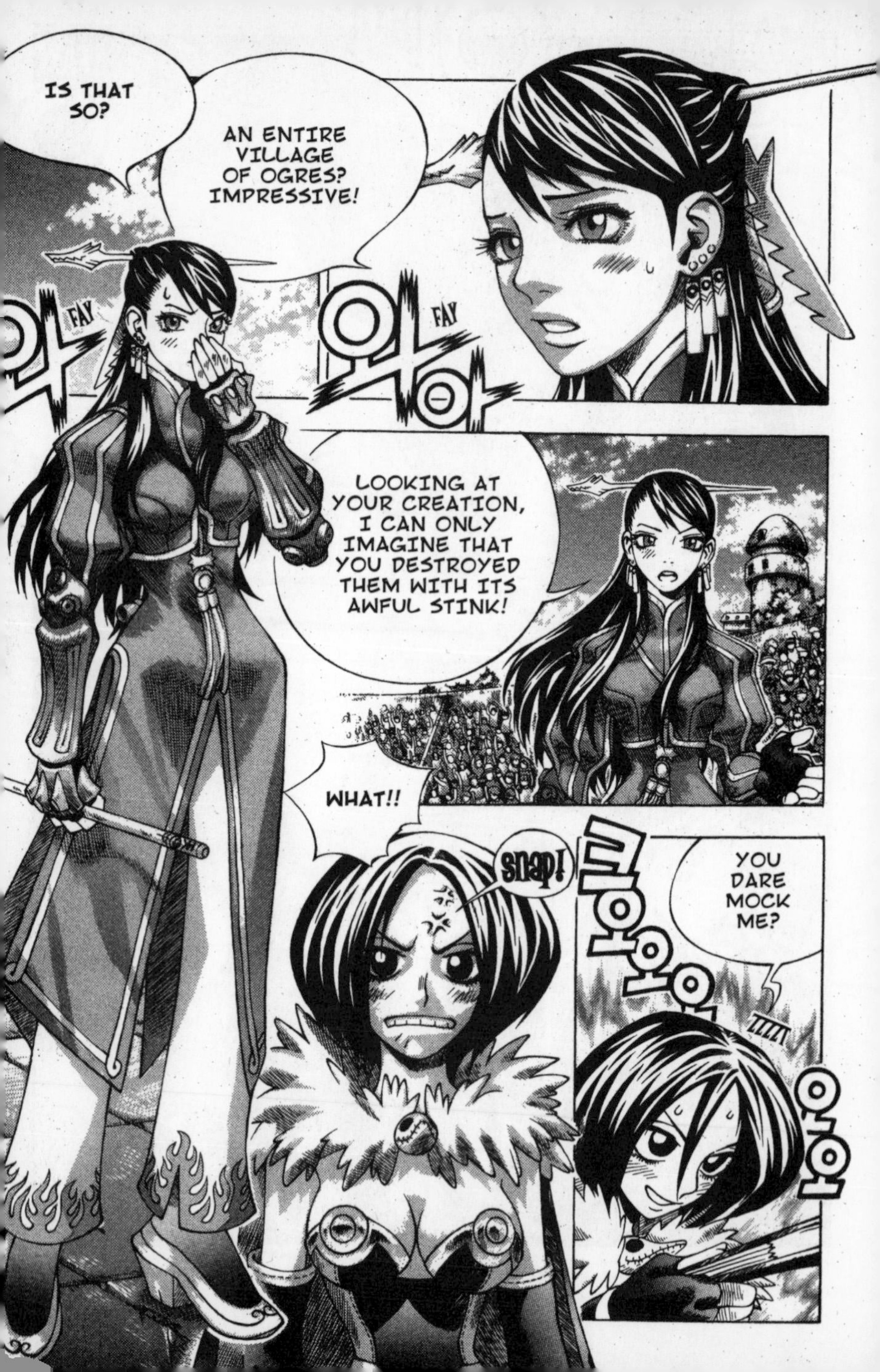
IS THAT SO?
AN ENTIRE VILLAGE OF OGRES? IMPRESSIVE!
FAY
FAY
LOOKING AT YOUR CREATION, I CAN ONLY IMAGINE THAT YOU DESTROYED THEM WITH ITS AWFUL STINK!
WHAT!!
snap!
YOU DARE MOCK ME?

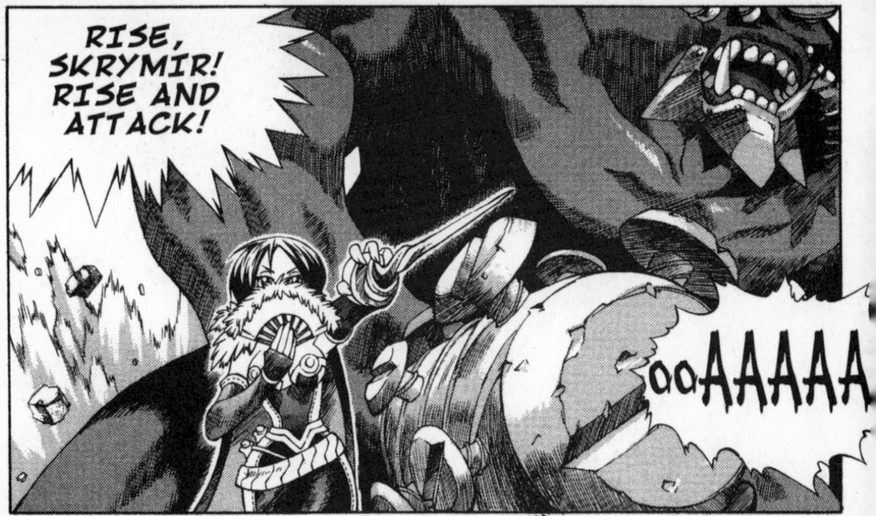
RISE, SKRYMIR! RISE AND ATTACK!
aaAAAAA

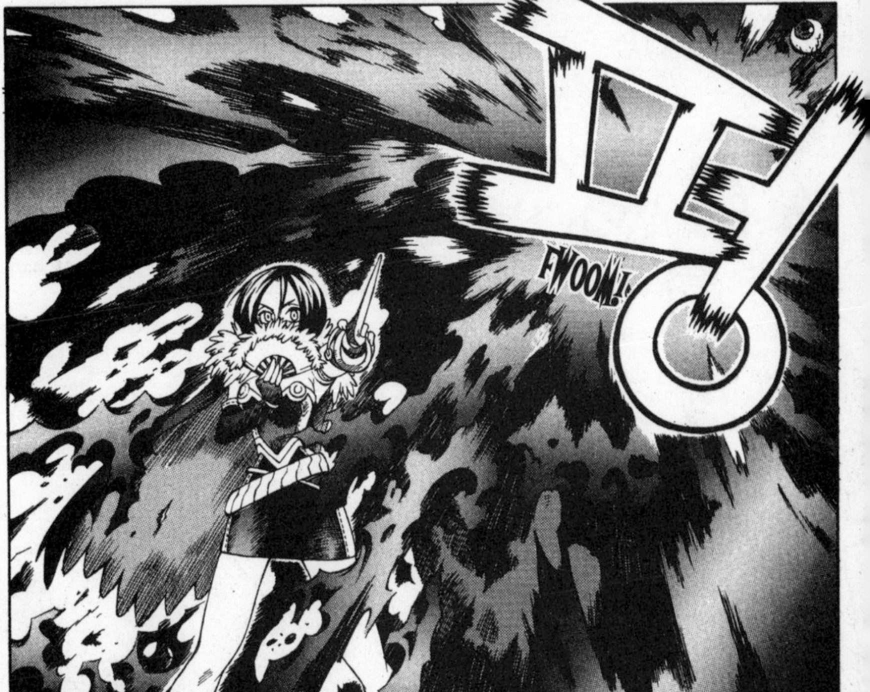
FWOOM!!

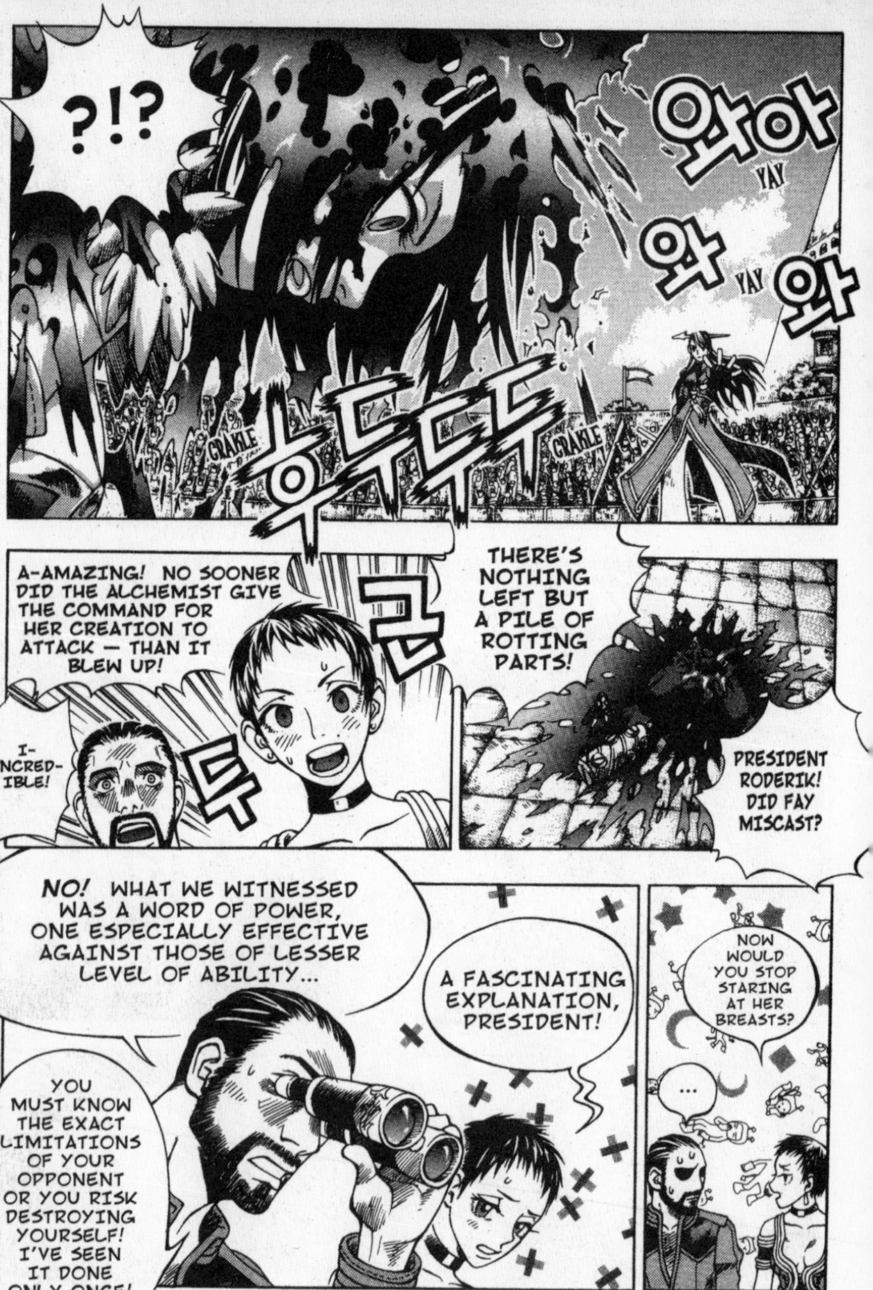

?!?
와아
YAY
와
YAY
와
CRAKLE
CRAKLE
A-AMAZING! NO SOONER DID THE ALCHEMIST GIVE THE COMMAND FOR HER CREATION TO ATTACK — THAN IT BLEW UP!
I-INCRED-IBLE!
THERE'S NOTHING LEFT BUT A PILE OF ROTTING PARTS!
PRESIDENT RODERIK! DID FAY MISCAST?
NO! WHAT WE WITNESSED WAS A WORD OF POWER, ONE ESPECIALLY EFFECTIVE AGAINST THOSE OF LESSER LEVEL OF ABILITY...
YOU MUST KNOW THE EXACT LIMITATIONS OF YOUR OPPONENT OR YOU RISK DESTROYING YOURSELF! I'VE SEEN IT DONE ONLY ONCE!
A FASCINATING EXPLANATION, PRESIDENT!
NOW WOULD YOU STOP STARING AT HER BREASTS?
...

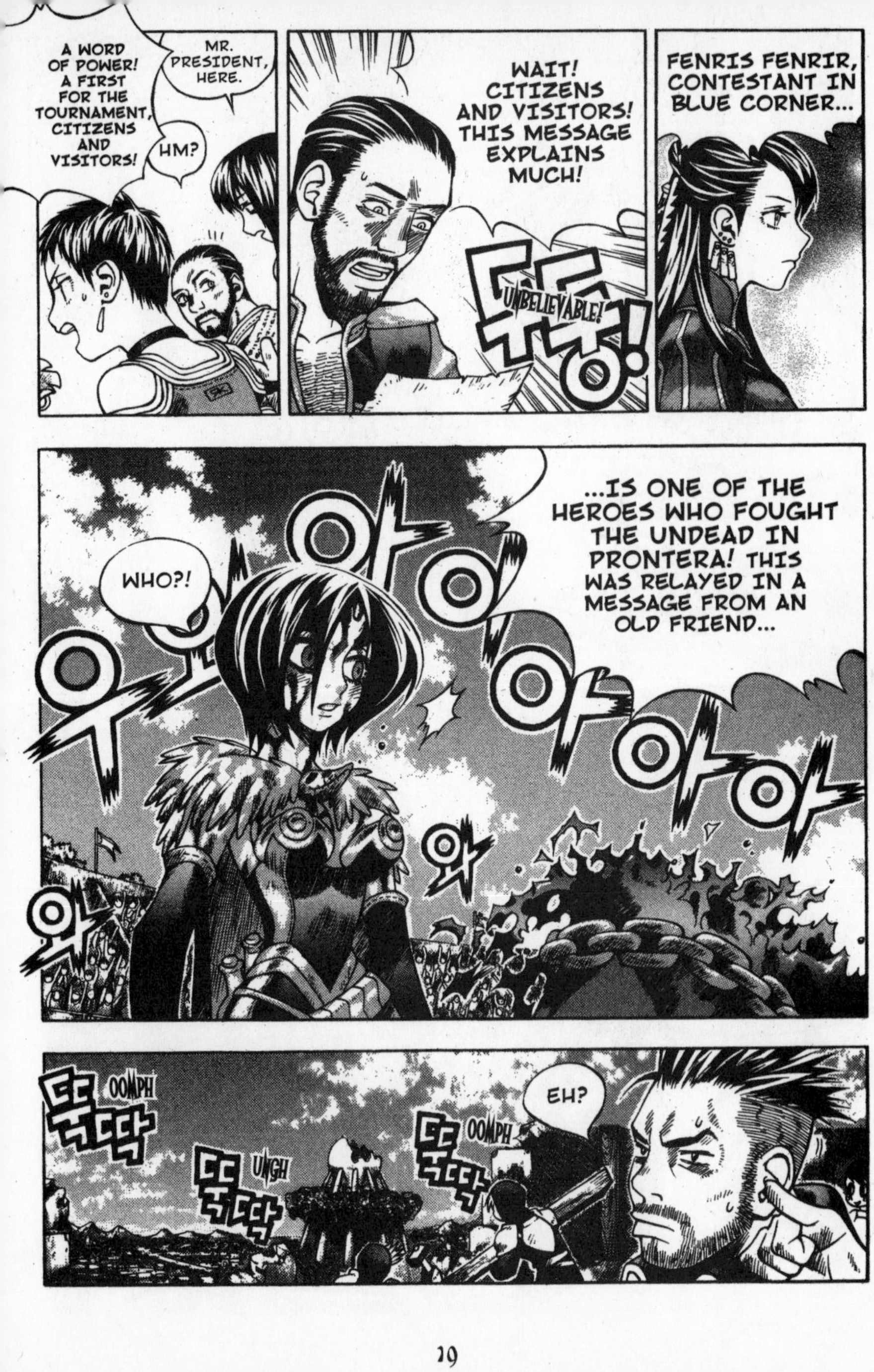
A WORD OF POWER! A FIRST FOR THE TOURNAMENT, CITIZENS AND VISITORS!
MR. PRESIDENT, HERE.
HM?
WAIT! CITIZENS AND VISITORS! THIS MESSAGE EXPLAINS MUCH!
UNBELIEVABLE!
FENRIS FENRIR, CONTESTANT IN BLUE CORNER...
...IS ONE OF THE HEROES WHO FOUGHT THE UNDEAD IN PRONTERA! THIS WAS RELAYED IN A MESSAGE FROM AN OLD FRIEND...
WHO?!
OOMPH
UNGH
OOMPH
EH?

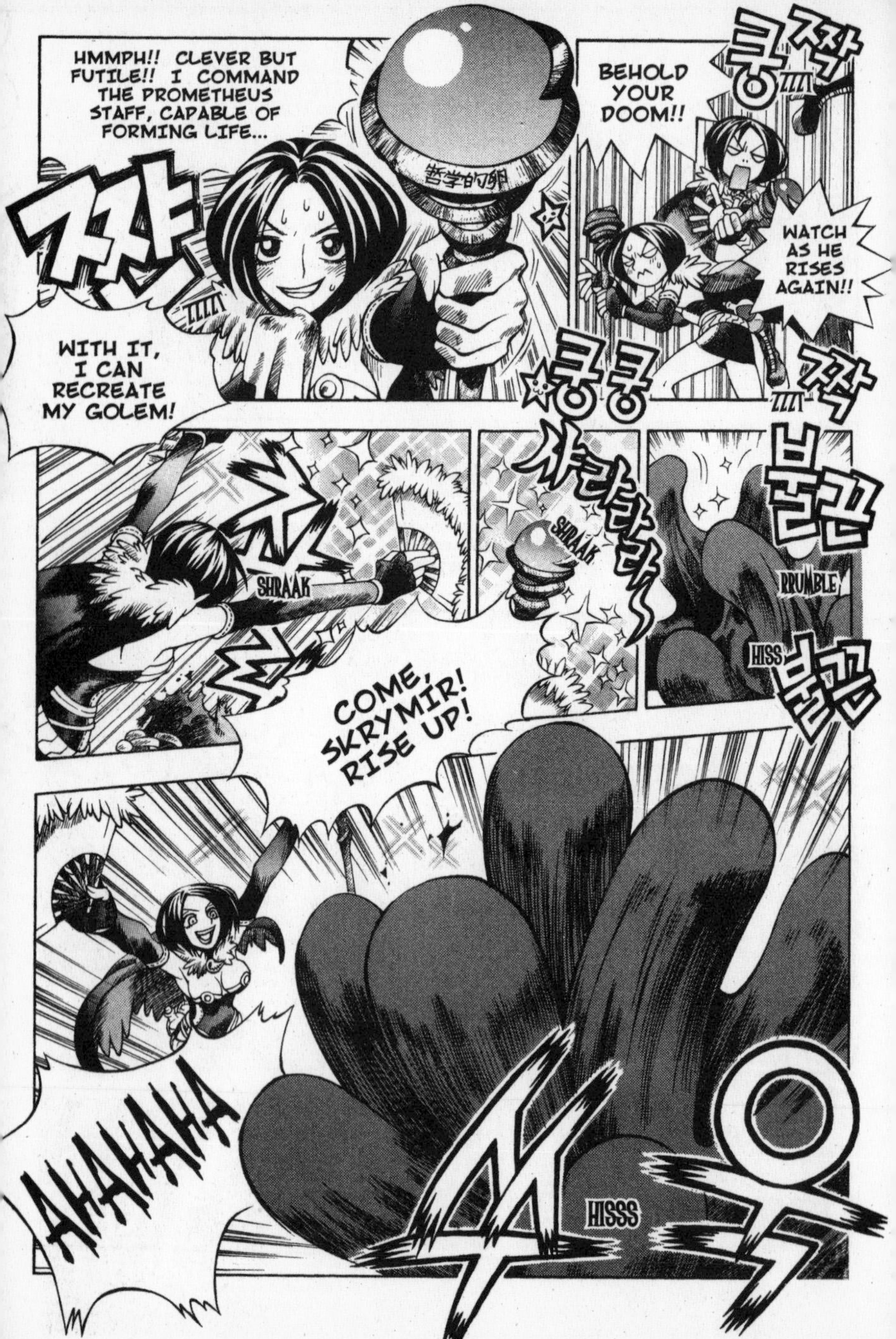
HMMPH!! CLEVER BUT FUTILE!! I COMMAND THE PROMETHEUS STAFF, CAPABLE OF FORMING LIFE...
WITH IT, I CAN RECREATE MY GOLEM!
BEHOLD YOUR DOOM!!
WATCH AS HE RISES AGAIN!!
SHRAAK
SHRAAK
RRUMBLE
HISS
COME, SKRYMIR! RISE UP!
AHAHAHA
HISSS

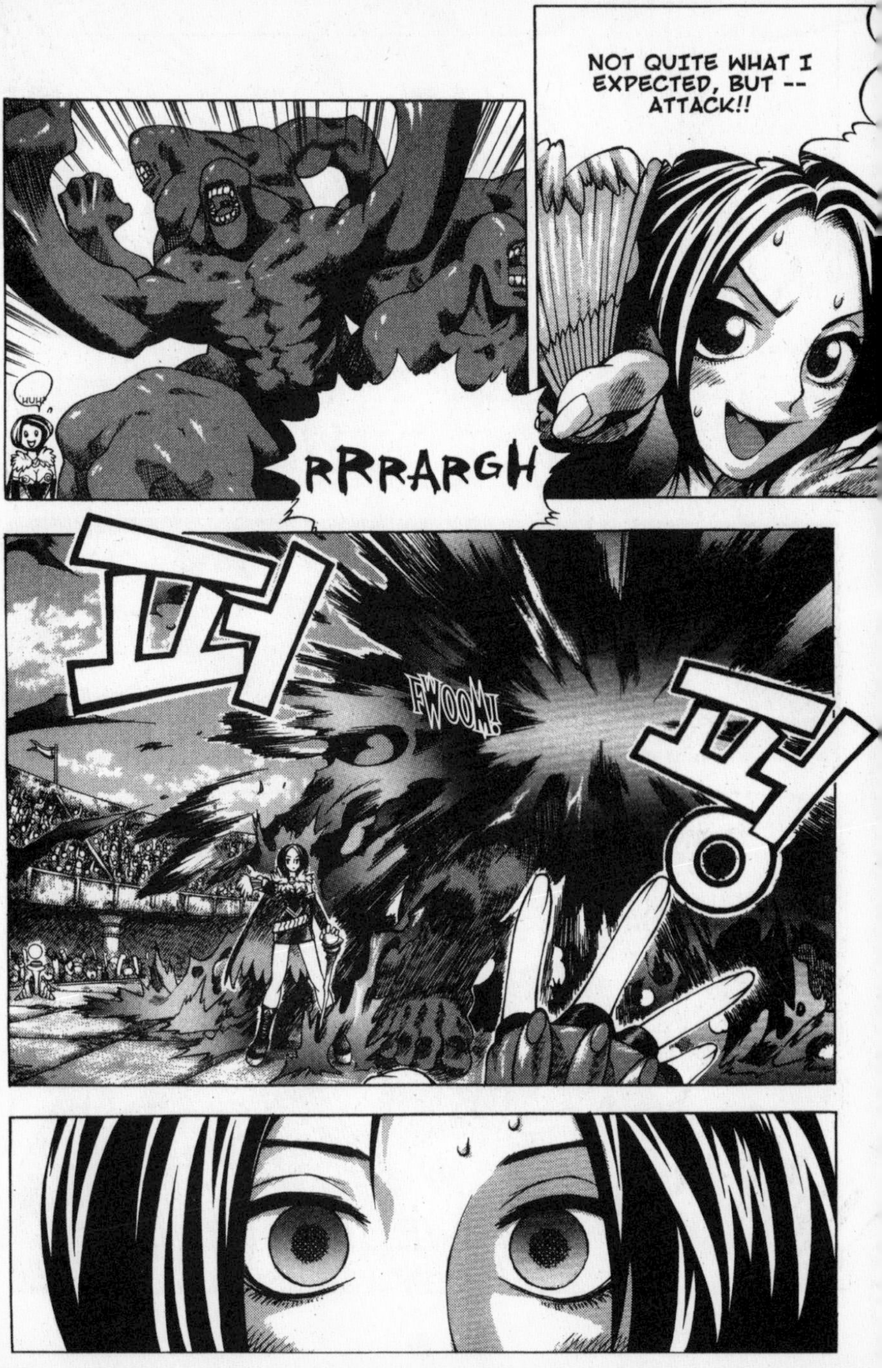
NOT QUITE WHAT I EXPECTED, BUT -- ATTACK!!
HUH?
RRRARGH
FWOOM!

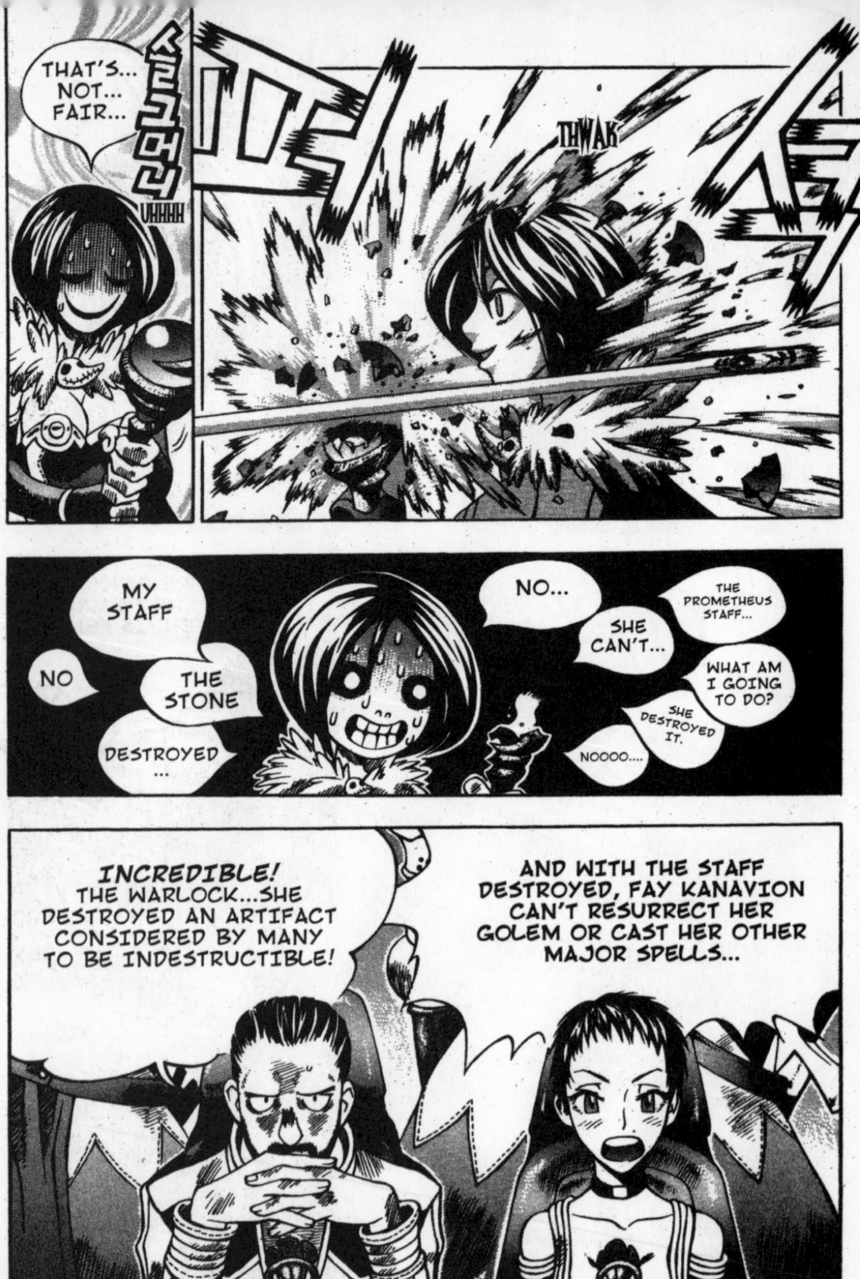
THAT'S... NOT... FAIR...
으흐흐흐
UHHHH
THWAK
MY STAFF
NO
THE STONE
DESTROYED ...
NO...
SHE CAN'T...
THE PROMETHEUS STAFF...
WHAT AM I GOING TO DO?
SHE DESTROYED IT.
NOOOO....
INCREDIBLE! THE WARLOCK...SHE DESTROYED AN ARTIFACT CONSIDERED BY MANY TO BE INDESTRUCTIBLE!
AND WITH THE STAFF DESTROYED, FAY KANAVION CAN'T RESURRECT HER GOLEM OR CAST HER OTHER MAJOR SPELLS...

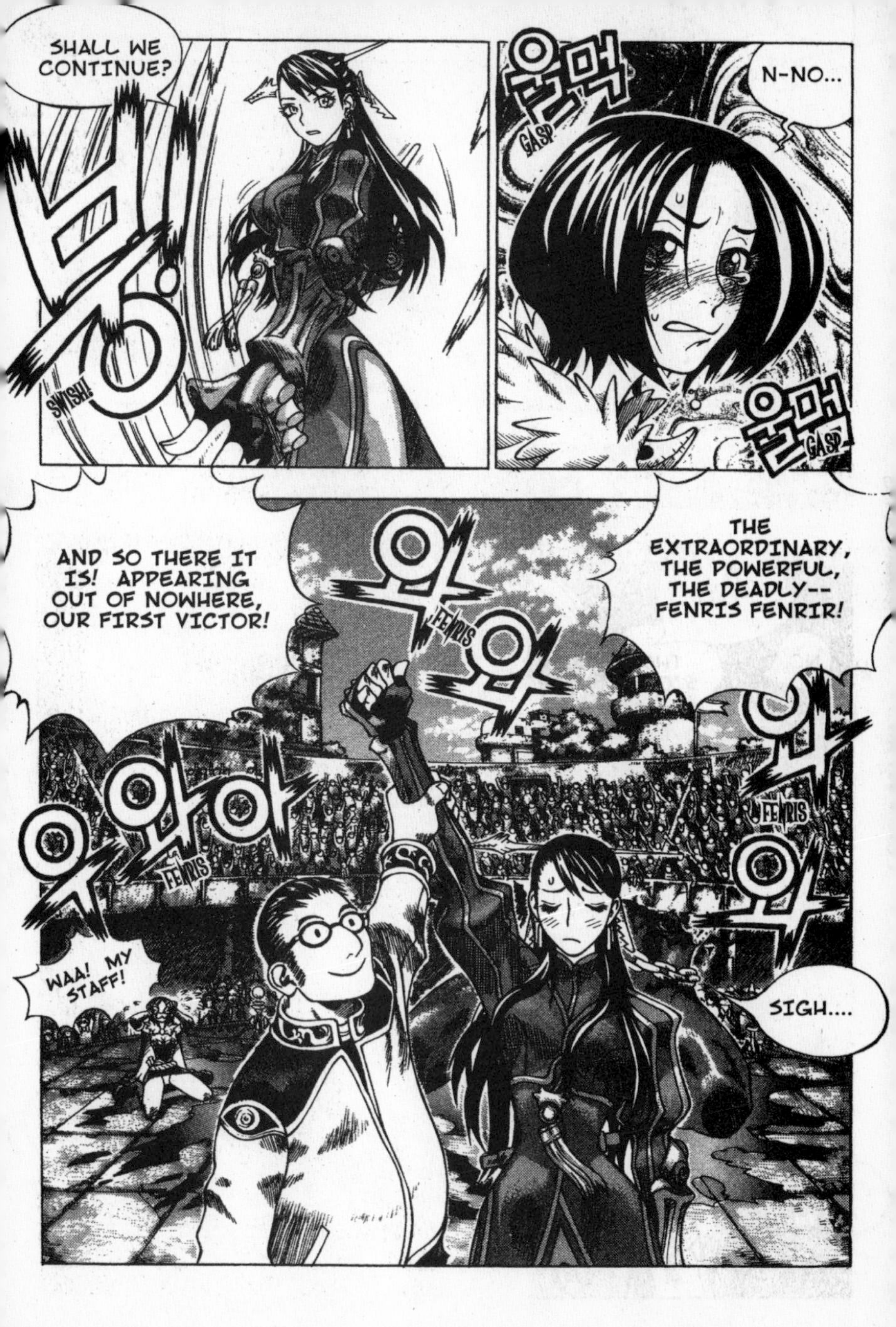
SHALL WE CONTINUE?
SWISH!
N-NO...
GASP
GASP
AND SO THERE IT IS! APPEARING OUT OF NOWHERE, OUR FIRST VICTOR!
THE EXTRAORDINARY, THE POWERFUL, THE DEADLY-- FENRIS FENRIR!
FENRIS
FENRIS
FENRIS
FENRIS
WAA! MY STAFF!
SIGH....

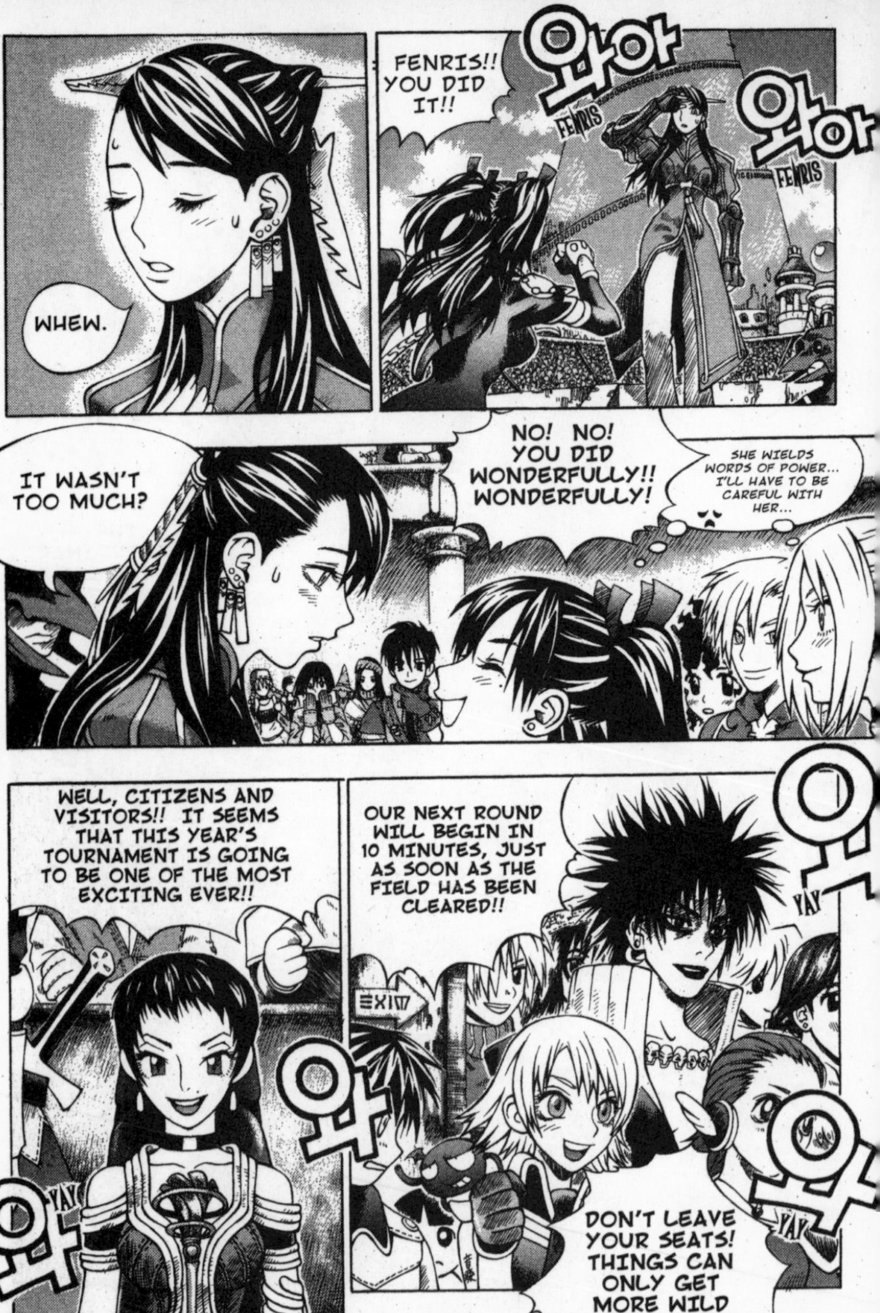
WHEW.
FENRIS!! YOU DID IT!!
와아
FENRIS
와아
FENRIS
IT WASN'T TOO MUCH?
NO! NO! YOU DID WONDERFULLY!! WONDERFULLY!
SHE WIELDS WORDS OF POWER... I'LL HAVE TO BE CAREFUL WITH HER...
WELL, CITIZENS AND VISITORS!! IT SEEMS THAT THIS YEAR'S TOURNAMENT IS GOING TO BE ONE OF THE MOST EXCITING EVER!!
와
YAY
OUR NEXT ROUND WILL BEGIN IN 10 MINUTES, JUST AS SOON AS THE FIELD HAS BEEN CLEARED!!
와
YAY
EXIT
와
YAY
DON'T LEAVE YOUR SEATS! THINGS CAN ONLY GET MORE WILD FROM HERE!

RAGNAROK
라그나로크
IN TO THE ABYSS

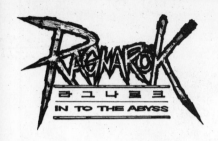

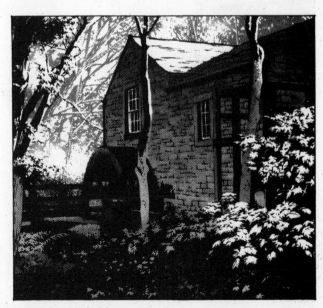

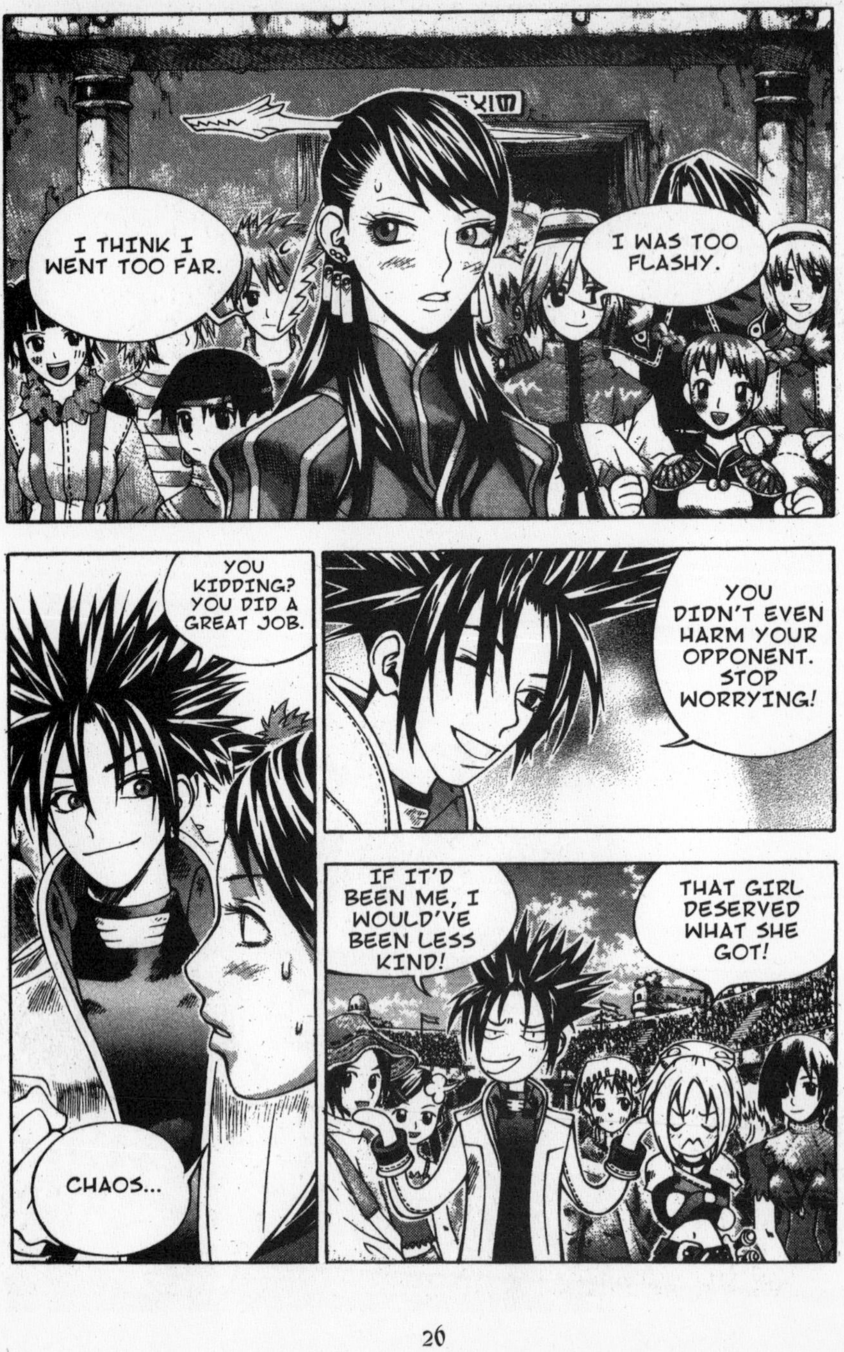
I THINK I WENT TOO FAR.
I WAS TOO FLASHY.
YOU KIDDING? YOU DID A GREAT JOB.
CHAOS...
YOU DIDN'T EVEN HARM YOUR OPPONENT. STOP WORRYING!
IF IT'D BEEN ME, I WOULD'VE BEEN LESS KIND!
THAT GIRL DESERVED WHAT SHE GOT!

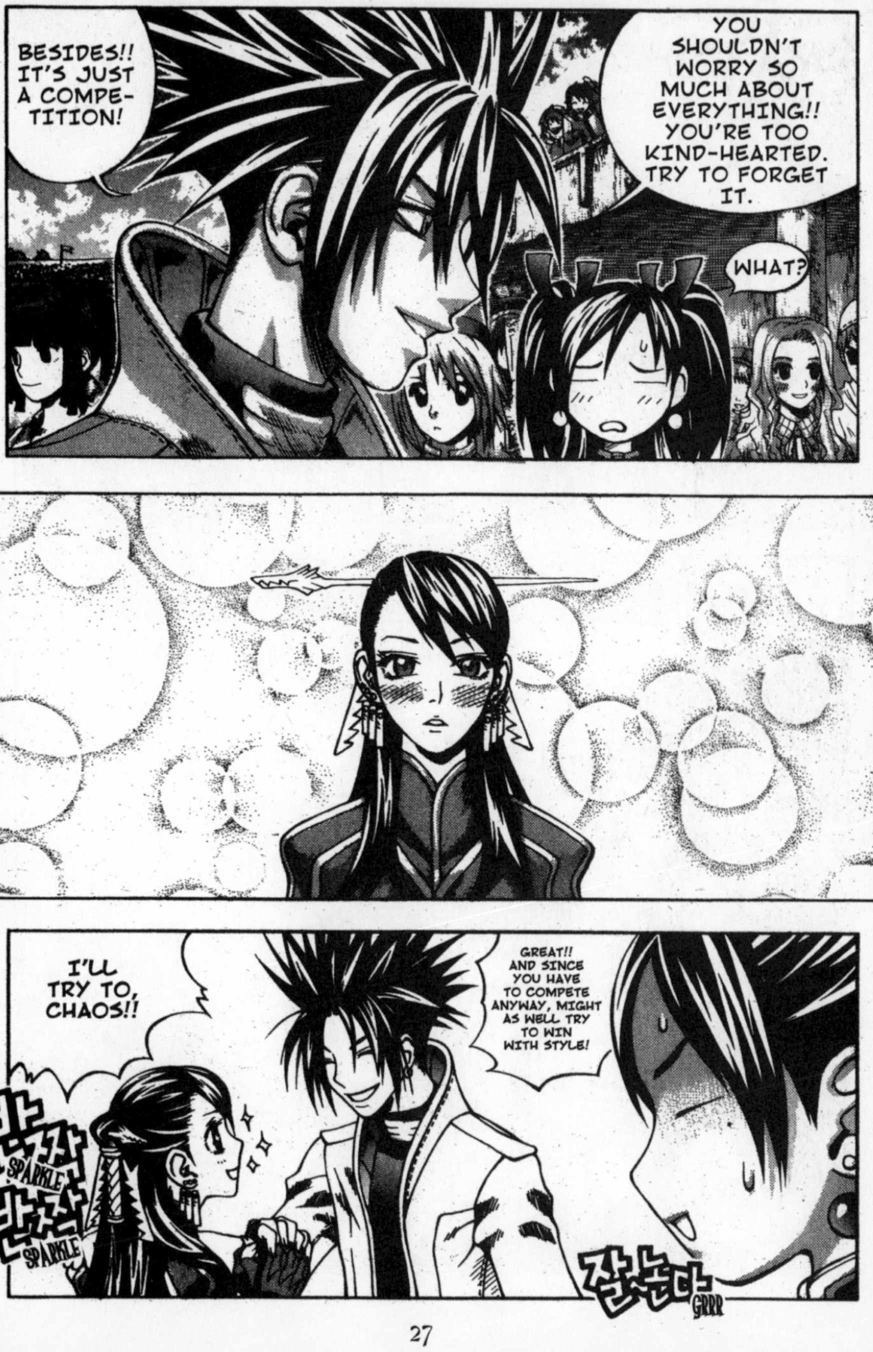
BESIDES!! IT'S JUST A COMPE-TITION!
YOU SHOULDN'T WORRY SO MUCH ABOUT EVERYTHING!! YOU'RE TOO KIND-HEARTED. TRY TO FORGET IT.
WHAT?
I'LL TRY TO, CHAOS!!
GREAT!! AND SINCE YOU HAVE TO COMPETE ANYWAY, MIGHT AS WELL TRY TO WIN WITH STYLE!
SPARKLE
SPARKLE
GRRR

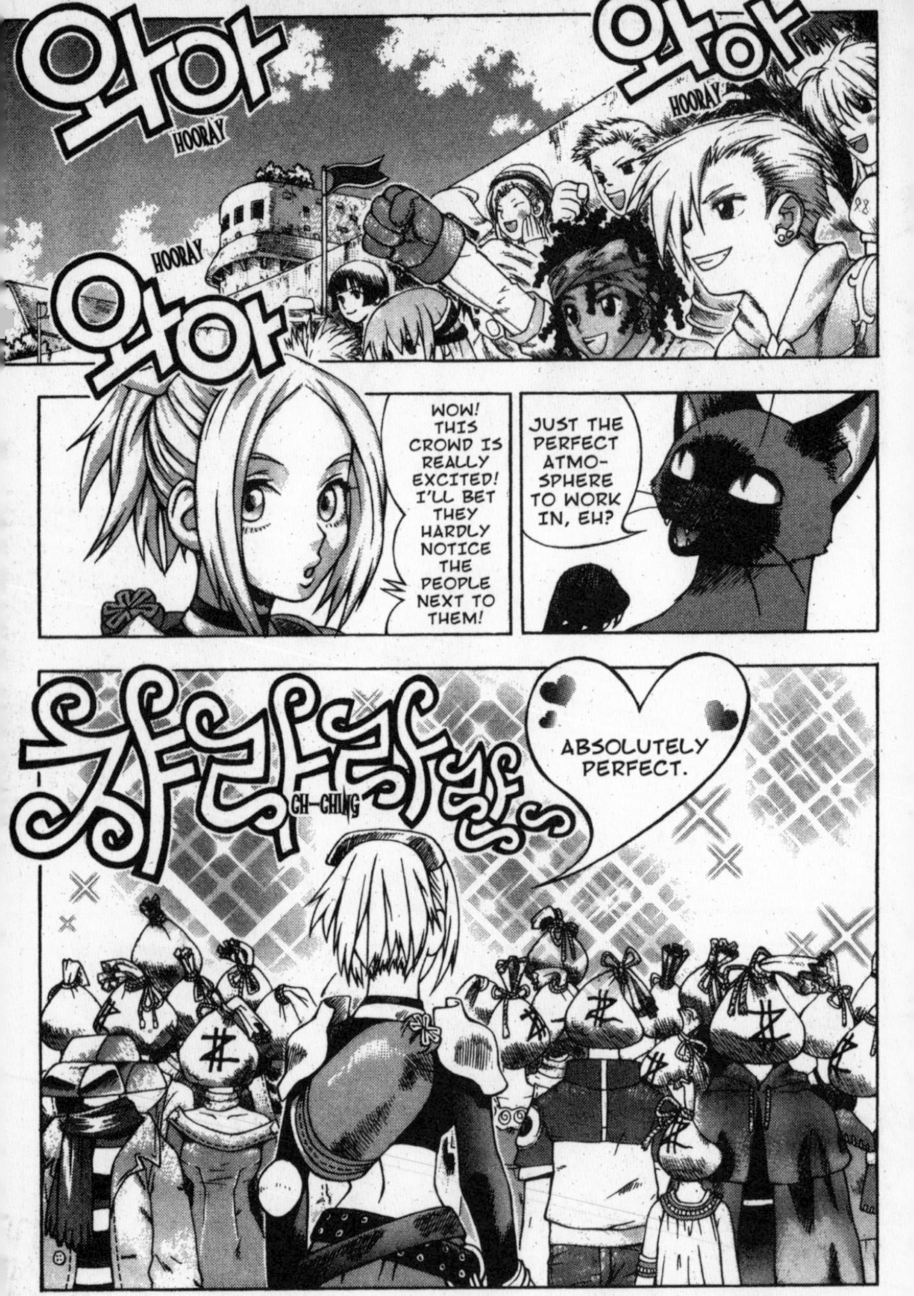
와아
HOORAY
와아
HOORAY
HOORAY
와아
WOW! THIS CROWD IS REALLY EXCITED! I'LL BET THEY HARDLY NOTICE THE PEOPLE NEXT TO THEM!
JUST THE PERFECT ATMO-SPHERE TO WORK IN, EH?
CH-CHING
ABSOLUTELY PERFECT.

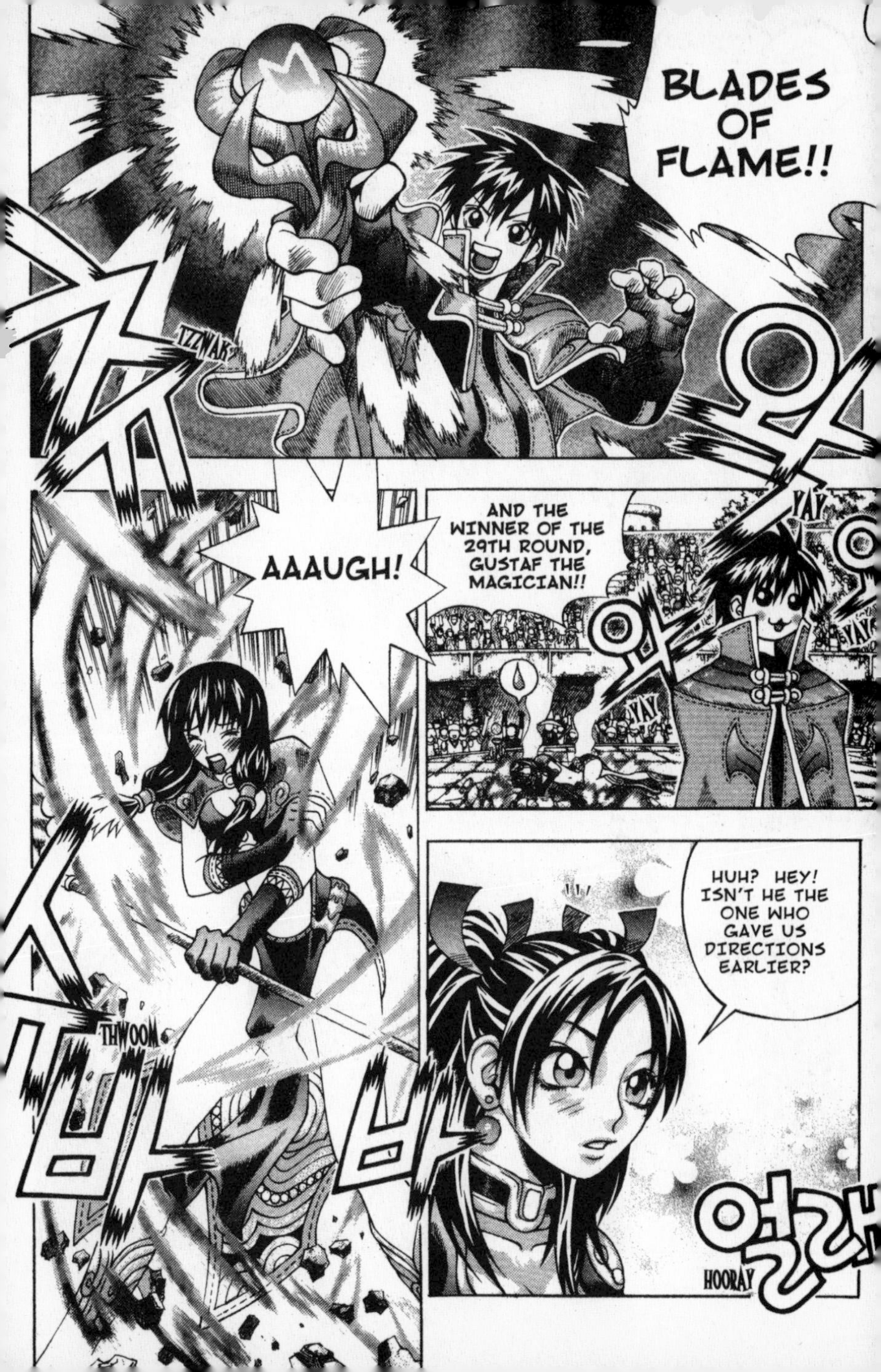
BLADES OF FLAME!!
TZZWAK
AAAUGH!
THWOOM
AND THE WINNER OF THE 29TH ROUND, GUSTAF THE MAGICIAN!!
YAY
YAY
YAY
HUH? HEY! ISN'T HE THE ONE WHO GAVE US DIRECTIONS EARLIER?
HOORAY

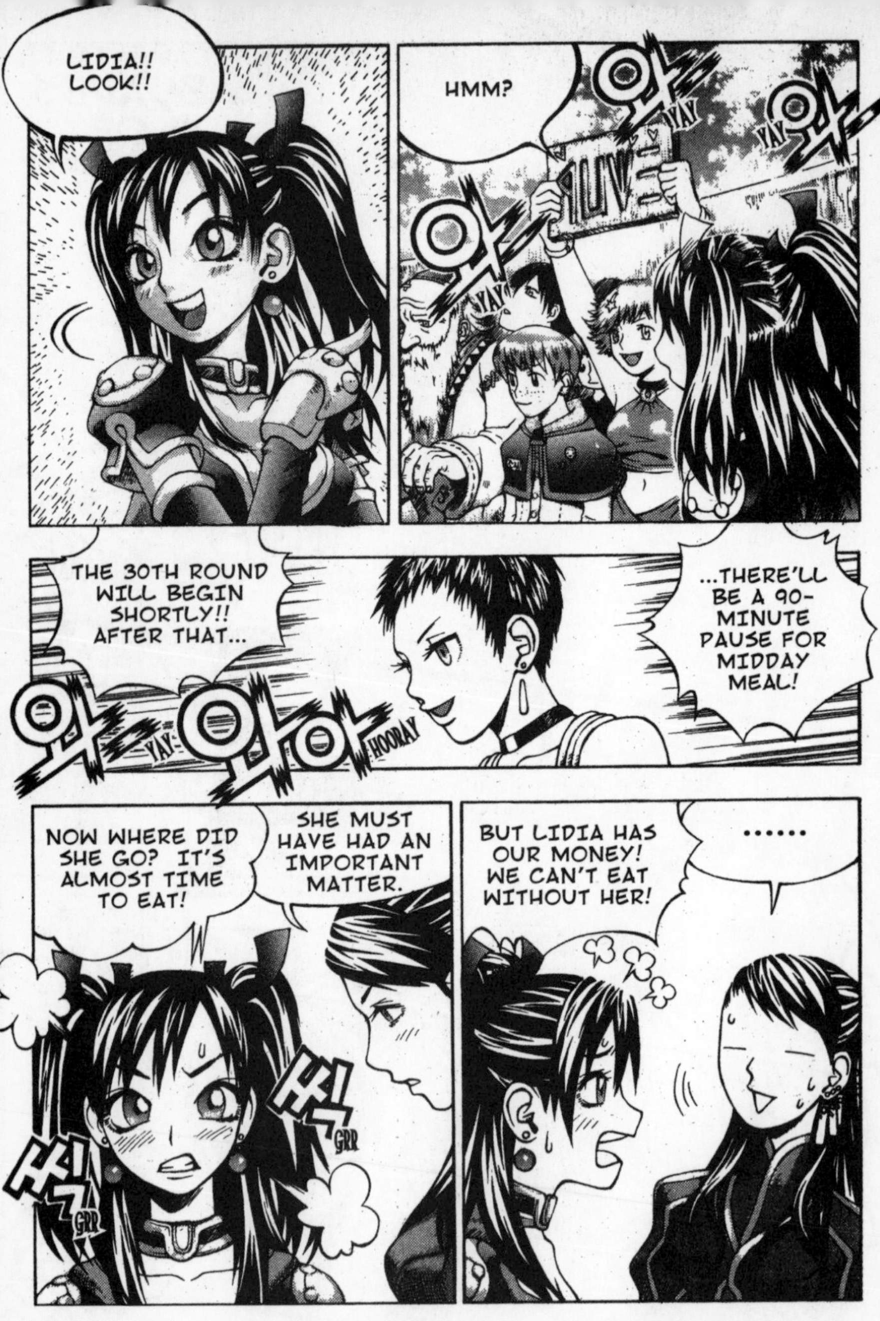
LIDIA!! LOOK!!
HMM?
YAY
YAY
YAY
THE 30TH ROUND WILL BEGIN SHORTLY!! AFTER THAT...
...THERE'LL BE A 90-MINUTE PAUSE FOR MIDDAY MEAL!
YAY
HOORAY
NOW WHERE DID SHE GO? IT'S ALMOST TIME TO EAT!
SHE MUST HAVE HAD AN IMPORTANT MATTER.
GRR
GRR
BUT LIDIA HAS OUR MONEY! WE CAN'T EAT WITHOUT HER!
......

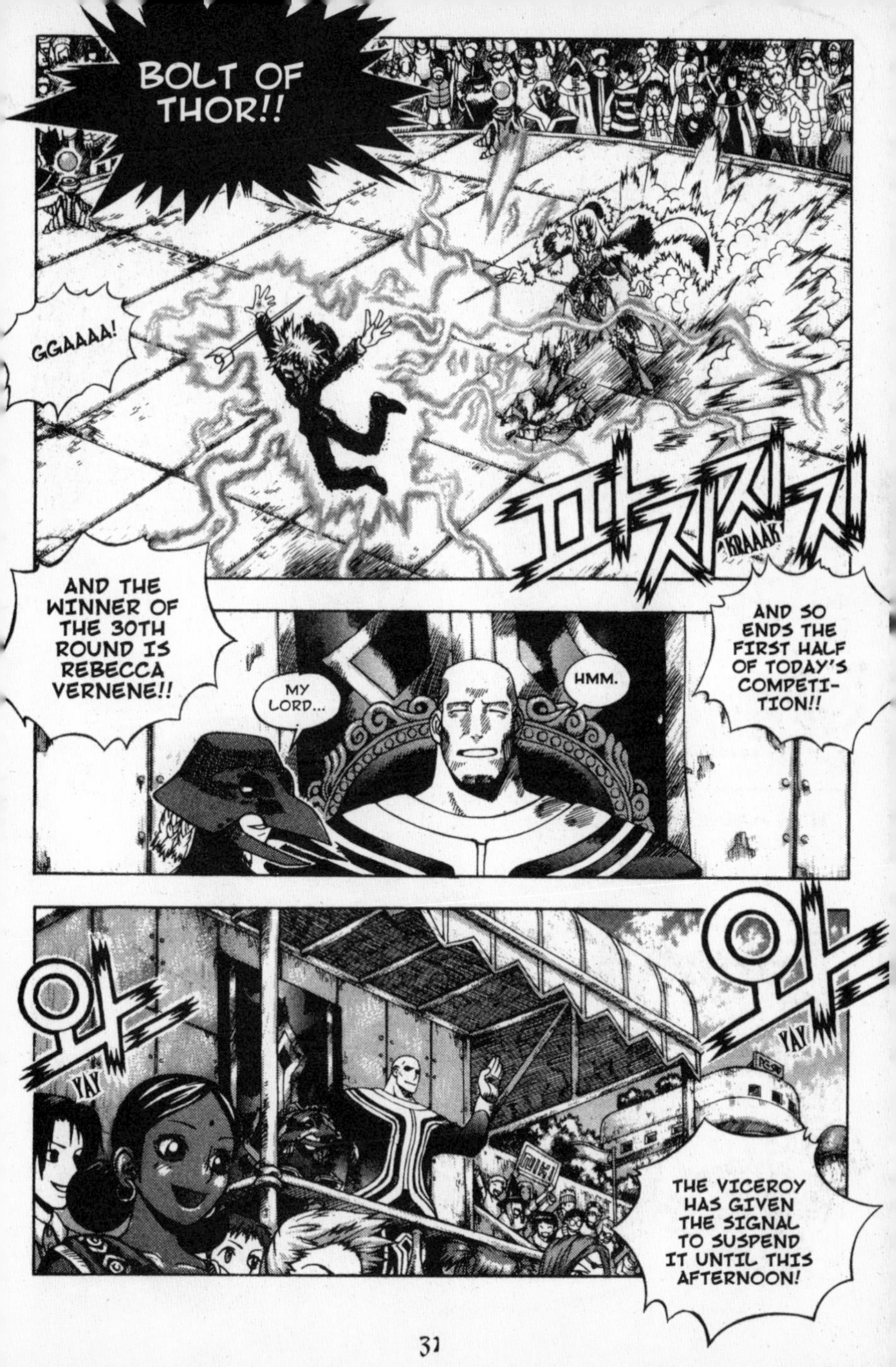
BOLT OF THOR!!
GGAAAA!
KRAAAK
AND THE WINNER OF THE 30TH ROUND IS REBECCA VERNENE!!
MY LORD...
HMM.
AND SO ENDS THE FIRST HALF OF TODAY'S COMPETITION!!
YAY
YAY
THE VICEROY HAS GIVEN THE SIGNAL TO SUSPEND IT UNTIL THIS AFTERNOON!

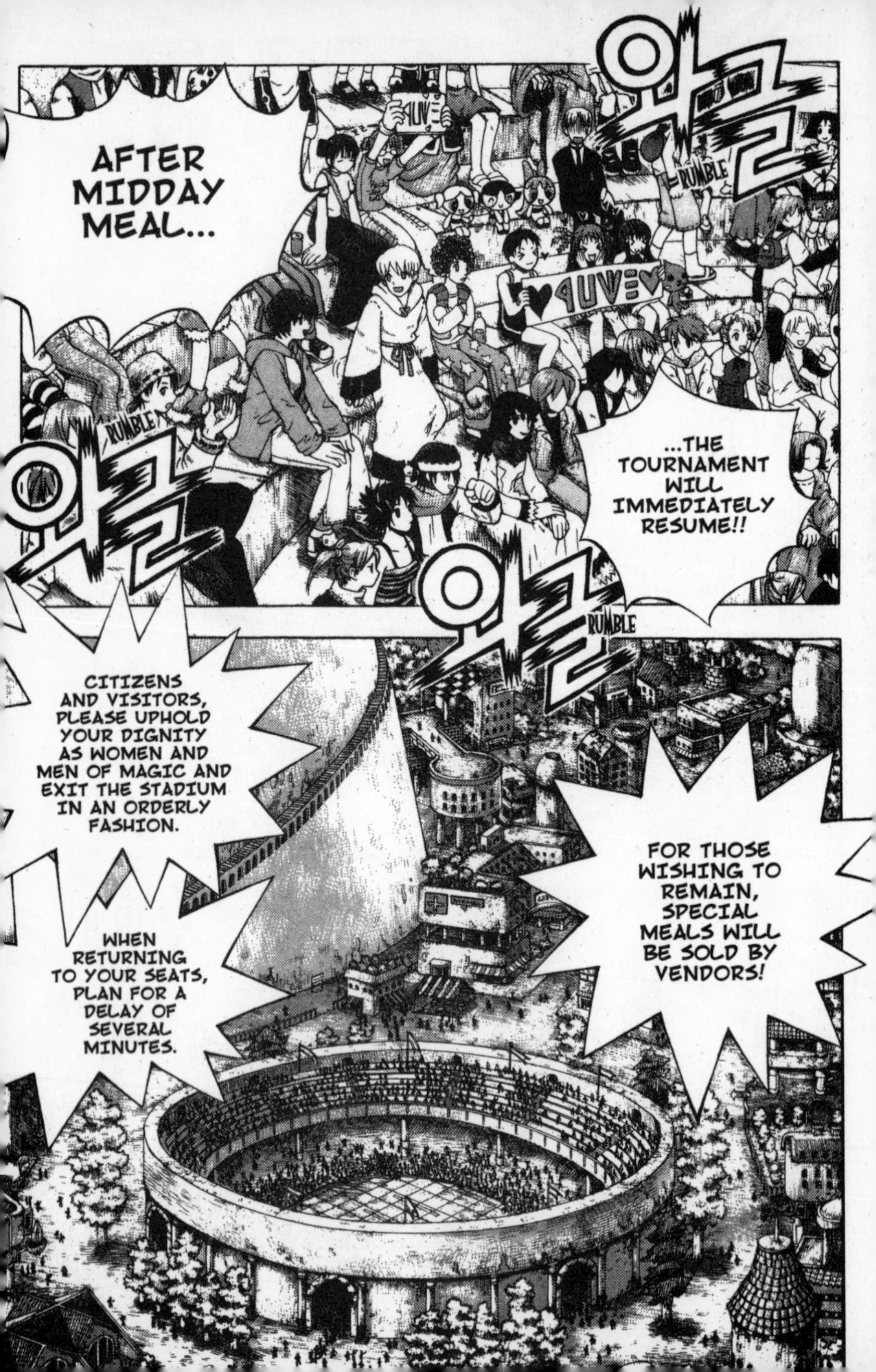
AFTER MIDDAY MEAL...
RUMBLE
RUMBLE
...THE TOURNAMENT WILL IMMEDIATELY RESUME!!
RUMBLE
CITIZENS AND VISITORS, PLEASE UPHOLD YOUR DIGNITY AS WOMEN AND MEN OF MAGIC AND EXIT THE STADIUM IN AN ORDERLY FASHION.
FOR THOSE WISHING TO REMAIN, SPECIAL MEALS WILL BE SOLD BY VENDORS!
WHEN RETURNING TO YOUR SEATS, PLAN FOR A DELAY OF SEVERAL MINUTES.

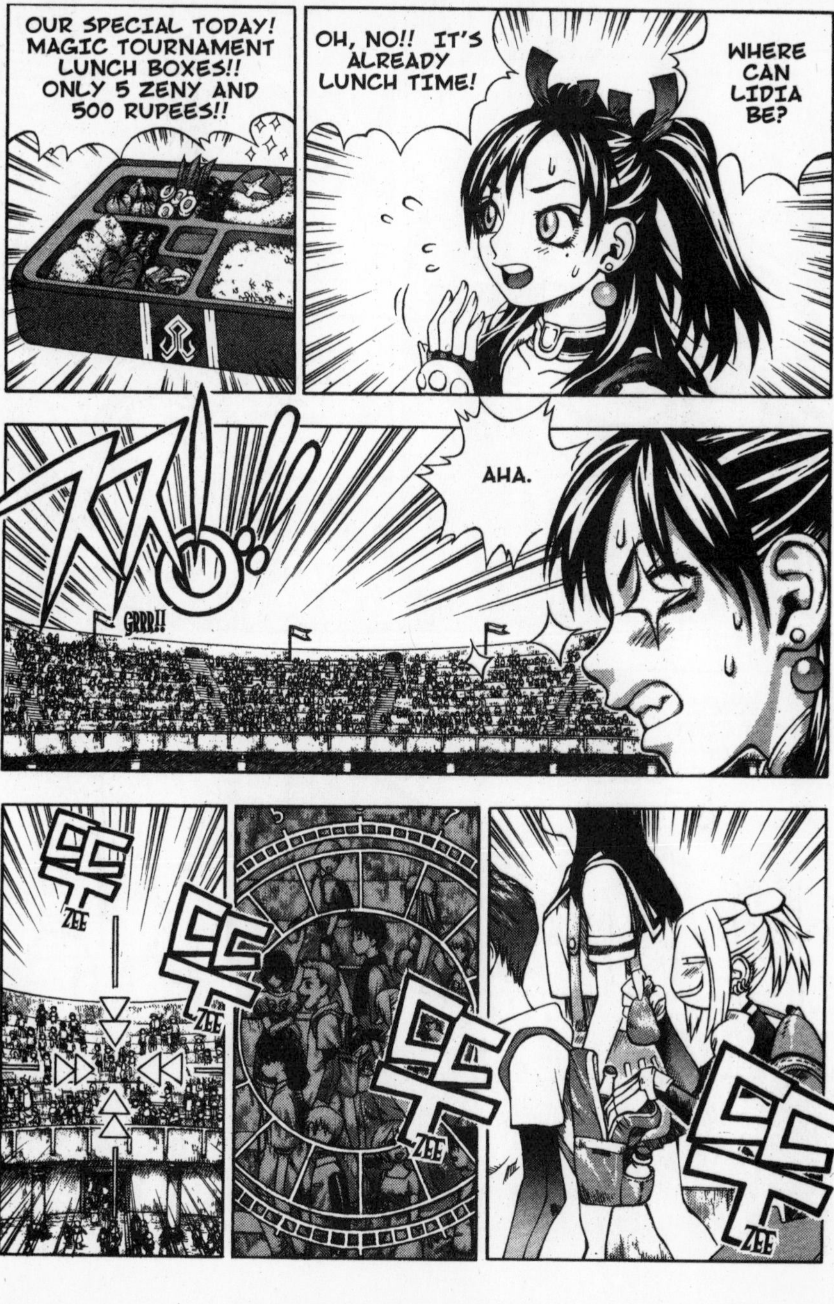
OUR SPECIAL TODAY! MAGIC TOURNAMENT LUNCH BOXES!! ONLY 5 ZENY AND 500 RUPEES!!
OH, NO!! IT'S ALREADY LUNCH TIME!
WHERE CAN LIDIA BE?
AHA.
GRRR!!
ZEE
ZEE
ZEE
ZEE

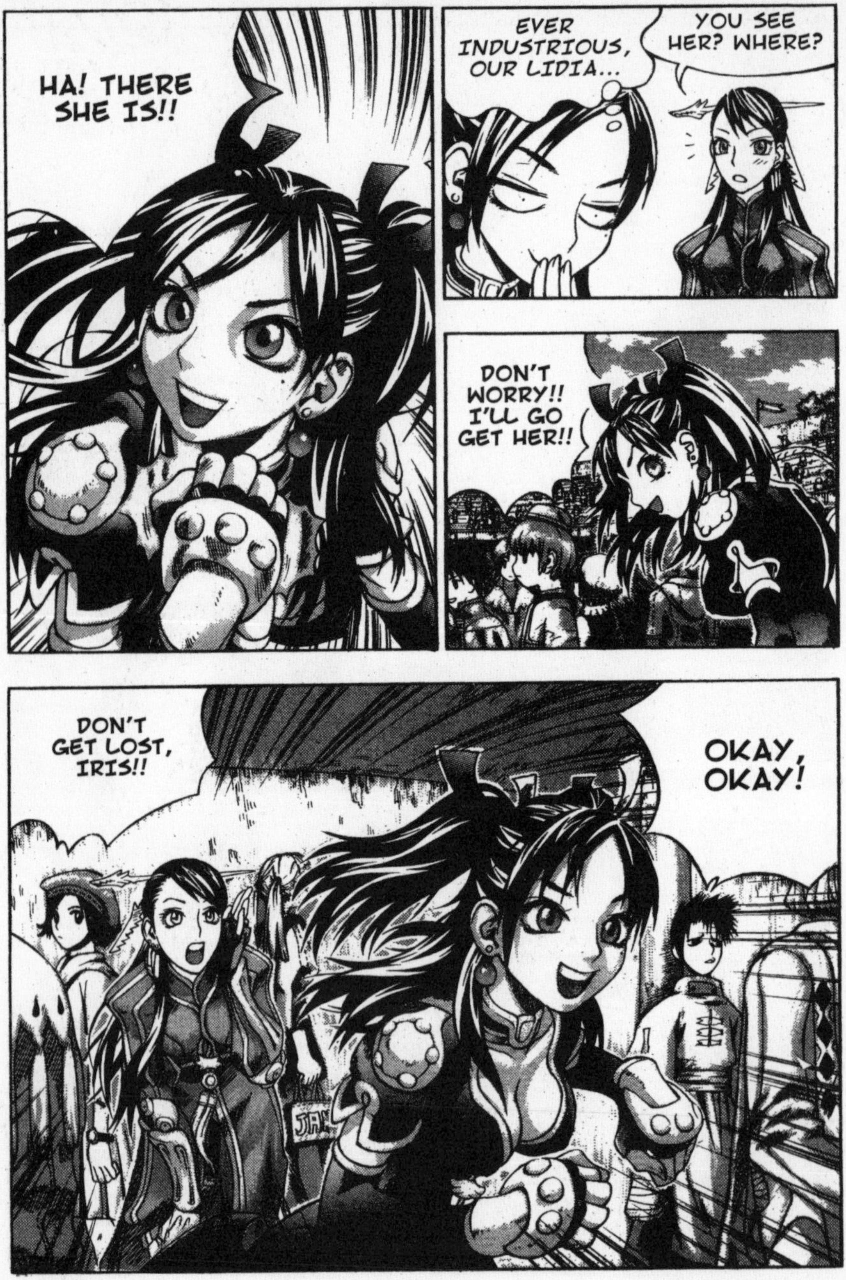
HA! THERE SHE IS!!
EVER INDUSTRIOUS, OUR LIDIA...
YOU SEE HER? WHERE?
DON'T WORRY!! I'LL GO GET HER!!
DON'T GET LOST, IRIS!!
OKAY, OKAY!

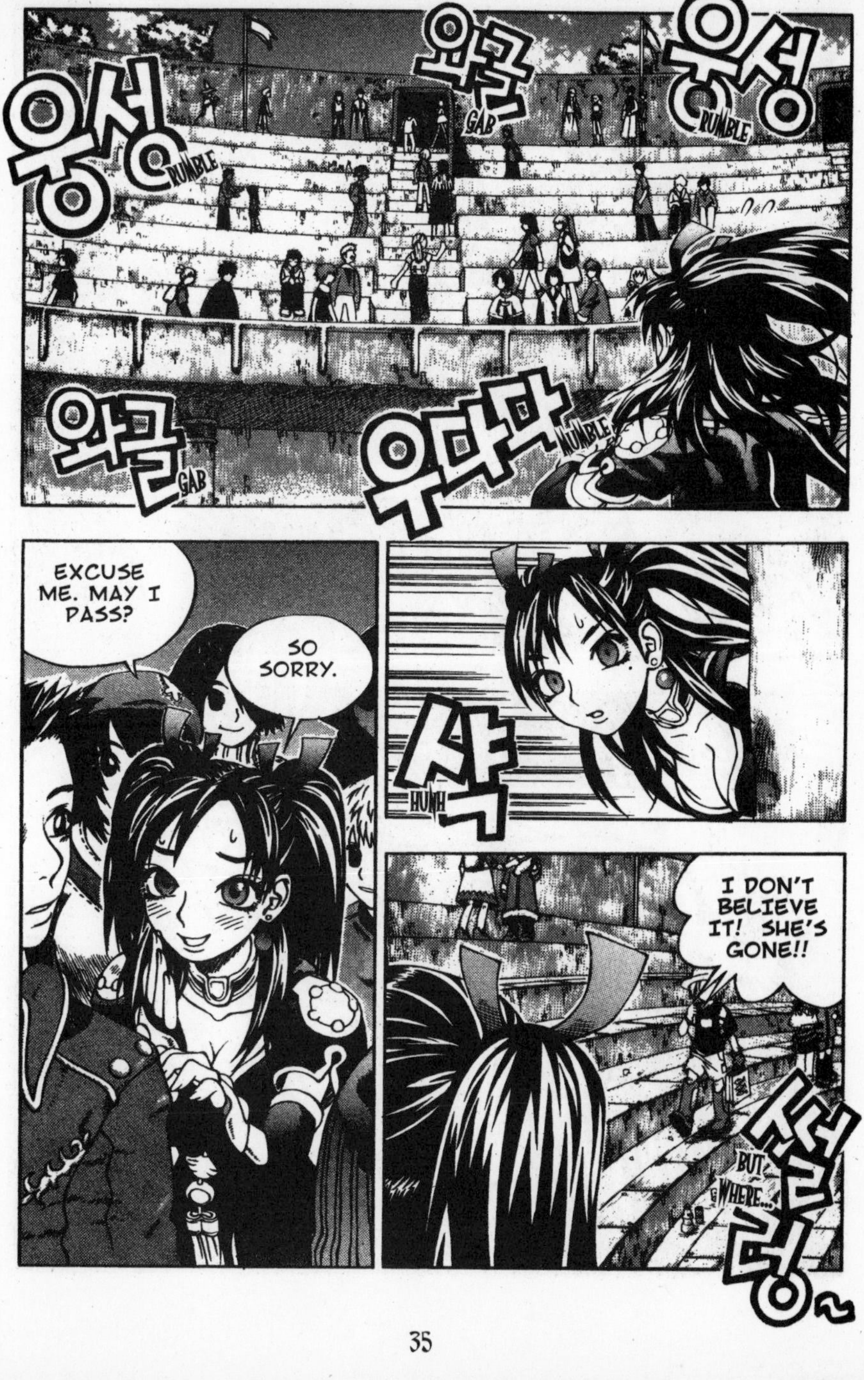
웅성 RUMBLE
와글 GAB
웅성 RUMBLE
와글 GAB
우다닥 NUMBLE
EXCUSE ME. MAY I PASS?
SO SORRY.
샥 HUNH
I DON'T BELIEVE IT! SHE'S GONE!!
BUT WHERE...

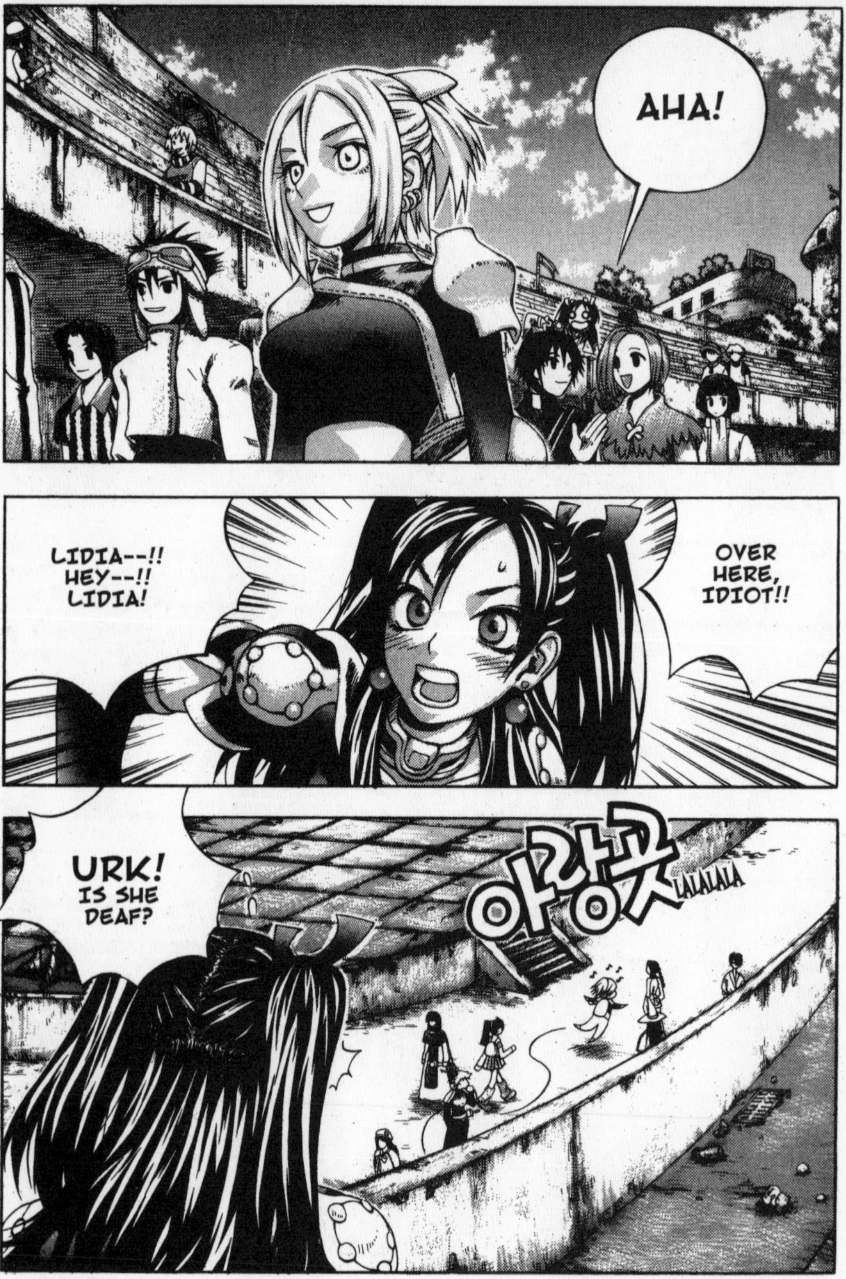
AHA!
LIDIA--!! HEY--!! LIDIA!
OVER HERE, IDIOT!!
URK! IS SHE DEAF?
야랑꿋
LALALALA

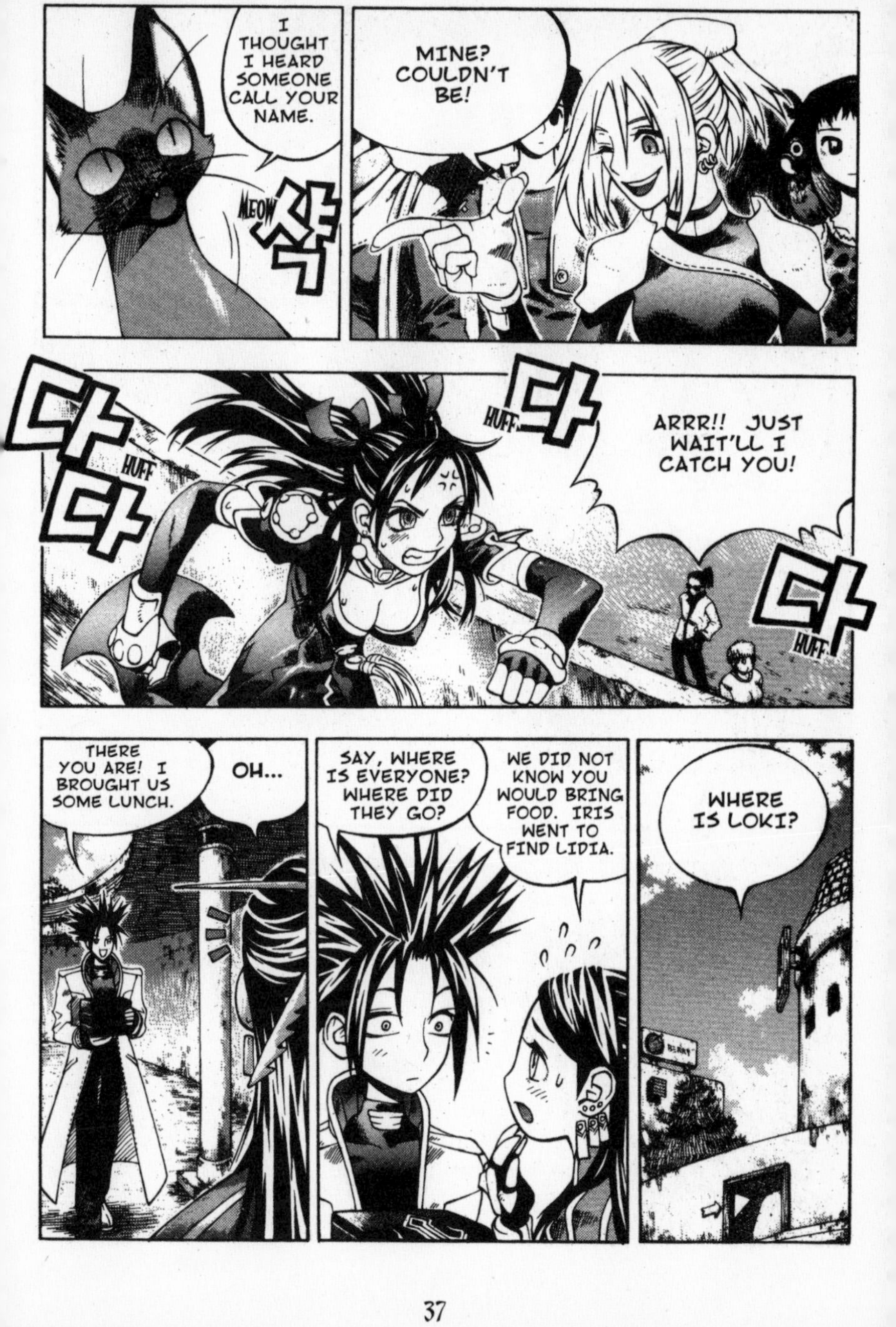
I THOUGHT I HEARD SOMEONE CALL YOUR NAME.
MEOW
샥
MINE? COULDN'T BE!
다
HUFF
다
HUFF
다
ARRR!! JUST WAIT'LL I CATCH YOU!
다
HUFF
THERE YOU ARE! I BROUGHT US SOME LUNCH.
OH...
SAY, WHERE IS EVERYONE? WHERE DID THEY GO?
WE DID NOT KNOW YOU WOULD BRING FOOD. IRIS WENT TO FIND LIDIA.
WHERE IS LOKI?

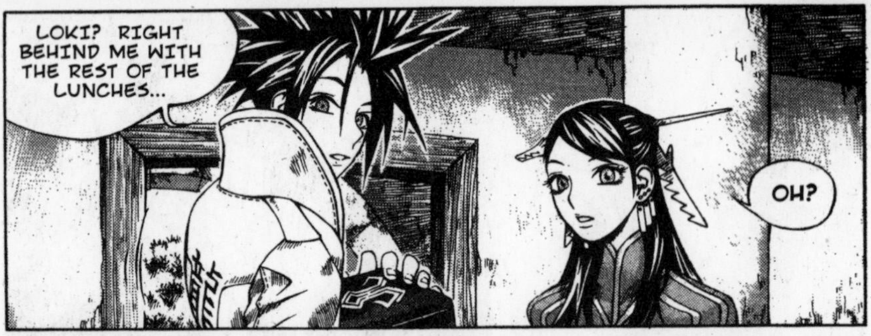
LOKI? RIGHT BEHIND ME WITH THE REST OF THE LUNCHES...
OH?

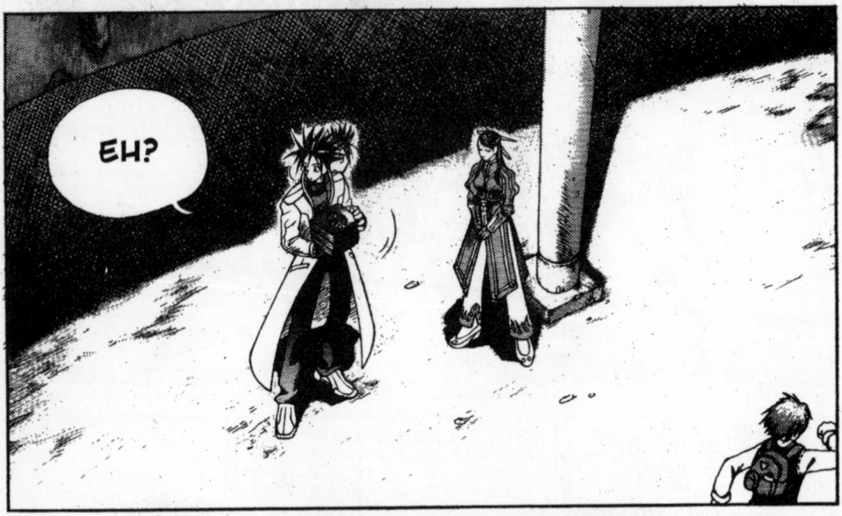
EH?

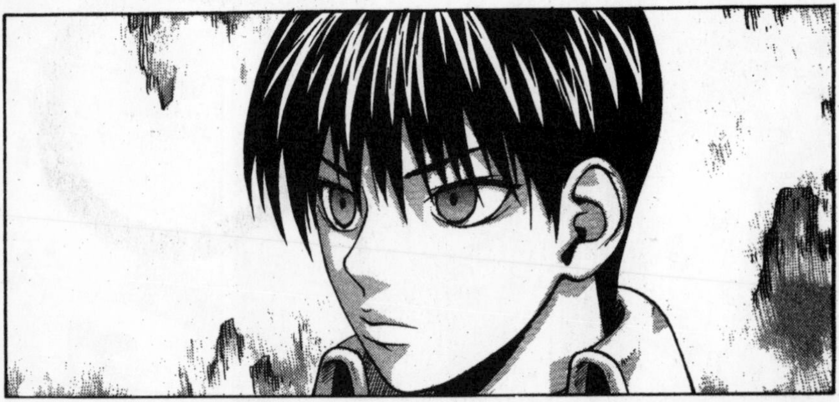

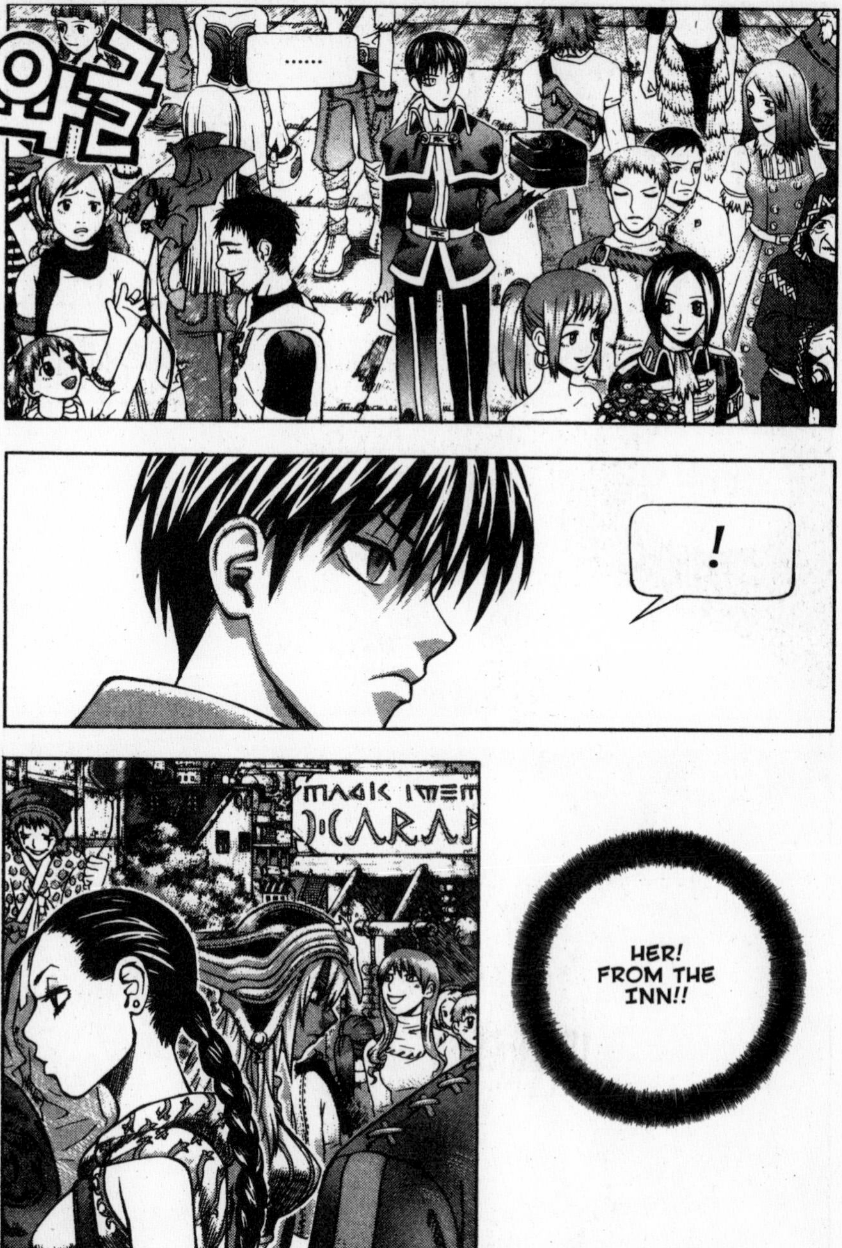
와글
......
!
HER! FROM THE INN!!

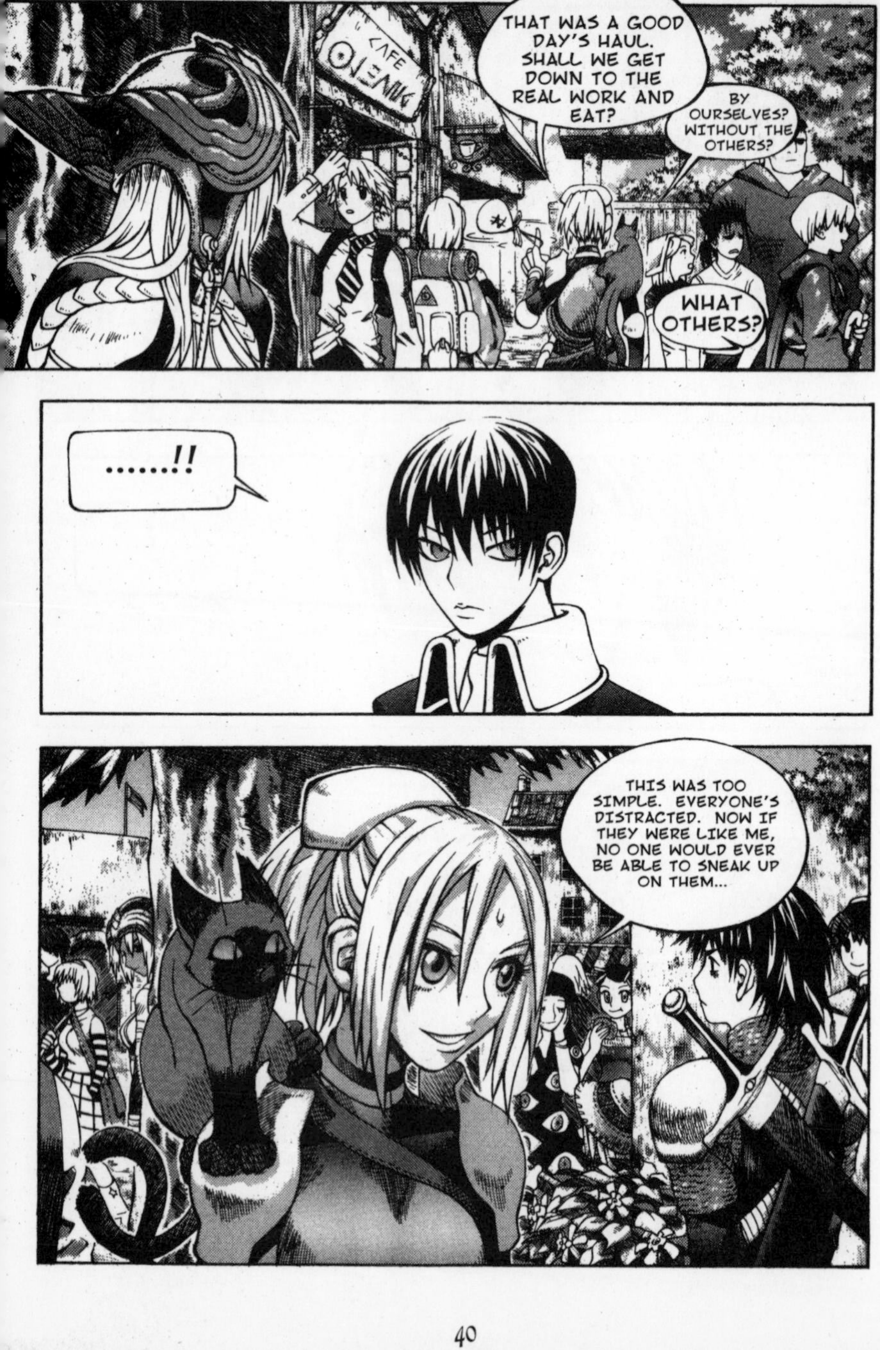
CAFE
THAT WAS A GOOD DAY'S HAUL. SHALL WE GET DOWN TO THE REAL WORK AND EAT?
BY OURSELVES? WITHOUT THE OTHERS?
WHAT OTHERS?
......!!
THIS WAS TOO SIMPLE. EVERYONE'S DISTRACTED. NOW IF THEY WERE LIKE ME, NO ONE WOULD EVER BE ABLE TO SNEAK UP ON THEM...

RAGNAROK
라그나로크
IN TO THE ABYSS

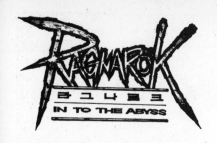

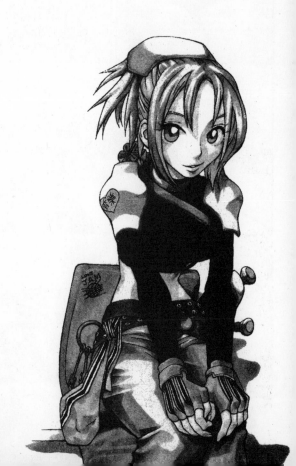

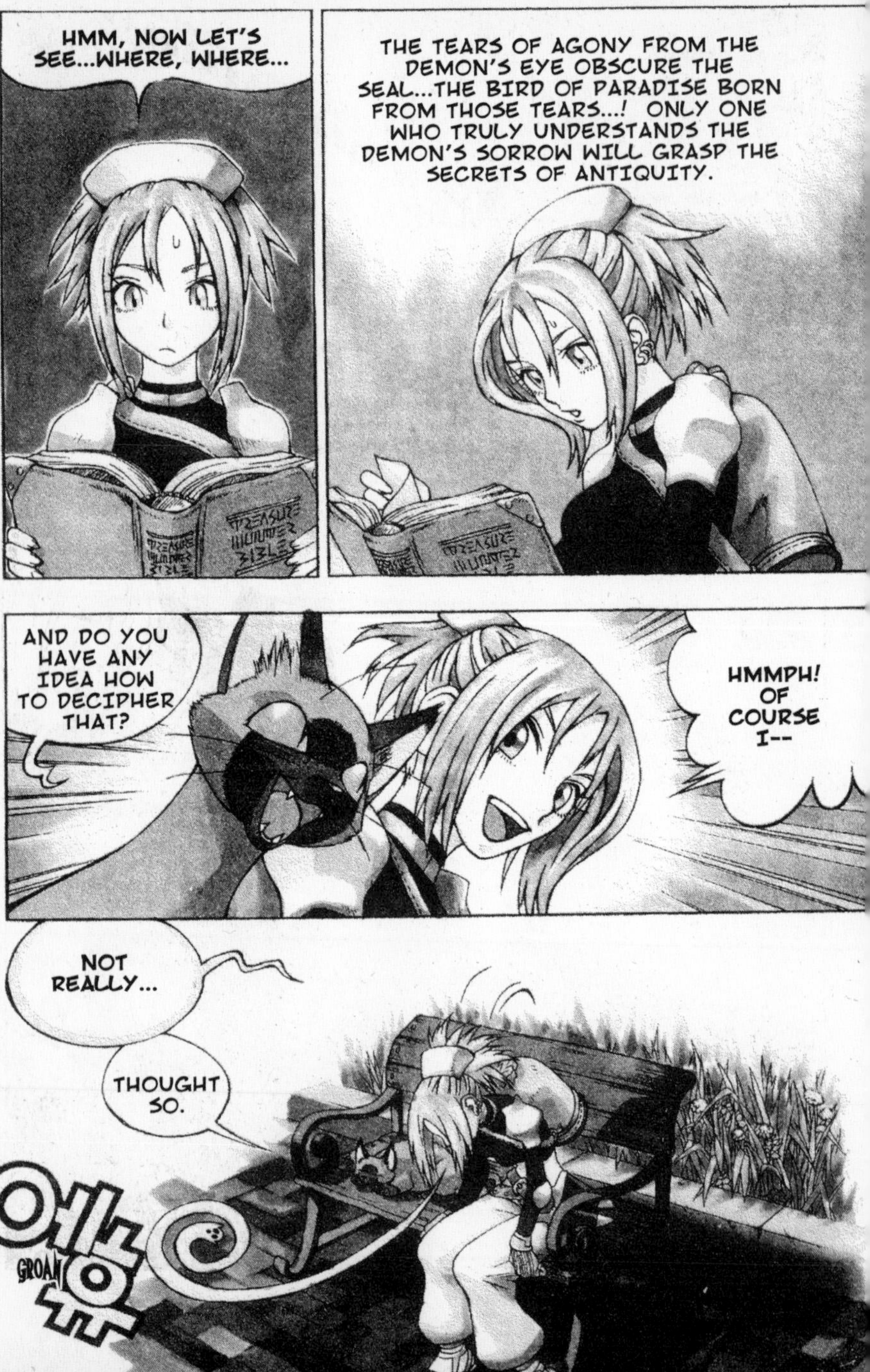
HMM, NOW LET'S SEE...WHERE, WHERE...
THE TEARS OF AGONY FROM THE DEMON'S EYE OBSCURE THE SEAL...THE BIRD OF PARADISE BORN FROM THOSE TEARS...! ONLY ONE WHO TRULY UNDERSTANDS THE DEMON'S SORROW WILL GRASP THE SECRETS OF ANTIQUITY.
TREASURE HUNTER BIBLE
AND DO YOU HAVE ANY IDEA HOW TO DECIPHER THAT?
HMMPH! OF COURSE I--
NOT REALLY...
THOUGHT SO.
GROAN

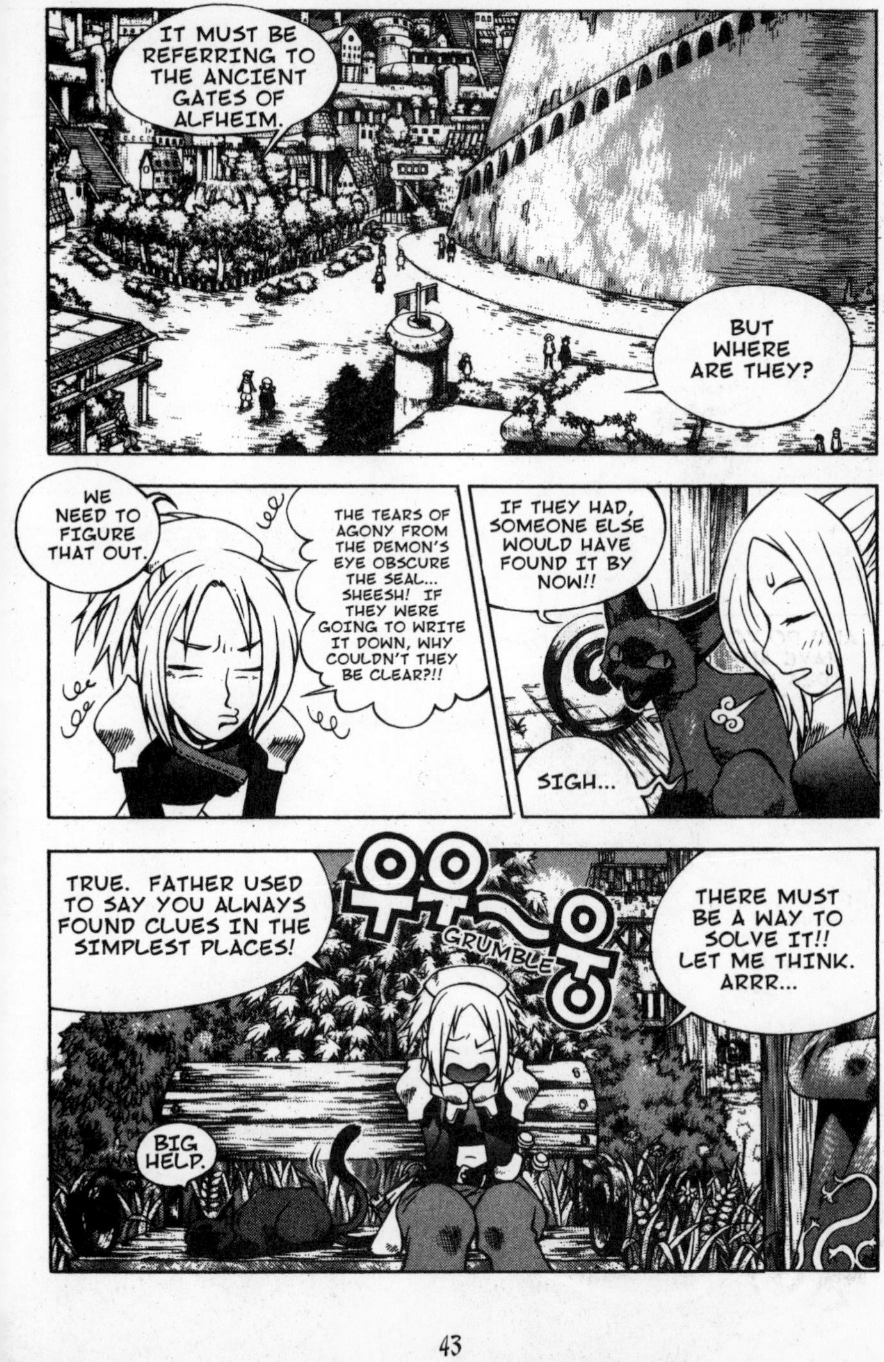
IT MUST BE REFERRING TO THE ANCIENT GATES OF ALFHEIM.
BUT WHERE ARE THEY?
WE NEED TO FIGURE THAT OUT.
THE TEARS OF AGONY FROM THE DEMON'S EYE OBSCURE THE SEAL... SHEESH! IF THEY WERE GOING TO WRITE IT DOWN, WHY COULDN'T THEY BE CLEAR?!!
IF THEY HAD, SOMEONE ELSE WOULD HAVE FOUND IT BY NOW!!
SIGH...
TRUE. FATHER USED TO SAY YOU ALWAYS FOUND CLUES IN THE SIMPLEST PLACES!
GRUMBLE
THERE MUST BE A WAY TO SOLVE IT!! LET ME THINK. ARRR...
BIG HELP.

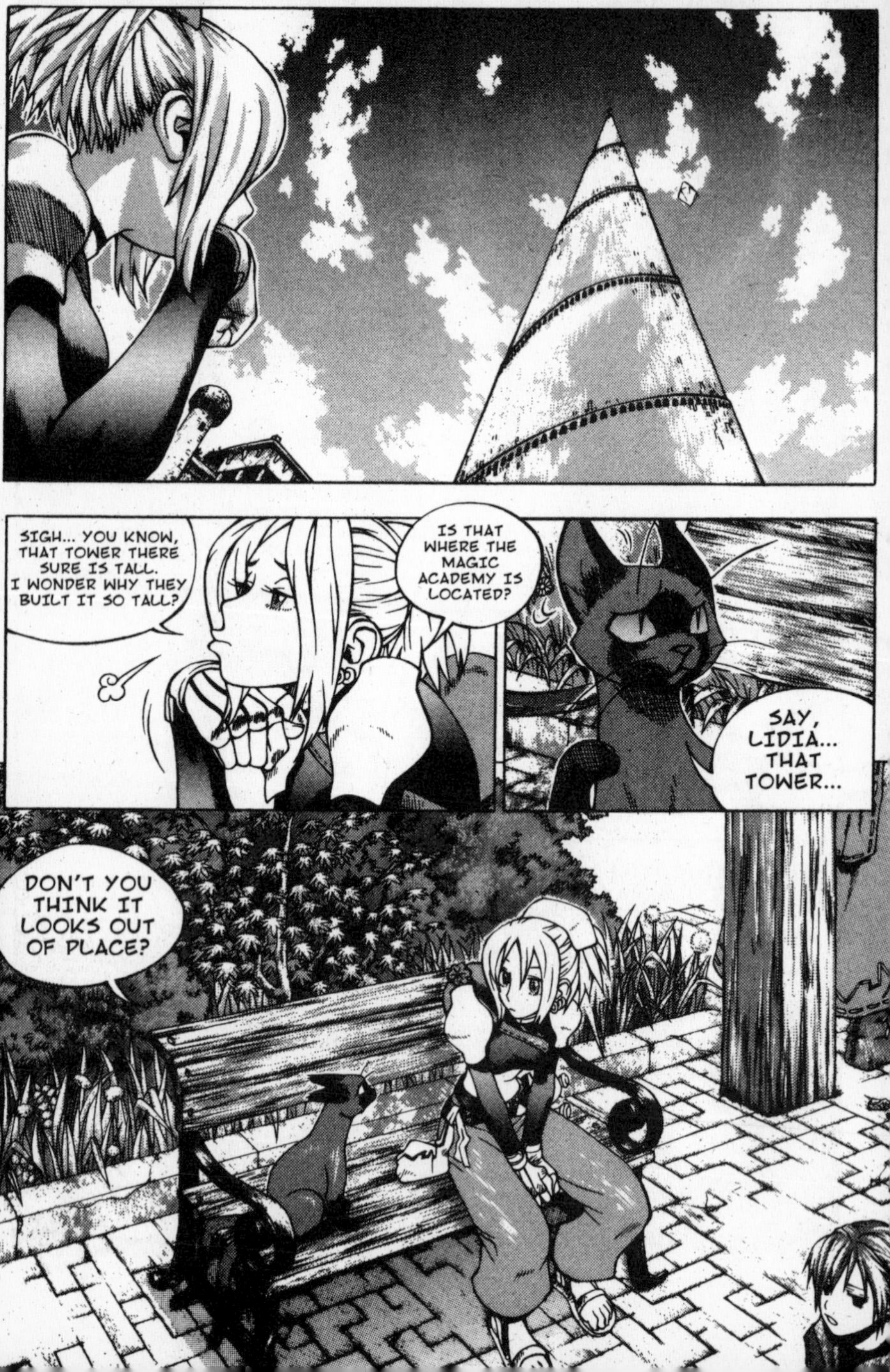
SIGH... YOU KNOW, THAT TOWER THERE SURE IS TALL. I WONDER WHY THEY BUILT IT SO TALL?
IS THAT WHERE THE MAGIC ACADEMY IS LOCATED?
SAY, LIDIA... THAT TOWER...
DON'T YOU THINK IT LOOKS OUT OF PLACE?

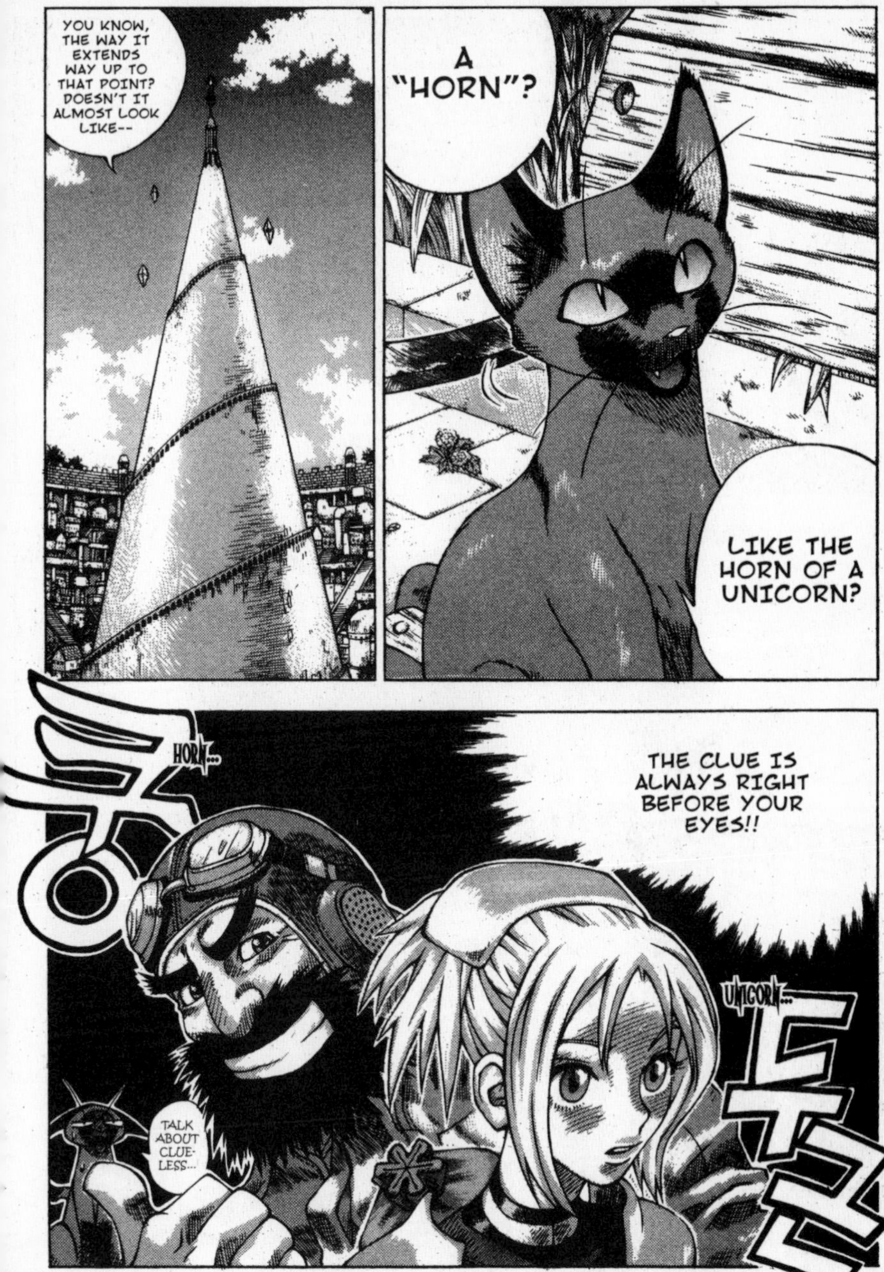
YOU KNOW, THE WAY IT EXTENDS WAY UP TO THAT POINT? DOESN'T IT ALMOST LOOK LIKE--
A "HORN"?
LIKE THE HORN OF A UNICORN?
HORN...
THE CLUE IS ALWAYS RIGHT BEFORE YOUR EYES!!
TALK ABOUT CLUE-LESS...
UNICORN...

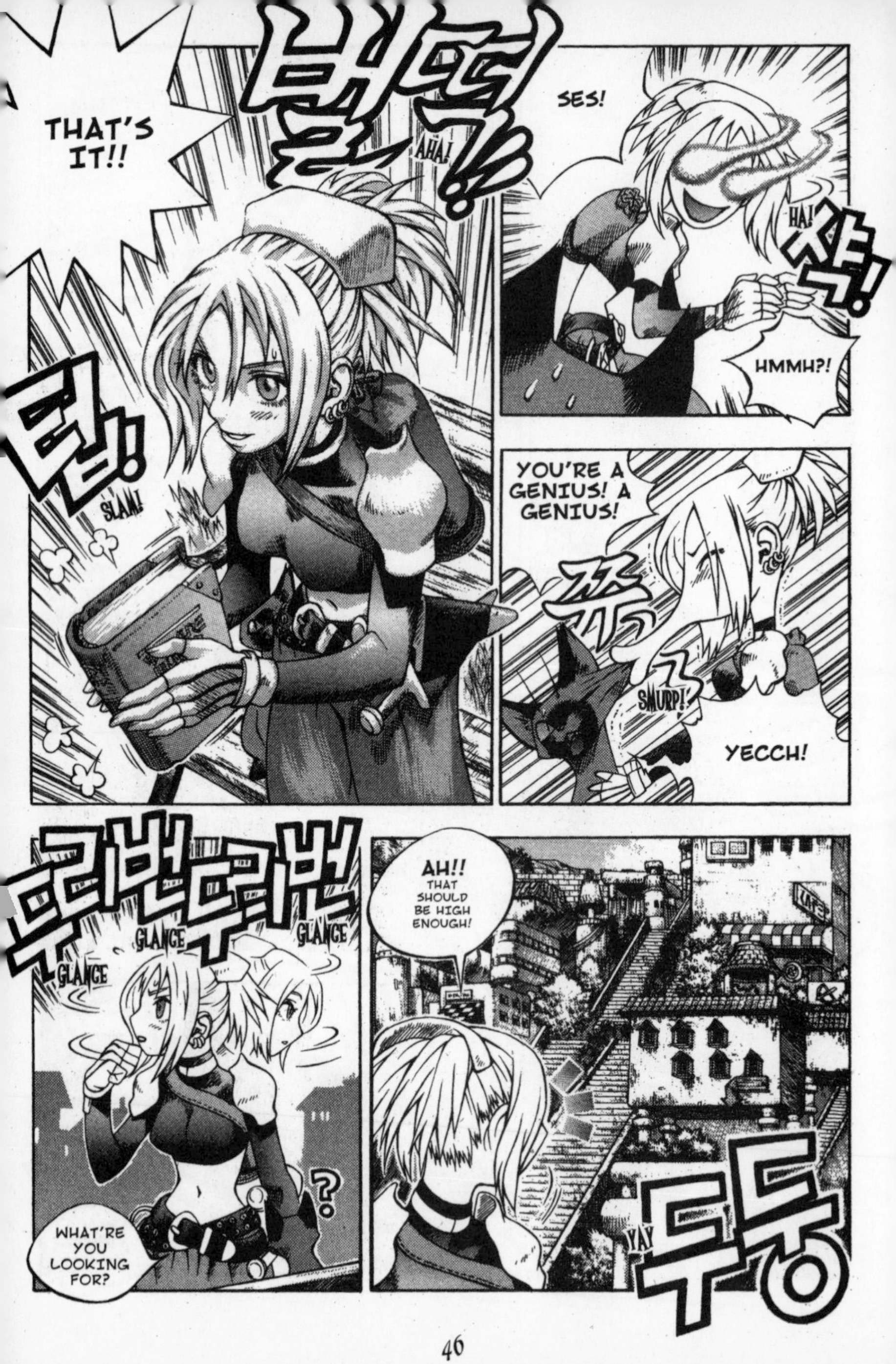
THAT'S IT!!
AHA!
SLAM!
SES!
HA!
HMMH?!
YOU'RE A GENIUS! A GENIUS!
SMURP!
YECCH!
GLANCE
GLANCE
GLANCE
?
WHAT'RE YOU LOOKING FOR?
AH!! THAT SHOULD BE HIGH ENOUGH!
YAY

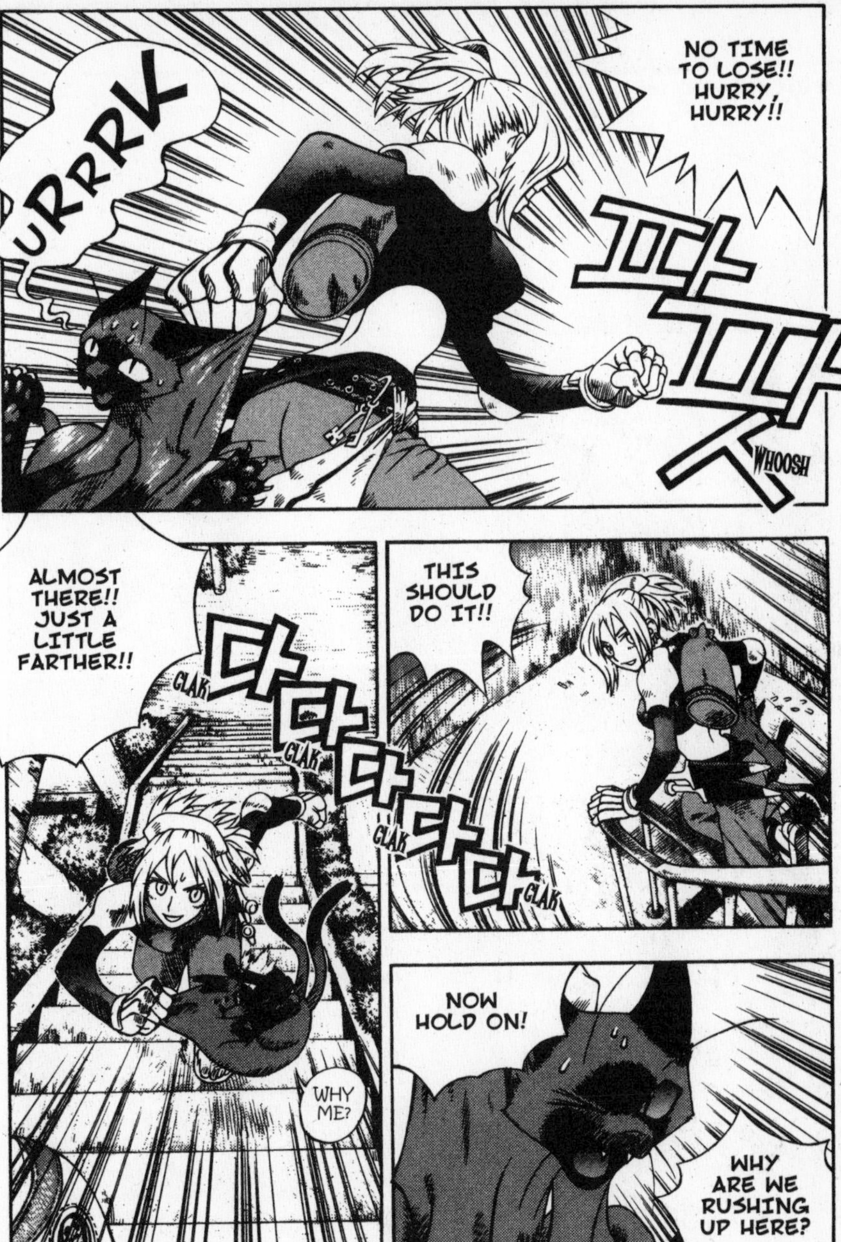
URRRK
NO TIME TO LOSE!! HURRY, HURRY!!
WHOOSH
ALMOST THERE!! JUST A LITTLE FARTHER!!
CLAK
CLAK
CLAK
CLAK
WHY ME?
THIS SHOULD DO IT!!
NOW HOLD ON!
WHY ARE WE RUSHING UP HERE?

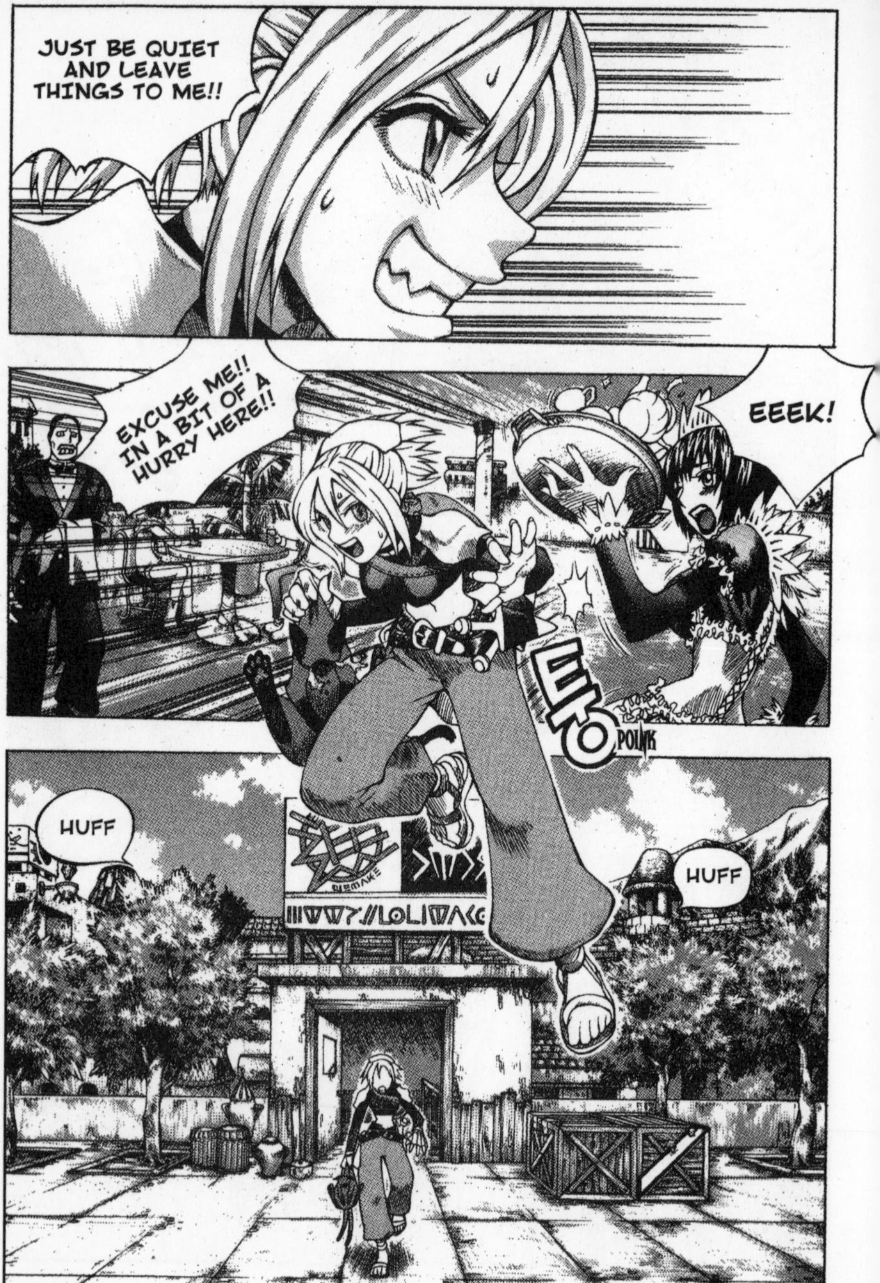
JUST BE QUIET AND LEAVE THINGS TO ME!!
EXCUSE ME!! IN A BIT OF A HURRY HERE!!
EEEK!
POINK
HUFF
HUFF

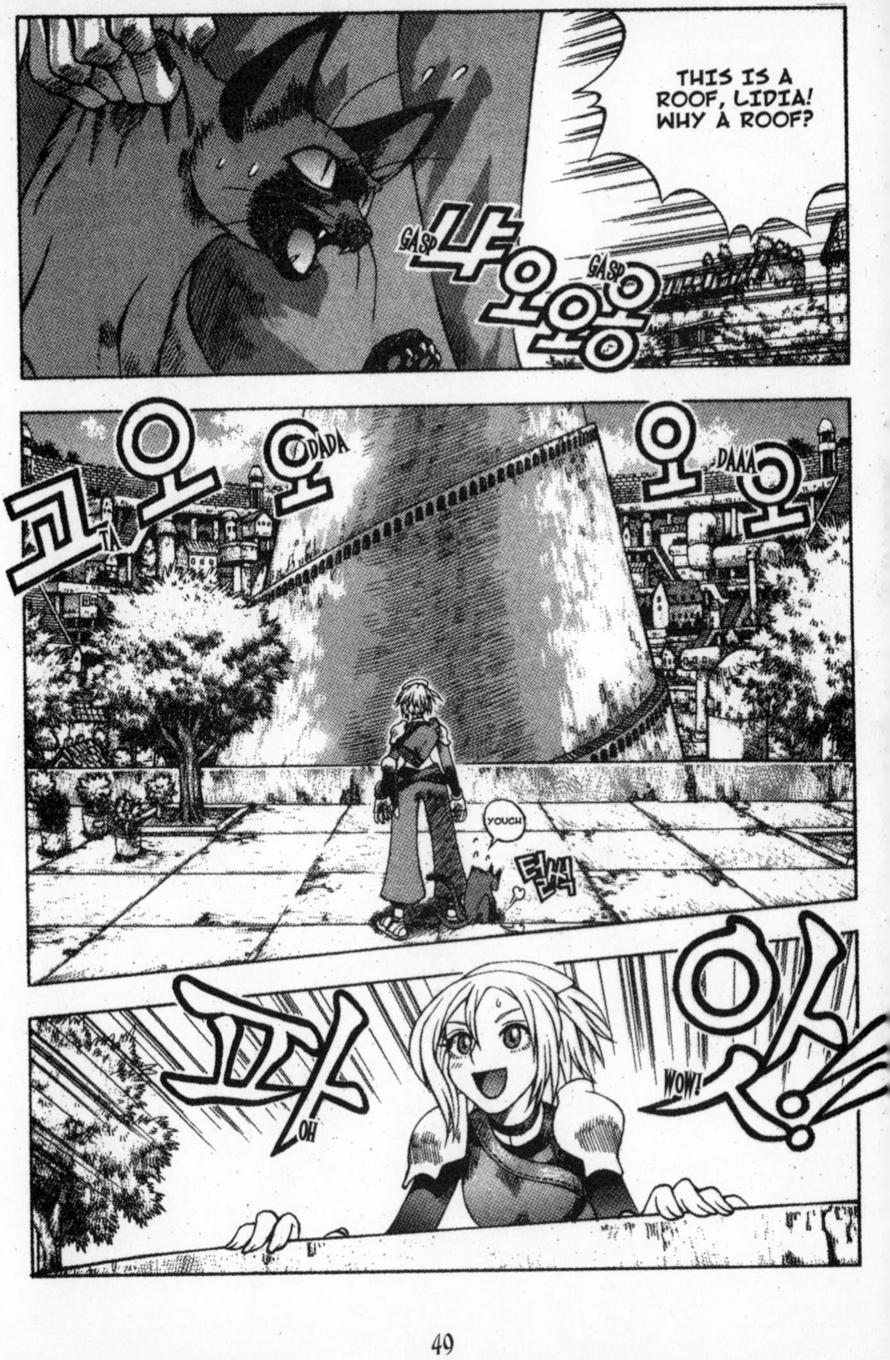
THIS IS A ROOF, LIDIA! WHY A ROOF?
GASP
GASP
DADA
DAAA
YOUCH
OH
WOW!

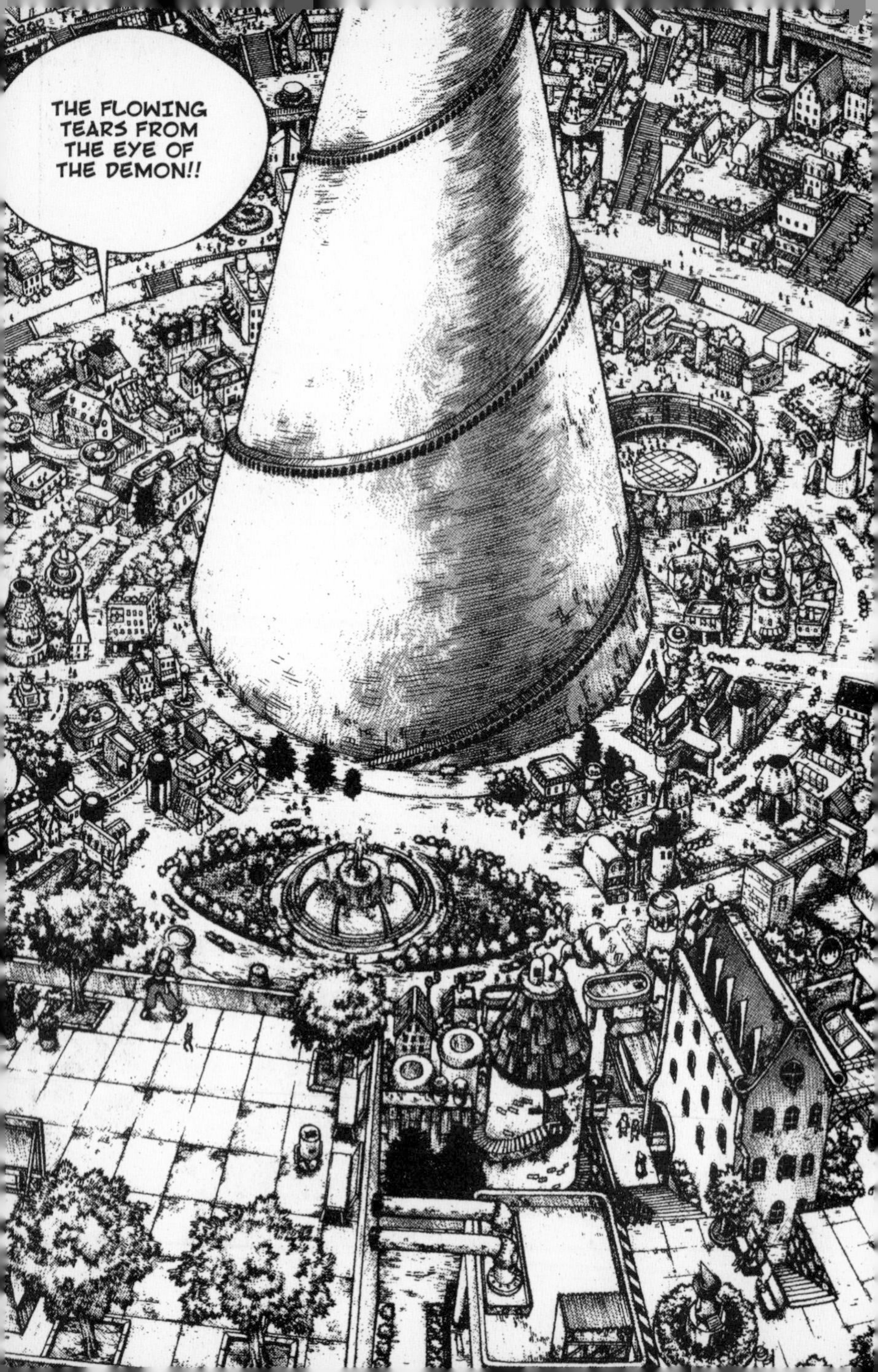
THE FLOWING TEARS FROM THE EYE OF THE DEMON!!

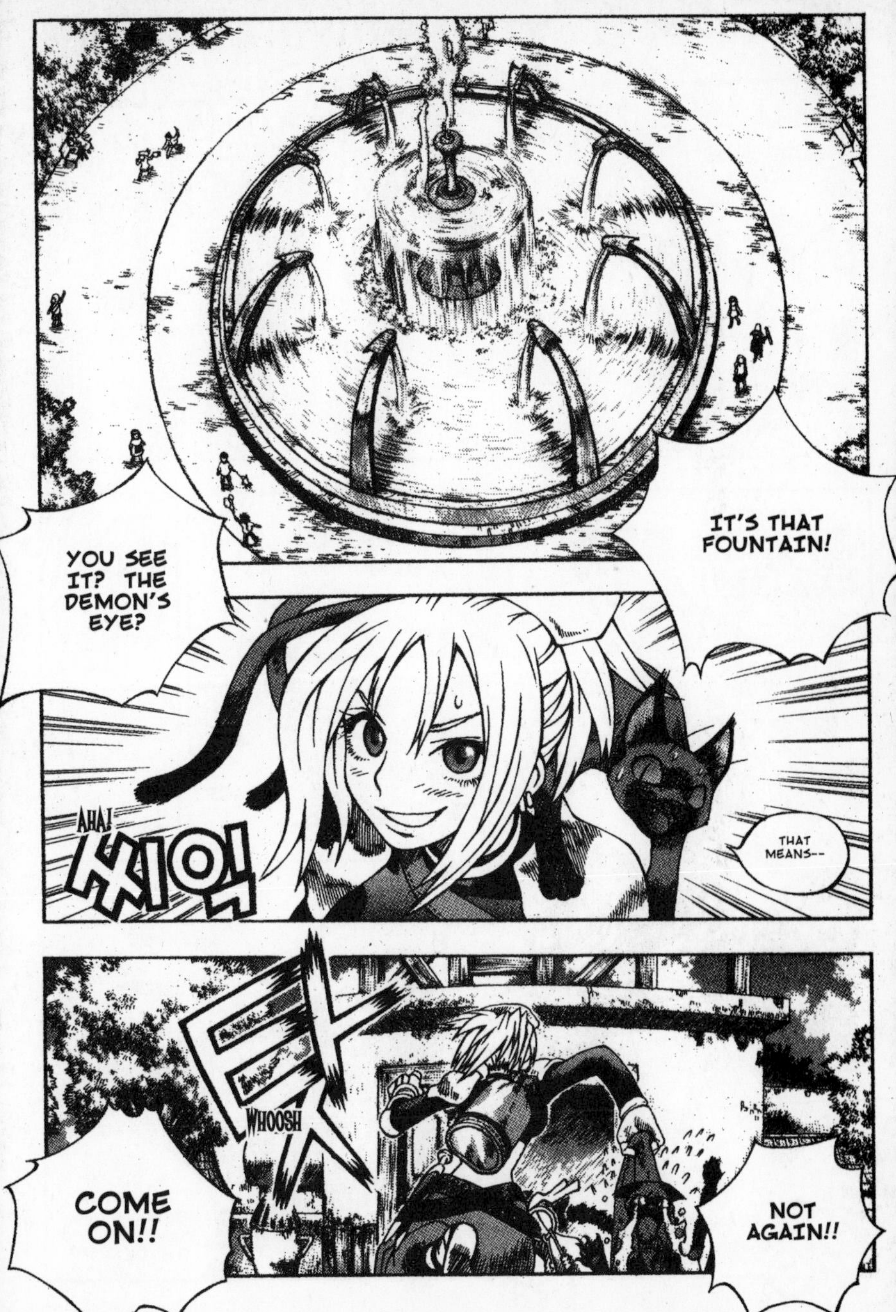
YOU SEE IT? THE DEMON'S EYE?
IT'S THAT FOUNTAIN!
AHA!
THAT MEANS--
WHOOSH
COME ON!!
NOT AGAIN!!

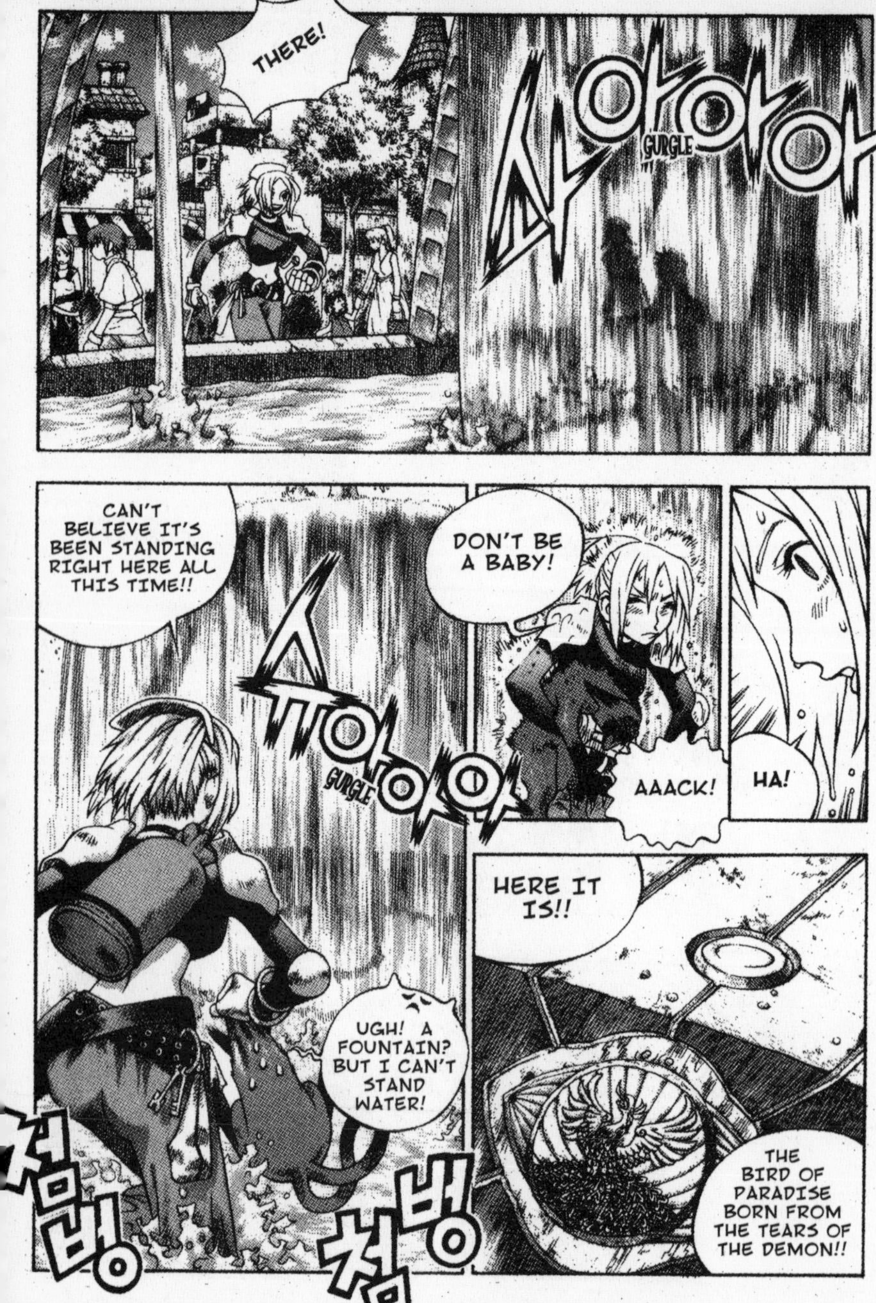

THERE!
GURGLE
CAN'T BELIEVE IT'S BEEN STANDING RIGHT HERE ALL THIS TIME!!
GURGLE
UGH! A FOUNTAIN? BUT I CAN'T STAND WATER!
첨벙
첨벙
DON'T BE A BABY!
AAACK!
HA!
HERE IT IS!!
THE BIRD OF PARADISE BORN FROM THE TEARS OF THE DEMON!!

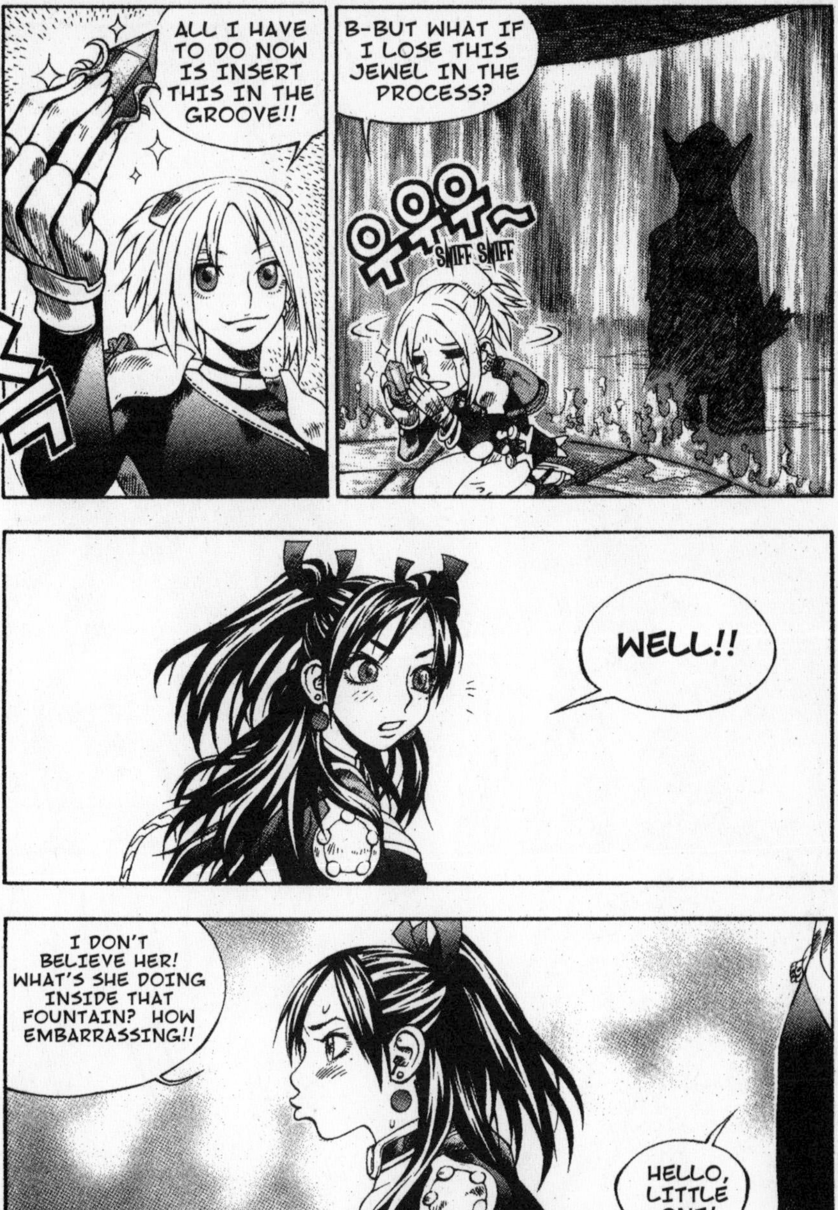
ALL I HAVE TO DO NOW IS INSERT THIS IN THE GROOVE!!
B-BUT WHAT IF I LOSE THIS JEWEL IN THE PROCESS?
SNIFF SNIFF
WELL!!
I DON'T BELIEVE HER! WHAT'S SHE DOING INSIDE THAT FOUNTAIN? HOW EMBARRASSING!!
HELLO, LITTLE ONE!

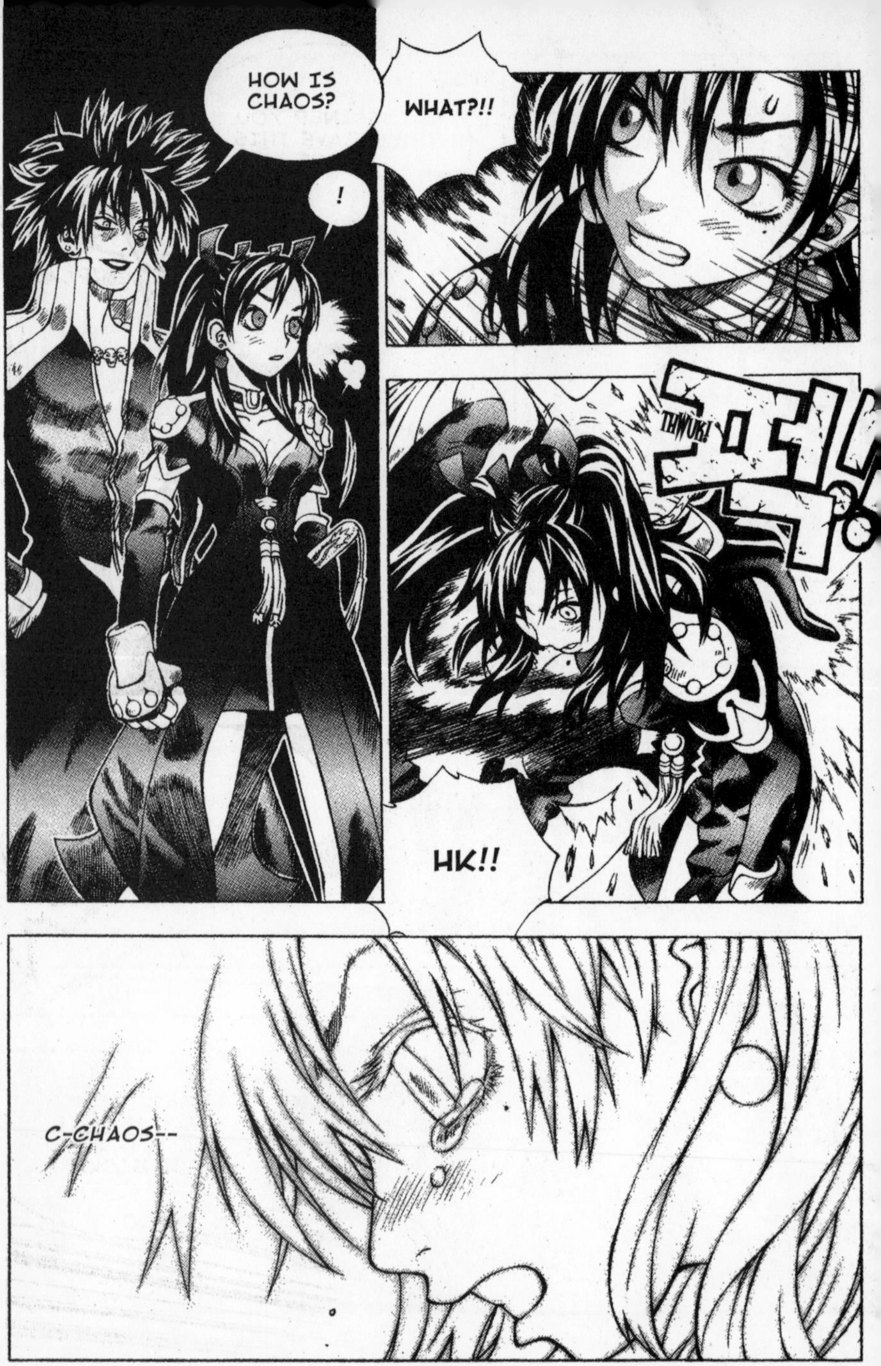
HOW IS CHAOS?
!
WHAT?!!
THWUK!
HK!!
C-CHAOS--

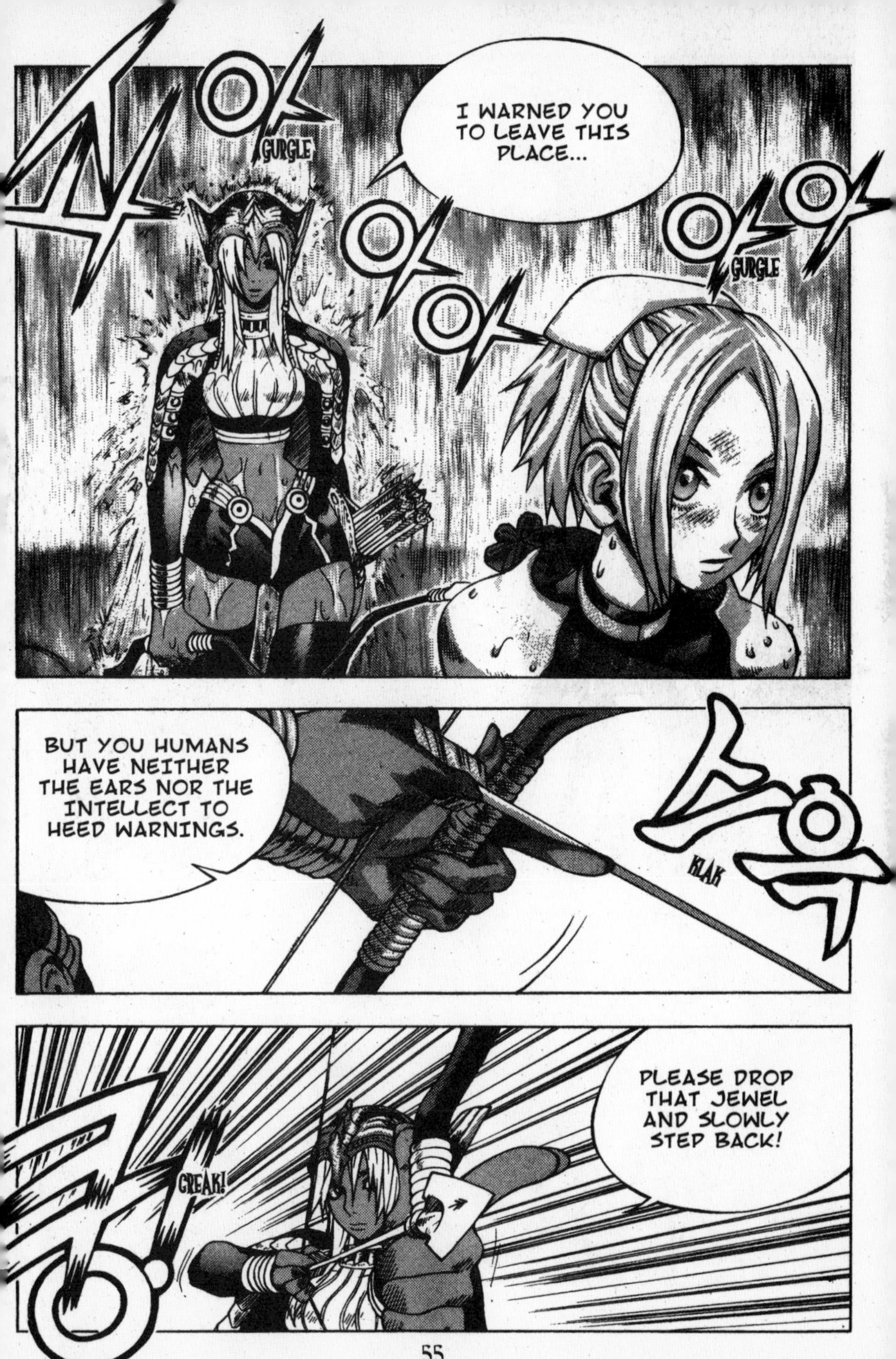
GURGLE
I WARNED YOU TO LEAVE THIS PLACE...
GURGLE
BUT YOU HUMANS HAVE NEITHER THE EARS NOR THE INTELLECT TO HEED WARNINGS.
KLAK
CREAK!
PLEASE DROP THAT JEWEL AND SLOWLY STEP BACK!

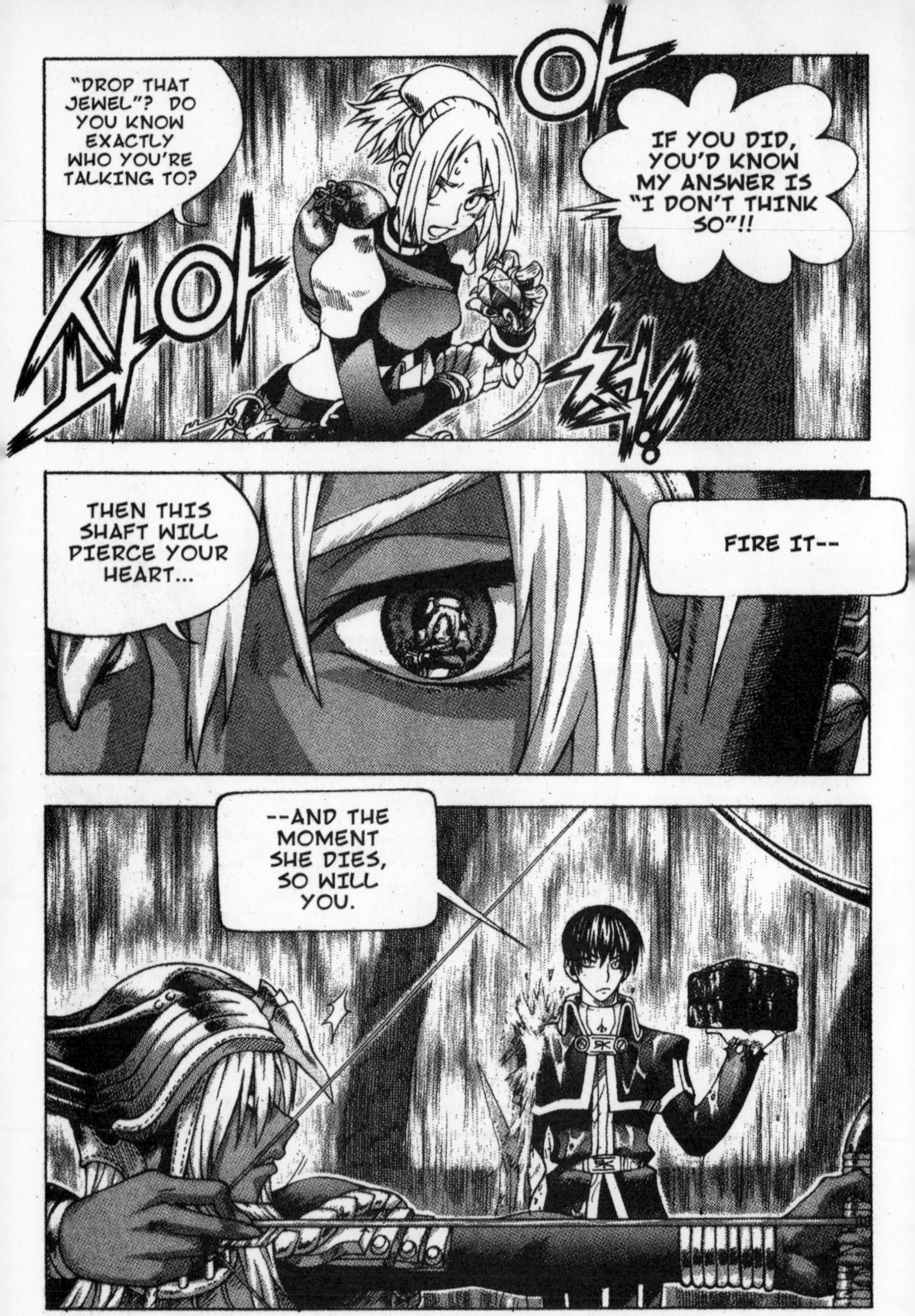
"DROP THAT JEWEL"? DO YOU KNOW EXACTLY WHO YOU'RE TALKING TO?
IF YOU DID, YOU'D KNOW MY ANSWER IS "I DON'T THINK SO"!!
THEN THIS SHAFT WILL PIERCE YOUR HEART...
FIRE IT--
--AND THE MOMENT SHE DIES, SO WILL YOU.

RAGNAROK
라그나로크
IN TO THE ABYSS

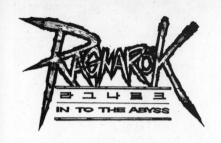

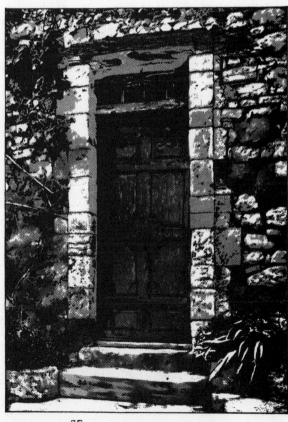

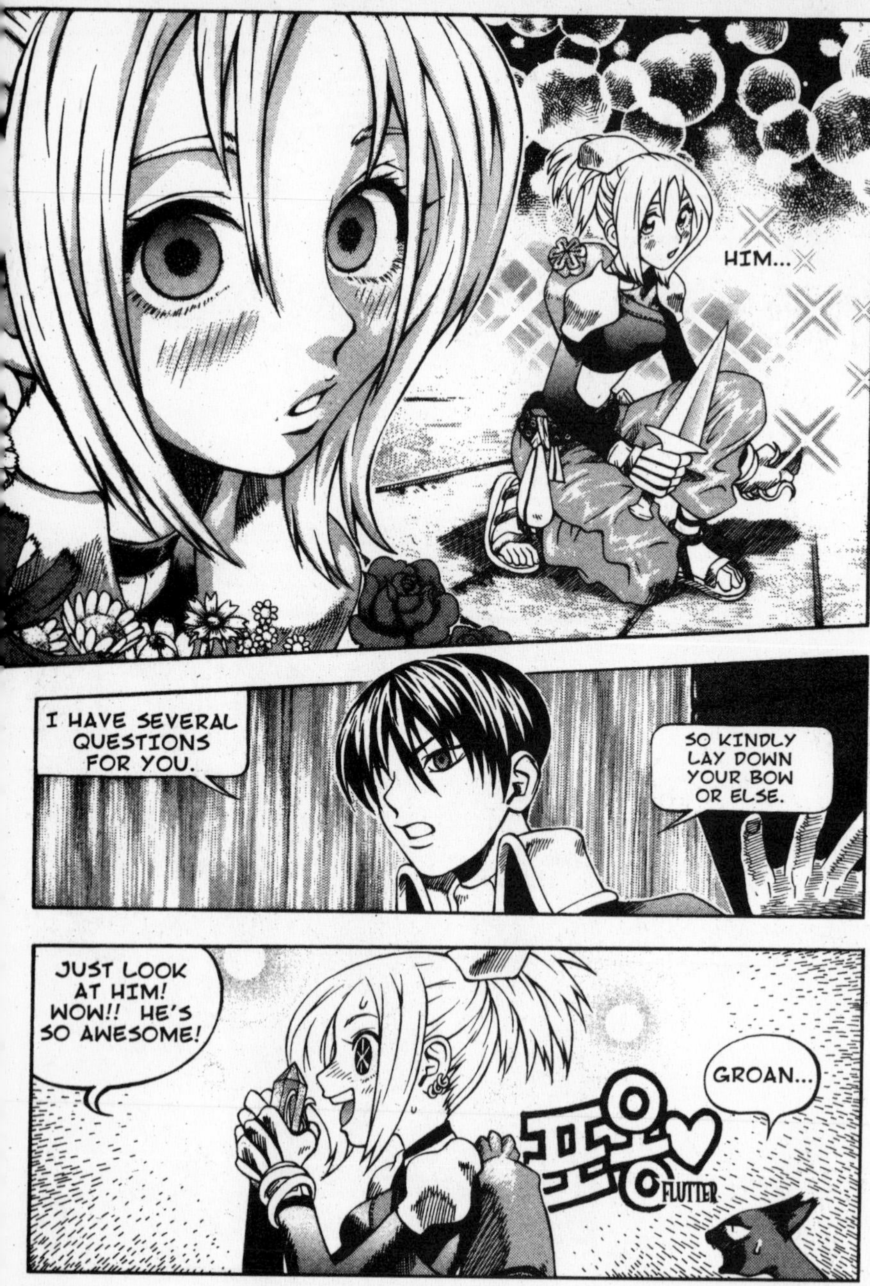
HIM...
I HAVE SEVERAL QUESTIONS FOR YOU.
SO KINDLY LAY DOWN YOUR BOW OR ELSE.
JUST LOOK AT HIM! WOW!! HE'S SO AWESOME!
FLUTTER
GROAN...

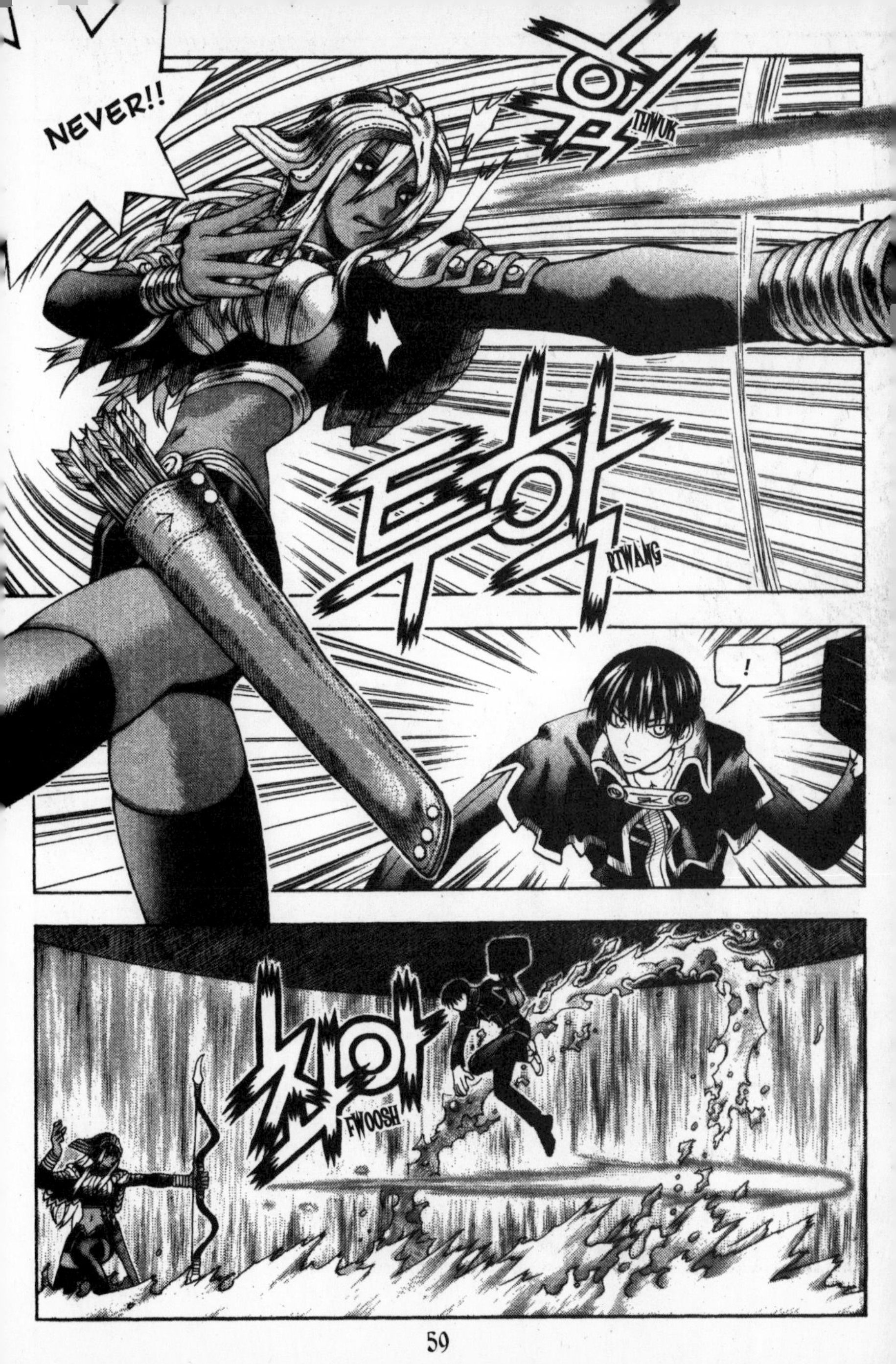
NEVER!!
THWUK
RTWANG
!
FWOOSH

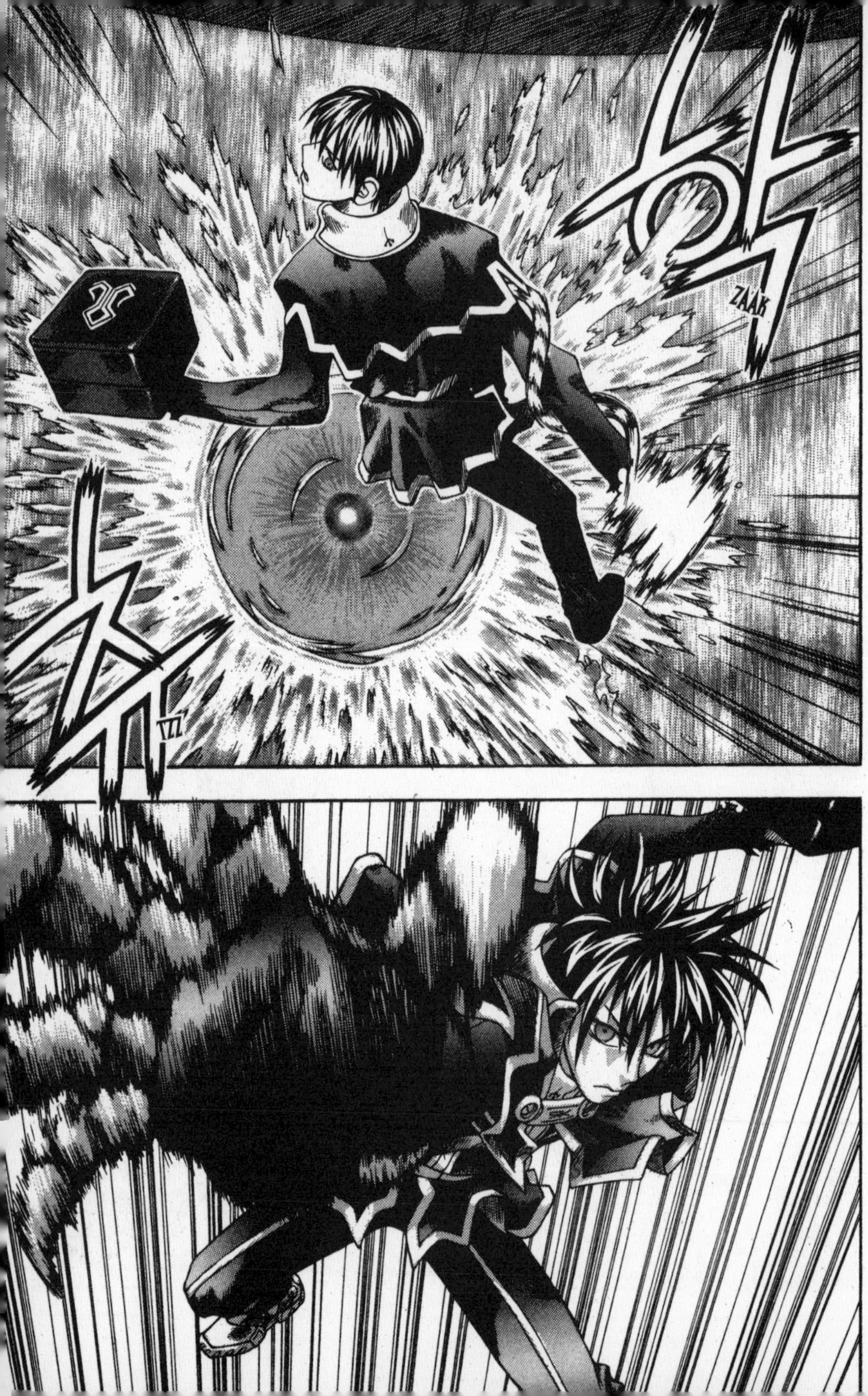
ZAAK
VZZ

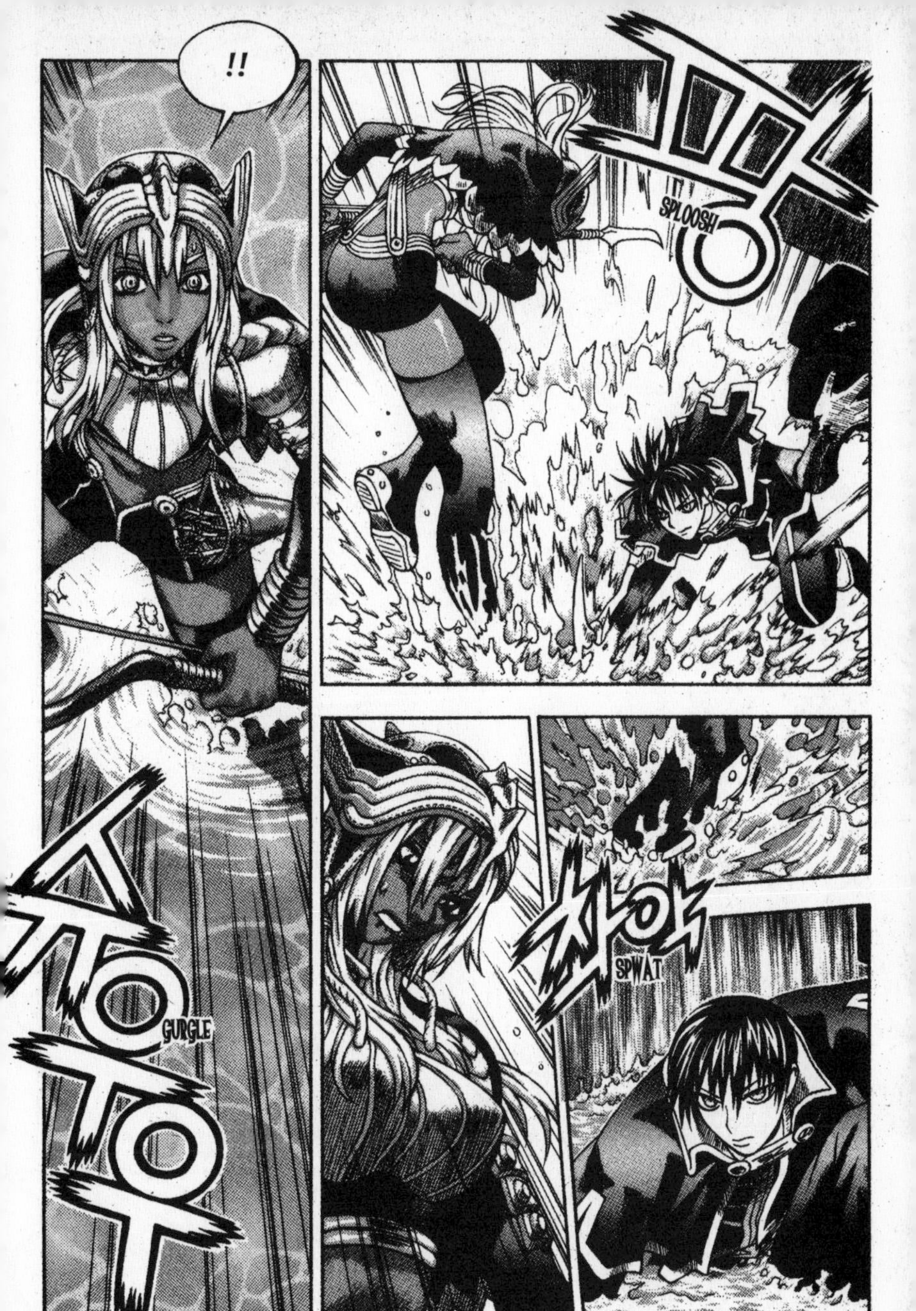
!!
GURGLE
SPLOOSH
SPWAT

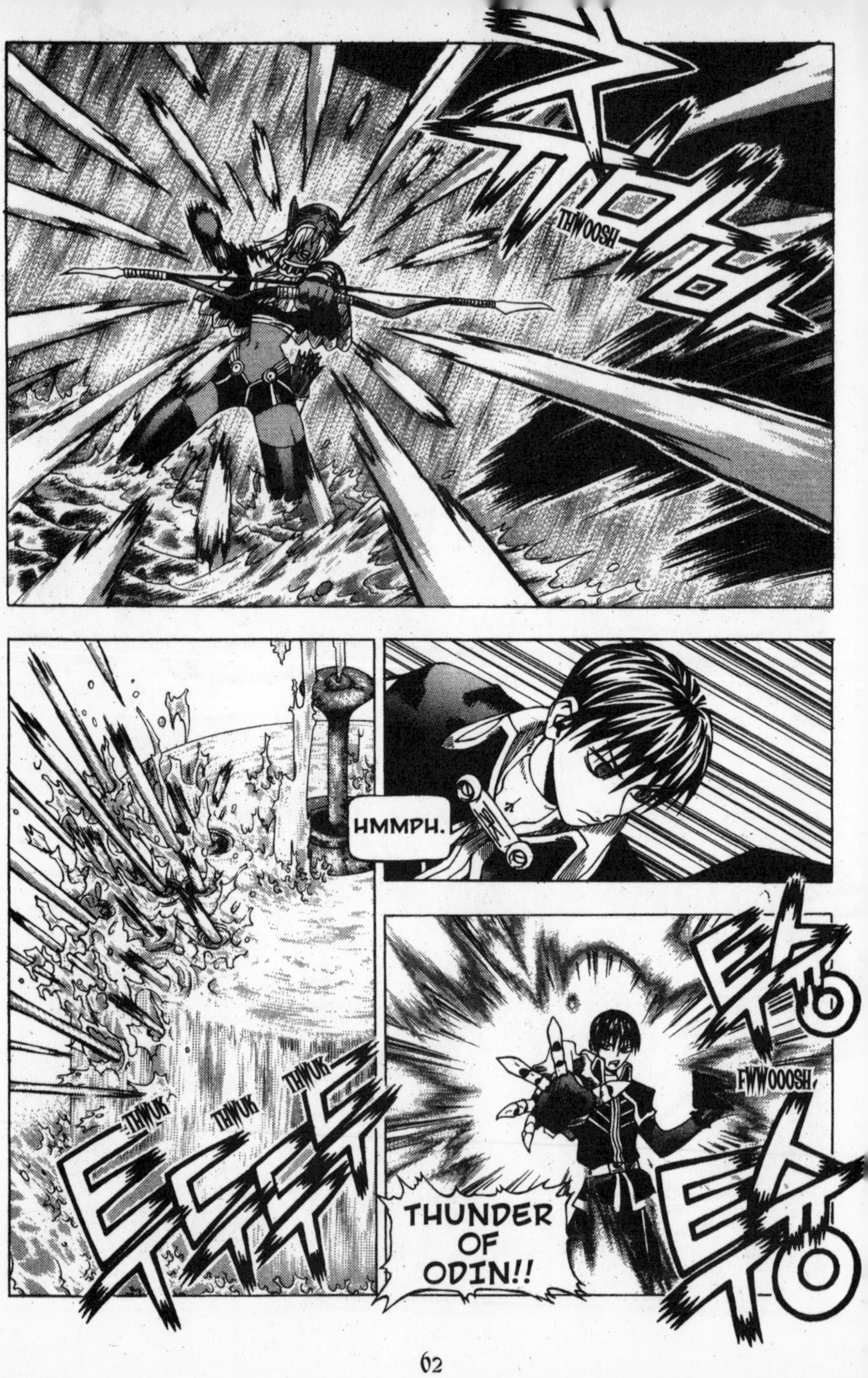
THWOOSH
THWUK
THWUK
THWUK
HMMPH.
FWWOOOSH
THUNDER OF ODIN!!

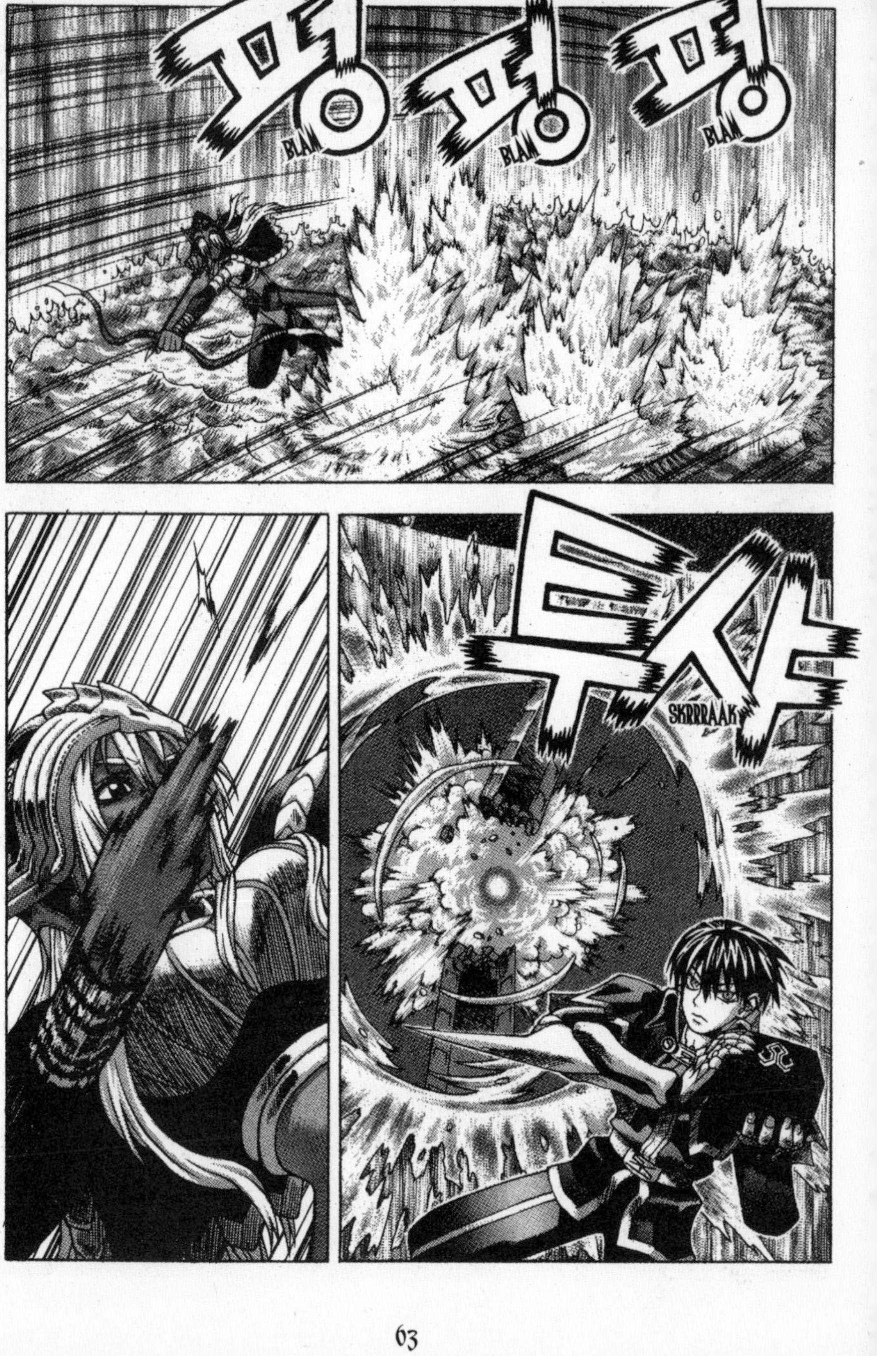
펑
BLAM
펑
BLAM
펑
BLAM
SKRRRAAK

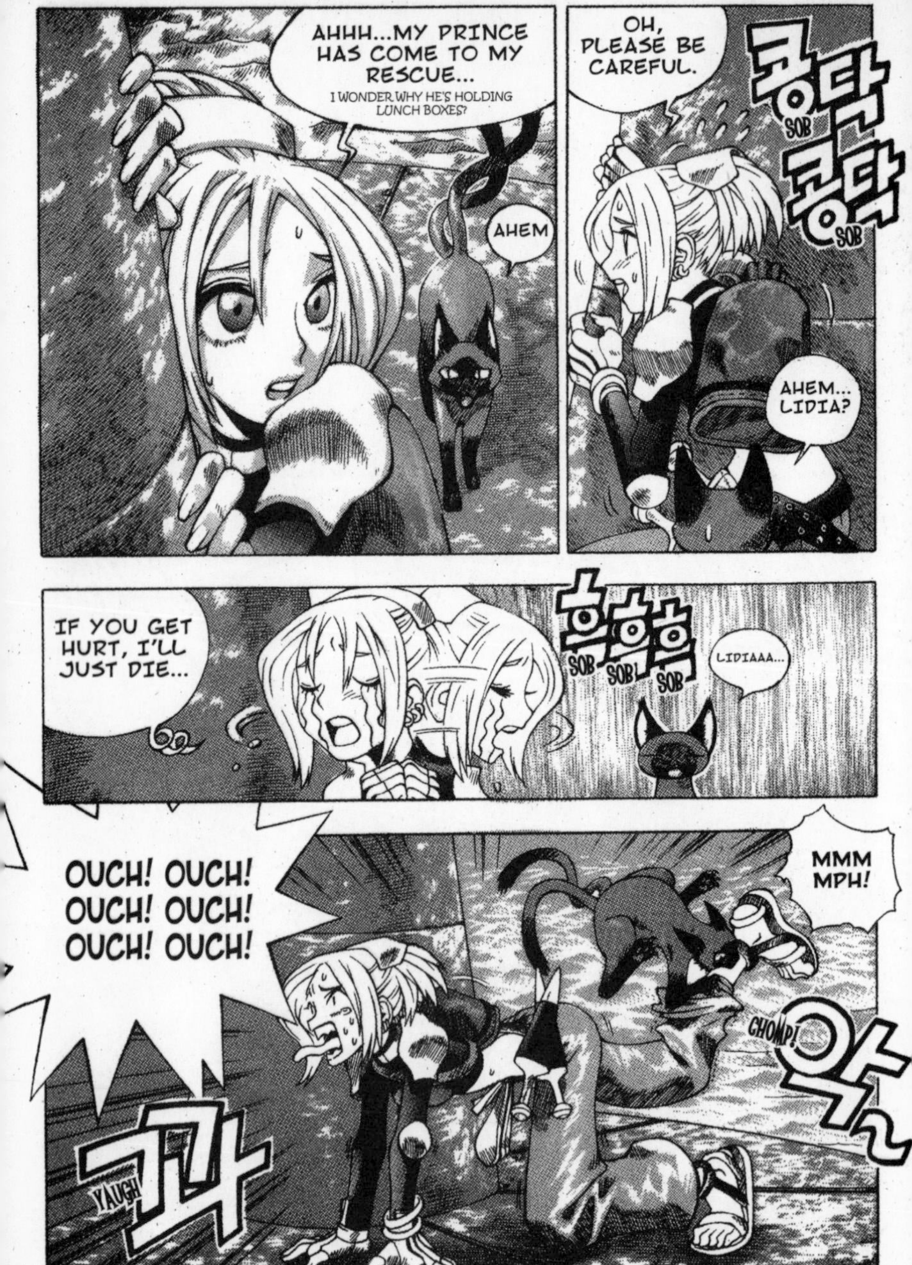
AHHH...MY PRINCE HAS COME TO MY RESCUE...
I WONDER WHY HE'S HOLDING LUNCH BOXES?
AHEM
OH, PLEASE BE CAREFUL.
콩닥 SOB
콩닥 SOB
AHEM... LIDIA?
IF YOU GET HURT, I'LL JUST DIE...
흐흐흐 SOB SOB SOB
LIDIAAA...
OUCH! OUCH! OUCH! OUCH! OUCH! OUCH!
MMM MPH!
CHOMP!
악~
YAUGH
꾸악

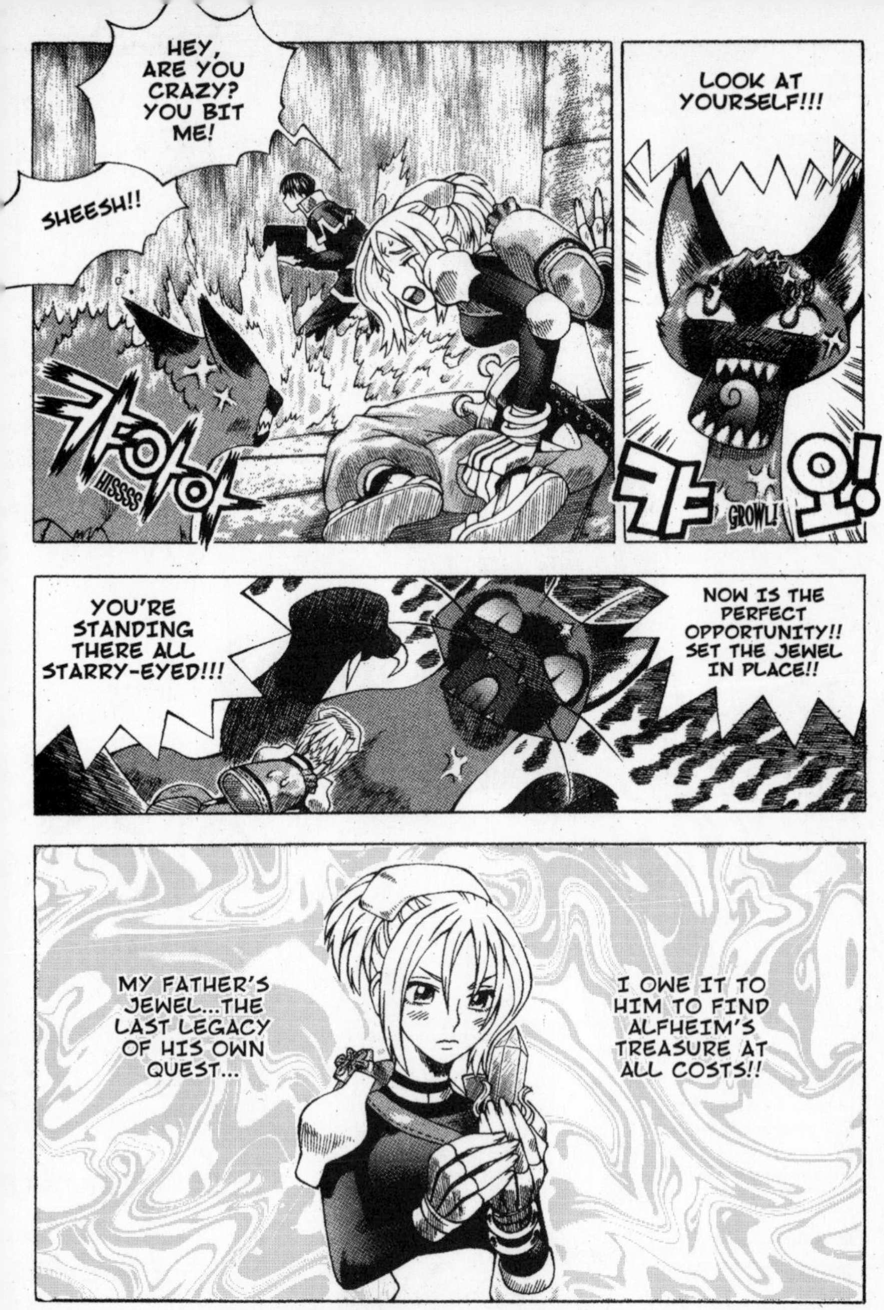
HEY, ARE YOU CRAZY? YOU BIT ME!
SHEESH!!
HISSSS
LOOK AT YOURSELF!!!
GROWL!
YOU'RE STANDING THERE ALL STARRY-EYED!!!
NOW IS THE PERFECT OPPORTUNITY!! SET THE JEWEL IN PLACE!!
MY FATHER'S JEWEL...THE LAST LEGACY OF HIS OWN QUEST...
I OWE IT TO HIM TO FIND ALFHEIM'S TREASURE AT ALL COSTS!!

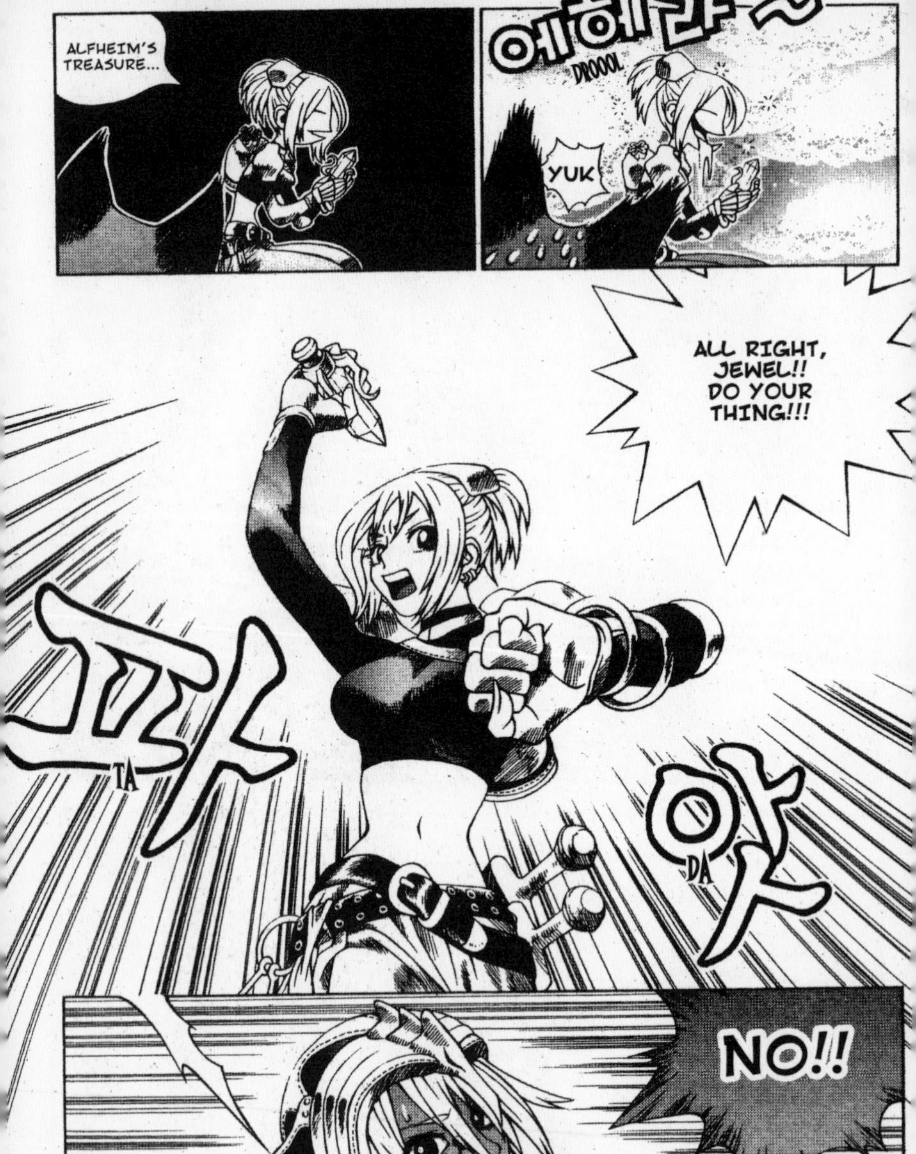
ALFHEIM'S TREASURE...
에헤라 ~
DROOOL
YUK
ALL RIGHT, JEWEL!! DO YOUR THING!!!
파
TA
앗
DA
NO!!

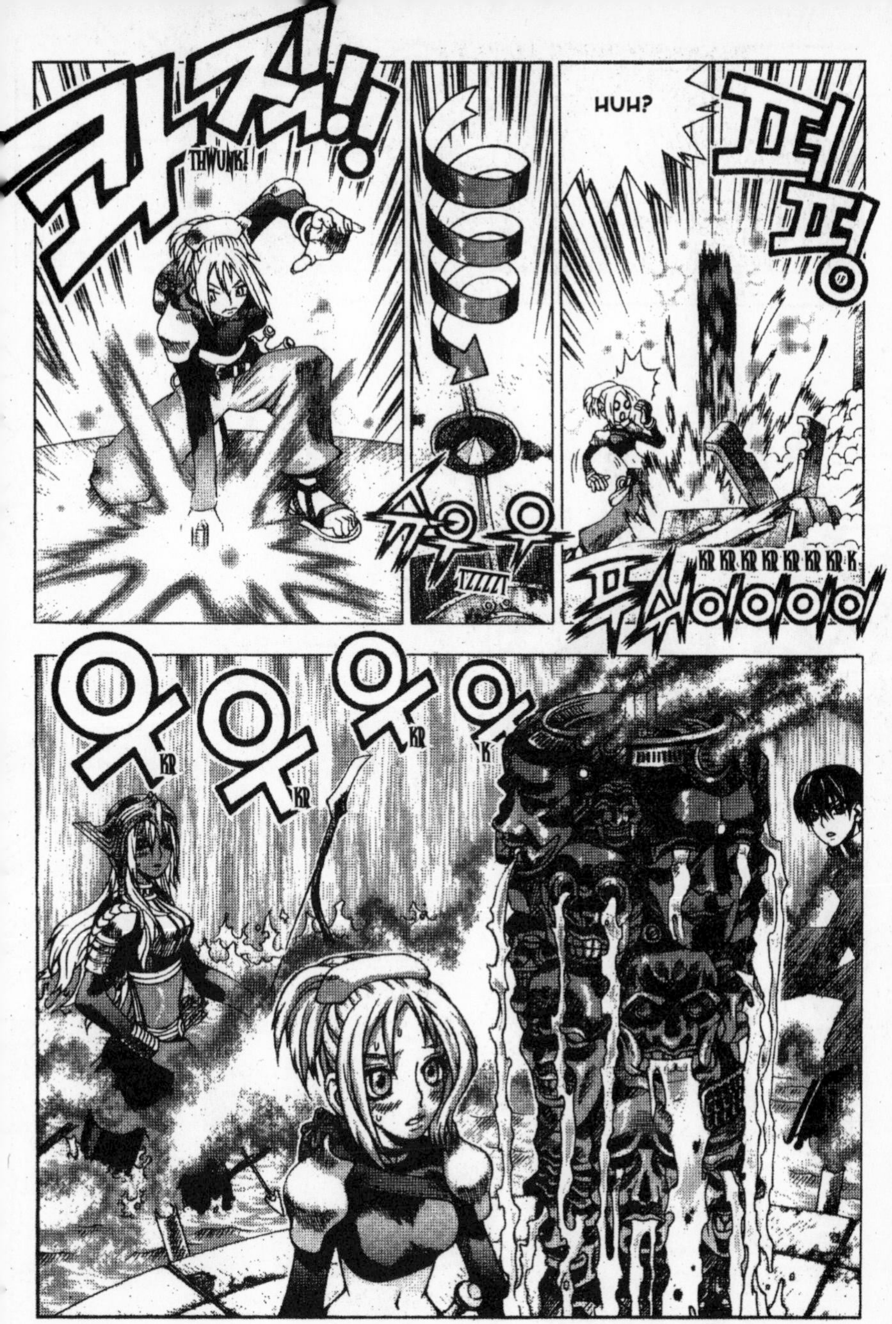
THWUNK!
ZZZZZT
HUH?
퍼펑!
KR KR KR KR KR KR KR K
푸쉬이이이이이
KR
KR
KR
K

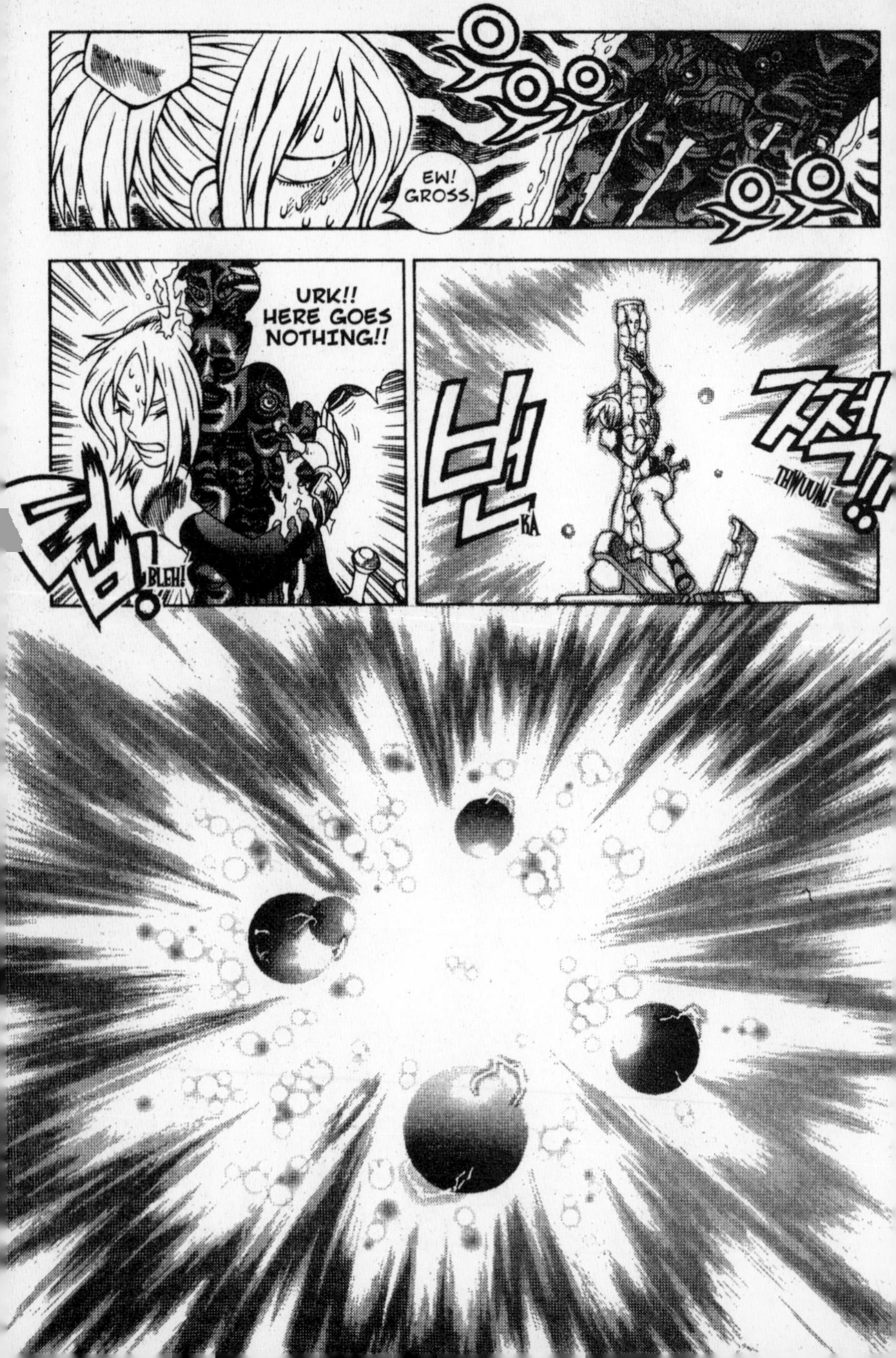
EW! GROSS.
URK!! HERE GOES NOTHING!!
BLEH!
번
KA
THWUUM!

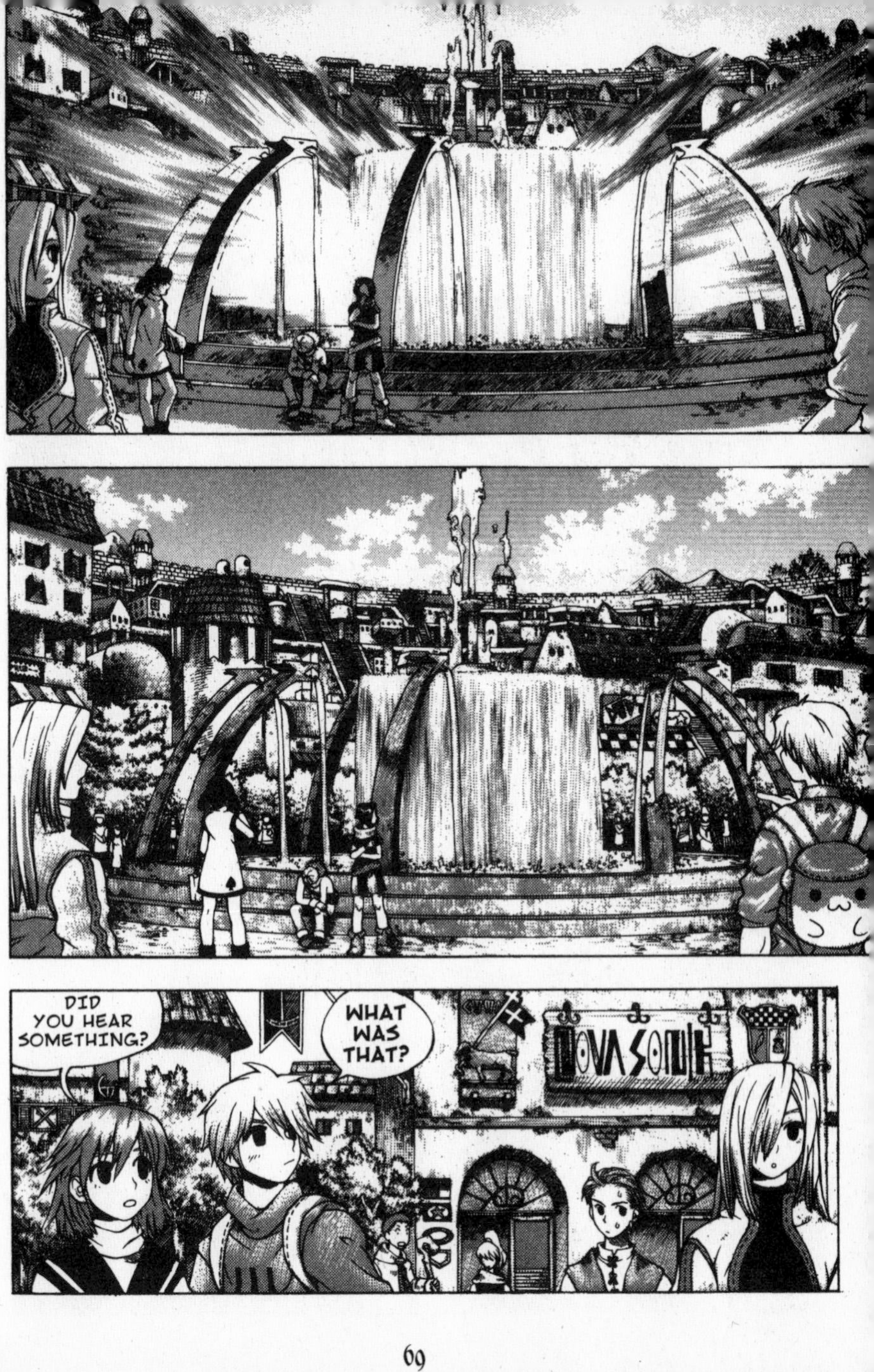
DID YOU HEAR SOMETHING?
WHAT WAS THAT?

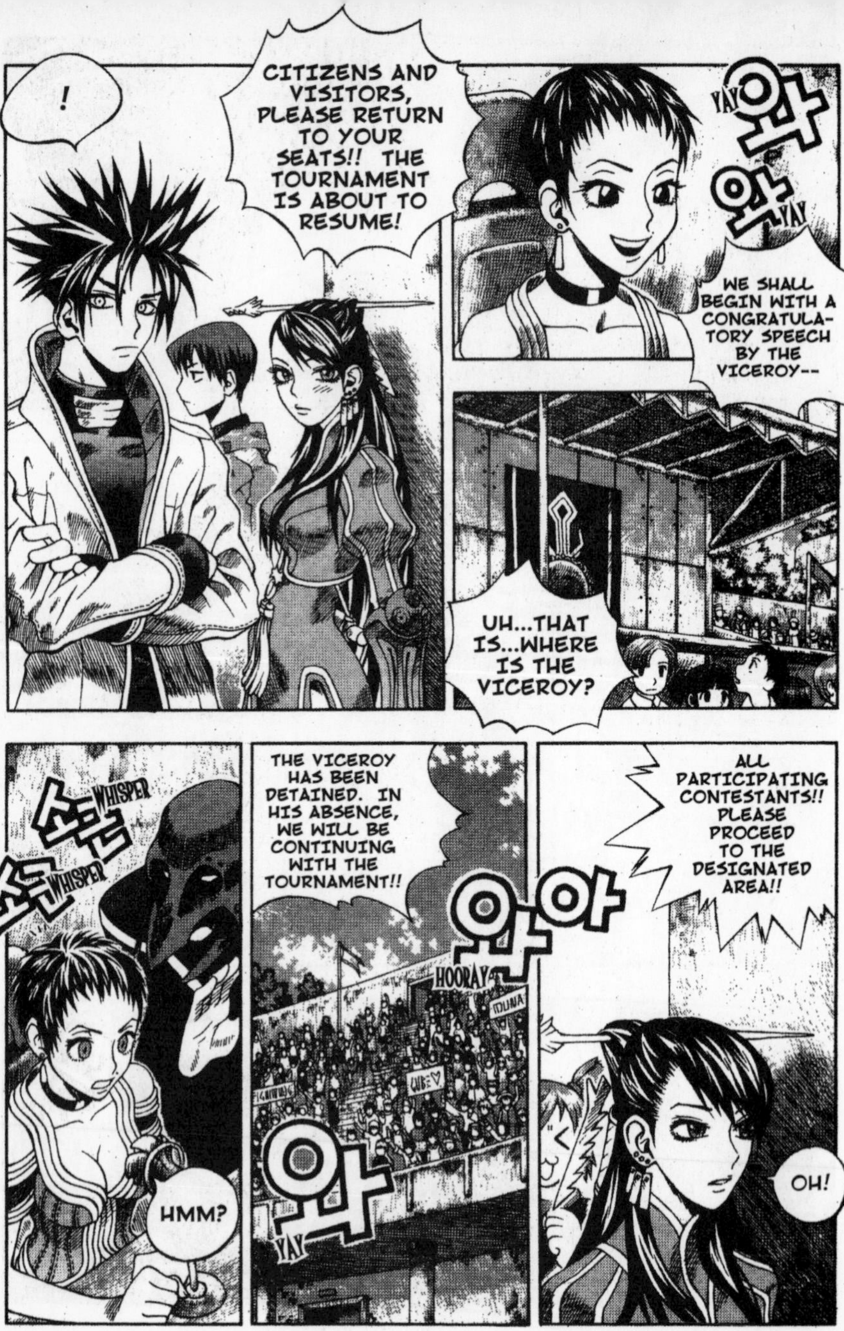
!
CITIZENS AND VISITORS, PLEASE RETURN TO YOUR SEATS!! THE TOURNAMENT IS ABOUT TO RESUME!
와 YAY
와 YAY
WE SHALL BEGIN WITH A CONGRATULATORY SPEECH BY THE VICEROY--
UH...THAT IS...WHERE IS THE VICEROY?
WHISPER
WHISPER
HMM?
THE VICEROY HAS BEEN DETAINED. IN HIS ABSENCE, WE WILL BE CONTINUING WITH THE TOURNAMENT!!
와아 HOORAY
와 YAY
ALL PARTICIPATING CONTESTANTS!! PLEASE PROCEED TO THE DESIGNATED AREA!!
OH!

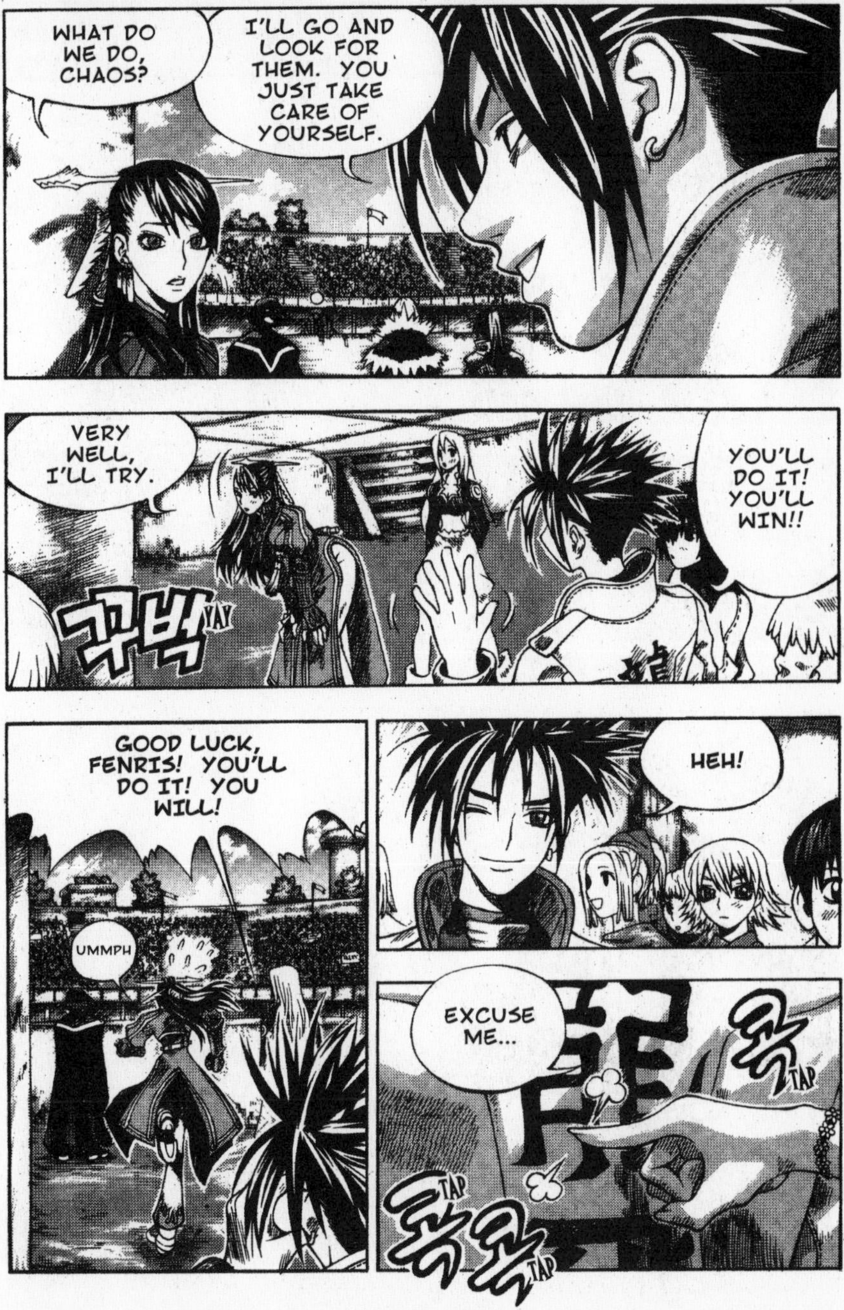
WHAT DO WE DO, CHAOS?
I'LL GO AND LOOK FOR THEM. YOU JUST TAKE CARE OF YOURSELF.
VERY WELL, I'LL TRY.
꾸벅 YAY
YOU'LL DO IT! YOU'LL WIN!!
GOOD LUCK, FENRIS! YOU'LL DO IT! YOU WILL!
UMMPH
HEH!
EXCUSE ME...
콕 TAP
콕 TAP
콕 TAP

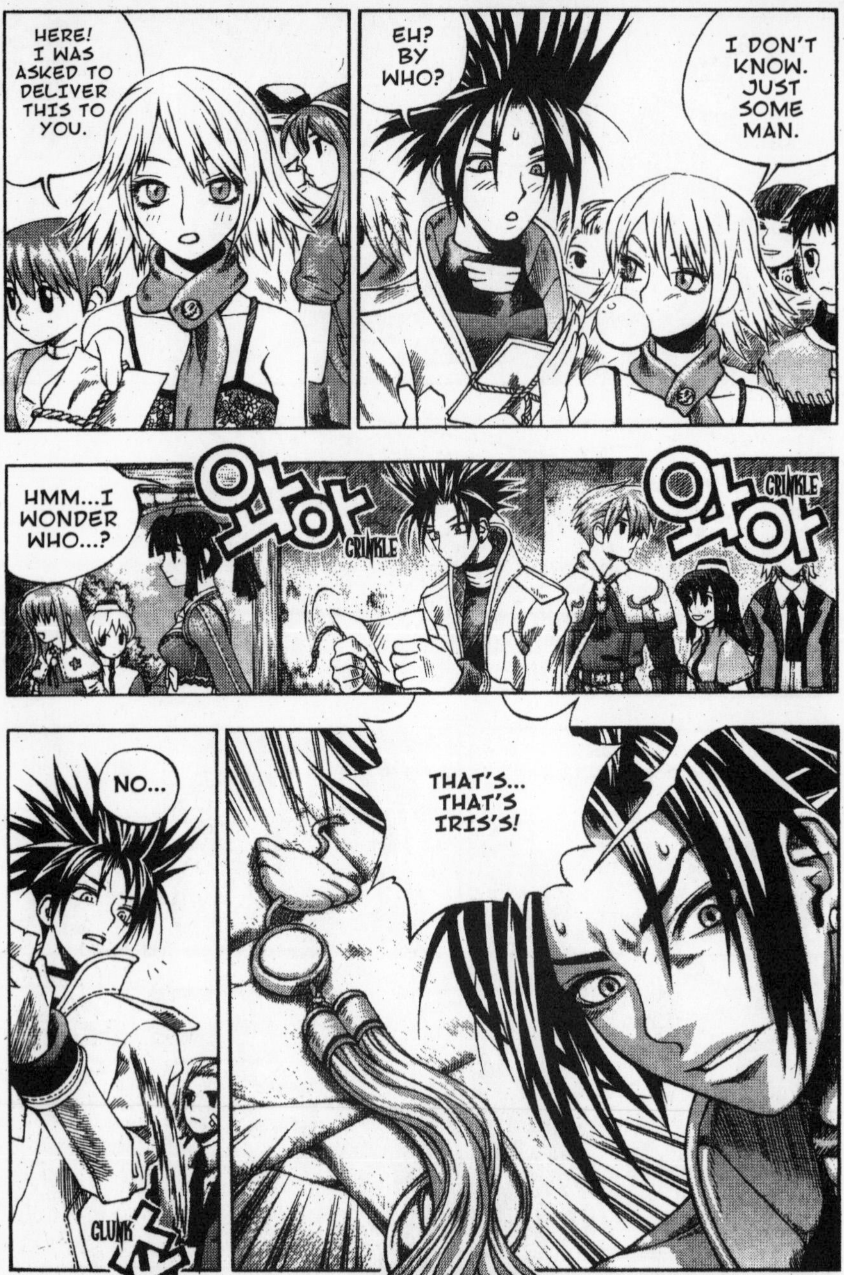
HERE! I WAS ASKED TO DELIVER THIS TO YOU.
EH? BY WHO?
I DON'T KNOW. JUST SOME MAN.
HMM...I WONDER WHO...?
와아
GRINKLE
와아
GRINKLE
NO...
THAT'S... THAT'S IRIS'S!
GLUNK

RAGNAROK

라그나로크

IN TO THE ABYSS

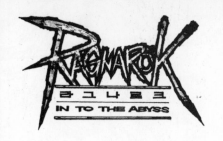

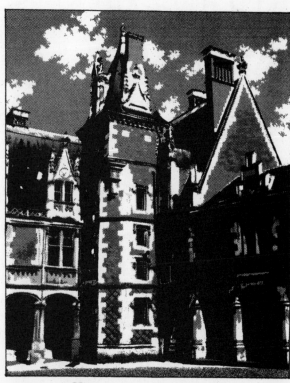

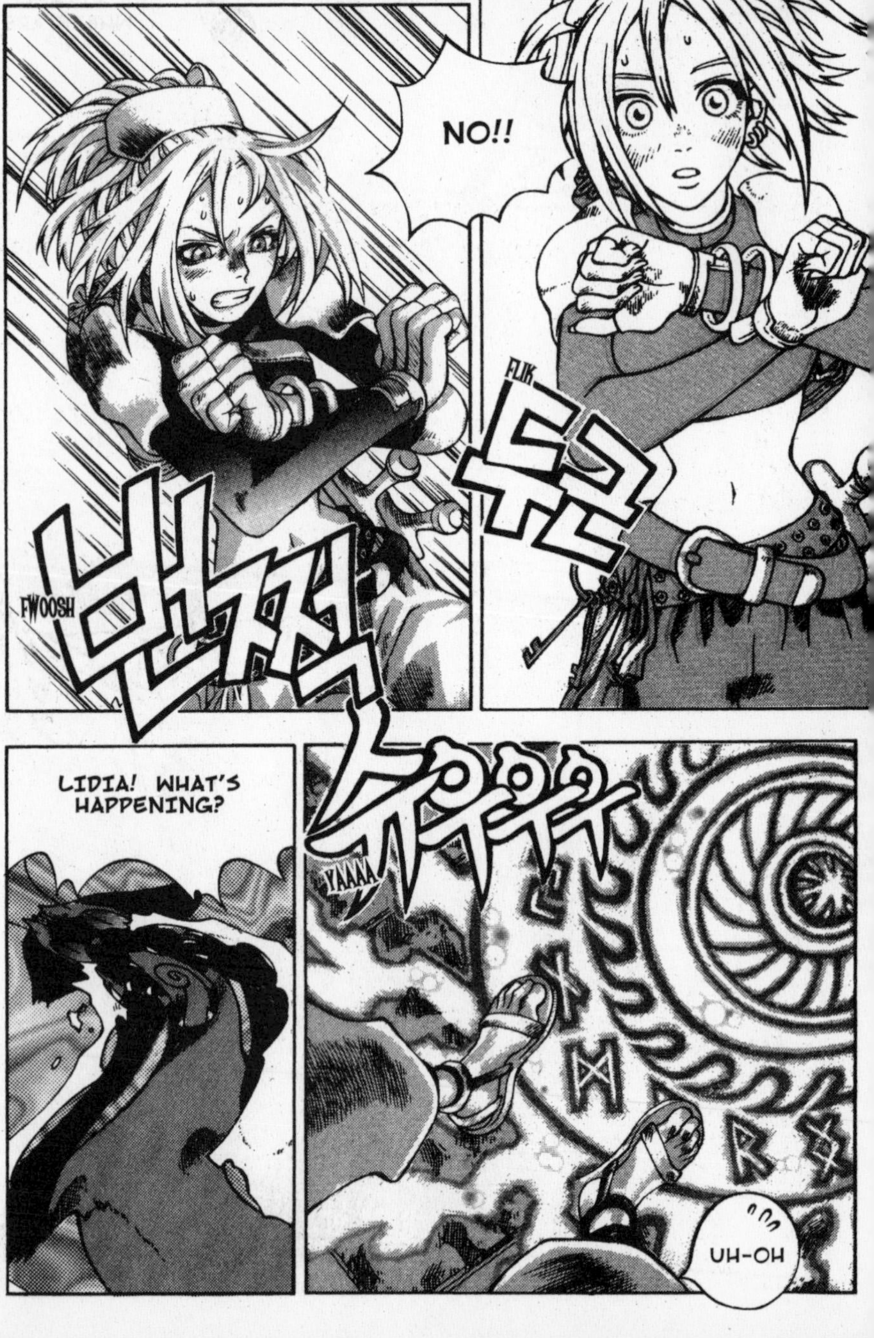
FWOOSH
NO!!
FLIK
LIDIA! WHAT'S HAPPENING?
YAAAA
UH-OH

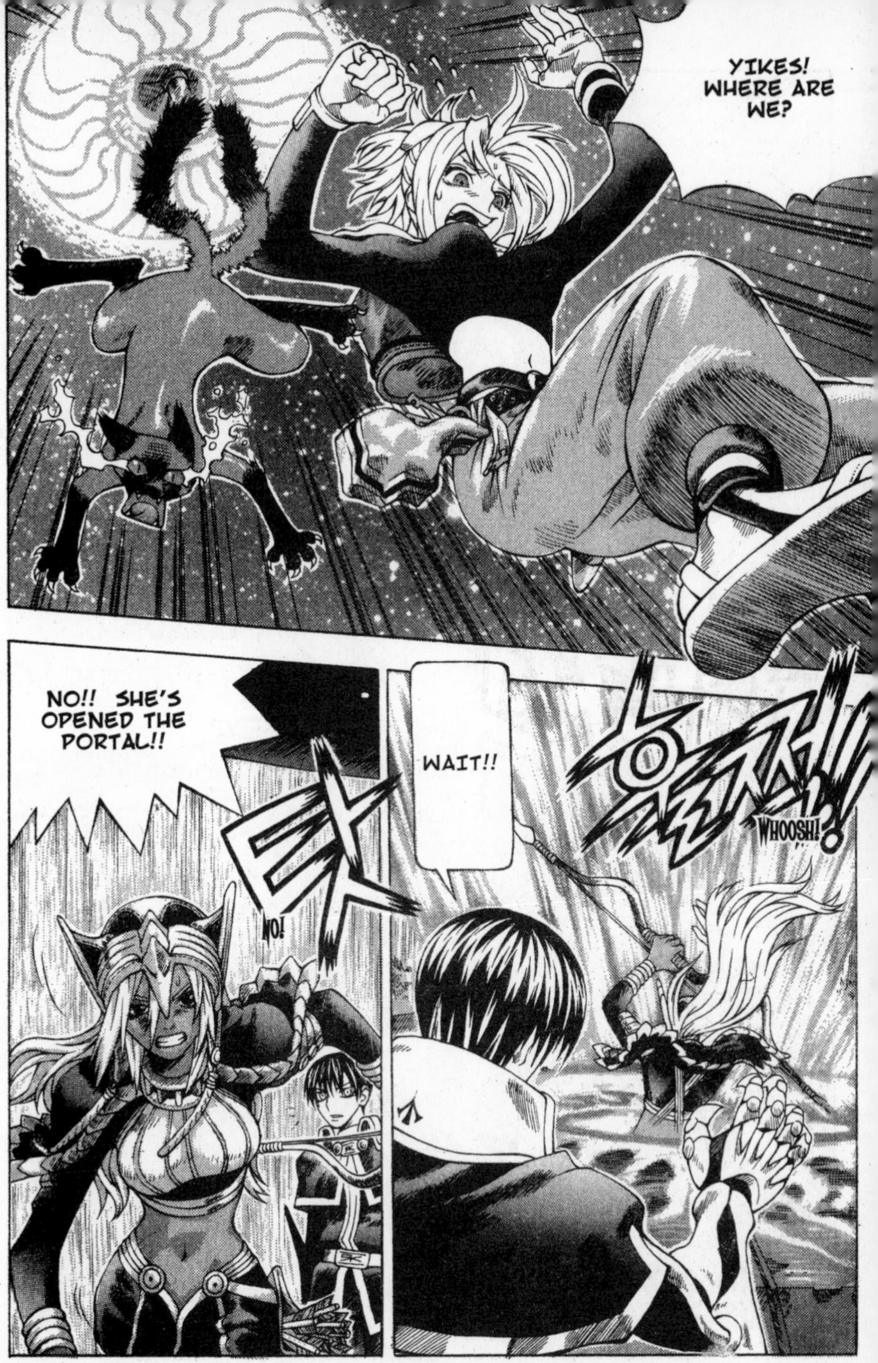
YIKES! WHERE ARE WE?
NO!! SHE'S OPENED THE PORTAL!!
NO!
WAIT!!
WHOOSH!

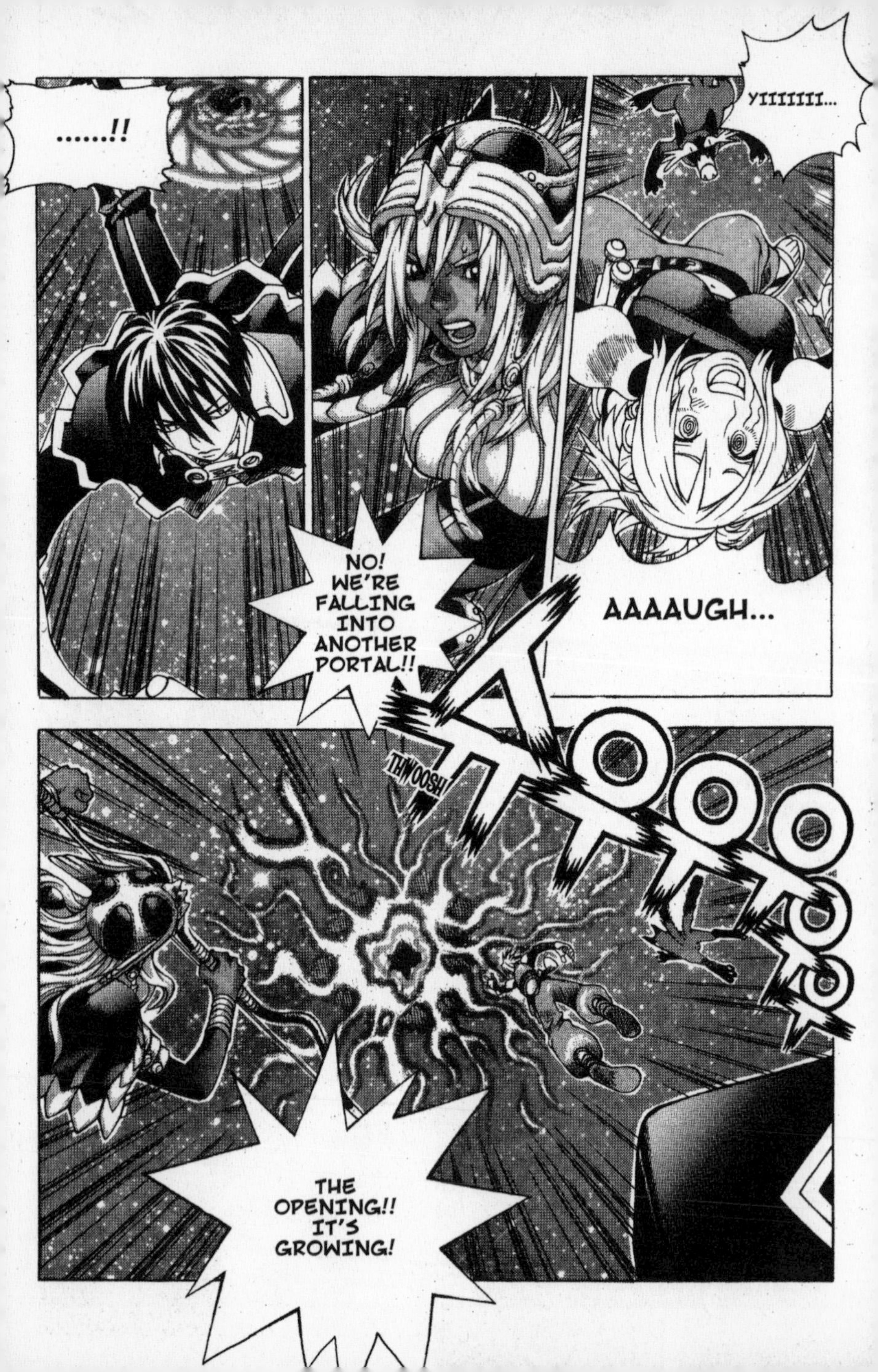

......!!
NO! WE'RE FALLING INTO ANOTHER PORTAL!!
YIIIIIII...
AAAAUGH...
THWOOSH
THE OPENING!! IT'S GROWING!

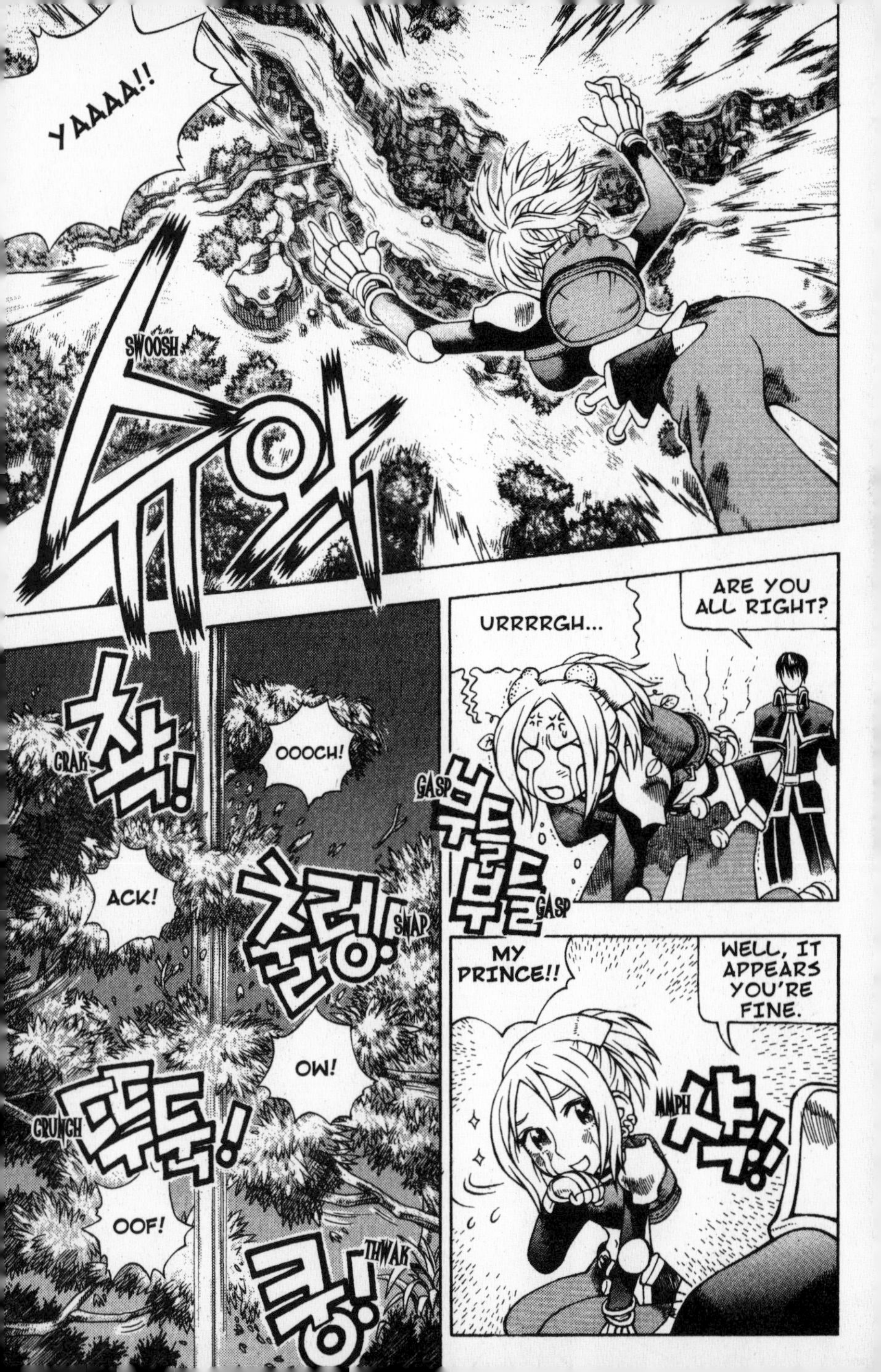
YAAAA!!
SWOOSH
CRAK
OOOCH!
ACK!
SNAP
OW!
CRUNCH
OOF!
THWAK
URRRRGH...
ARE YOU ALL RIGHT?
GASP
GASP
MY PRINCE!!
WELL, IT APPEARS YOU'RE FINE.
MMPH

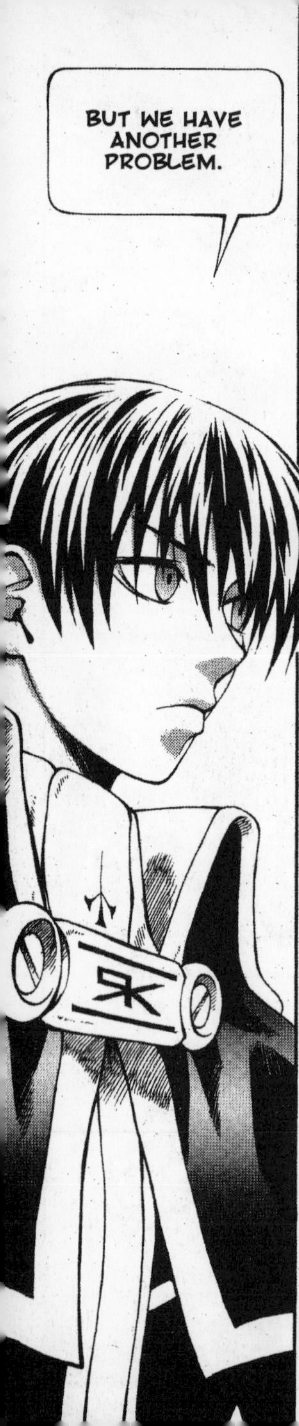
BUT WE HAVE ANOTHER PROBLEM.

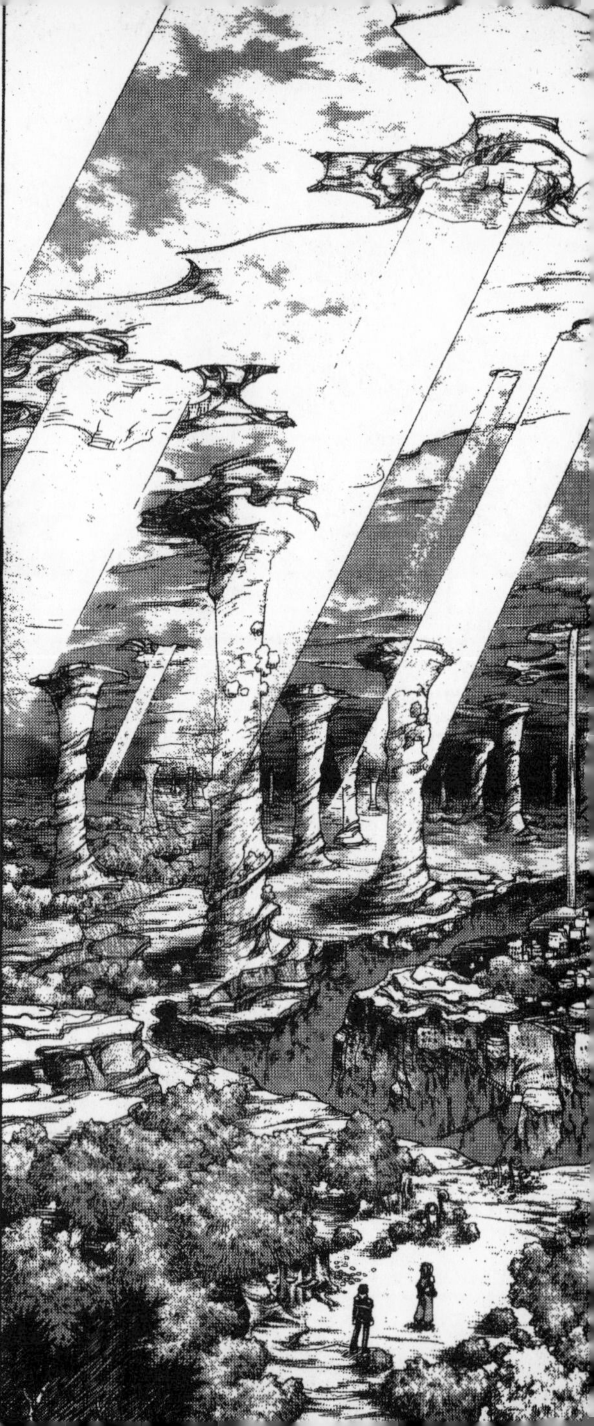

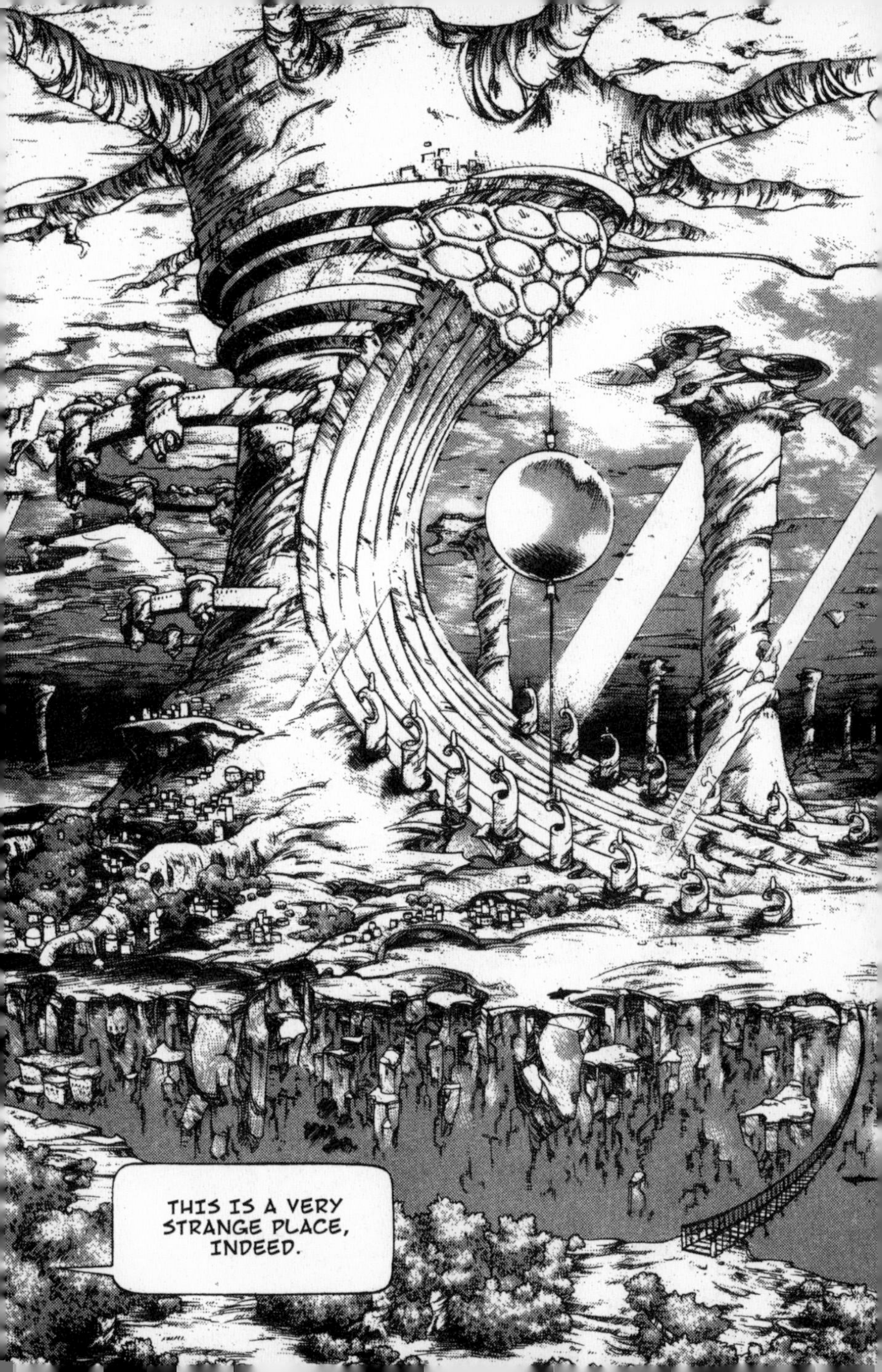
THIS IS A VERY STRANGE PLACE, INDEED.

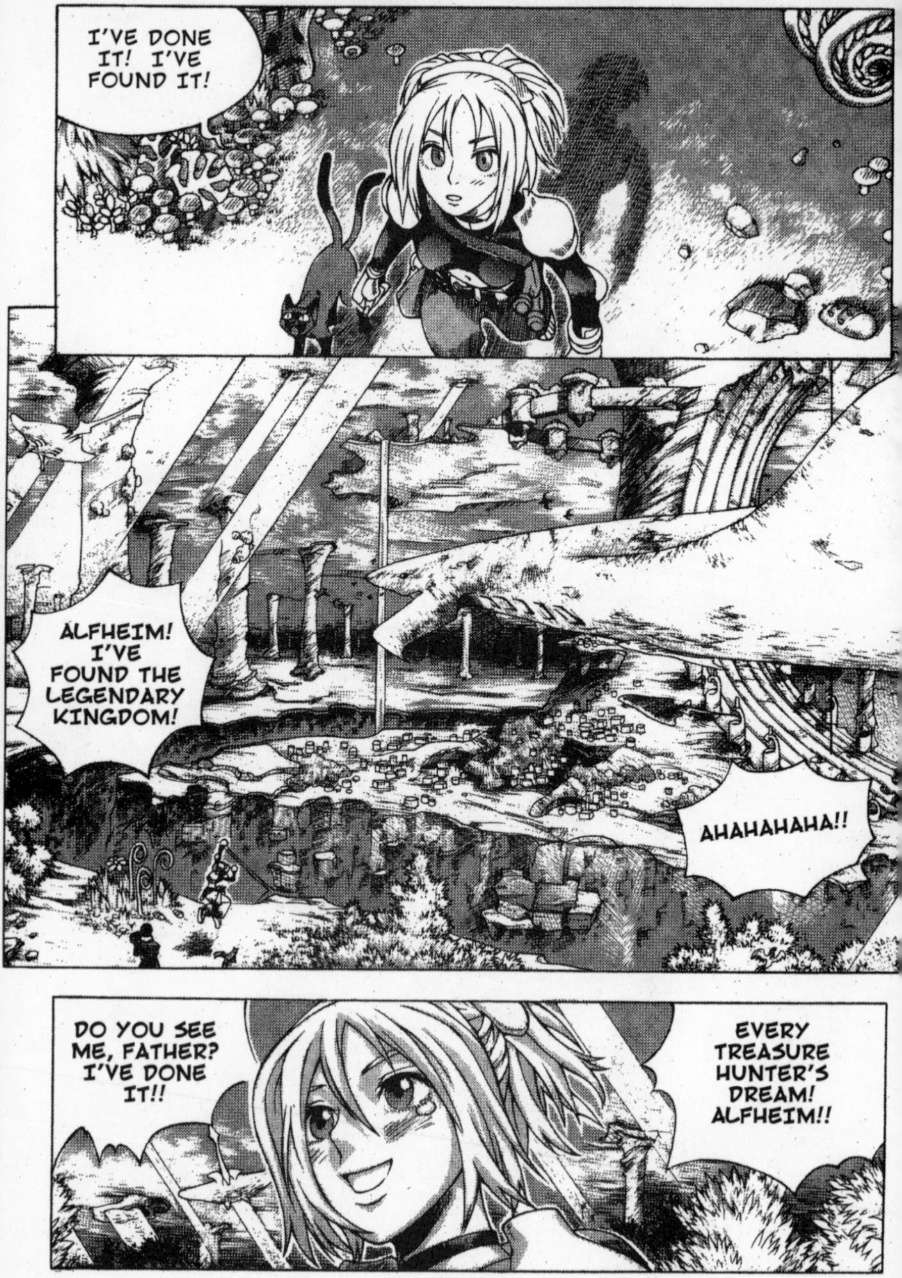
I'VE DONE IT! I'VE FOUND IT!
ALFHEIM! I'VE FOUND THE LEGENDARY KINGDOM!
AHAHAHAHA!!
DO YOU SEE ME, FATHER? I'VE DONE IT!!
EVERY TREASURE HUNTER'S DREAM! ALFHEIM!!

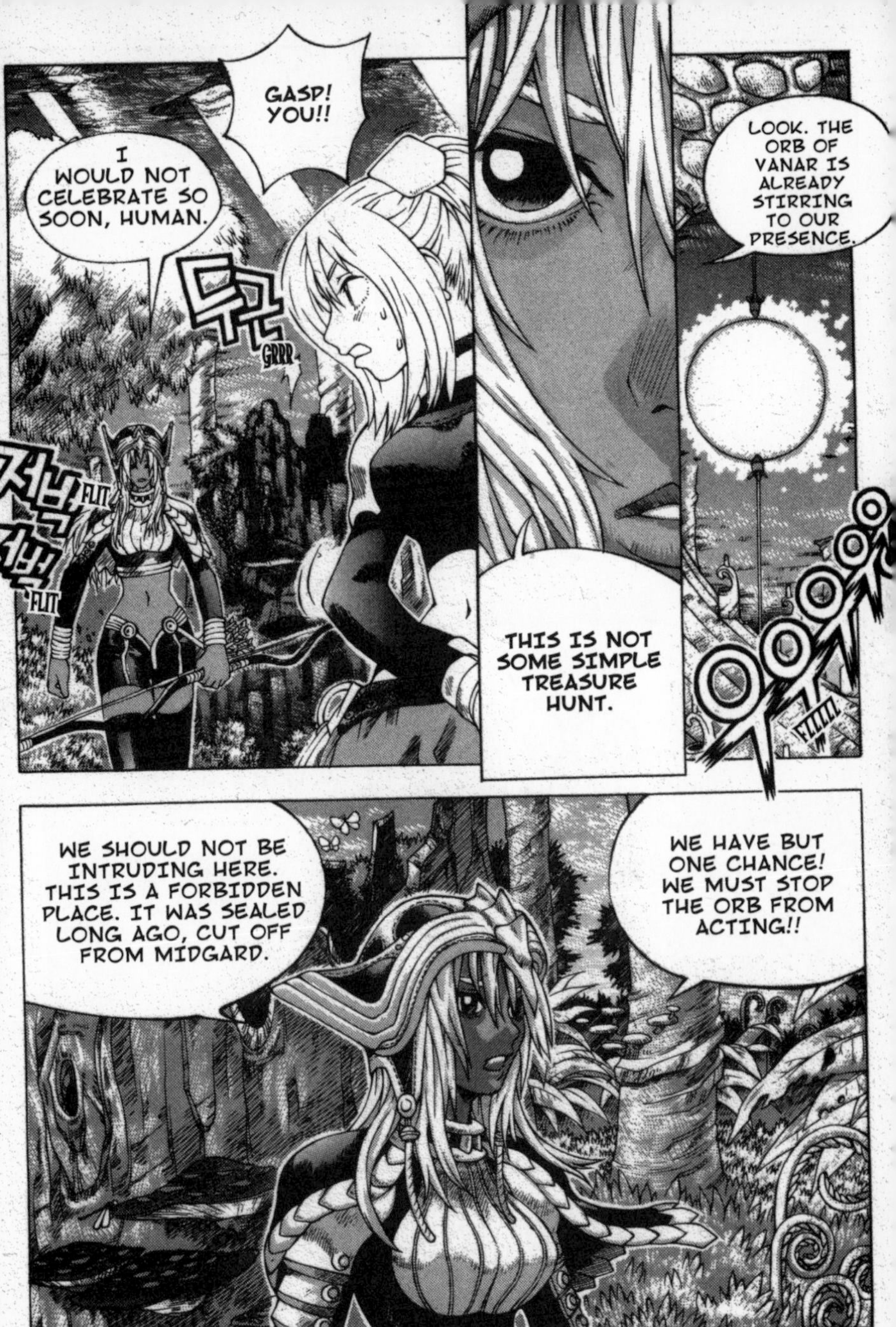
GASP! YOU!!
I WOULD NOT CELEBRATE SO SOON, HUMAN.
GRRR
FLIT
FLIT
THIS IS NOT SOME SIMPLE TREASURE HUNT.
LOOK. THE ORB OF VANAR IS ALREADY STIRRING TO OUR PRESENCE.
WE SHOULD NOT BE INTRUDING HERE. THIS IS A FORBIDDEN PLACE. IT WAS SEALED LONG AGO, CUT OFF FROM MIDGARD.
WE HAVE BUT ONE CHANCE! WE MUST STOP THE ORB FROM ACTING!!

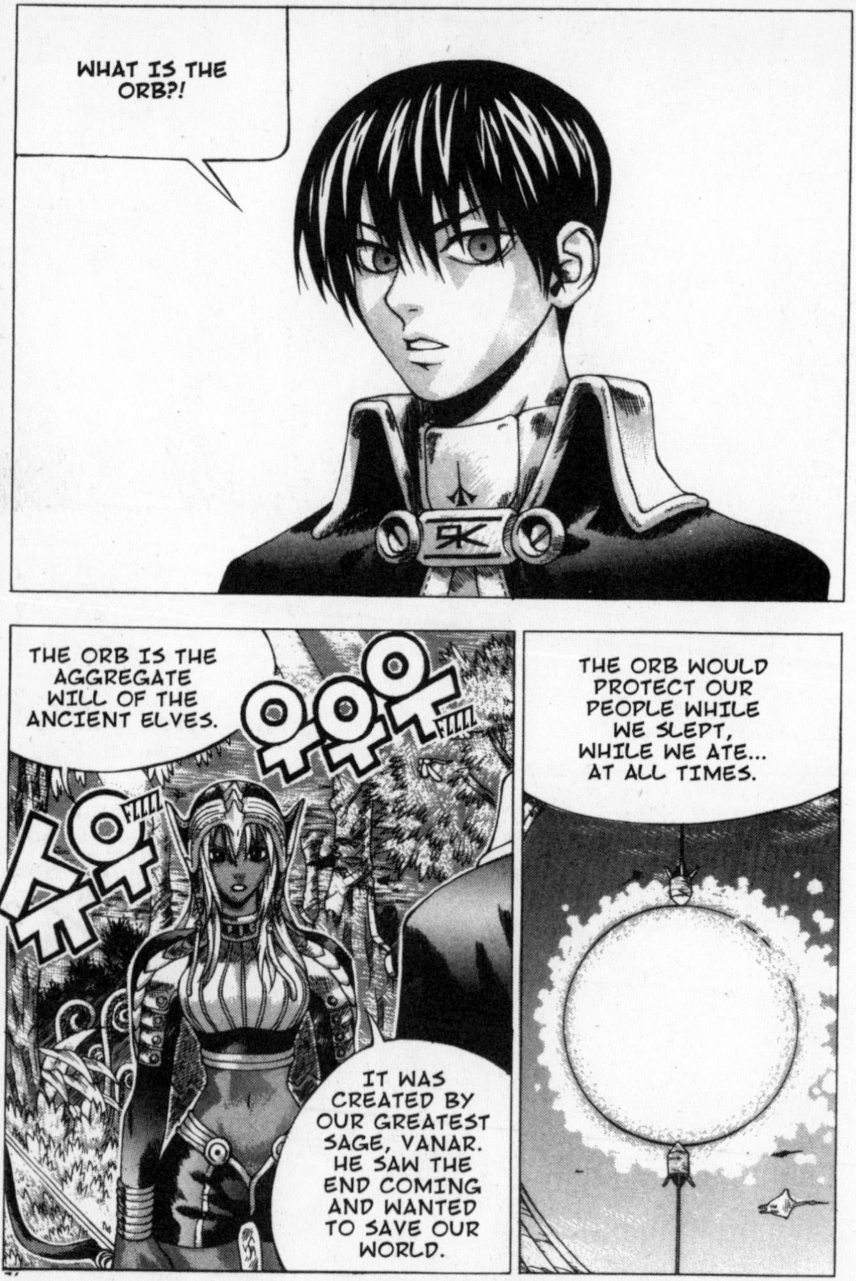
WHAT IS THE ORB?!
THE ORB IS THE AGGREGATE WILL OF THE ANCIENT ELVES.
IT WAS CREATED BY OUR GREATEST SAGE, VANAR. HE SAW THE END COMING AND WANTED TO SAVE OUR WORLD.
THE ORB WOULD PROTECT OUR PEOPLE WHILE WE SLEPT, WHILE WE ATE... AT ALL TIMES.

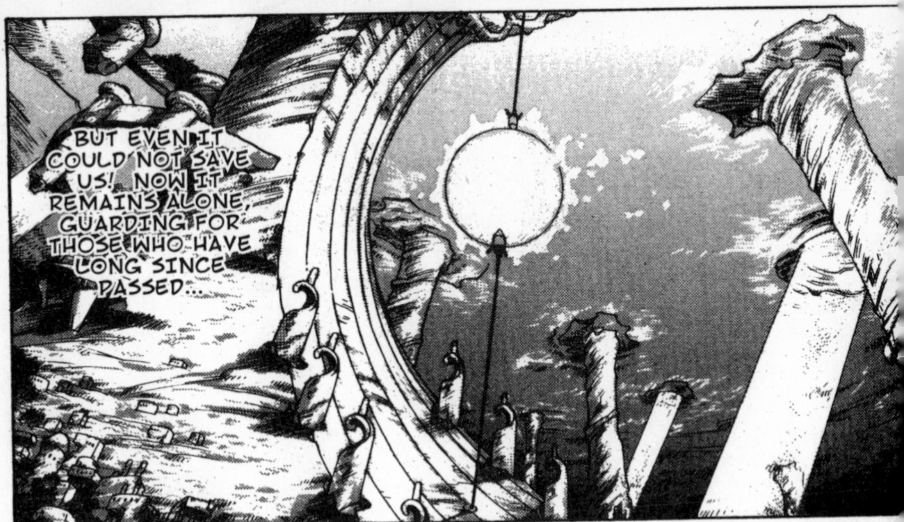
BUT EVEN IT COULD NOT SAVE US! NOW IT REMAINS ALONE, GUARDING FOR THOSE WHO HAVE LONG SINCE PASSED...

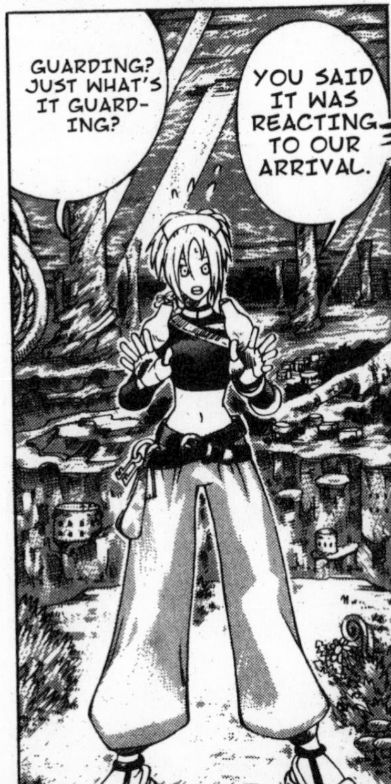
GUARDING? JUST WHAT'S IT GUARD-ING?
YOU SAID IT WAS REACTING TO OUR ARRIVAL.

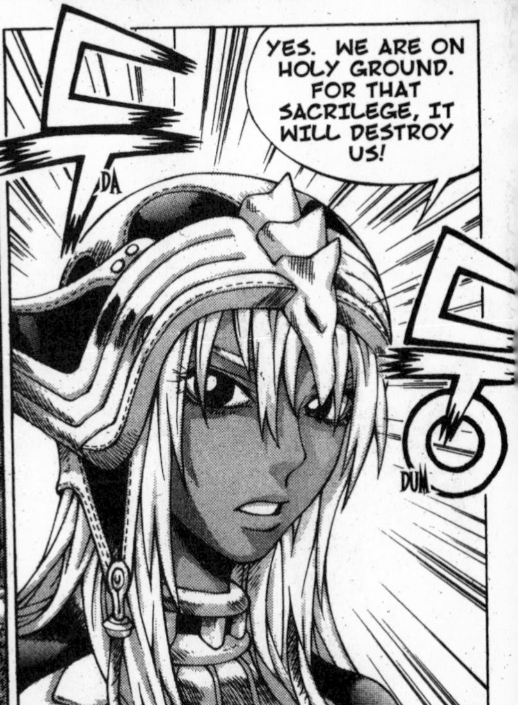
YES. WE ARE ON HOLY GROUND. FOR THAT SACRILEGE, IT WILL DESTROY US!
DA
DUM

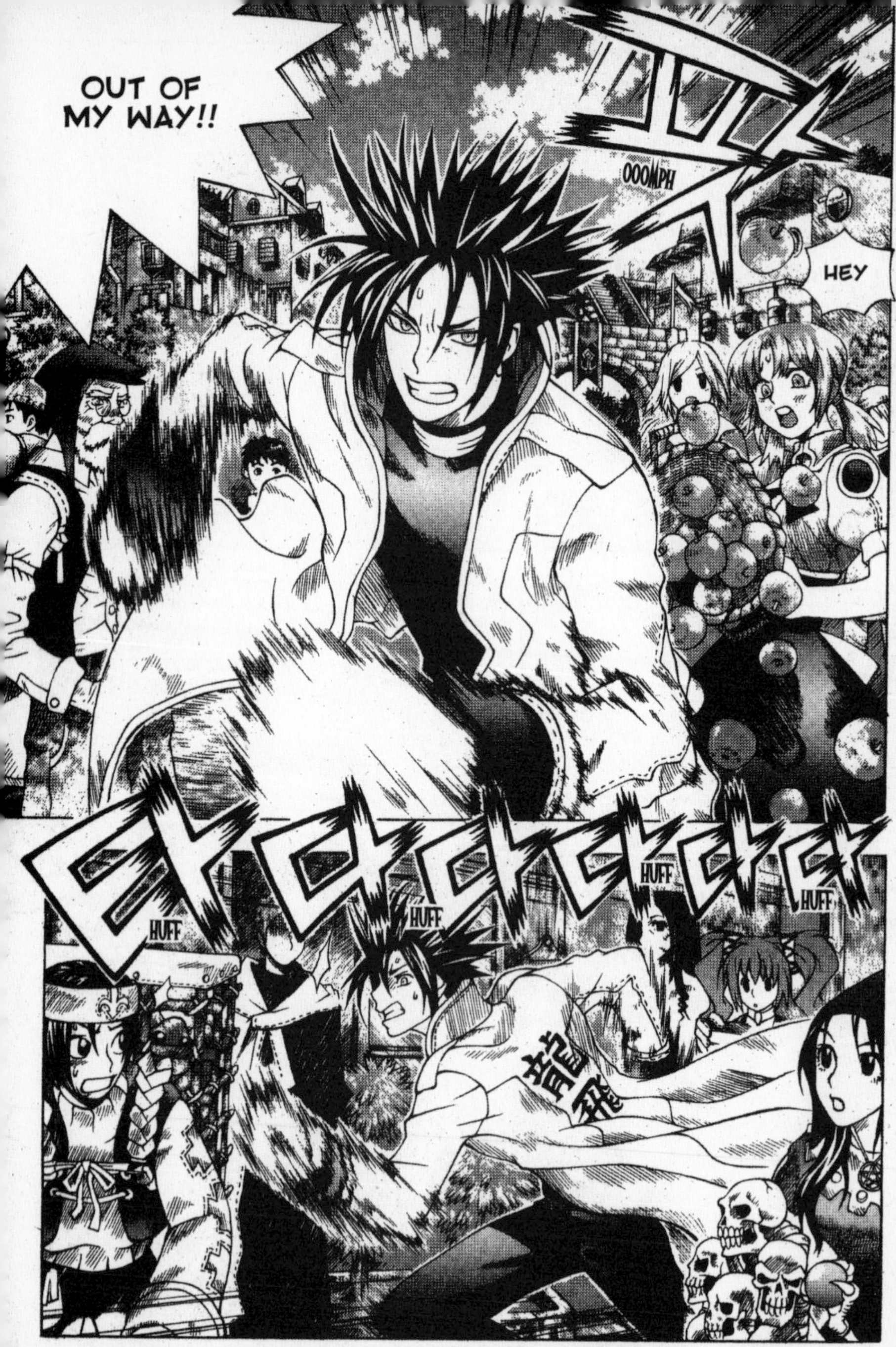
OUT OF MY WAY!!
OOOMPH
HEY
HUFF
HUFF
HUFF
HUFF

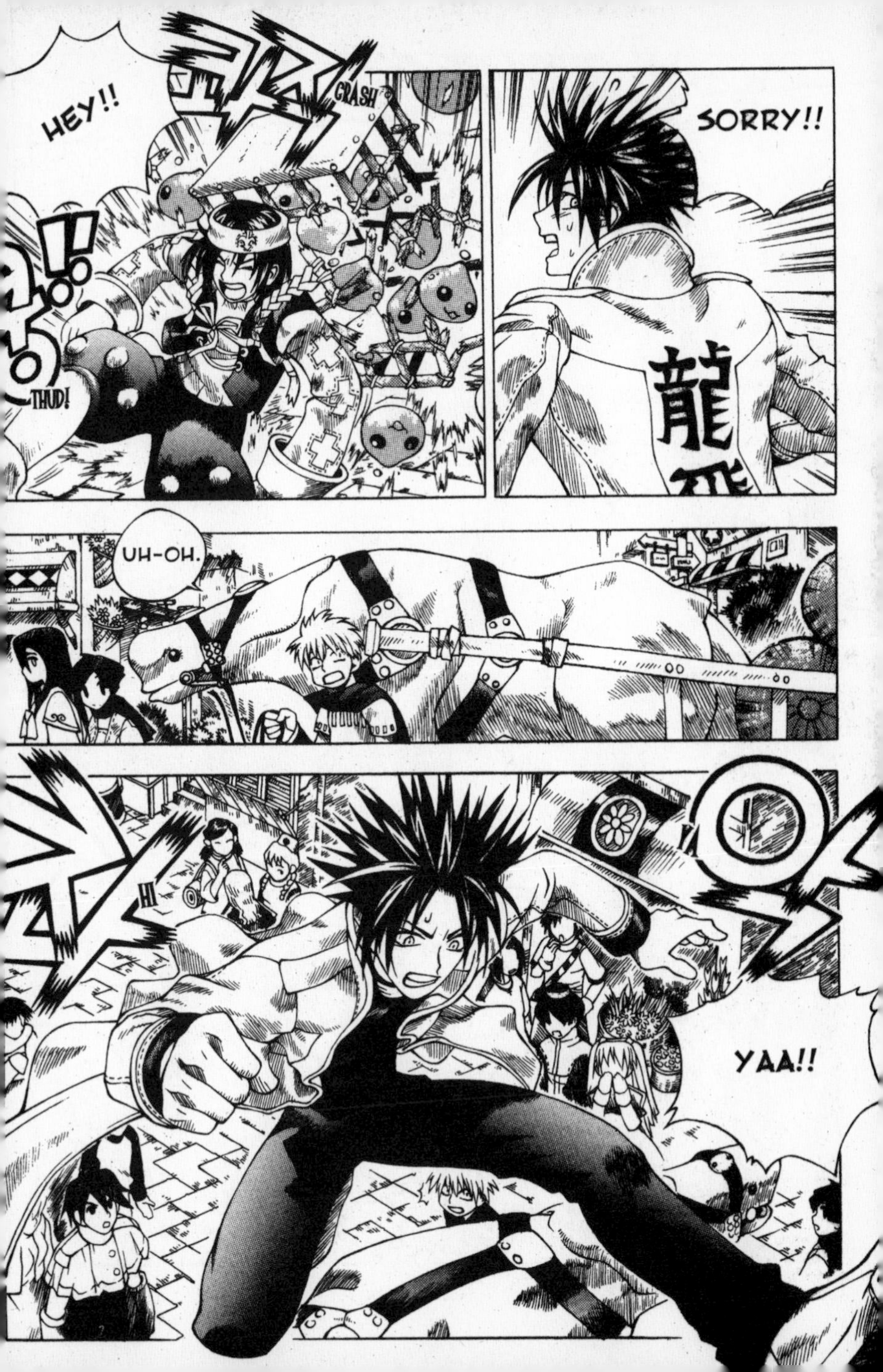
HEY!!
CRASH
THUD!
SORRY!!
龍
UH-OH.
HI
YAA!!

AAH, MY DEAR CHAOS... HOW HAVE YOU BEEN?

GASP!

I-I'M SORRY!

EEEK!!

YOU DO REMEMBER, DON'T YOU? PRONTERA... FEYON. YOU REMEMBER. SKURAI.

I'LL CRUSH HIM!!

DID YOU SEE THAT? HE NEARLY KILLED OUR GRAND-MOTHER!

ROAR

YOU! HOLD IT!!

YOU NEED TO LEARN SOME MANNERS!!

I'M WITH ANOTHER FRIEND FROM FAYON. A LITTLE DAMSEL CALLED IRIS...

SHE REALLY WANTS TO SEE YOU. SO DO I. ALONE...

86

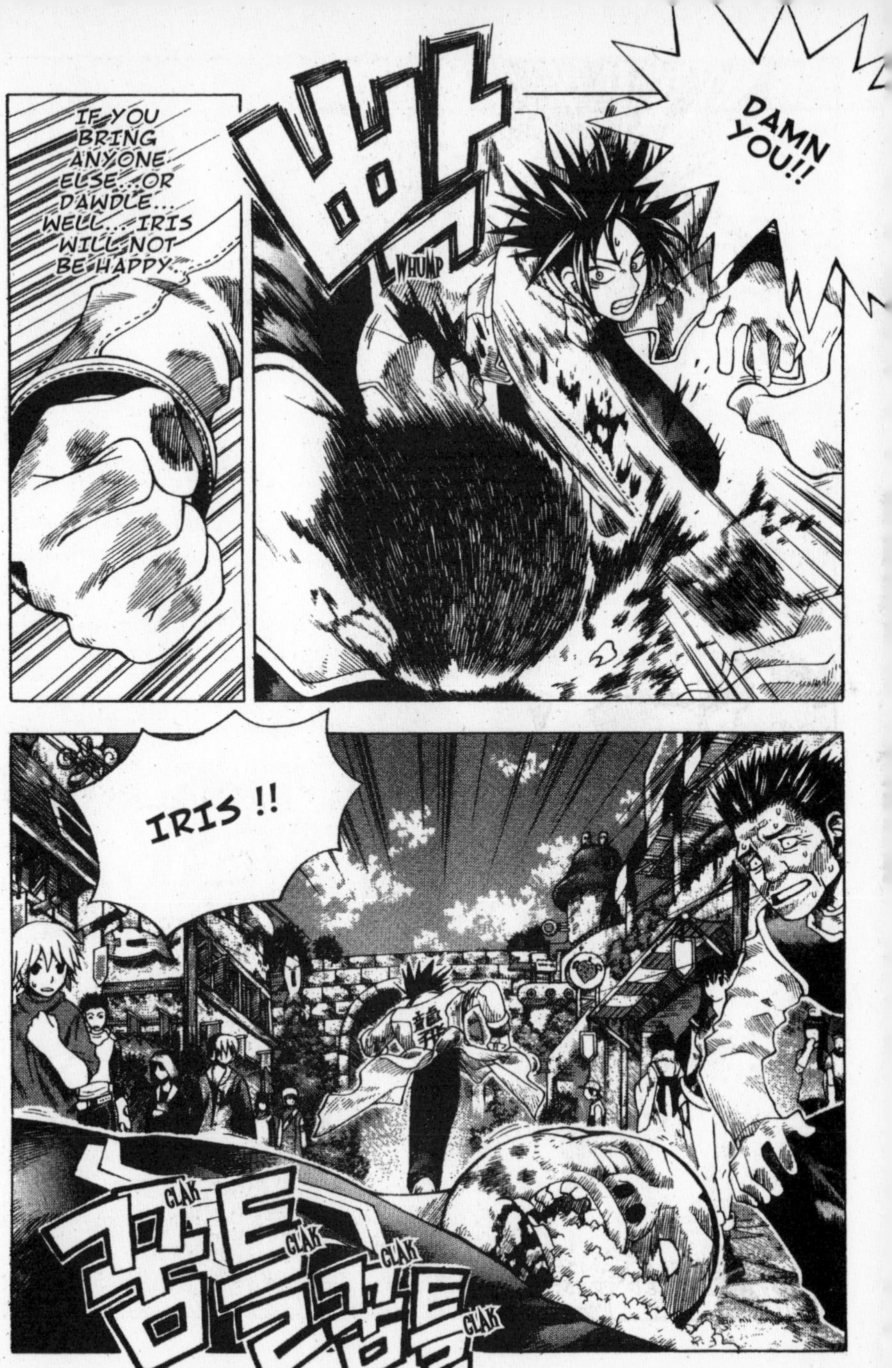
IF YOU BRING ANYONE ELSE... OR DAWDLE... WELL... IRIS WILL NOT BE HAPPY...
WHUMP
DAMN YOU!!
IRIS !!
CLAK
CLAK
CLAK
CLAK

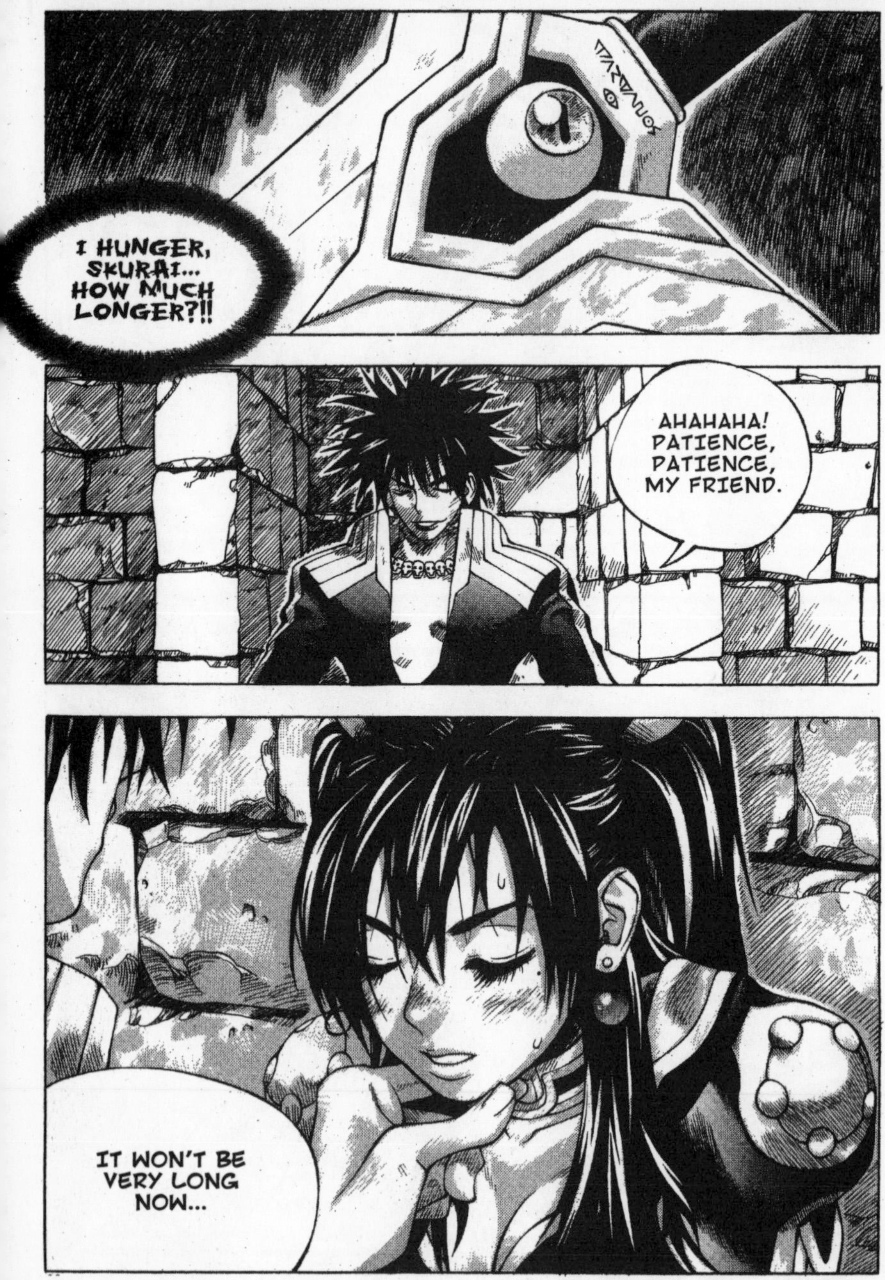
I HUNGER, SKURAI... HOW MUCH LONGER?!!
AHAHAHA! PATIENCE, PATIENCE, MY FRIEND.
IT WON'T BE VERY LONG NOW...

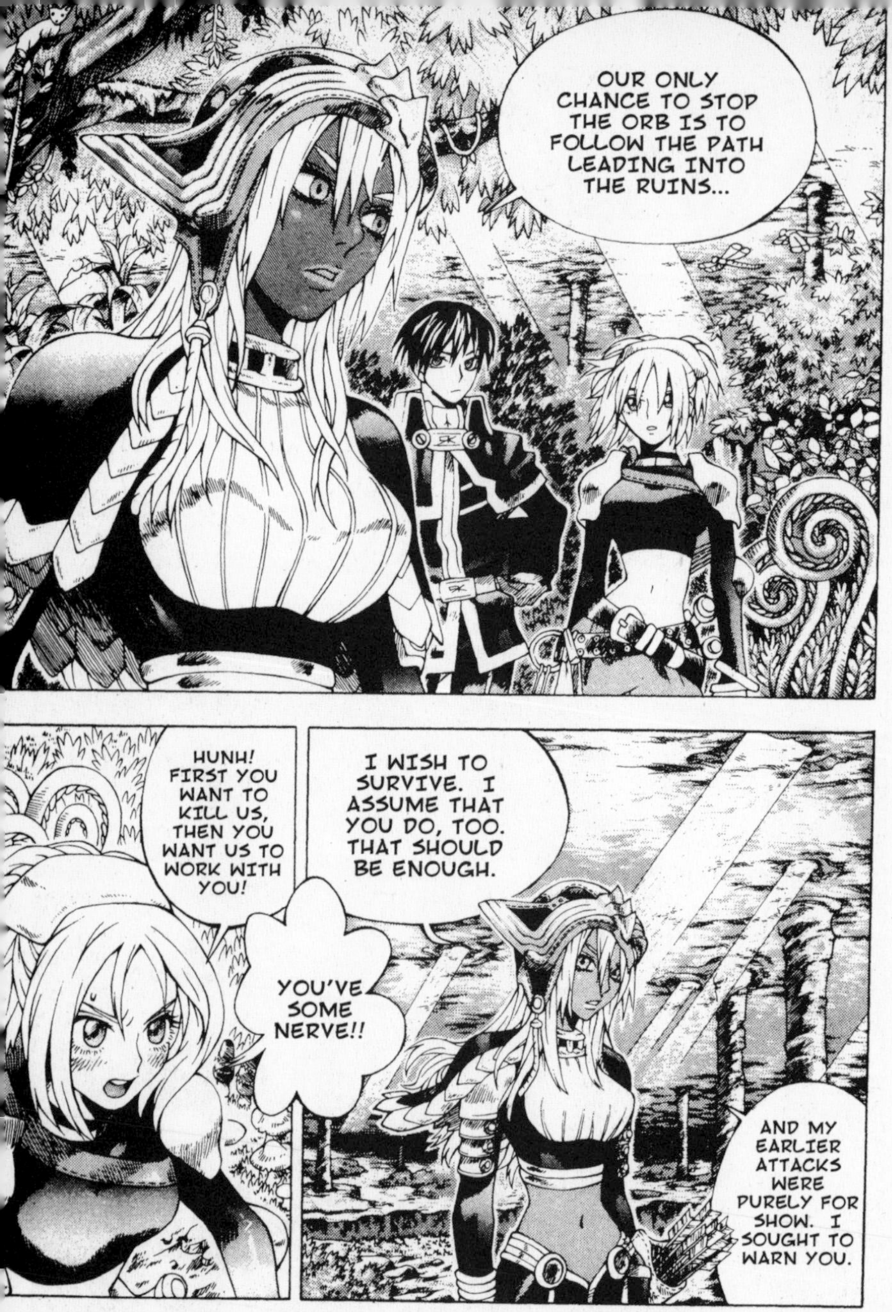
OUR ONLY CHANCE TO STOP THE ORB IS TO FOLLOW THE PATH LEADING INTO THE RUINS...
HUNH! FIRST YOU WANT TO KILL US, THEN YOU WANT US TO WORK WITH YOU!
YOU'VE SOME NERVE!!
I WISH TO SURVIVE. I ASSUME THAT YOU DO, TOO. THAT SHOULD BE ENOUGH.
AND MY EARLIER ATTACKS WERE PURELY FOR SHOW. I SOUGHT TO WARN YOU.

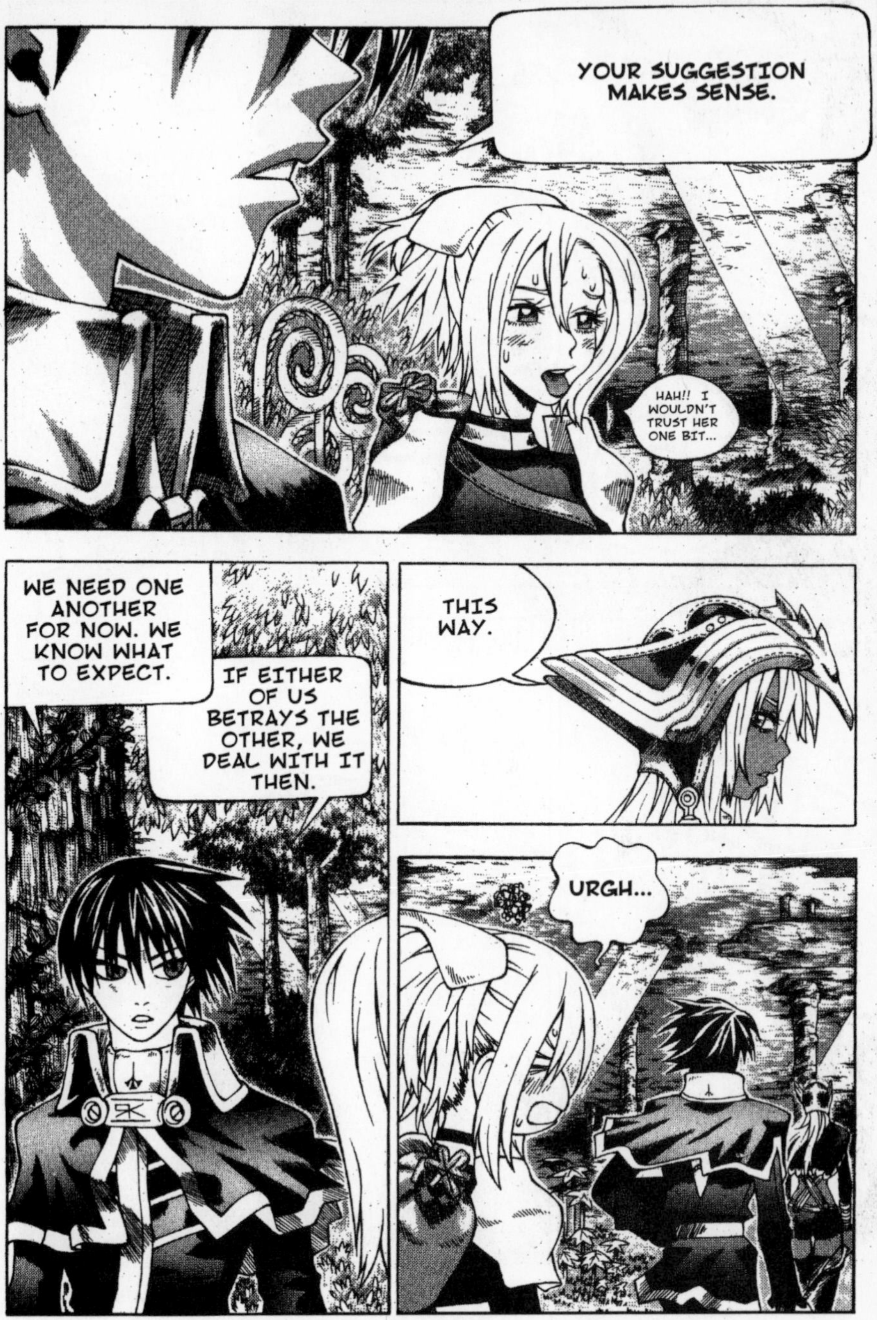
YOUR SUGGESTION MAKES SENSE.
HAH!! I WOULDN'T TRUST HER ONE BIT...
WE NEED ONE ANOTHER FOR NOW. WE KNOW WHAT TO EXPECT.
IF EITHER OF US BETRAYS THE OTHER, WE DEAL WITH IT THEN.
THIS WAY.
URGH...

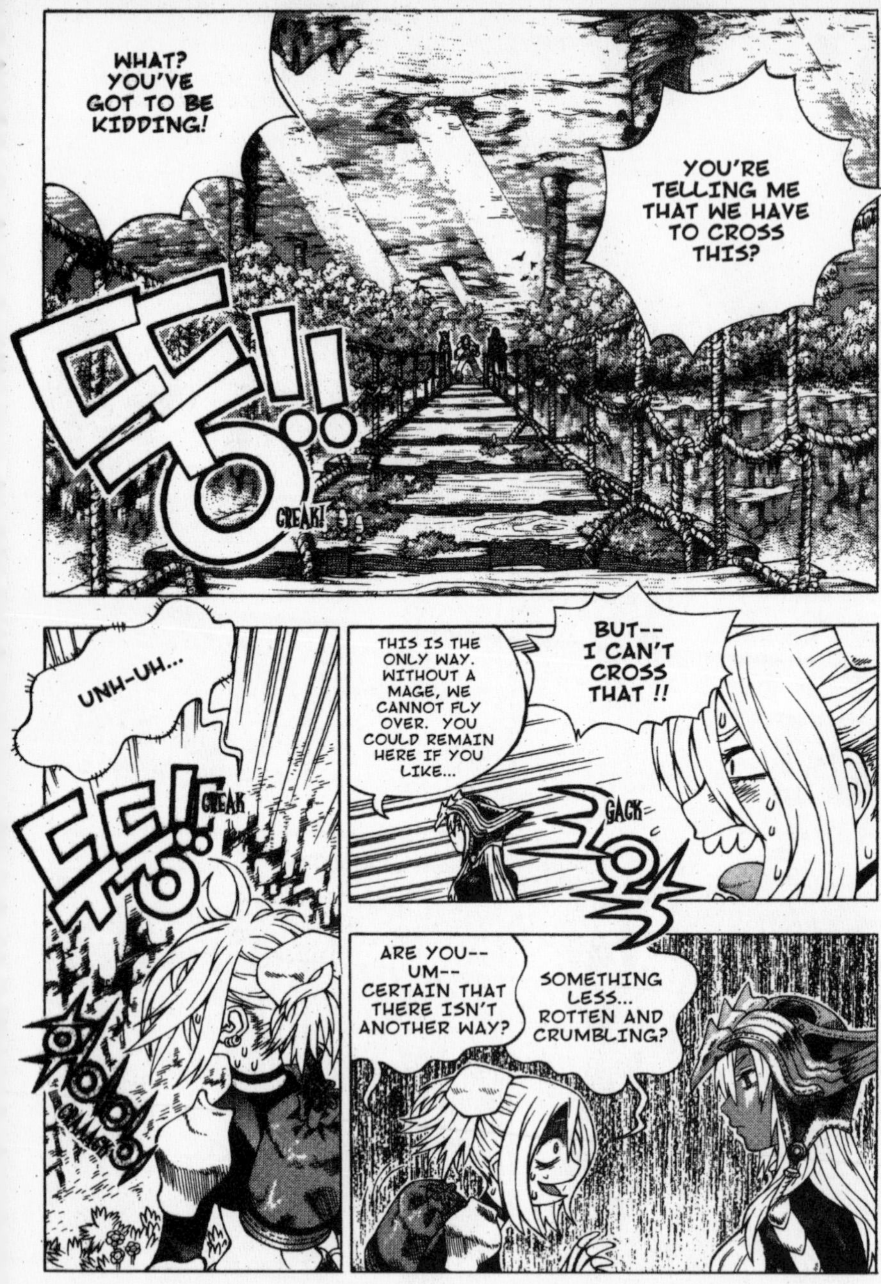
WHAT? YOU'VE GOT TO BE KIDDING!
YOU'RE TELLING ME THAT WE HAVE TO CROSS THIS?
CREAK!
UNH-UH...
CREAK
THIS IS THE ONLY WAY. WITHOUT A MAGE, WE CANNOT FLY OVER. YOU COULD REMAIN HERE IF YOU LIKE...
BUT-- I CAN'T CROSS THAT !!
GACK
ARE YOU-- UM-- CERTAIN THAT THERE ISN'T ANOTHER WAY?
SOMETHING LESS... ROTTEN AND CRUMBLING?

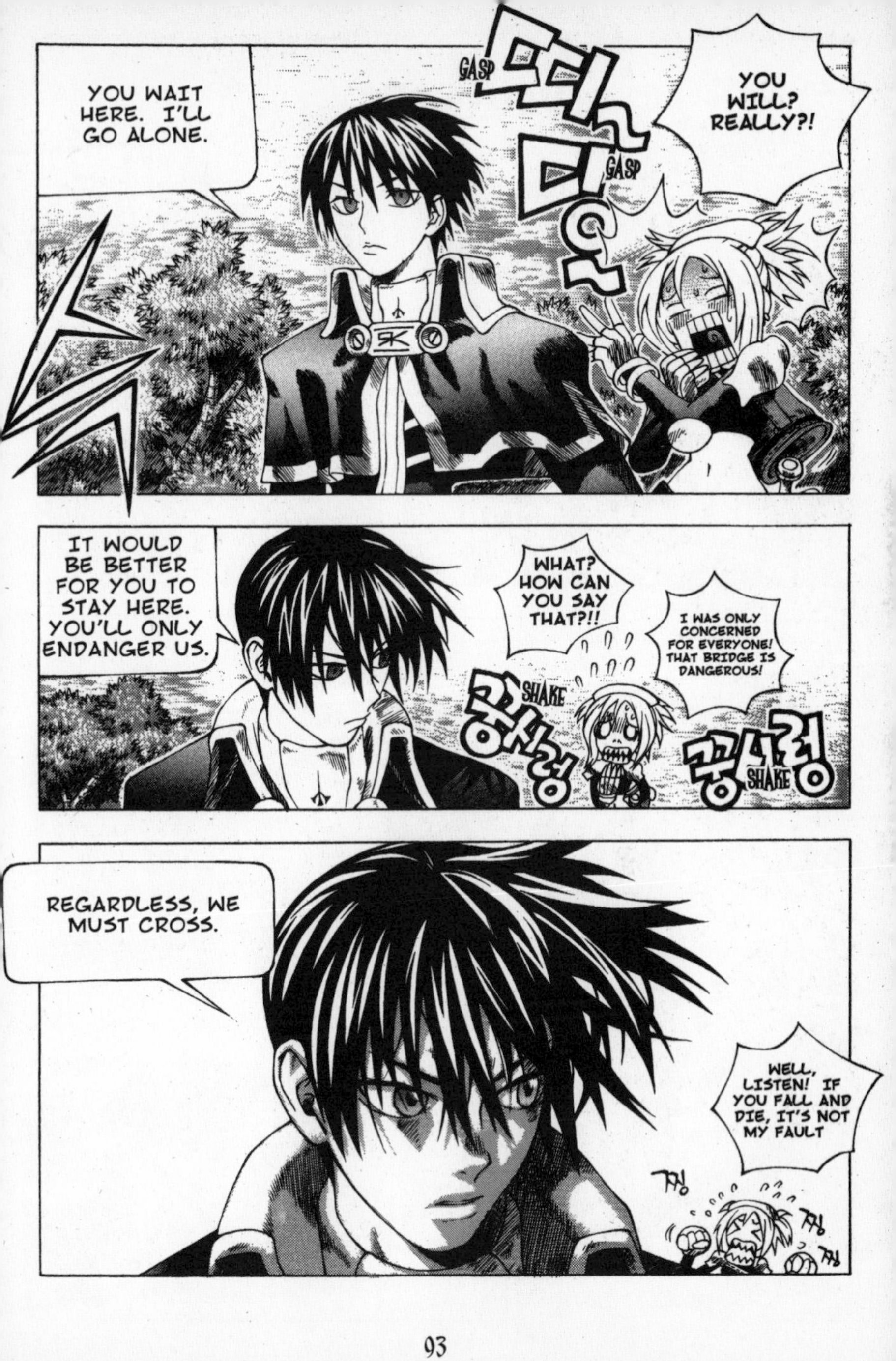
YOU WAIT HERE. I'LL GO ALONE.
GASP
GASP
YOU WILL? REALLY?!
IT WOULD BE BETTER FOR YOU TO STAY HERE. YOU'LL ONLY ENDANGER US.
WHAT? HOW CAN YOU SAY THAT?!!
I WAS ONLY CONCERNED FOR EVERYONE! THAT BRIDGE IS DANGEROUS!
SHAKE
SHAKE
REGARDLESS, WE MUST CROSS.
WELL, LISTEN! IF YOU FALL AND DIE, IT'S NOT MY FAULT

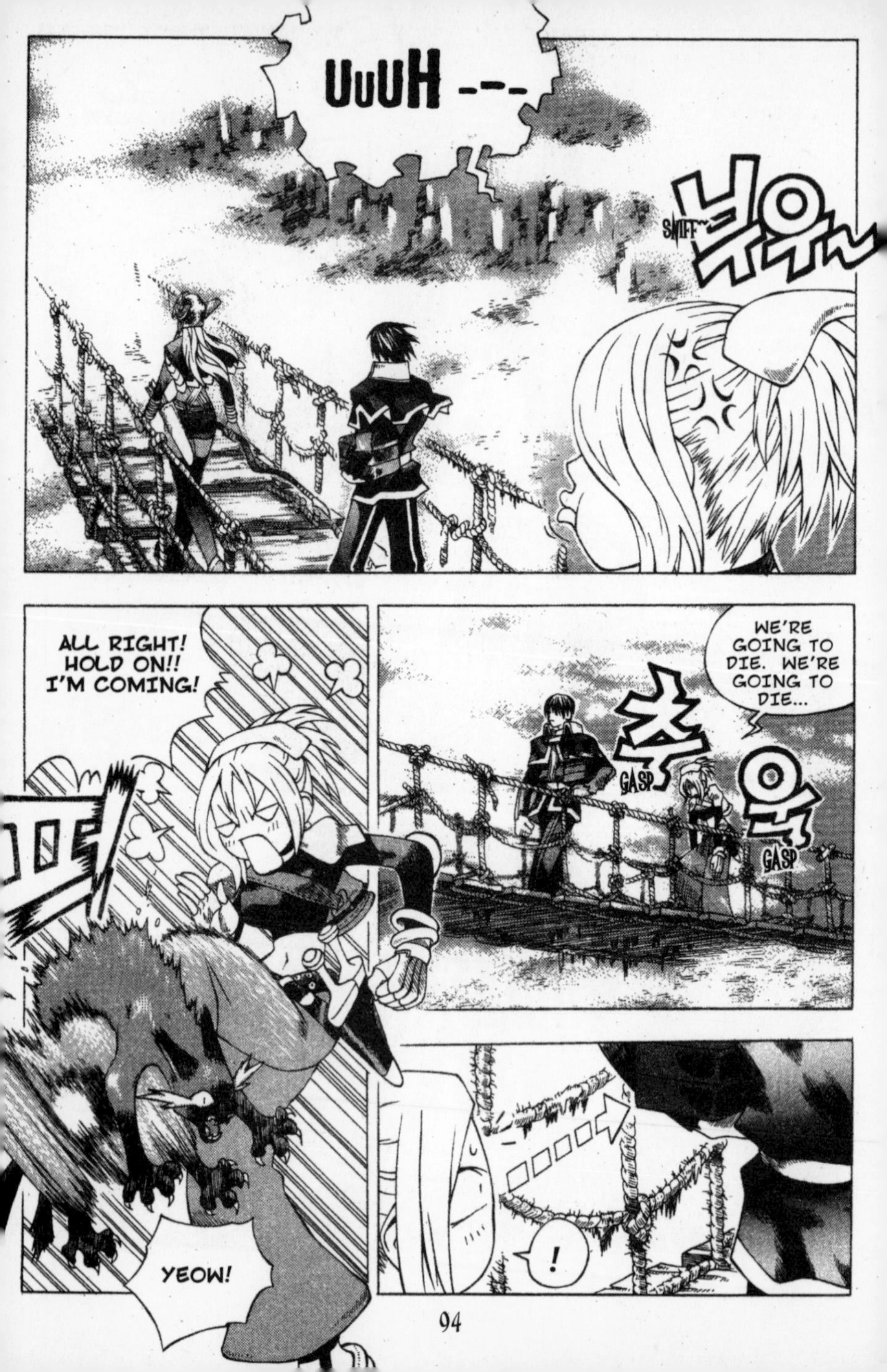
UuUH ---
SNIFF
ALL RIGHT! HOLD ON!! I'M COMING!
YEOW!
WE'RE GOING TO DIE. WE'RE GOING TO DIE...
GASP
GASP
!

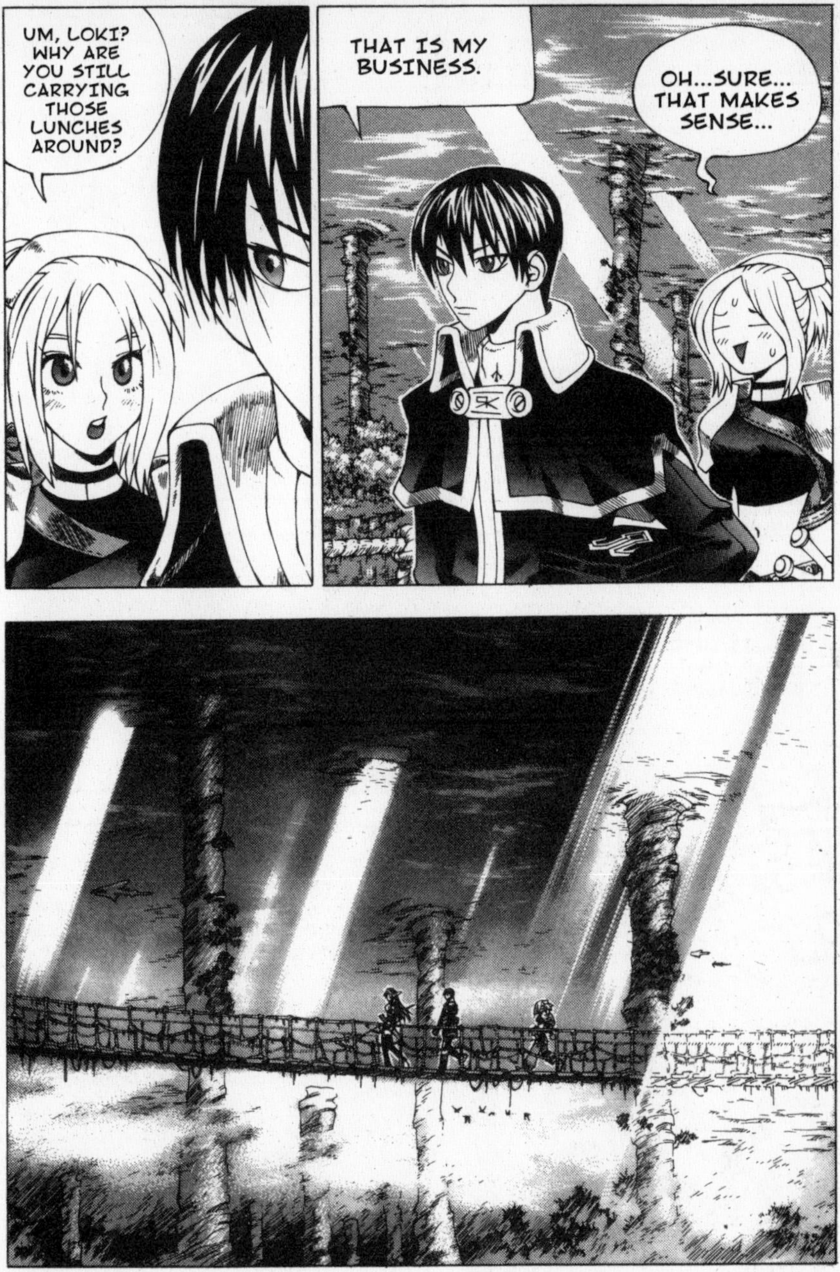
UM, LOKI? WHY ARE YOU STILL CARRYING THOSE LUNCHES AROUND?
THAT IS MY BUSINESS.
OH...SURE... THAT MAKES SENSE...

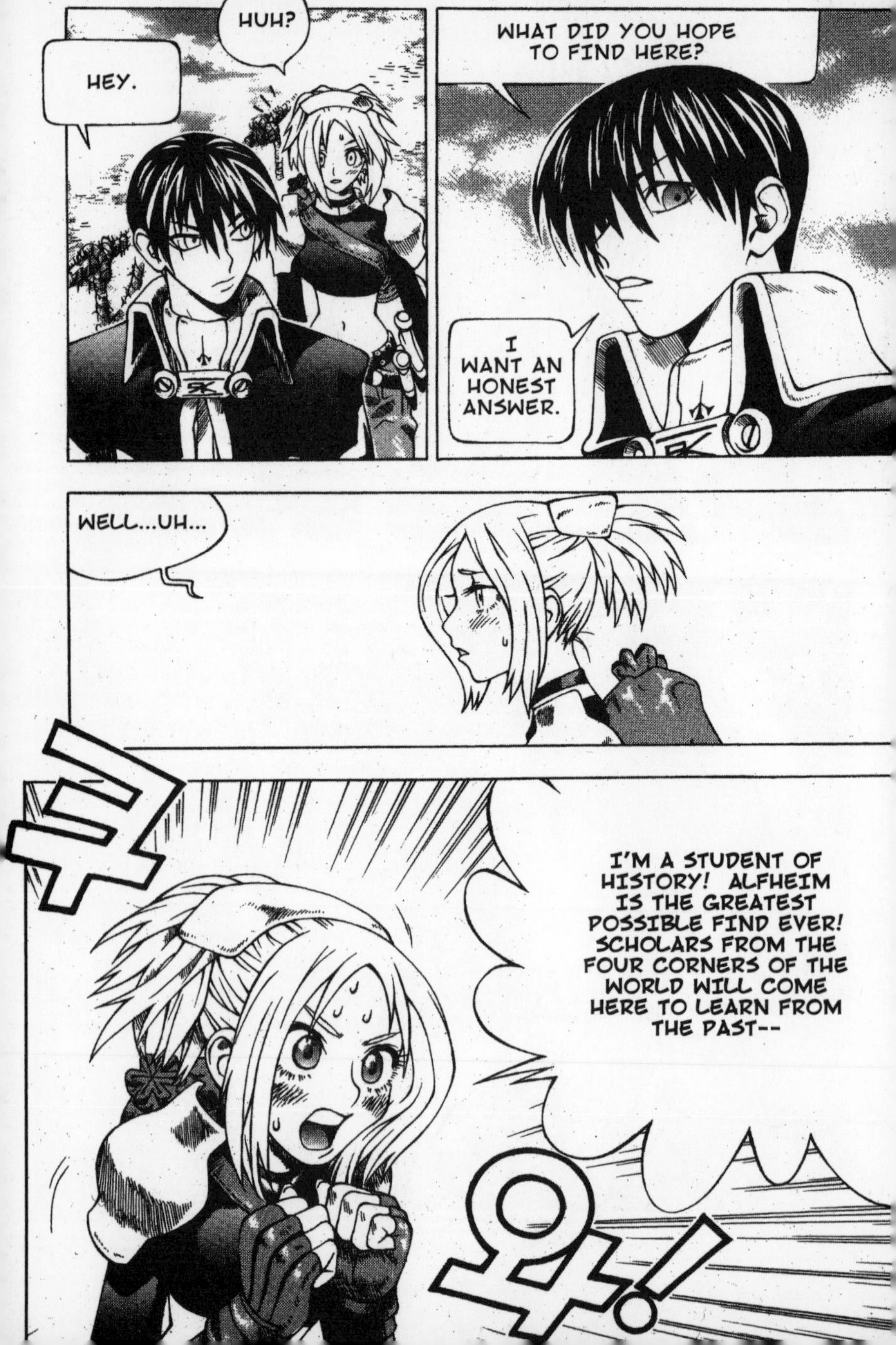
HEY.
HUH?
WHAT DID YOU HOPE TO FIND HERE?
I WANT AN HONEST ANSWER.
WELL...UH...
I'M A STUDENT OF HISTORY! ALFHEIM IS THE GREATEST POSSIBLE FIND EVER! SCHOLARS FROM THE FOUR CORNERS OF THE WORLD WILL COME HERE TO LEARN FROM THE PAST--

PATHETIC!!

TELL THE TRUTH!! TELL HIM YOU WANT THE RICHES OF ANCIENT ALFHEIM FOR YOURSELF!

SUCH ARROGANCE!!

YOU HUMANS!

YOU ARE ALL NOTHING BUT ANIMALS DRESSED UP AND PRETENDING TO BE BETTER THAN YOU ARE!!

WHEN YOU HUMANS WERE CRAWLING INTO CAVES, PICKING FLEAS OFF YOUR FURRY HIDES, WE ELVES FED YOU--TAUGHT YOU LANGUAGE AND SURVIVAL!!

97

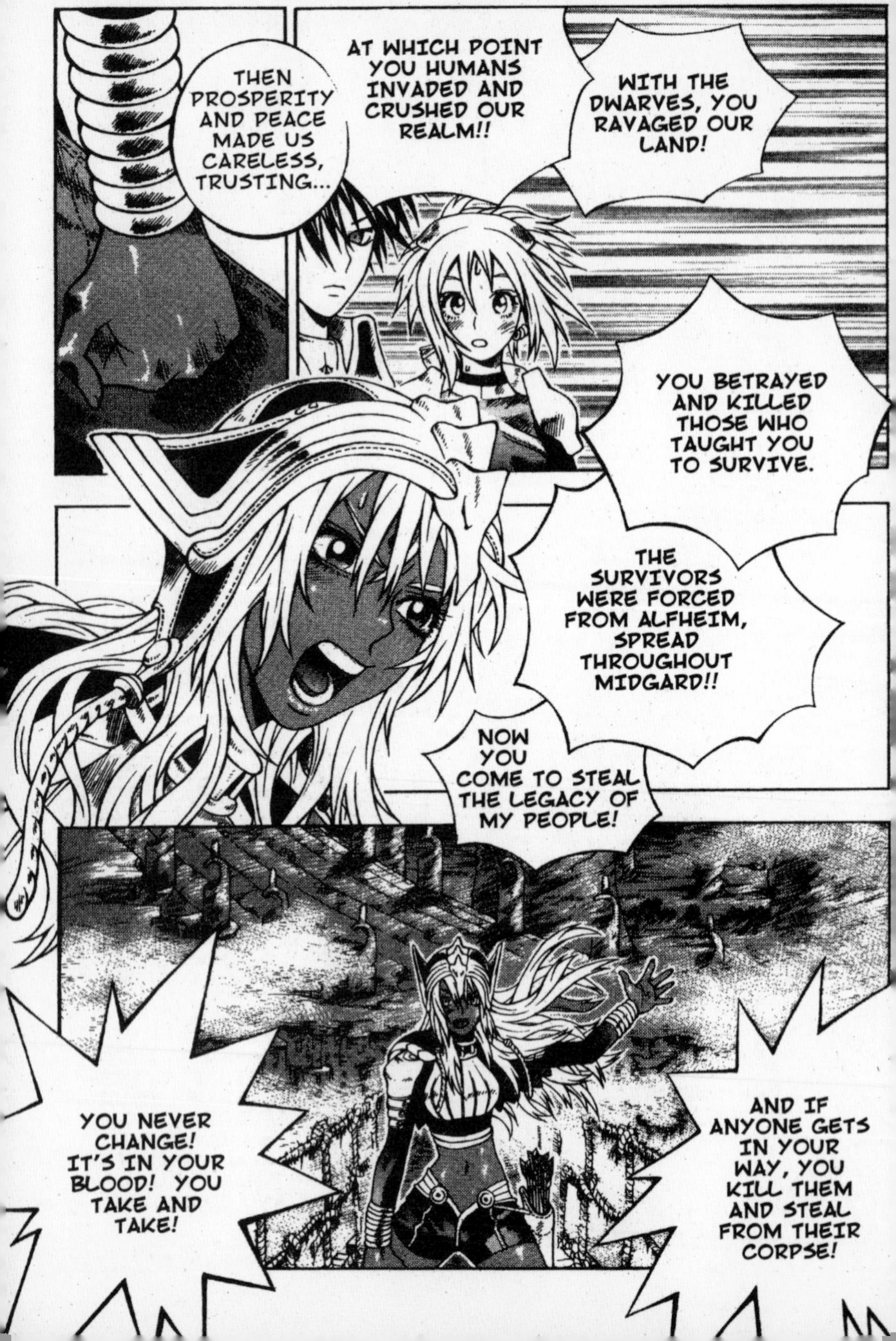
THEN PROSPERITY AND PEACE MADE US CARELESS, TRUSTING...
AT WHICH POINT YOU HUMANS INVADED AND CRUSHED OUR REALM!!
WITH THE DWARVES, YOU RAVAGED OUR LAND!
YOU BETRAYED AND KILLED THOSE WHO TAUGHT YOU TO SURVIVE.
THE SURVIVORS WERE FORCED FROM ALFHEIM, SPREAD THROUGHOUT MIDGARD!!
NOW YOU COME TO STEAL THE LEGACY OF MY PEOPLE!
YOU NEVER CHANGE! IT'S IN YOUR BLOOD! YOU TAKE AND TAKE!
AND IF ANYONE GETS IN YOUR WAY, YOU KILL THEM AND STEAL FROM THEIR CORPSE!

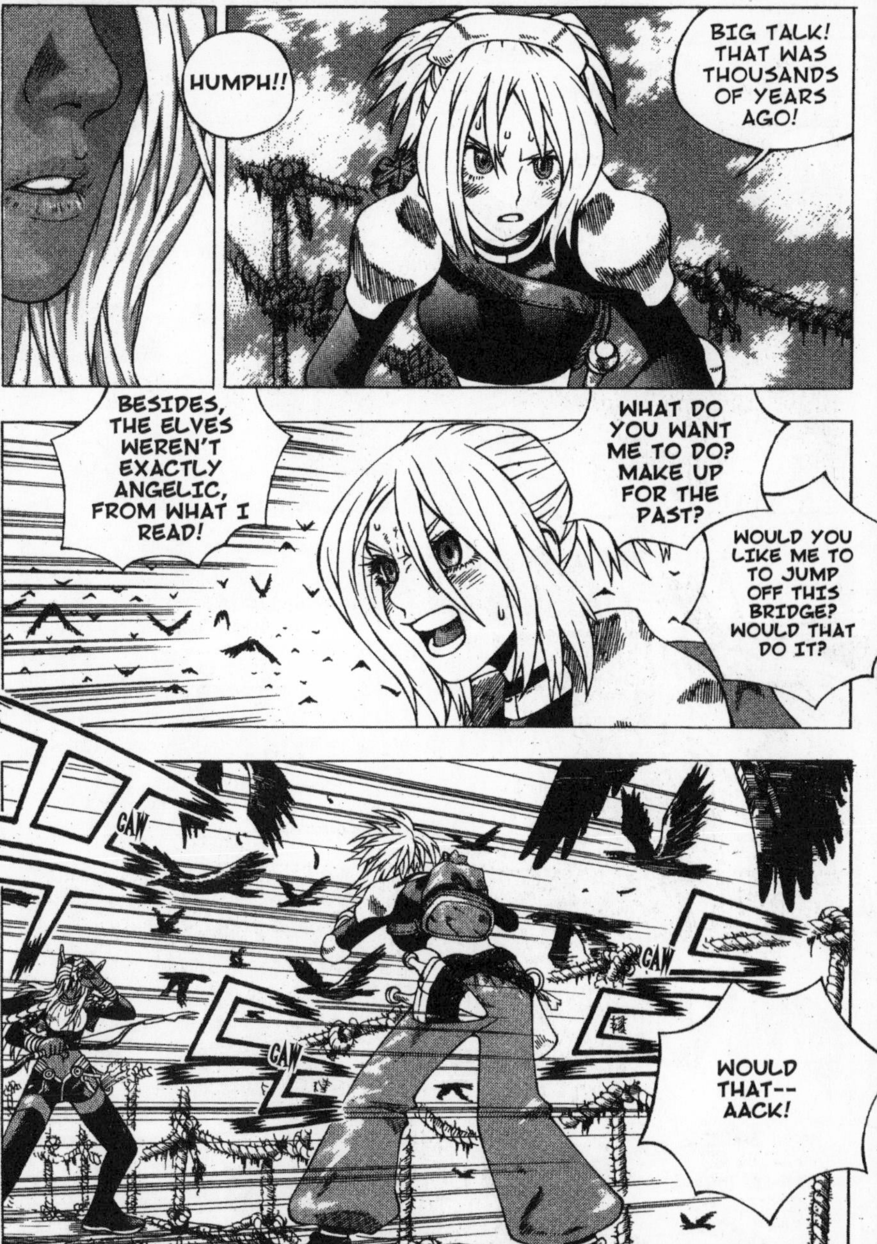
HUMPH!!
BIG TALK! THAT WAS THOUSANDS OF YEARS AGO!
BESIDES, THE ELVES WEREN'T EXACTLY ANGELIC, FROM WHAT I READ!
WHAT DO YOU WANT ME TO DO? MAKE UP FOR THE PAST?
WOULD YOU LIKE ME TO TO JUMP OFF THIS BRIDGE? WOULD THAT DO IT?
CAW
CAW
CAW
WOULD THAT-- AACK!

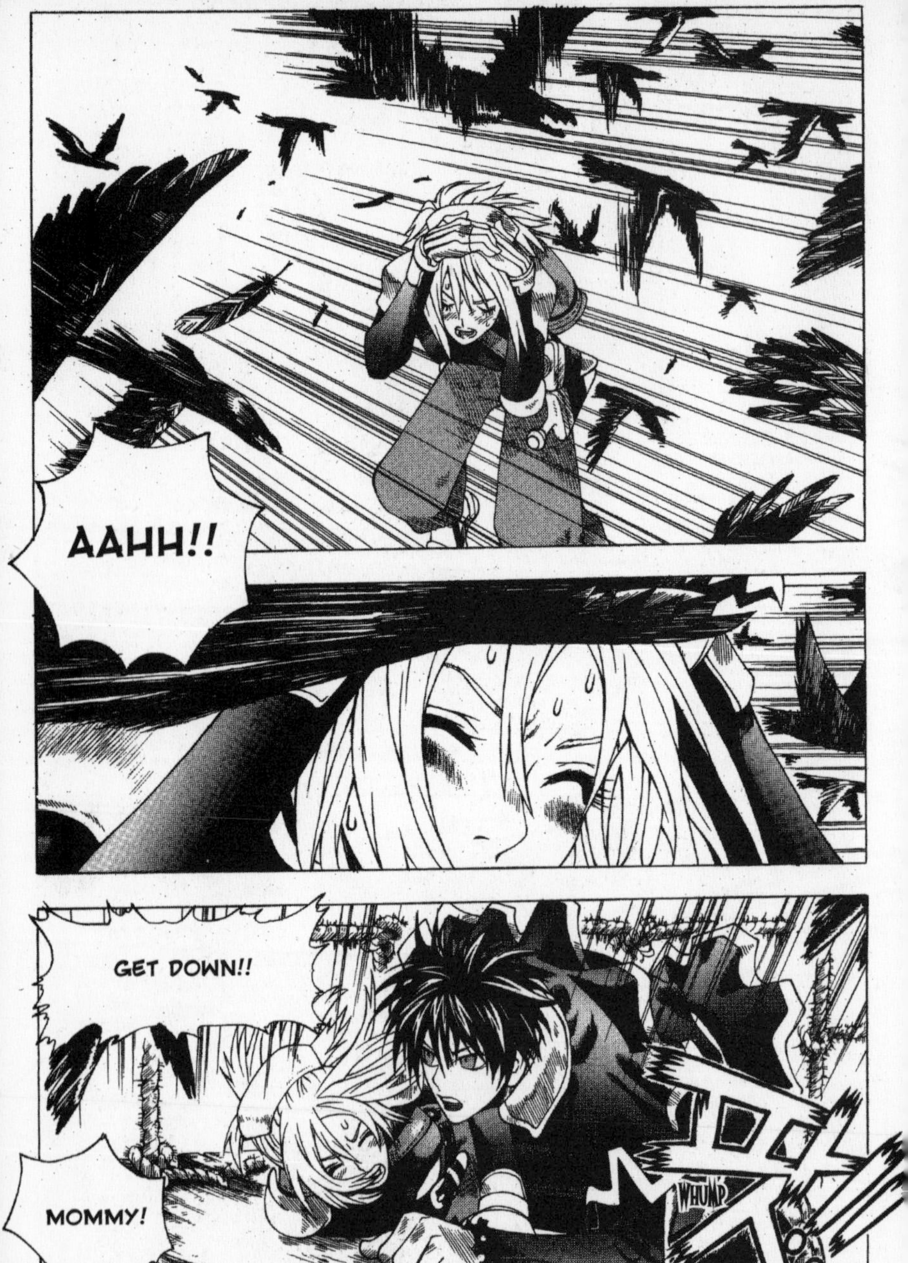
AAHH!!
GET DOWN!!
MOMMY!
WHUMP

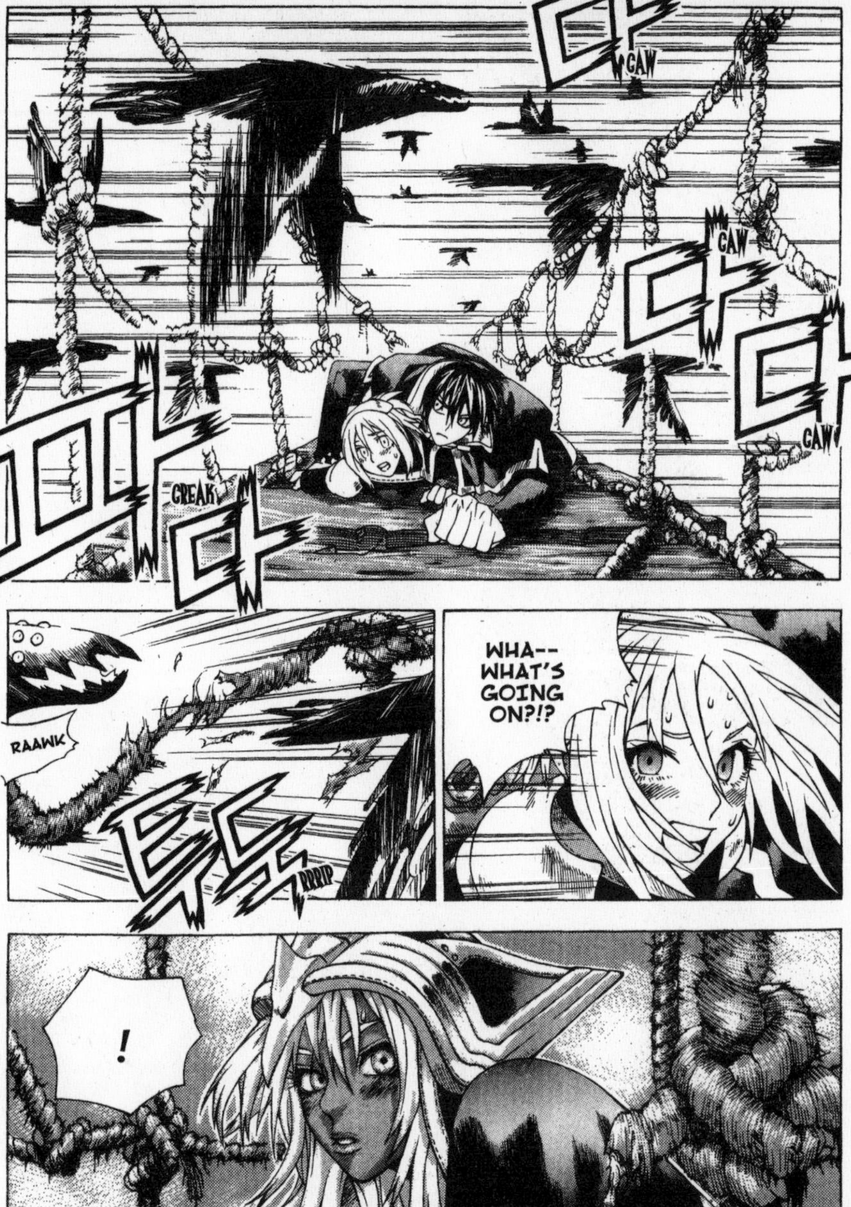
CAW
CAW
CAW
CREAK
RAAWK
RRRIP
WHA-- WHAT'S GOING ON?!?
!

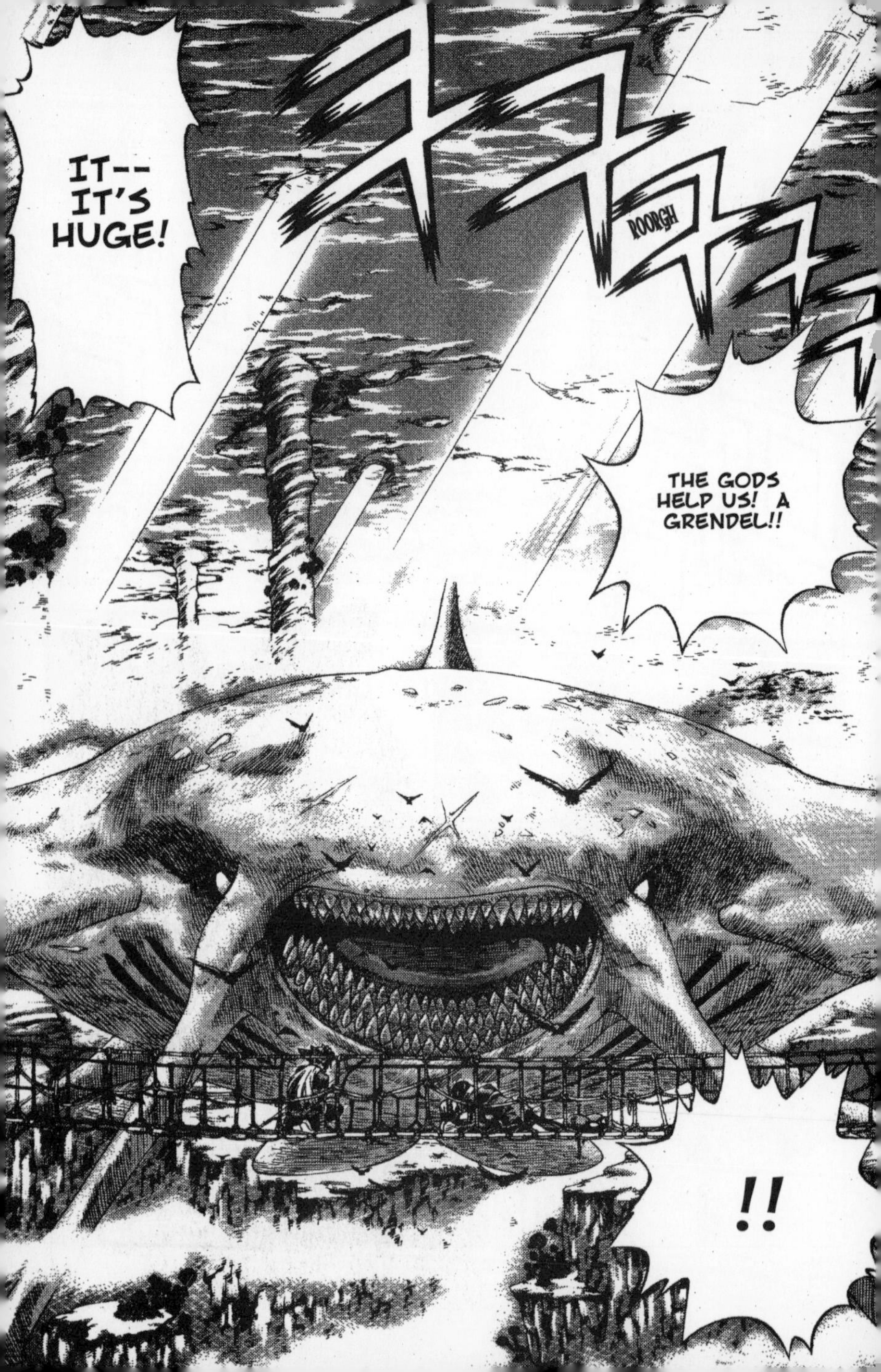
IT-- IT'S HUGE!
ROORGH
THE GODS HELP US! A GRENDEL!!
!!

RAGNARÖK
라그나로크
IN TO THE ABYSS

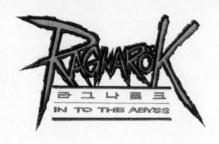

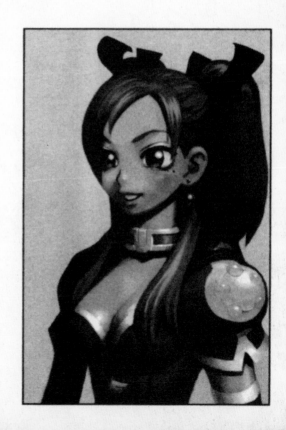

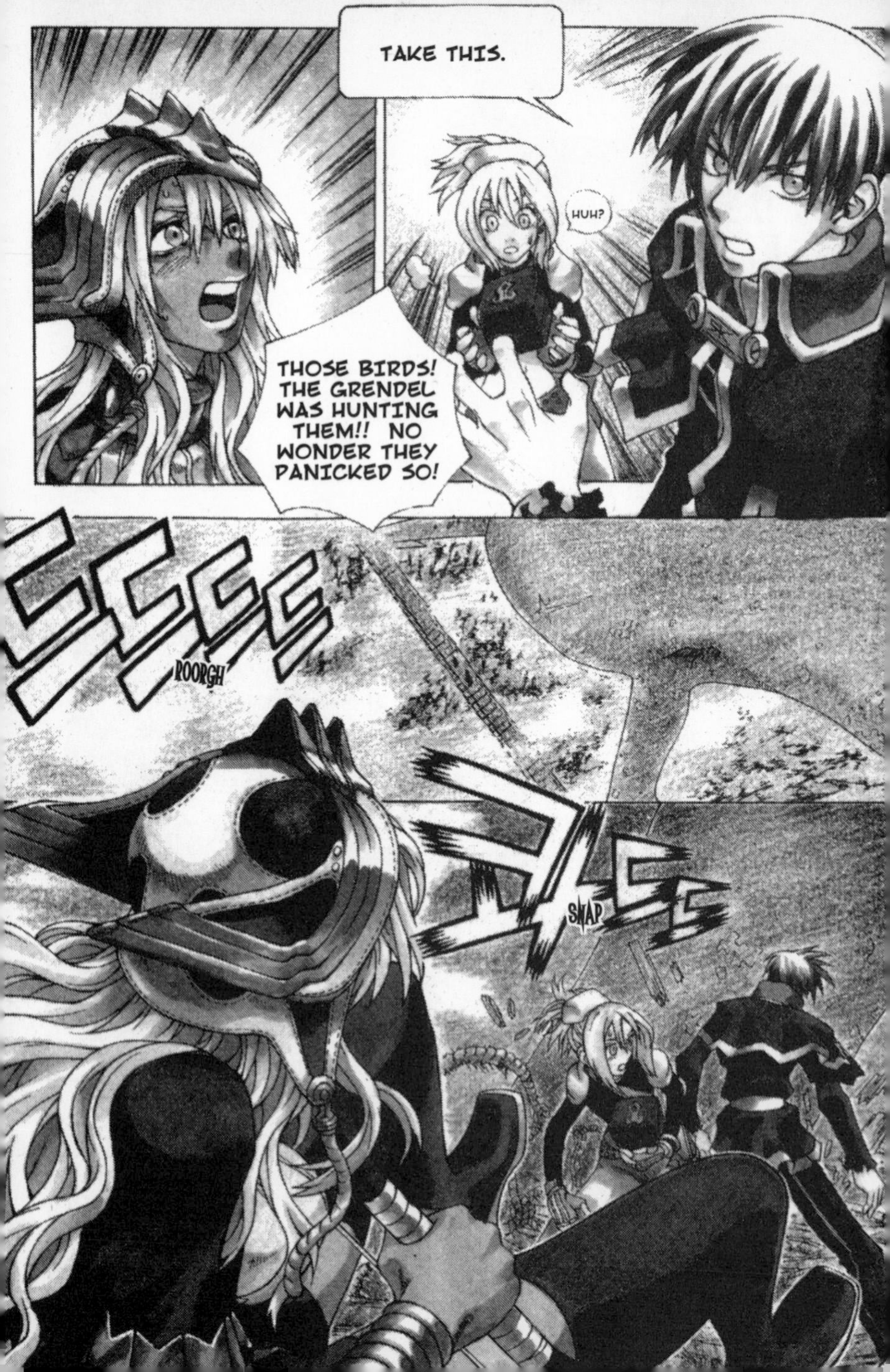
TAKE THIS.
HUH?
THOSE BIRDS! THE GRENDEL WAS HUNTING THEM!! NO WONDER THEY PANICKED SO!
ROORGH
SNAP

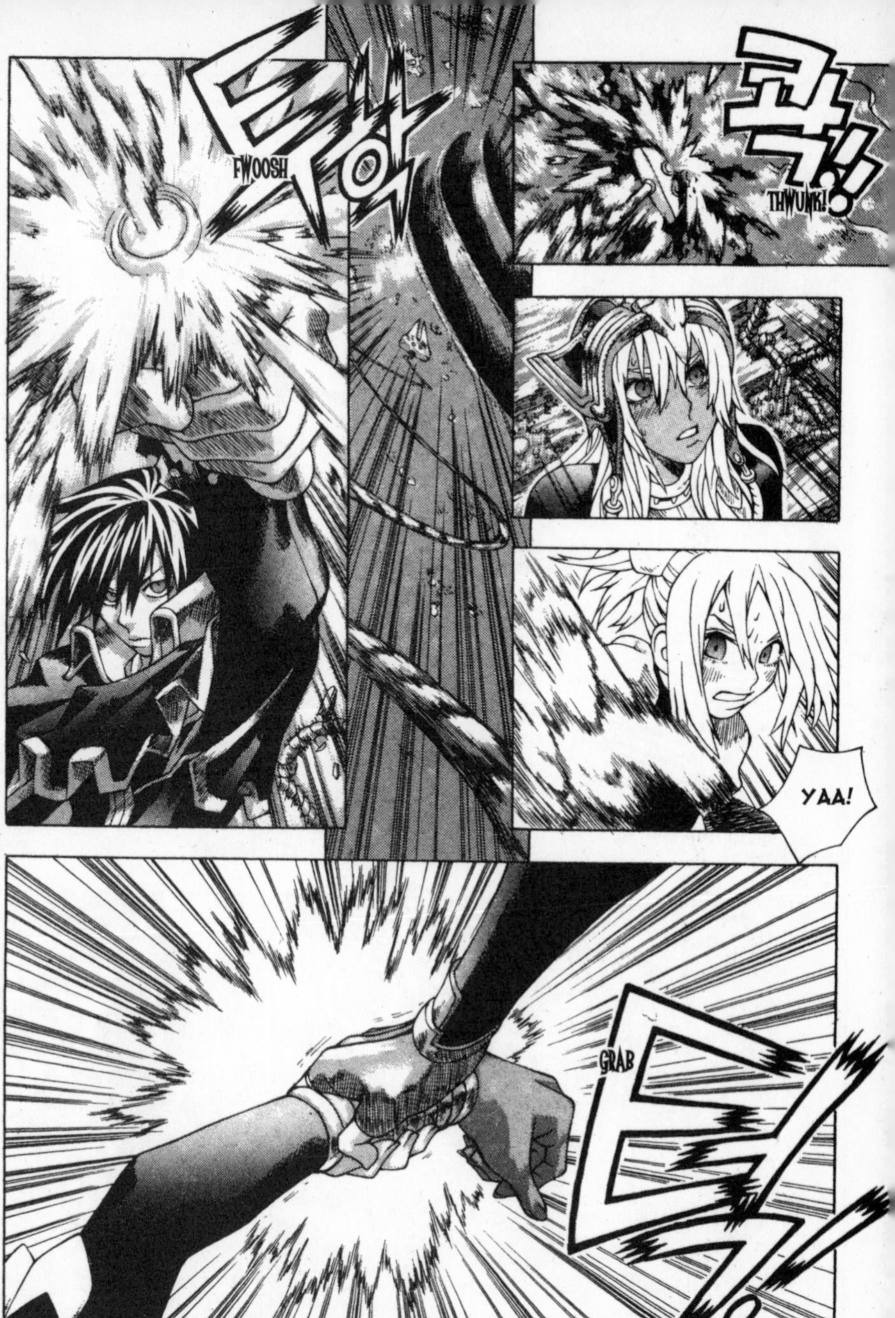
FWOOSH
THWUNK!
YAA!
GRAB

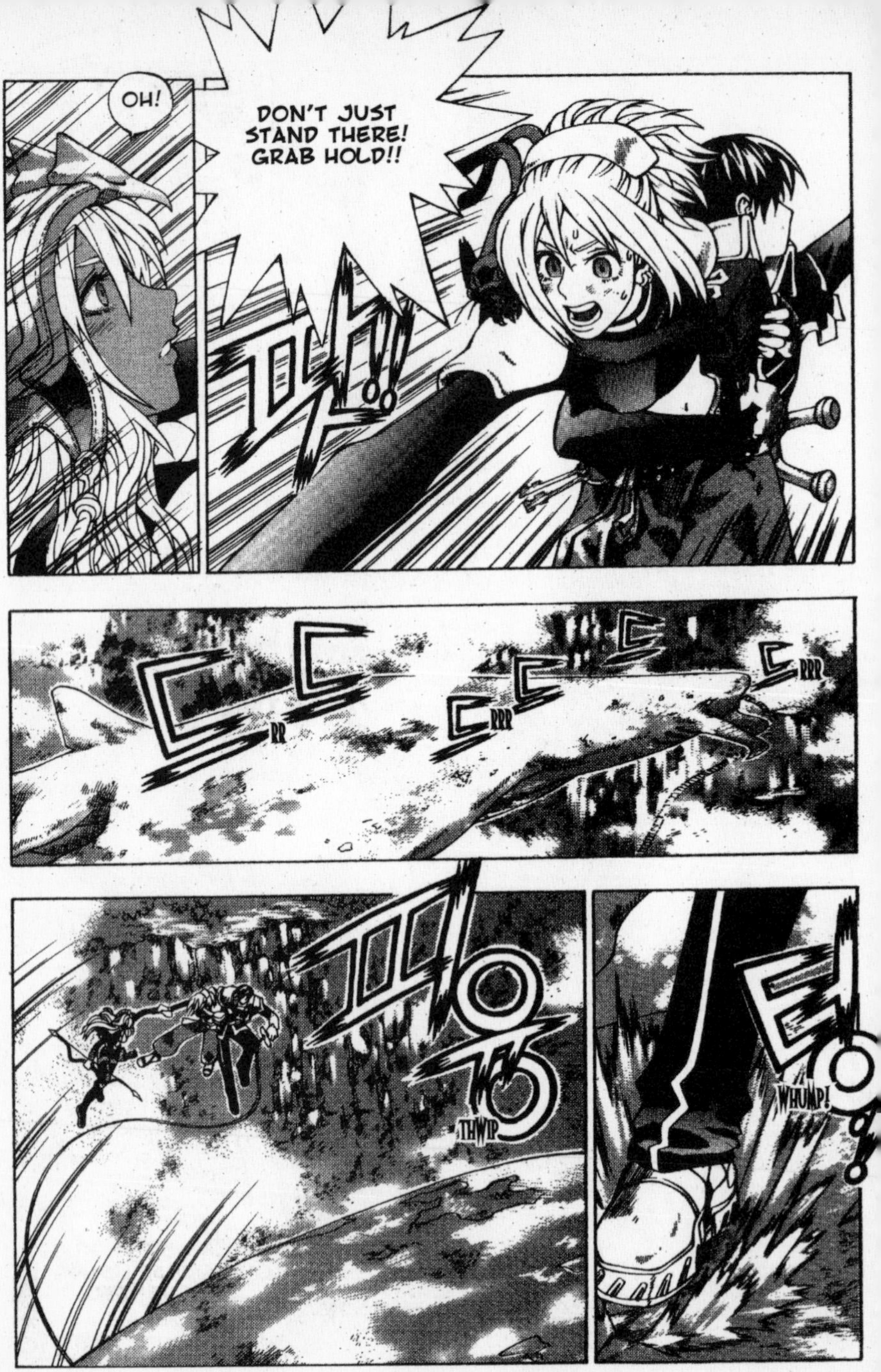
OH!
DON'T JUST STAND THERE! GRAB HOLD!!
RR
RRR
RRR
THWIP
WHUMP!

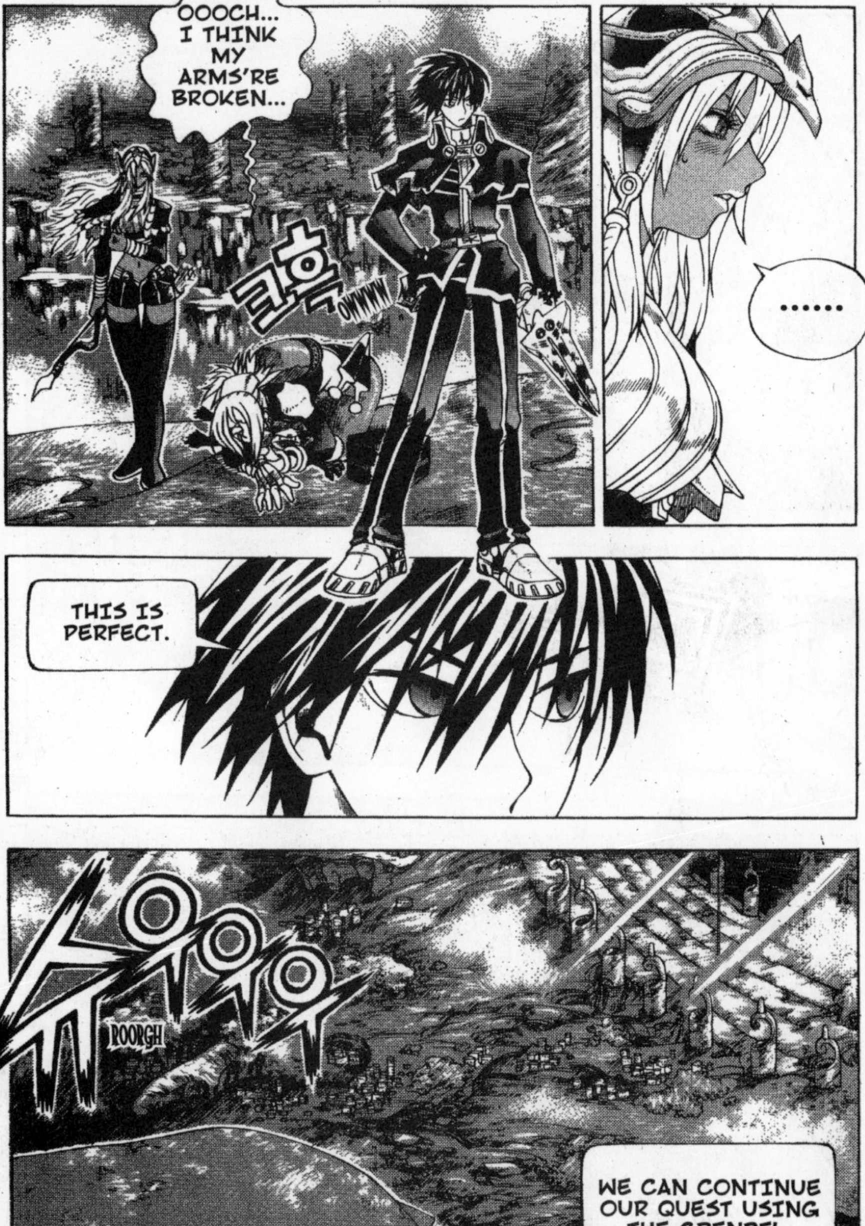
OOOCH... I THINK MY ARMS'RE BROKEN...
크흑
OWWWW
......
THIS IS PERFECT.
POORGH
WE CAN CONTINUE OUR QUEST USING THE GRENDEL.

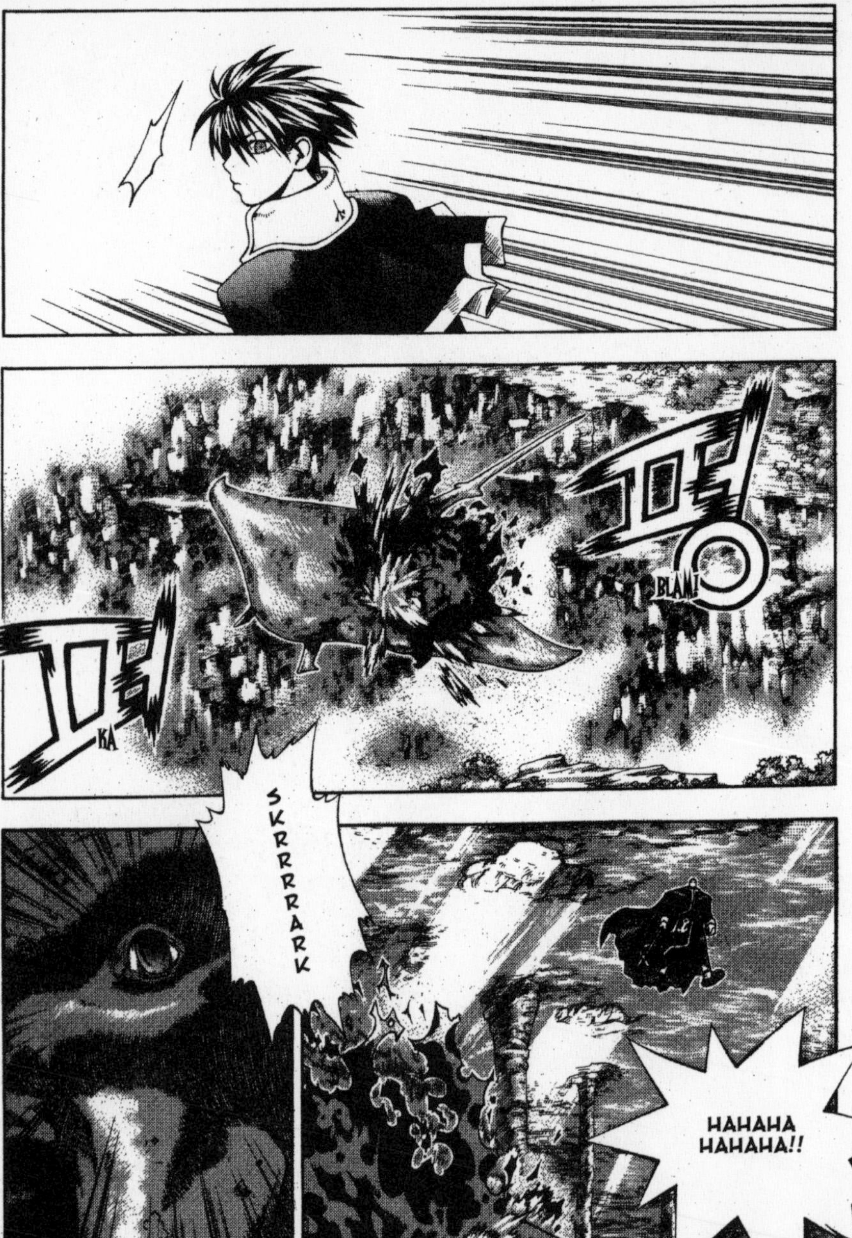
KA
BLAM!
SKRRRRARK
HAHAHA
HAHAHA!!

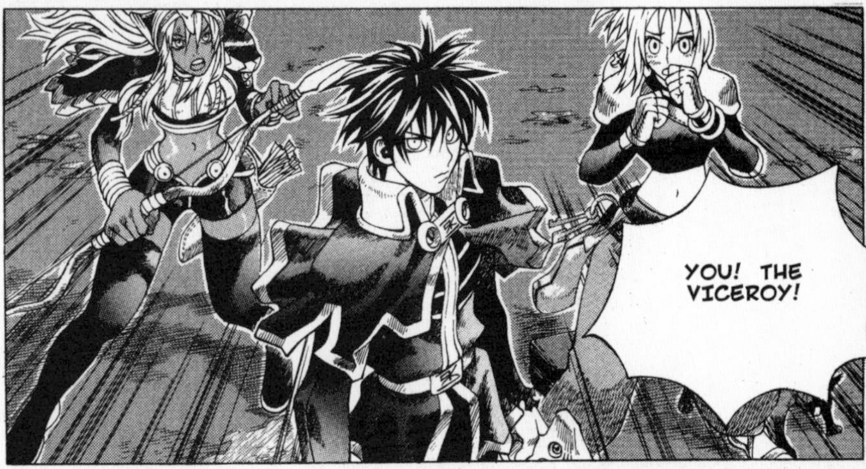
YOU! THE VICEROY!
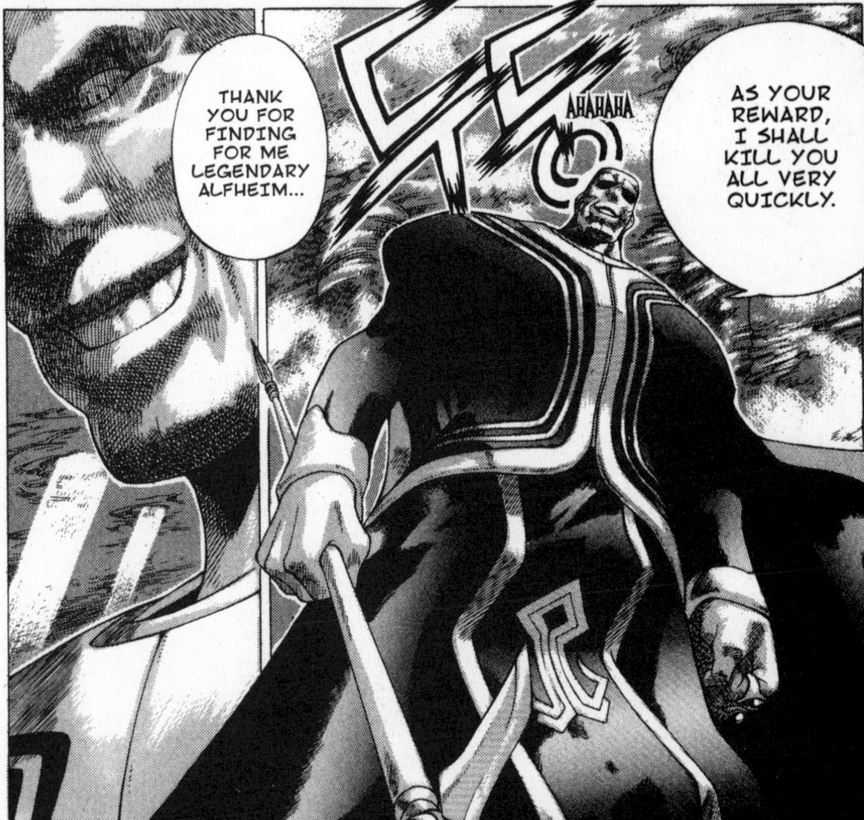
THANK YOU FOR FINDING FOR ME LEGENDARY ALFHEIM...
AHAHAHA
AS YOUR REWARD, I SHALL KILL YOU ALL VERY QUICKLY.

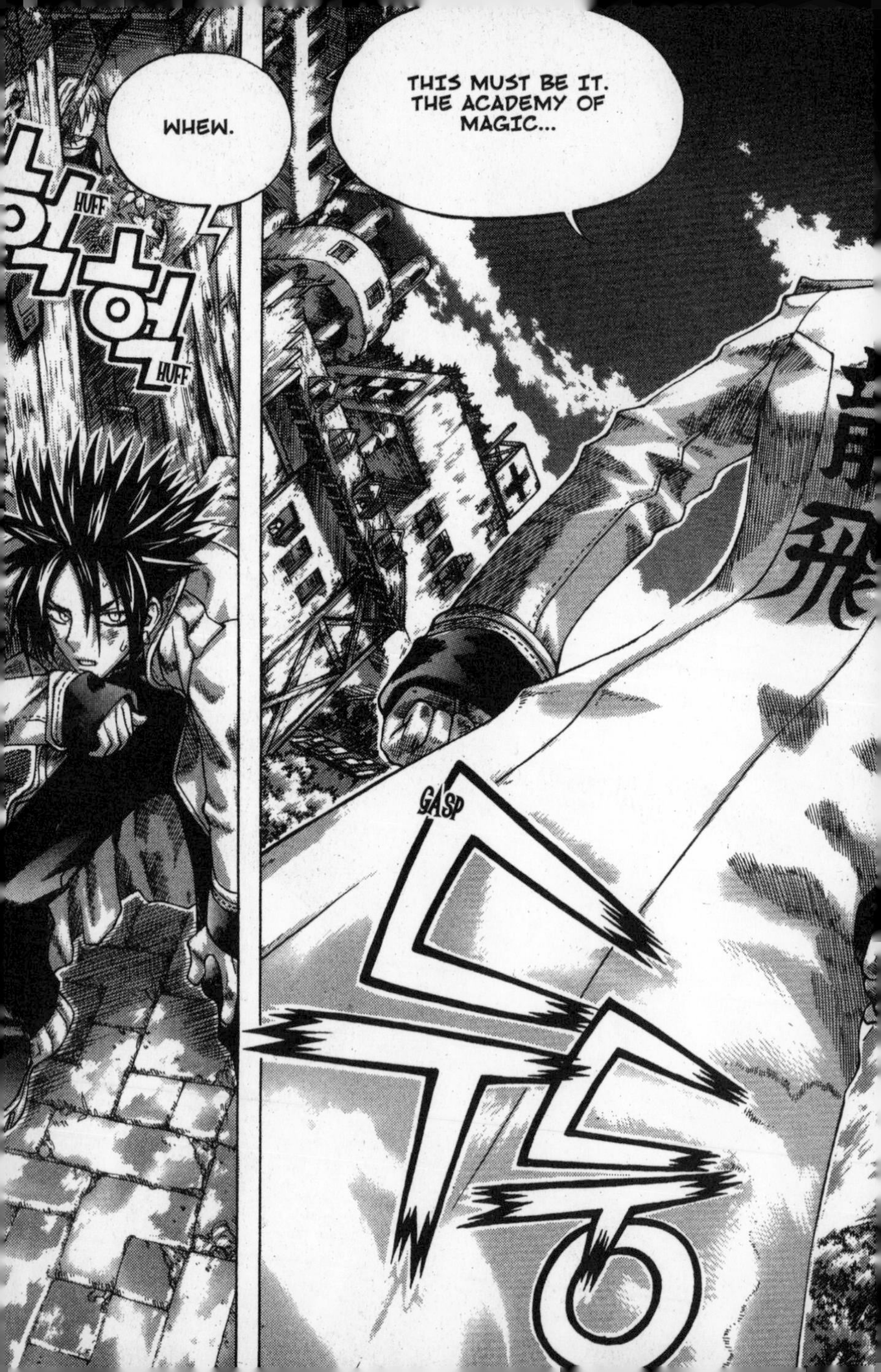
WHEW.
헉 헉
HUFF
HUFF
THIS MUST BE IT. THE ACADEMY OF MAGIC...
GASP

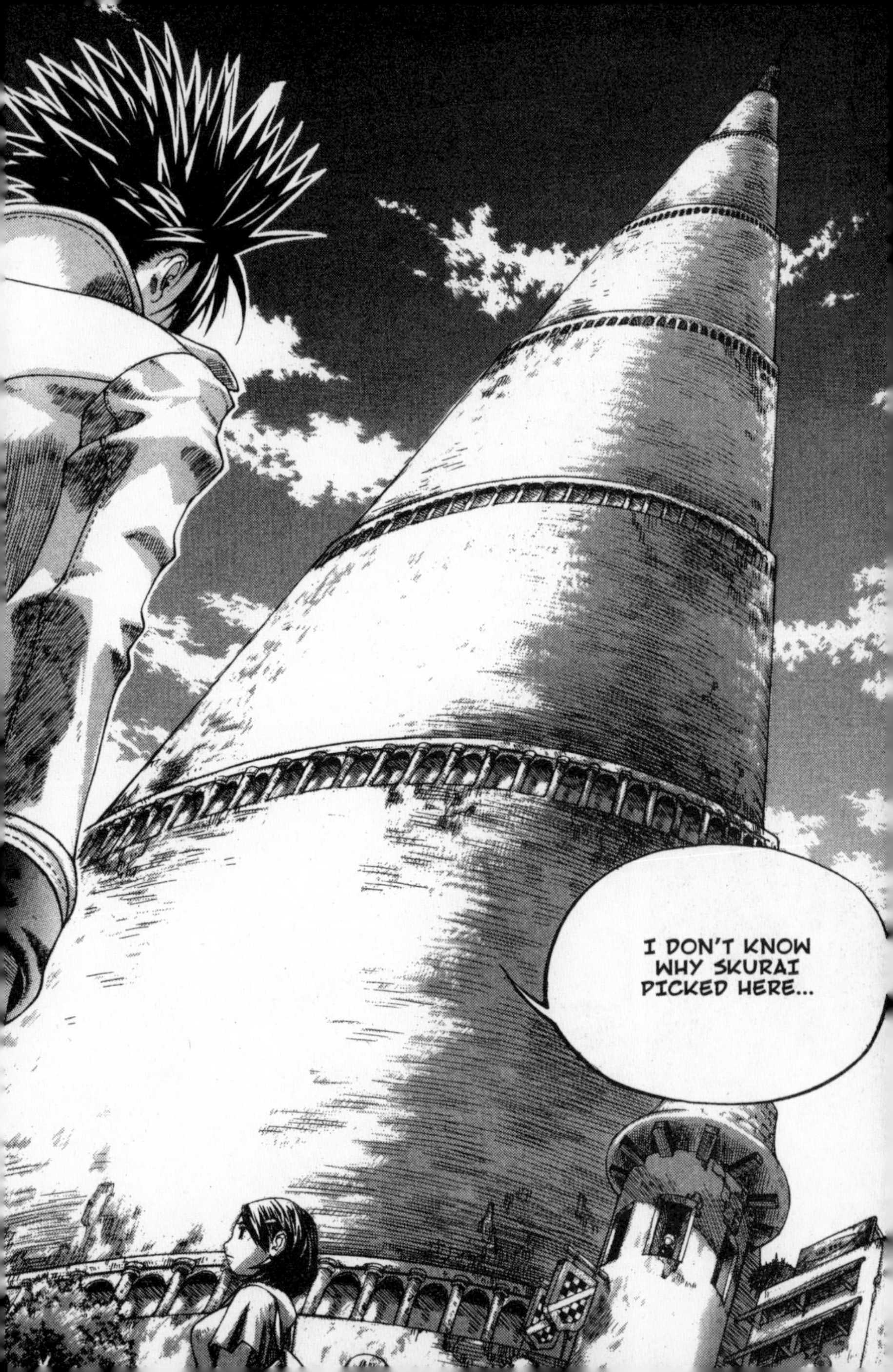
I DON'T KNOW WHY SKURAI PICKED HERE...

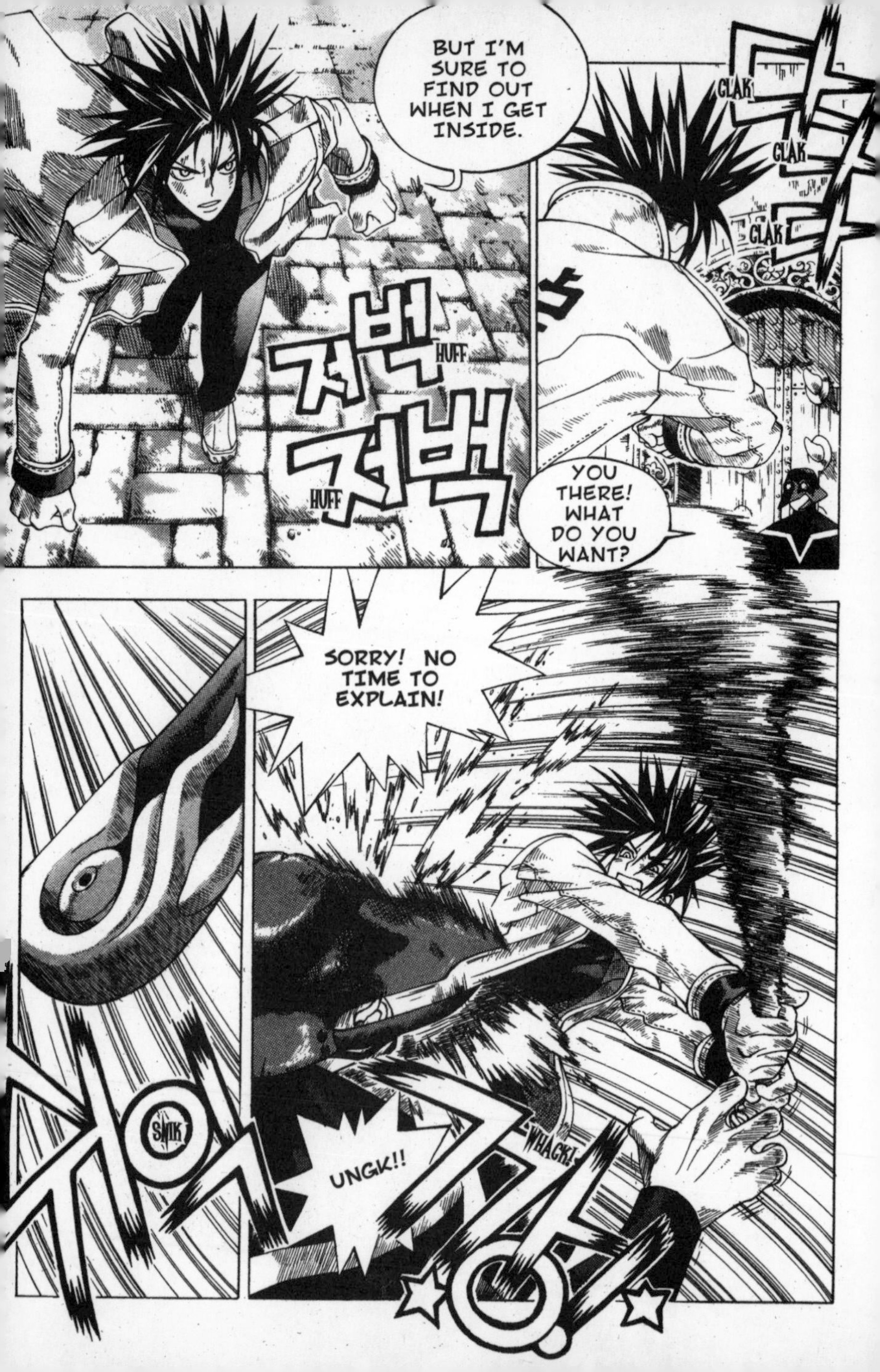
BUT I'M SURE TO FIND OUT WHEN I GET INSIDE.
저벅
HUFF
저벅
HUFF
CLAK
CLAK
CLAK
YOU THERE! WHAT DO YOU WANT?
SNIK
SORRY! NO TIME TO EXPLAIN!
WHACK!
UNGK!!

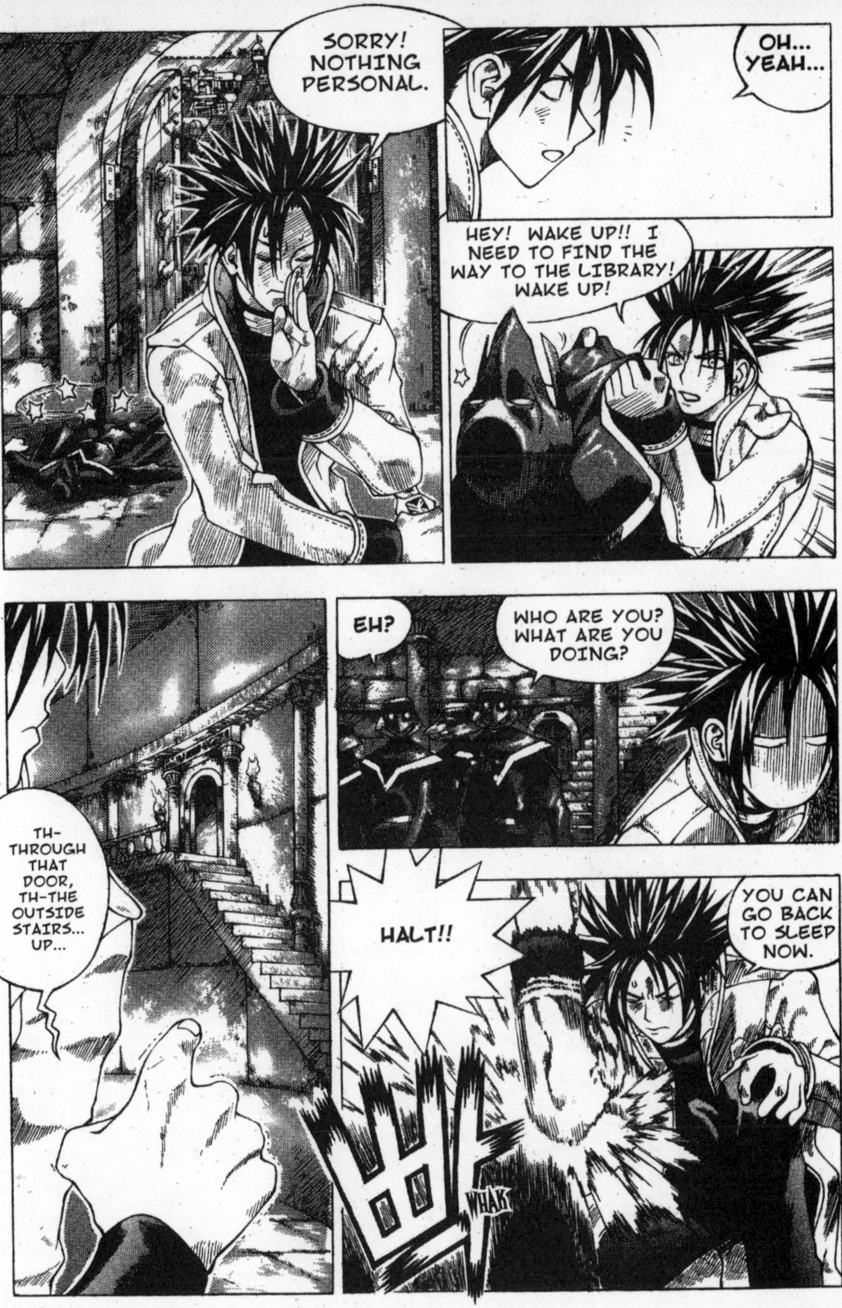
SORRY! NOTHING PERSONAL.
OH... YEAH...
HEY! WAKE UP!! I NEED TO FIND THE WAY TO THE LIBRARY! WAKE UP!
TH-THROUGH THAT DOOR, TH-THE OUTSIDE STAIRS... UP...
EH?
WHO ARE YOU? WHAT ARE YOU DOING?
HALT!!
YOU CAN GO BACK TO SLEEP NOW.
WHAK

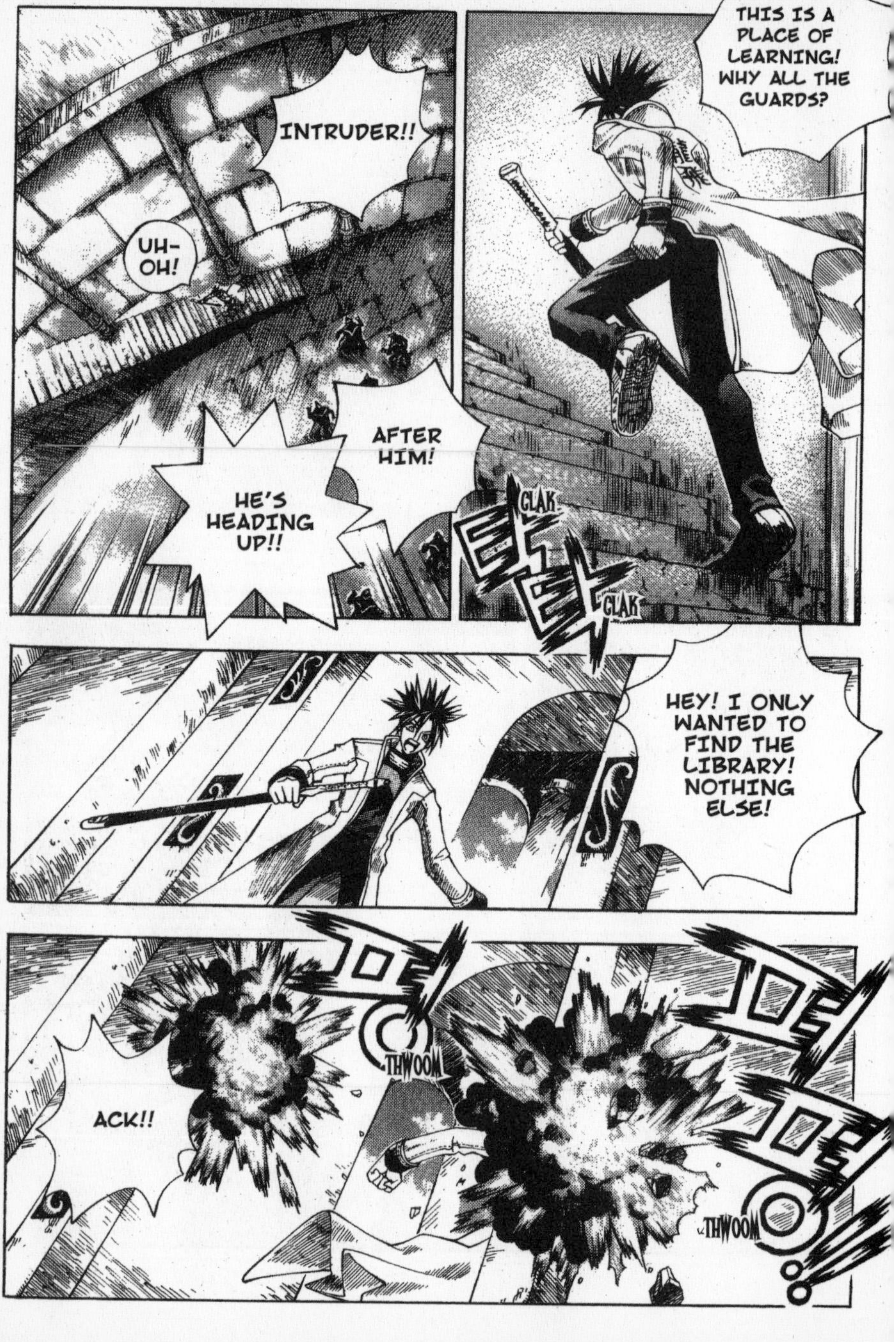
INTRUDER!!
UH-OH!
AFTER HIM!
HE'S HEADING UP!!
THIS IS A PLACE OF LEARNING! WHY ALL THE GUARDS?
CLAK
CLAK
HEY! I ONLY WANTED TO FIND THE LIBRARY! NOTHING ELSE!
ACK!!
THWOOM
THWOOM

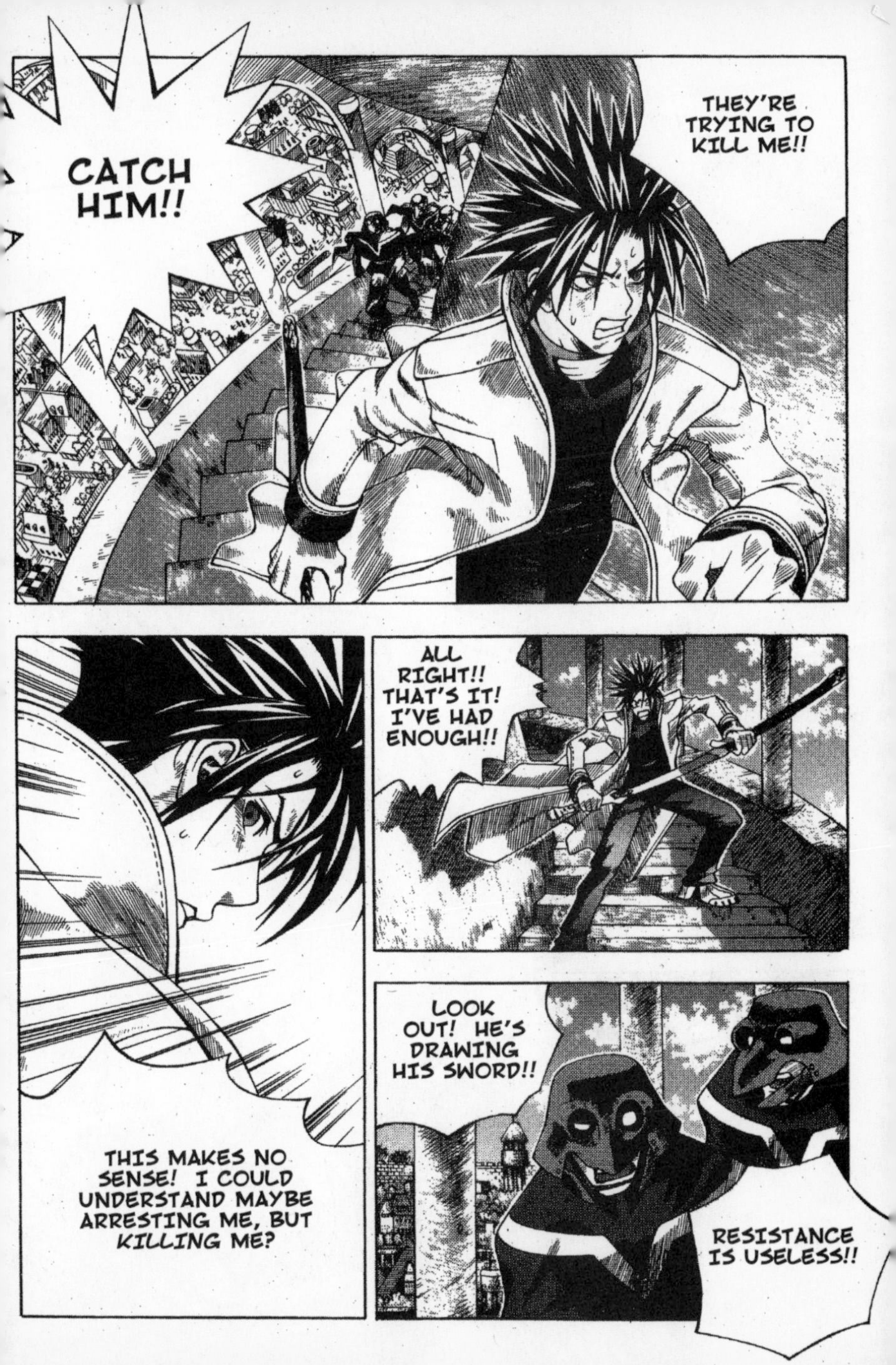
CATCH HIM!!
THEY'RE TRYING TO KILL ME!!
THIS MAKES NO SENSE! I COULD UNDERSTAND MAYBE ARRESTING ME, BUT KILLING ME?
ALL RIGHT!! THAT'S IT! I'VE HAD ENOUGH!!
LOOK OUT! HE'S DRAWING HIS SWORD!!
RESISTANCE IS USELESS!!

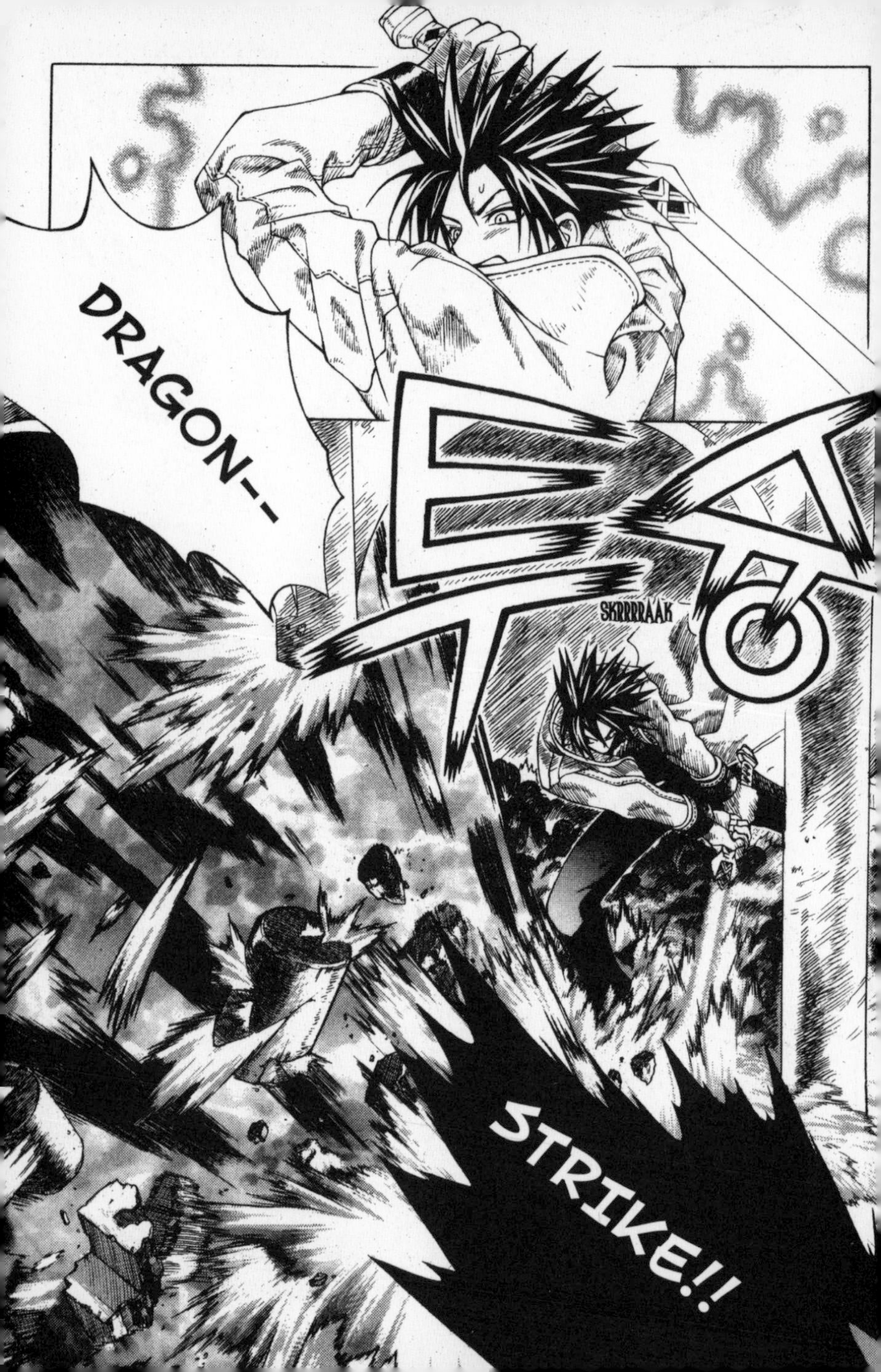
DRAGON--
SKRRRRAAK
STRIKE!!

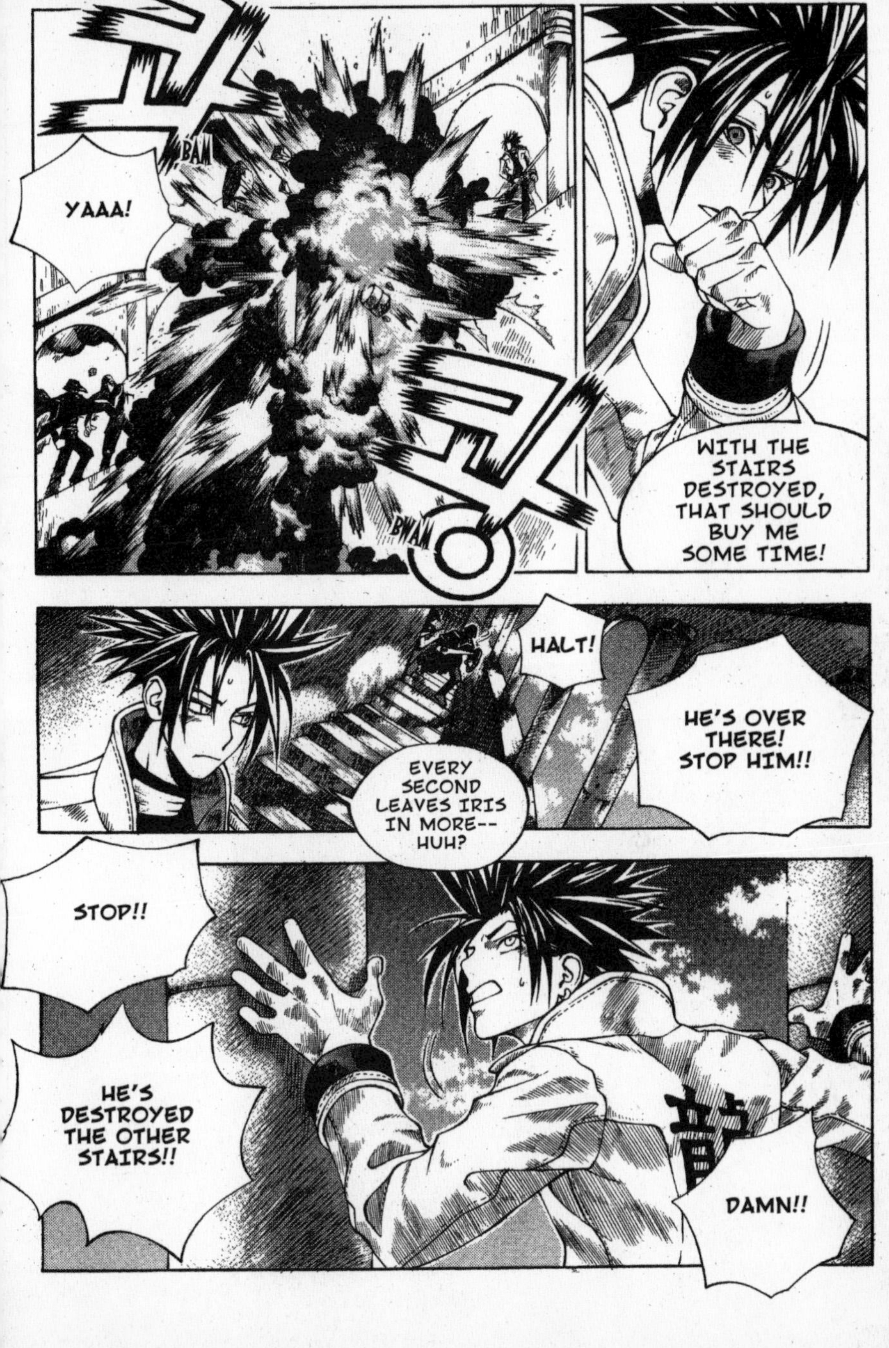
BAM
YAAA!
BWAM
WITH THE STAIRS DESTROYED, THAT SHOULD BUY ME SOME TIME!
HALT!
EVERY SECOND LEAVES IRIS IN MORE-- HUH?
HE'S OVER THERE! STOP HIM!!
STOP!!
HE'S DESTROYED THE OTHER STAIRS!!
DAMN!!

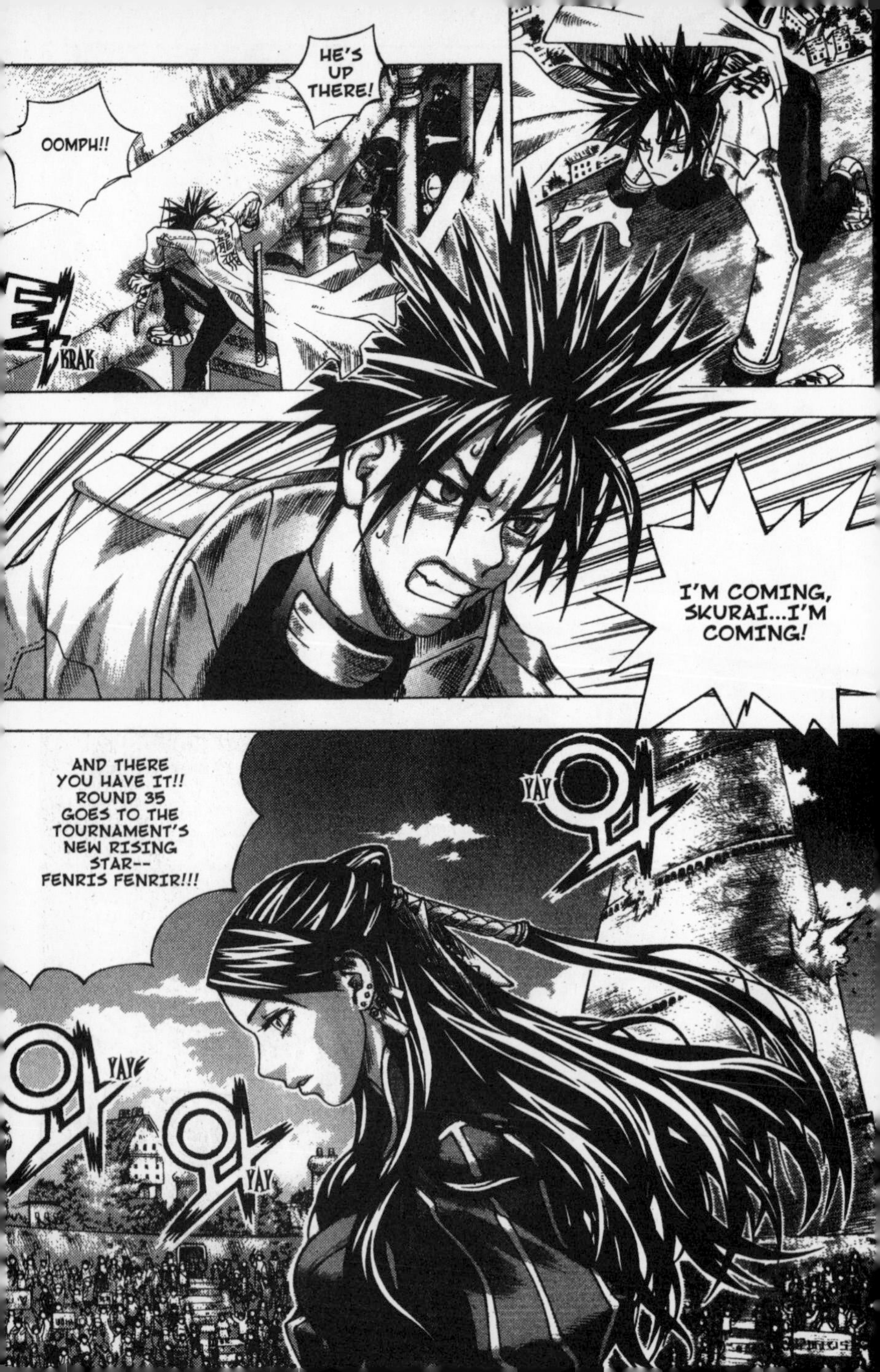
OOMPH!!
HE'S UP THERE!
KRAK
I'M COMING, SKURAI...I'M COMING!
AND THERE YOU HAVE IT!! ROUND 35 GOES TO THE TOURNAMENT'S NEW RISING STAR-- FENRIS FENRIR!!!
YAY
YAY
YAY

RAGNAROK
라그나로크
IN TO THE ABYSS

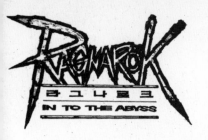

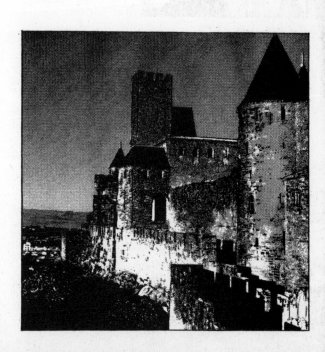

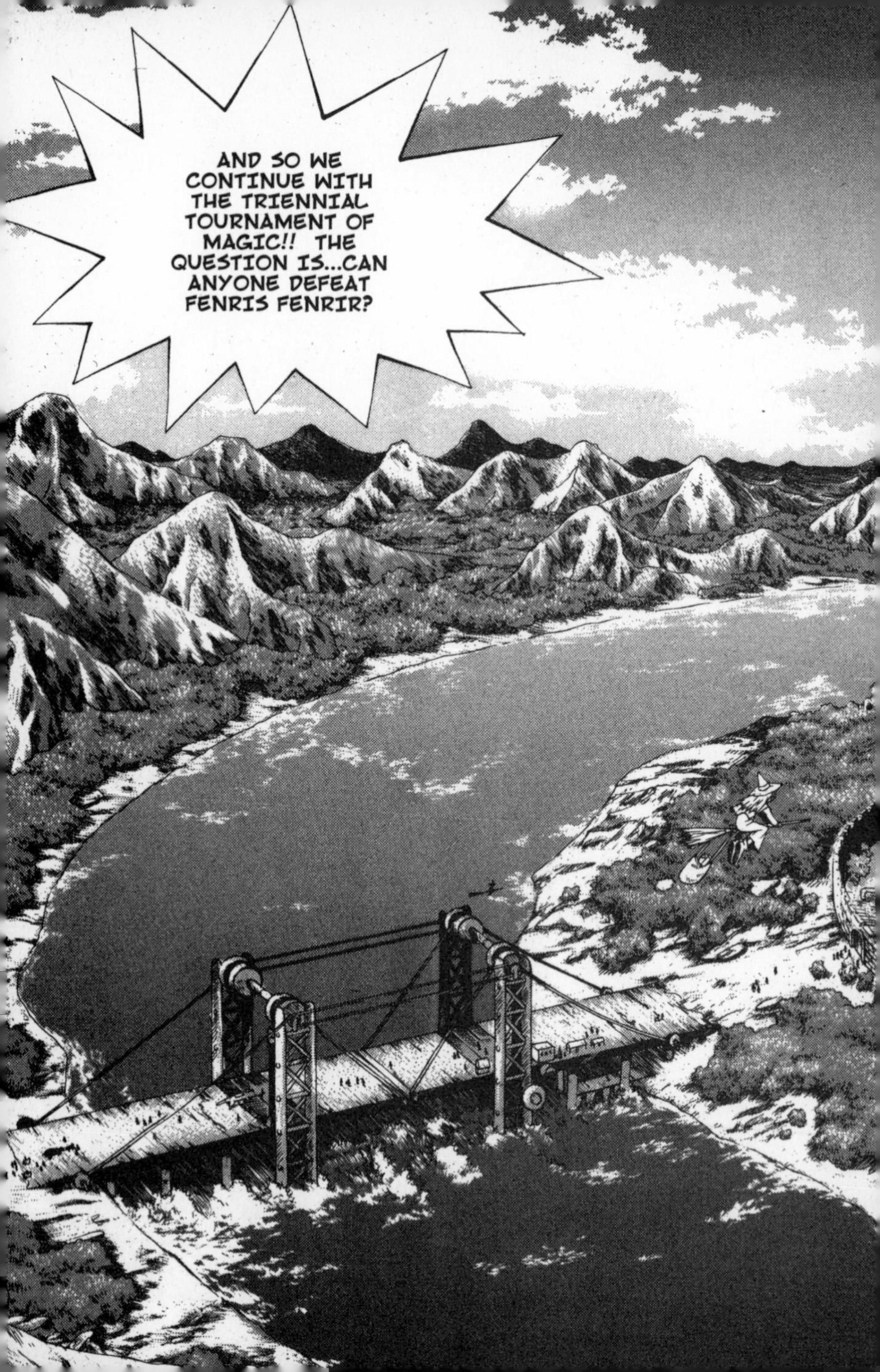
AND SO WE CONTINUE WITH THE TRIENNIAL TOURNAMENT OF MAGIC!! THE QUESTION IS...CAN ANYONE DEFEAT FENRIS FENRIR?

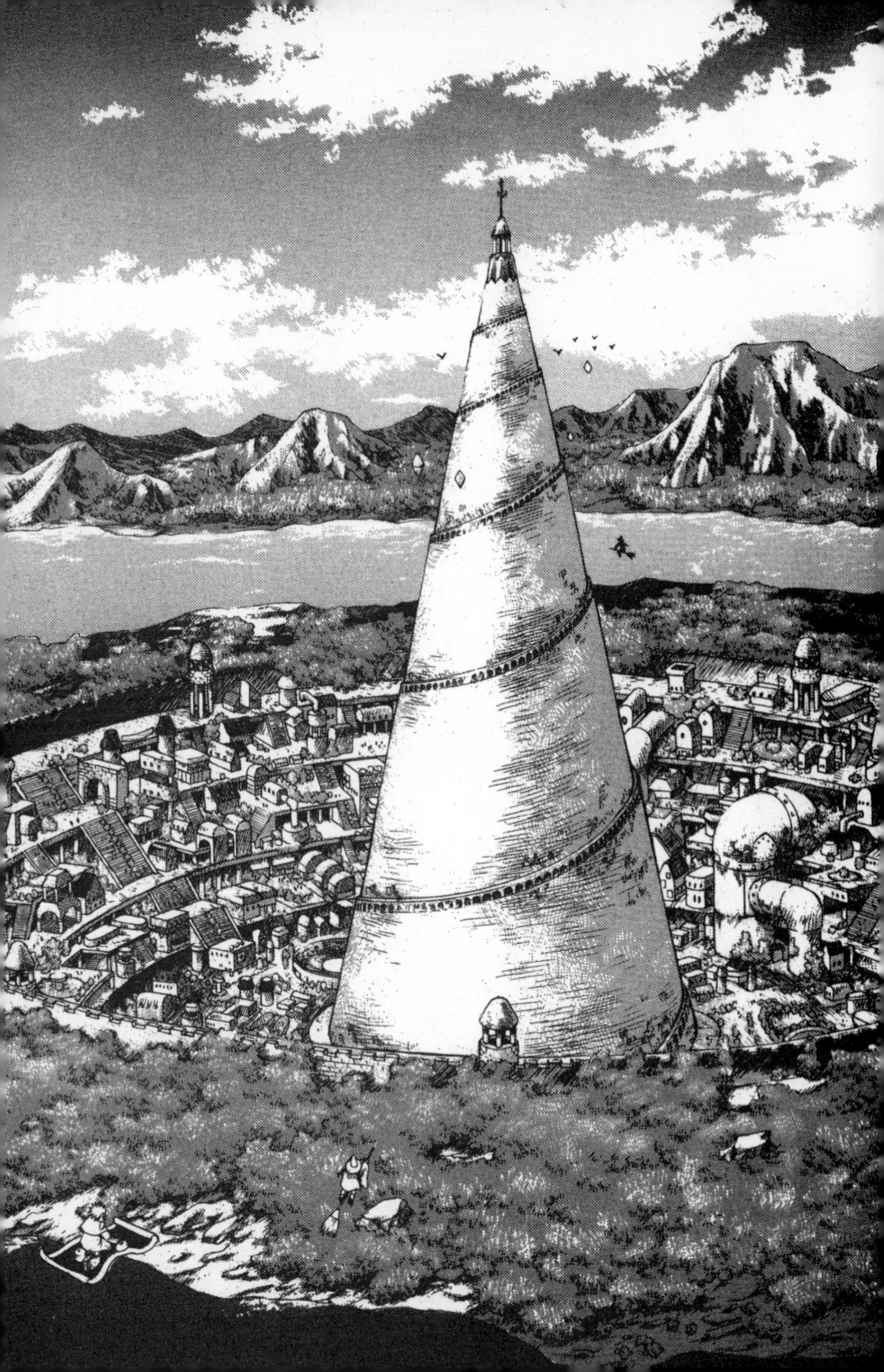

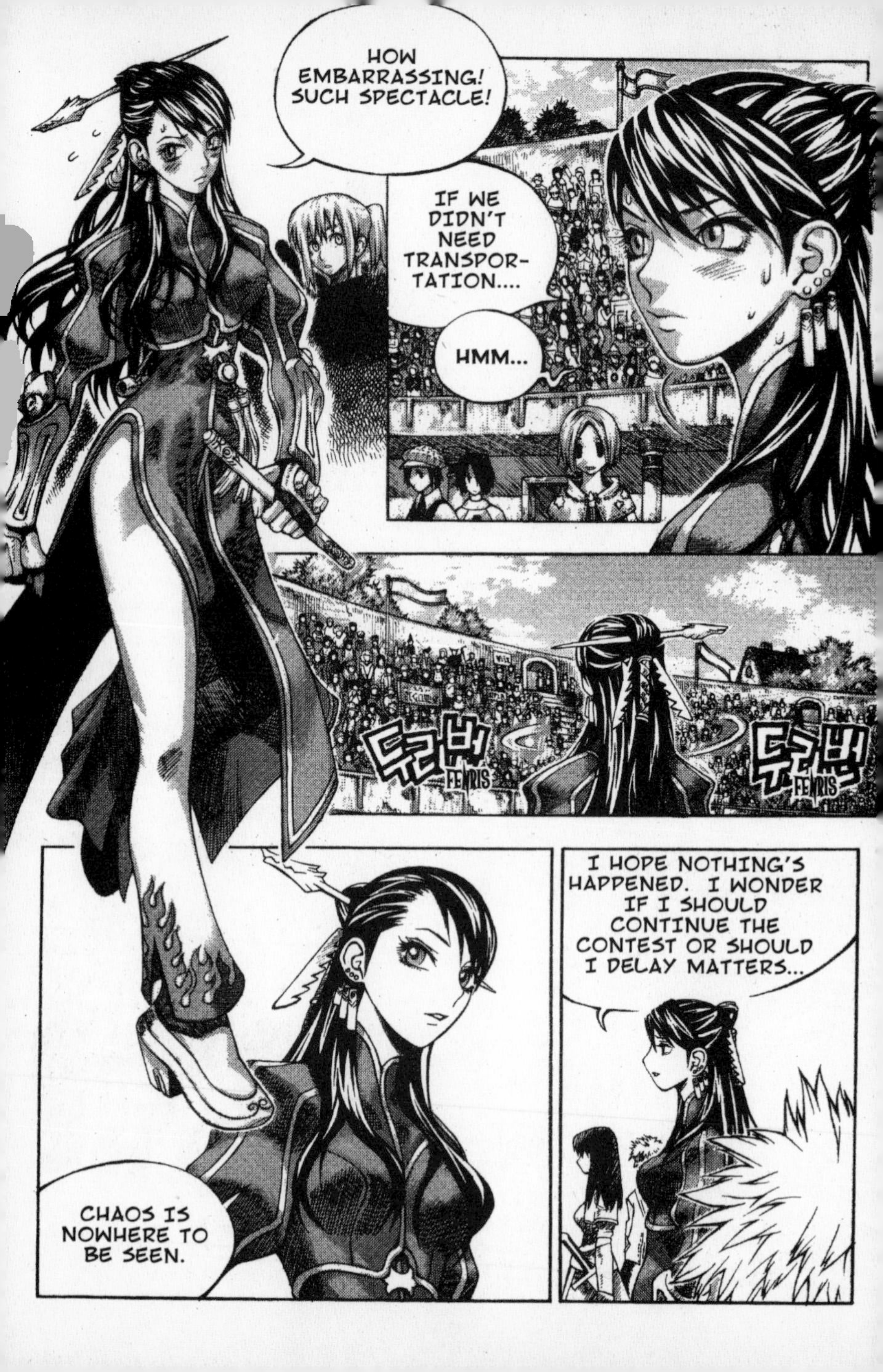
HOW EMBARRASSING! SUCH SPECTACLE!
IF WE DIDN'T NEED TRANSPOR-TATION....
HMM...
FENRIS
FENRIS
CHAOS IS NOWHERE TO BE SEEN.
I HOPE NOTHING'S HAPPENED. I WONDER IF I SHOULD CONTINUE THE CONTEST OR SHOULD I DELAY MATTERS...

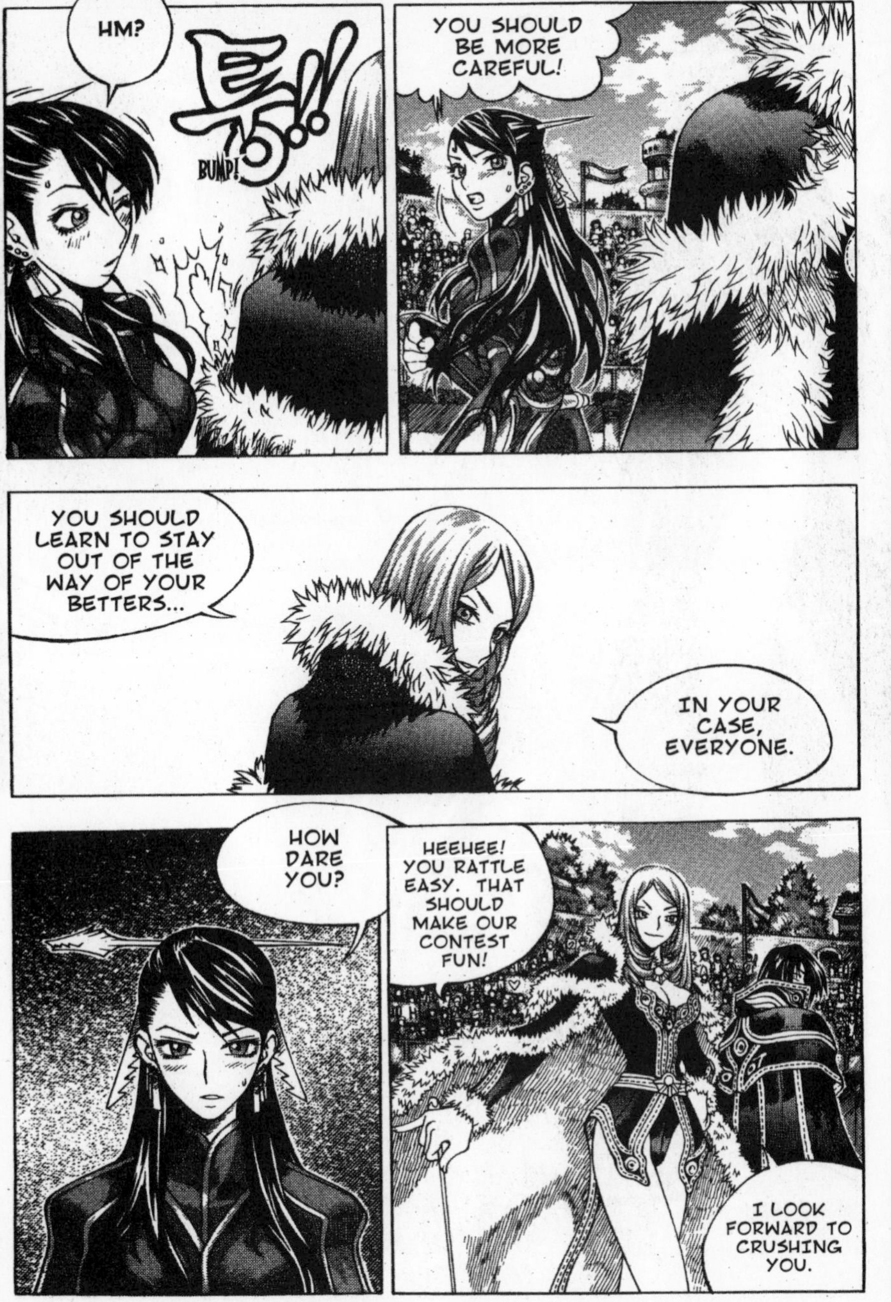
HM?
투
BUMP!
YOU SHOULD BE MORE CAREFUL!
YOU SHOULD LEARN TO STAY OUT OF THE WAY OF YOUR BETTERS...
IN YOUR CASE, EVERYONE.
HOW DARE YOU?
HEEHEE! YOU RATTLE EASY. THAT SHOULD MAKE OUR CONTEST FUN!
I LOOK FORWARD TO CRUSHING YOU.

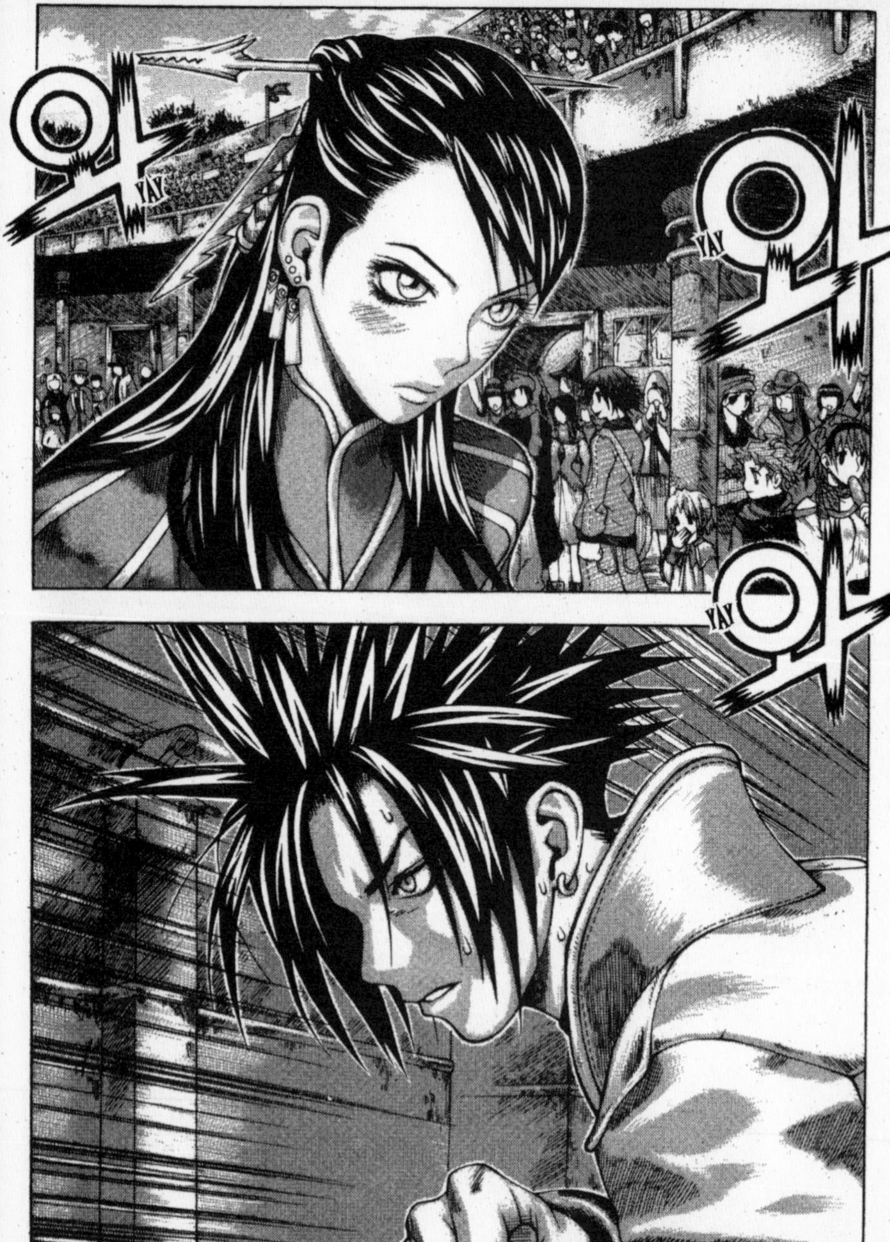
와
YAY
와
YAY
와
YAY

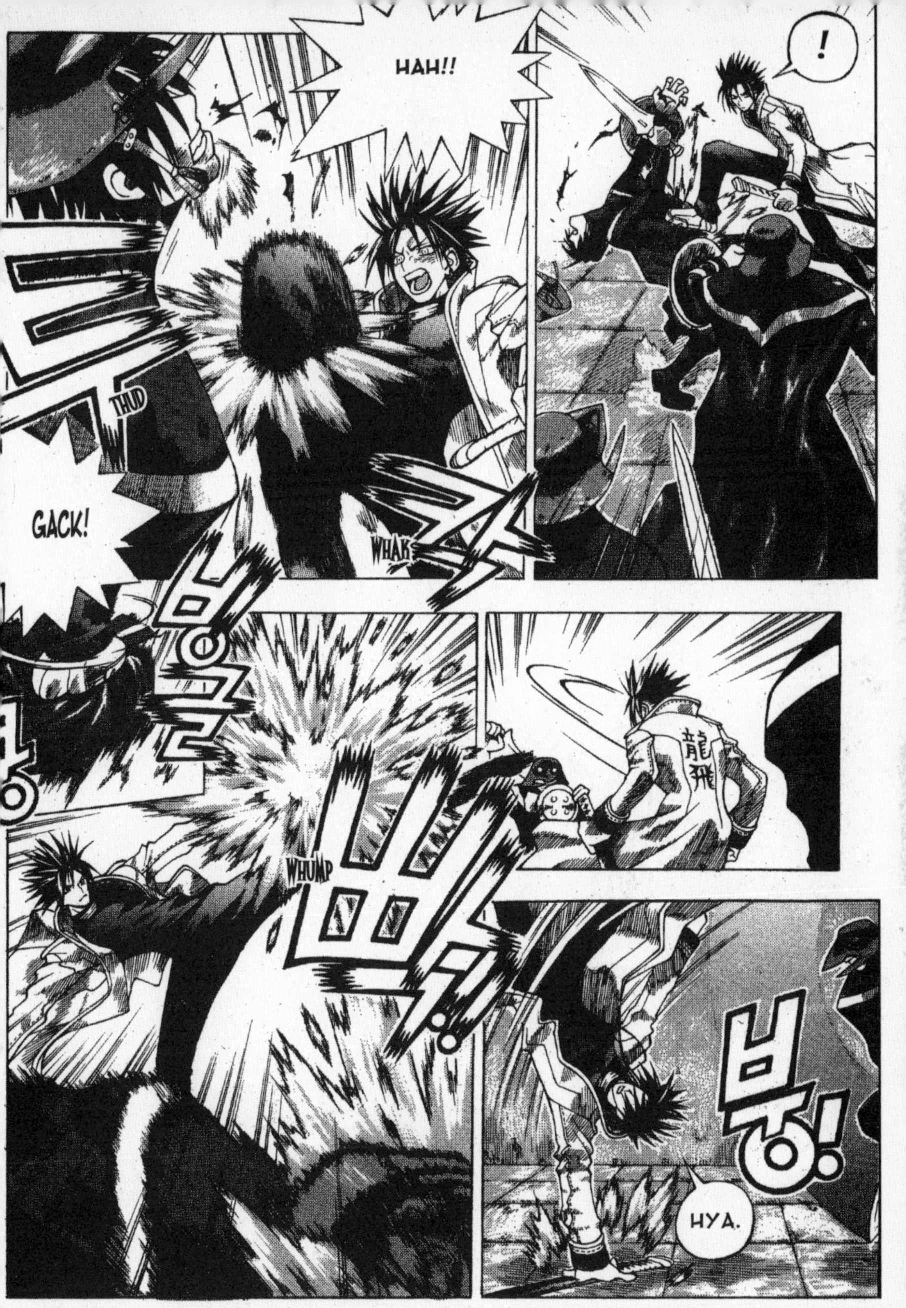
HAH!!
THUD
GACK!
WHAK
!
WHUMP
HYA.

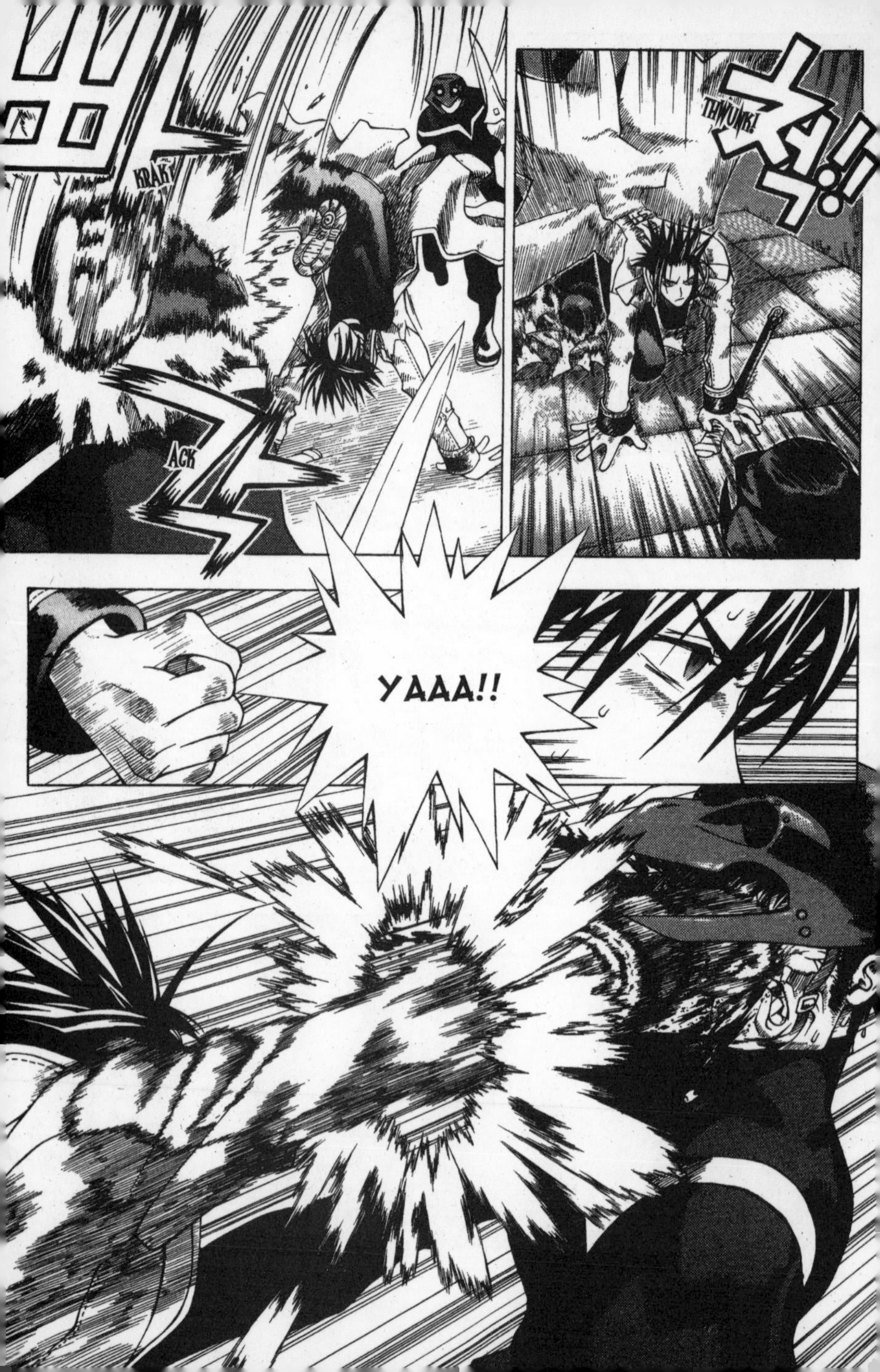
KRAK!
ACK
THWUNK!
YAAA!!

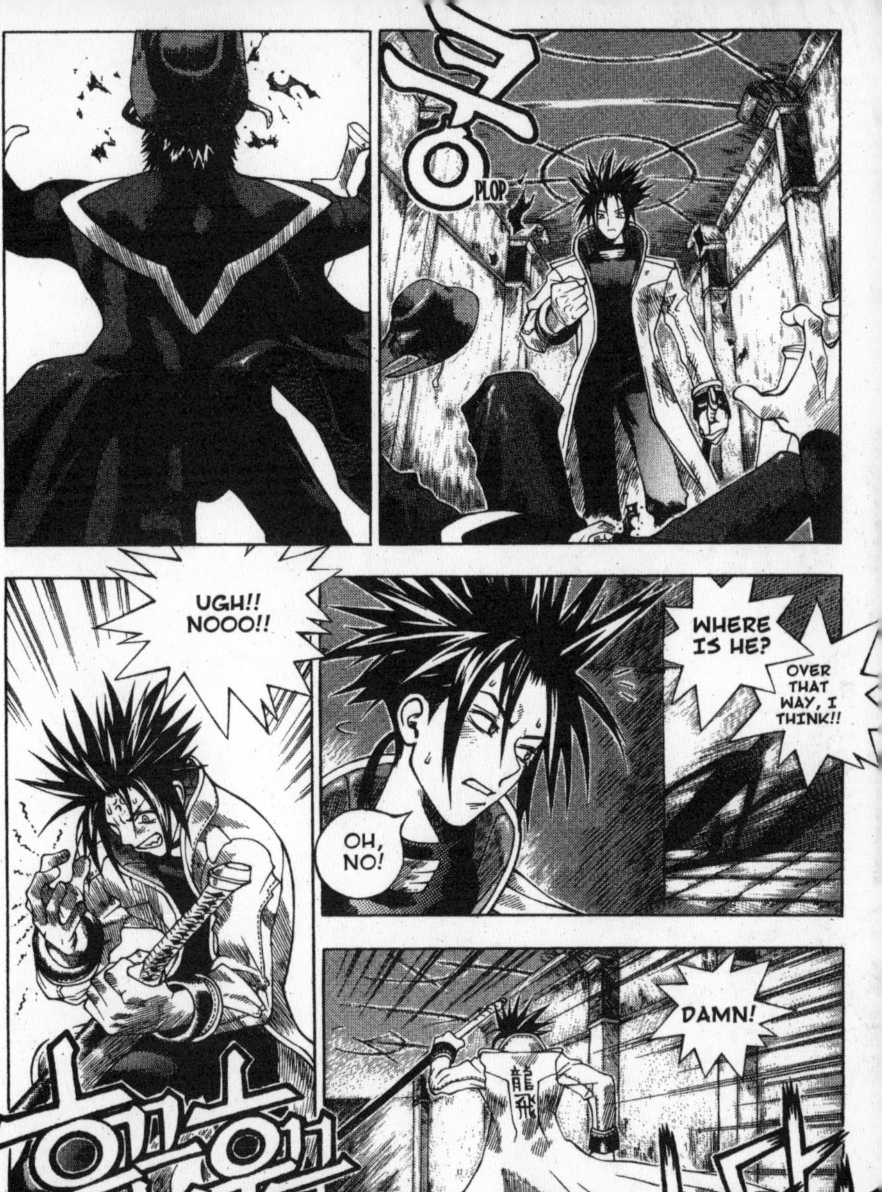
PLOP
UGH!! NOOO!!
BABUMP
BABUMP
WHERE IS HE?
OVER THAT WAY, I THINK!!
OH, NO!
DAMN!
CLAK
CLAK

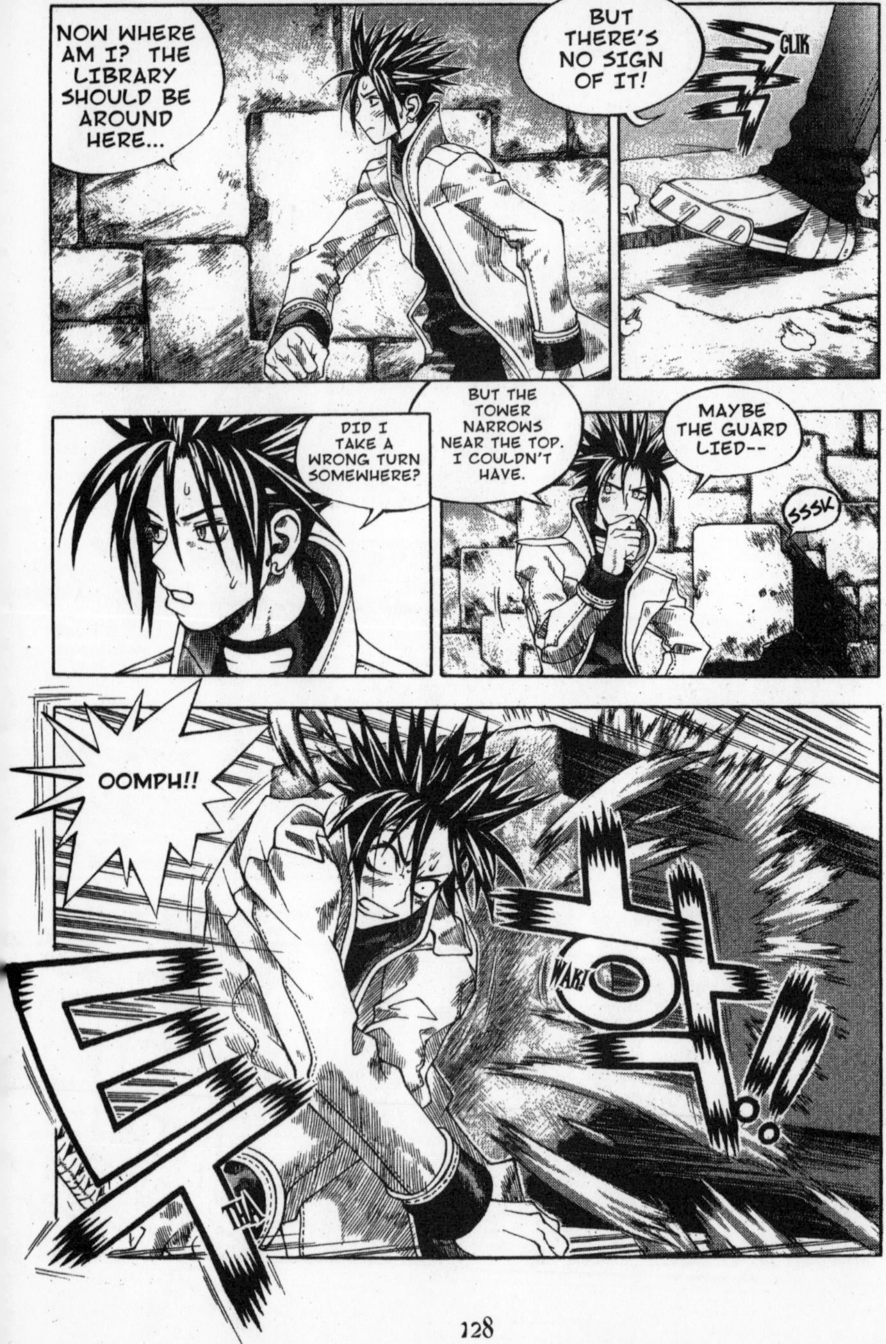
NOW WHERE AM I? THE LIBRARY SHOULD BE AROUND HERE...
BUT THERE'S NO SIGN OF IT!
GLIK
DID I TAKE A WRONG TURN SOMEWHERE?
BUT THE TOWER NARROWS NEAR THE TOP. I COULDN'T HAVE.
MAYBE THE GUARD LIED--
SSSK
OOMPH!!
WAK!
THA

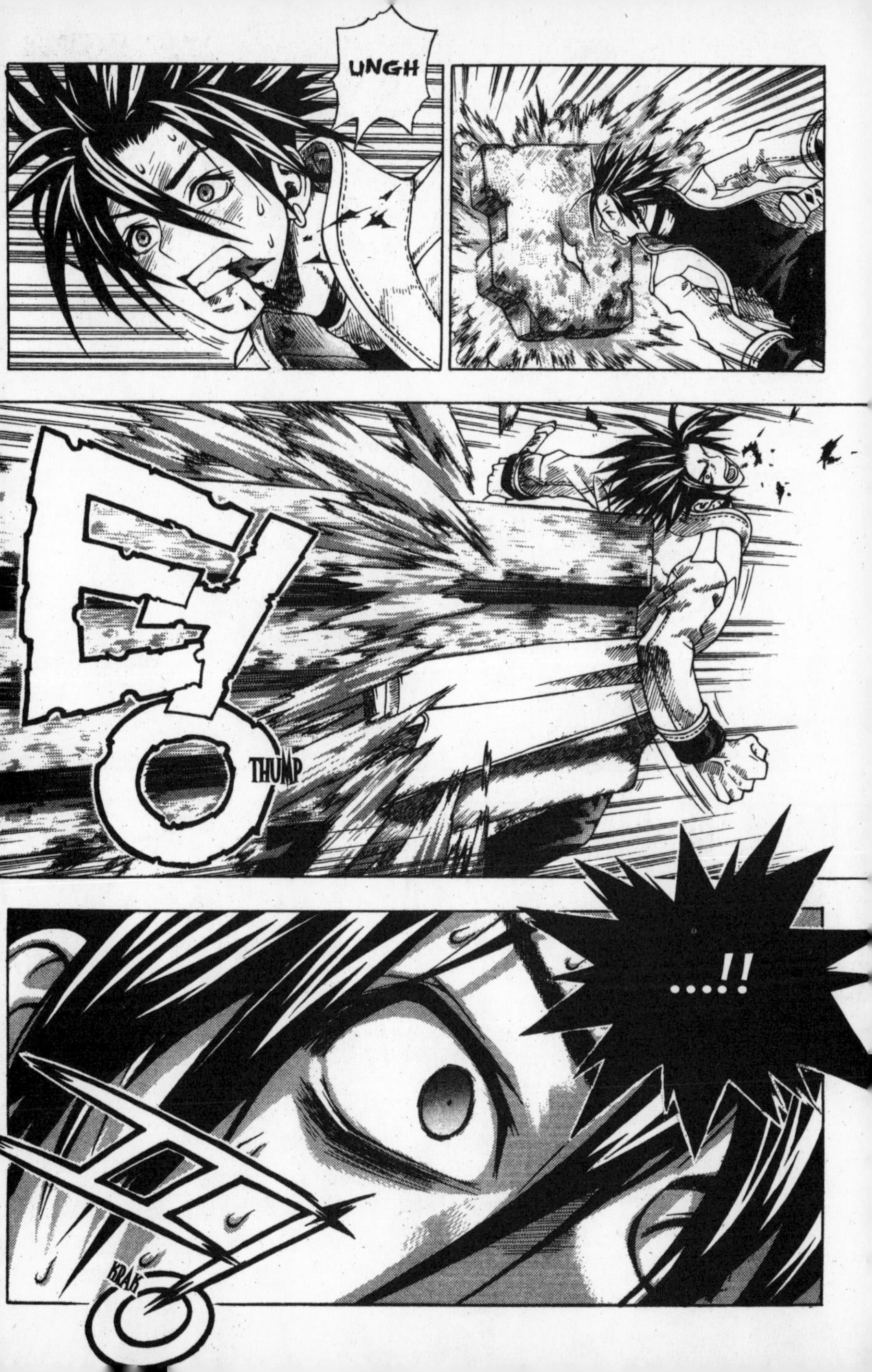
UNGH
THUMP
....!!
KRAK

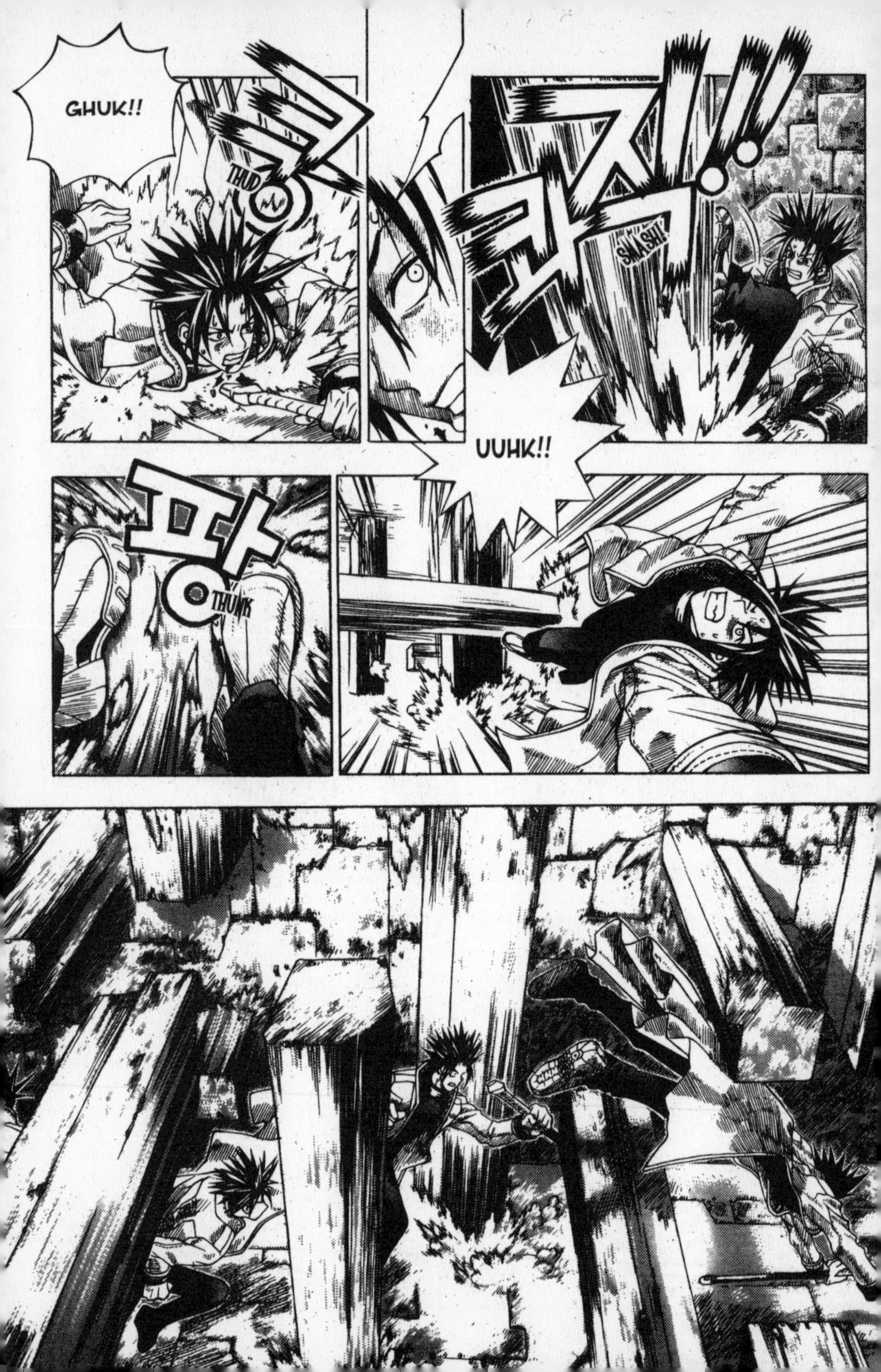
GHUK!!
THUD
SMASH!
UUHK!!
THUNK

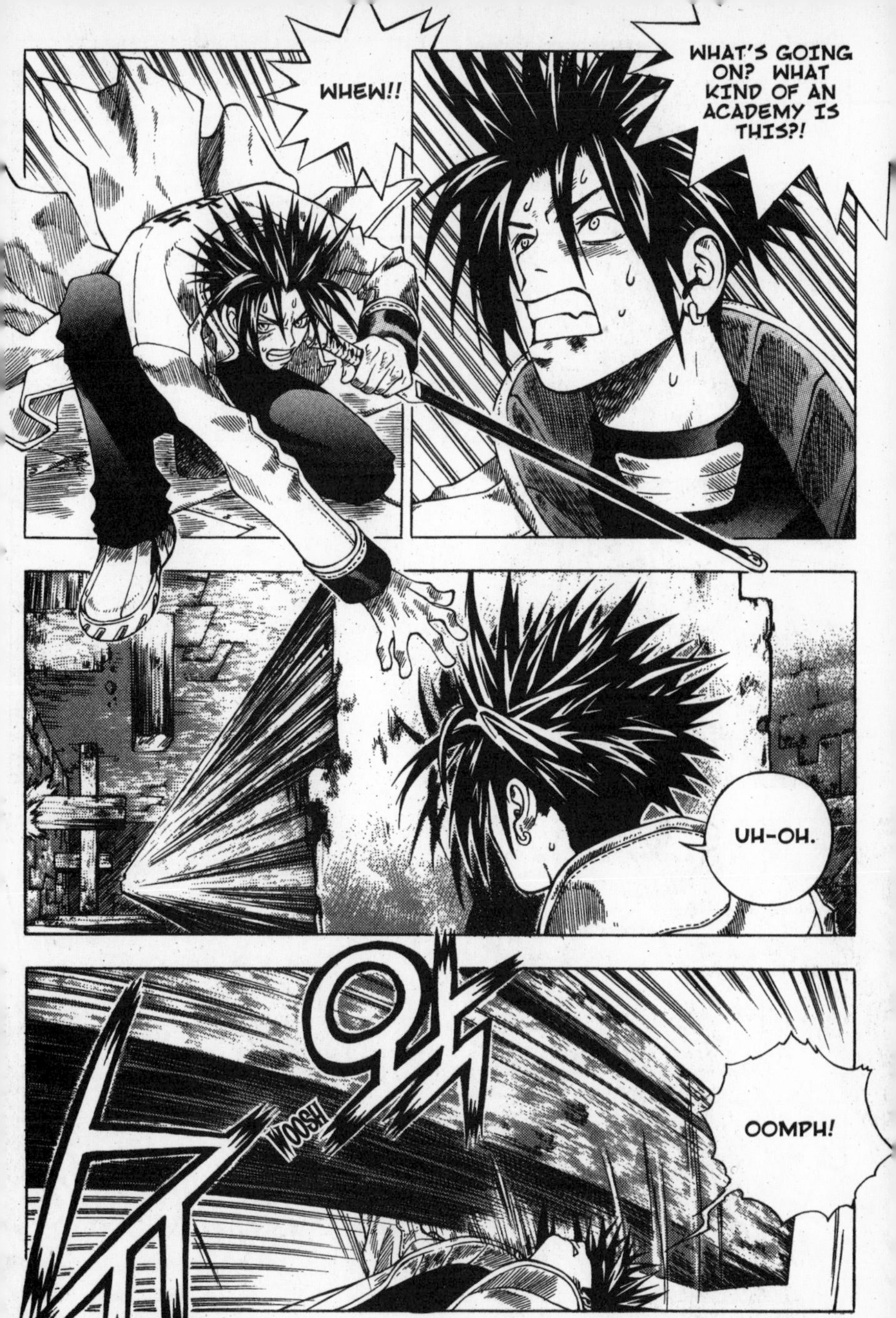
WHEW!!
WHAT'S GOING ON? WHAT KIND OF AN ACADEMY IS THIS?!
UH-OH.
WOOSH
OOMPH!

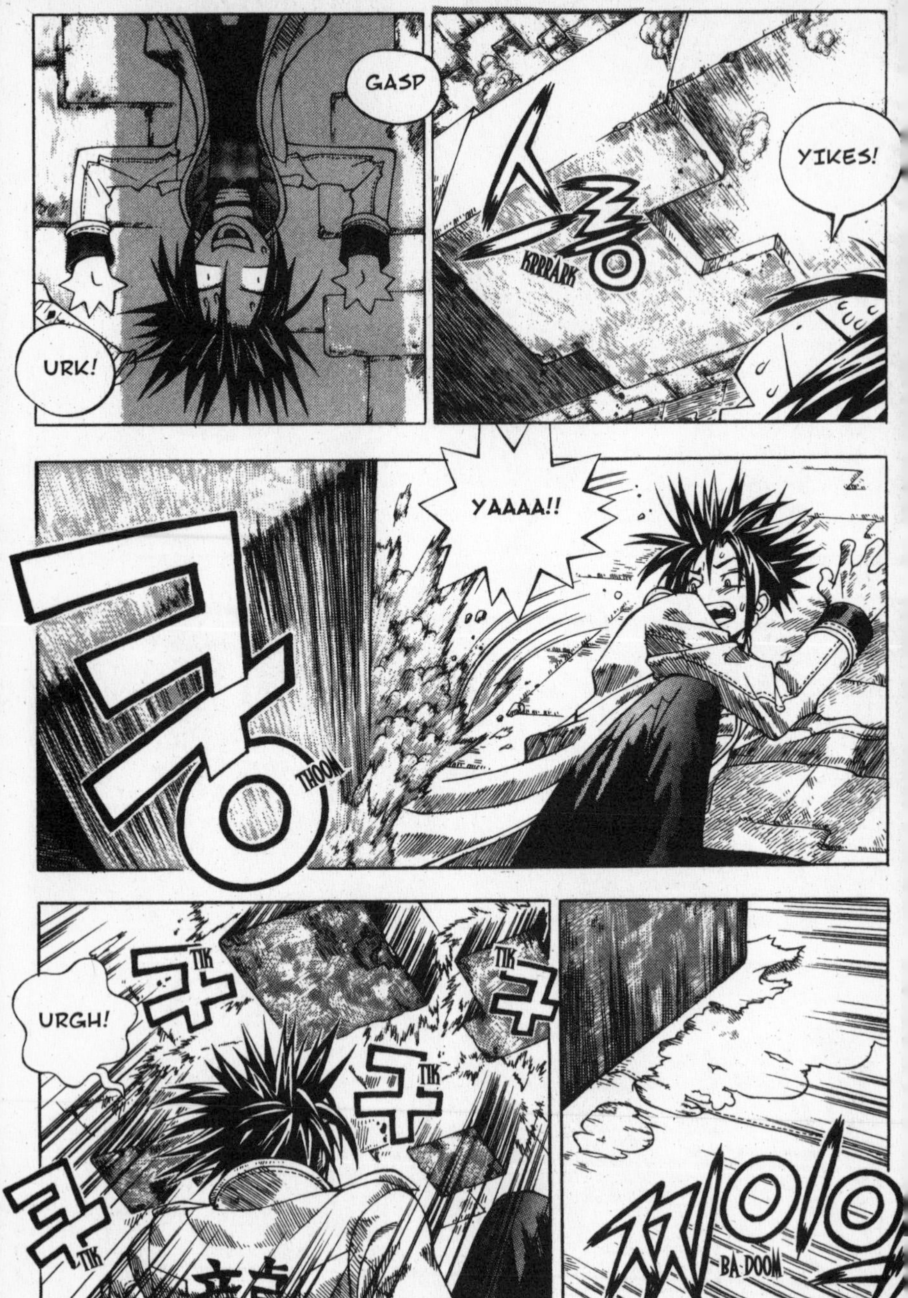
GASP
URK!
YIKES!
KRRRARK
YAAAA!!
THOOM
URGH!
TIK
TIK
TIK
TIK
BA-DOOM

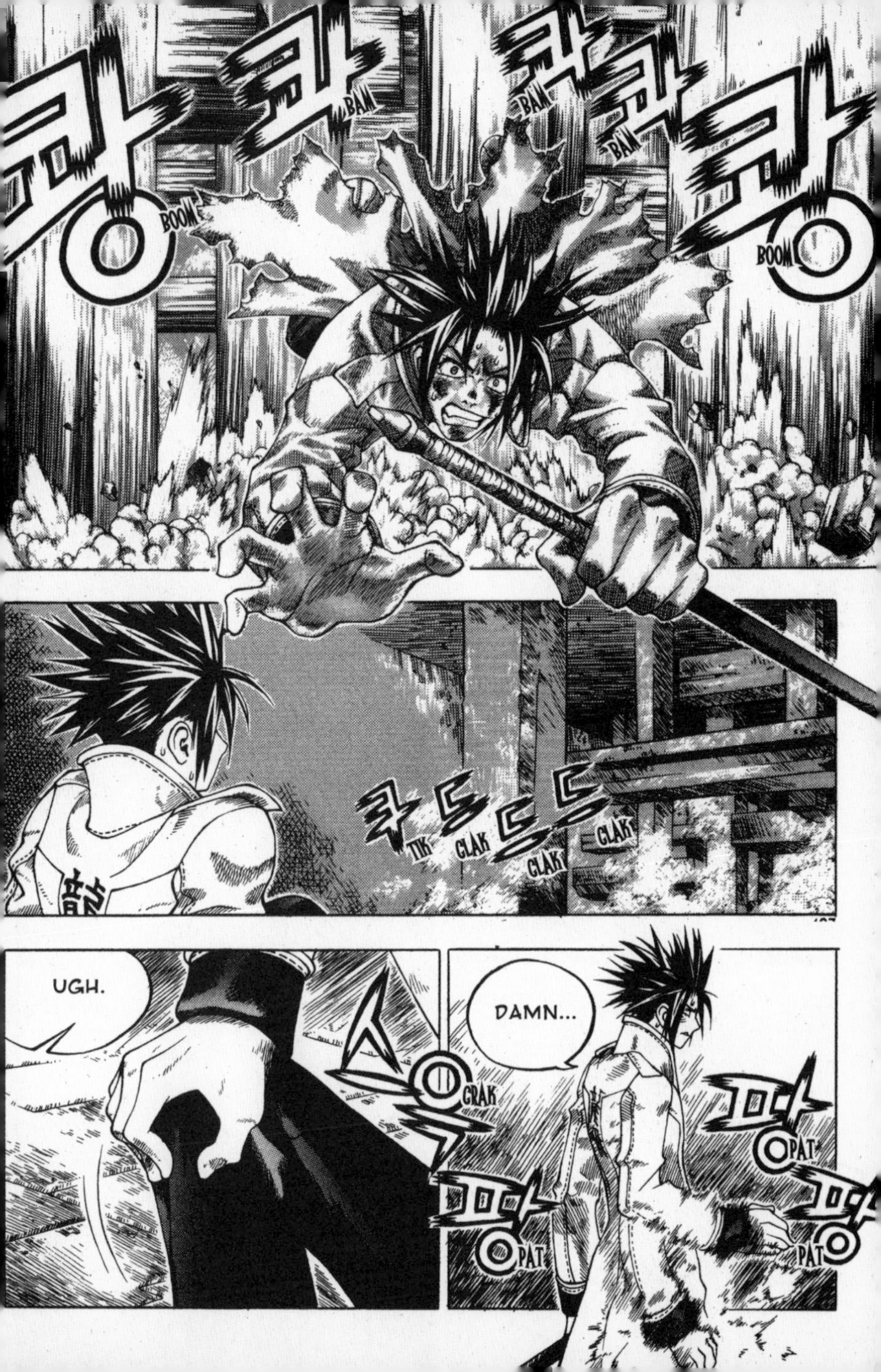
BOOM
BAM
BAM
BAM
BOOM
TIK
CLAK
CLAK
CLAK
UGH.
CRAK
DAMN...
PAT
PAT
PAT

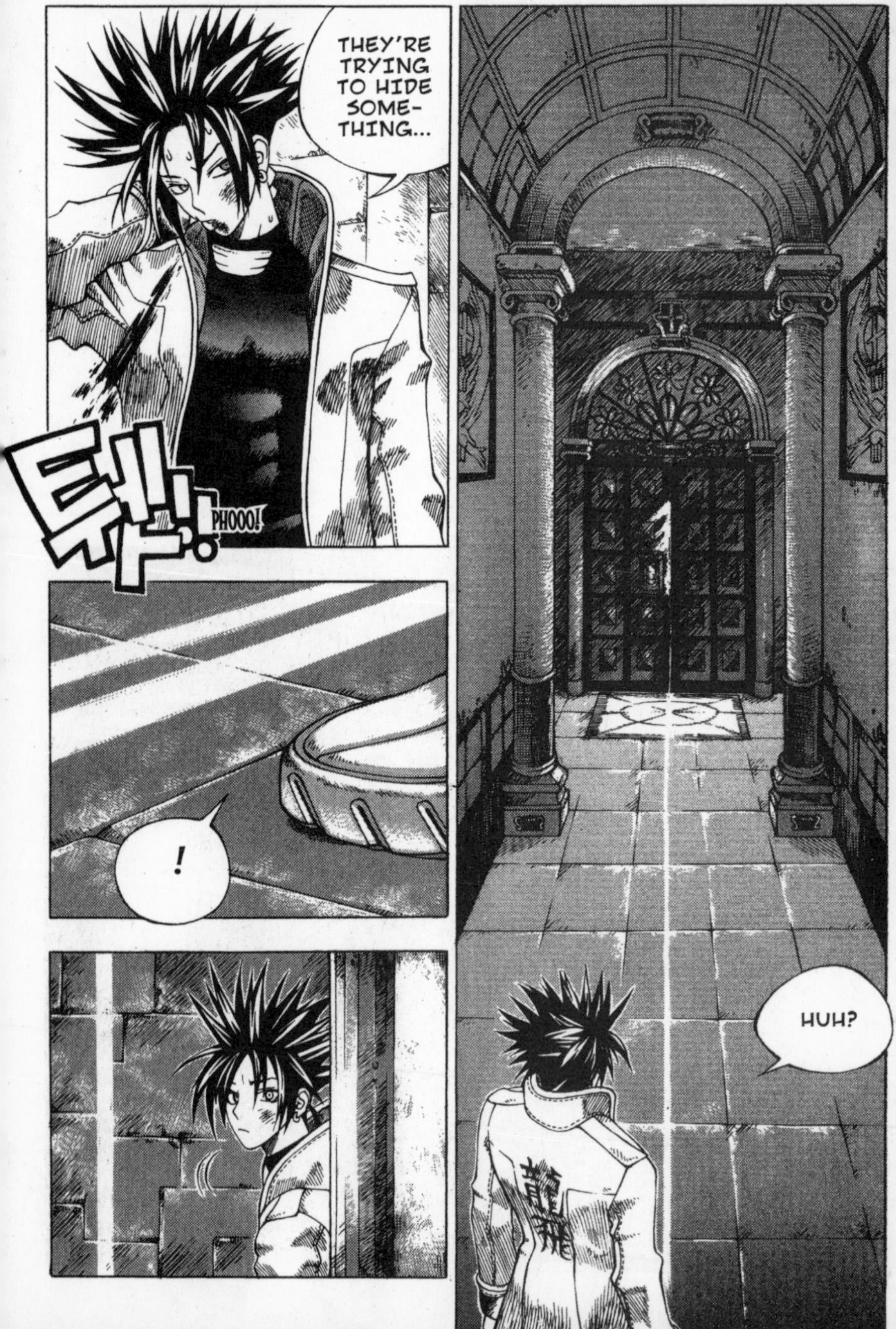
THEY'RE TRYING TO HIDE SOME-THING...
PHOOO!
!
HUH?

RAGNAROK
라그나로크
IN TO THE ABYSS

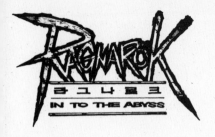

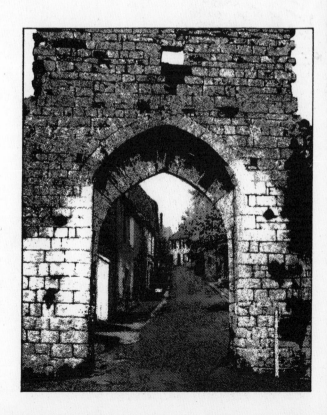

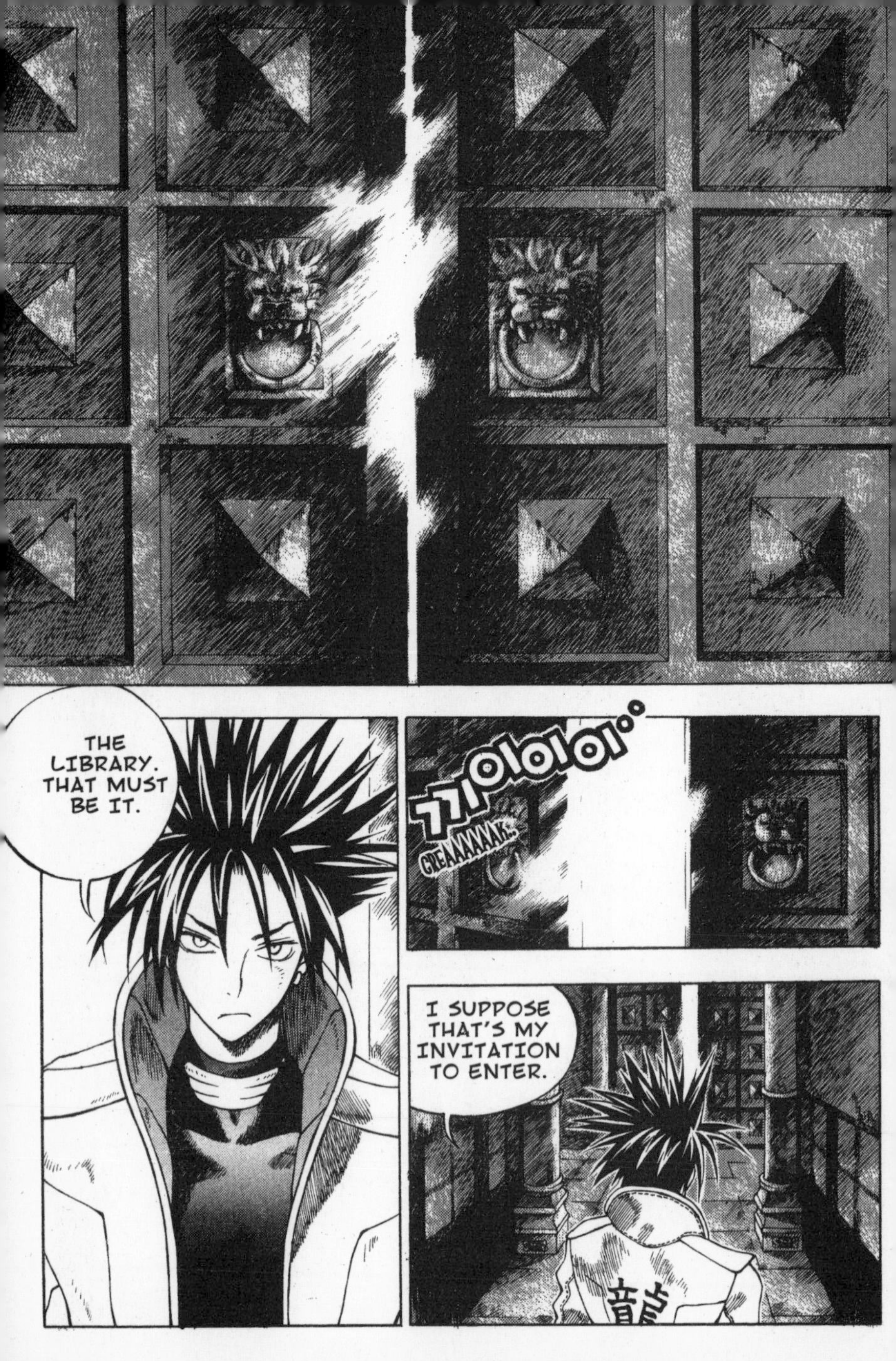
THE LIBRARY. THAT MUST BE IT.
끼이이이이
CREAAAAAAK..
I SUPPOSE THAT'S MY INVITATION TO ENTER.
龍

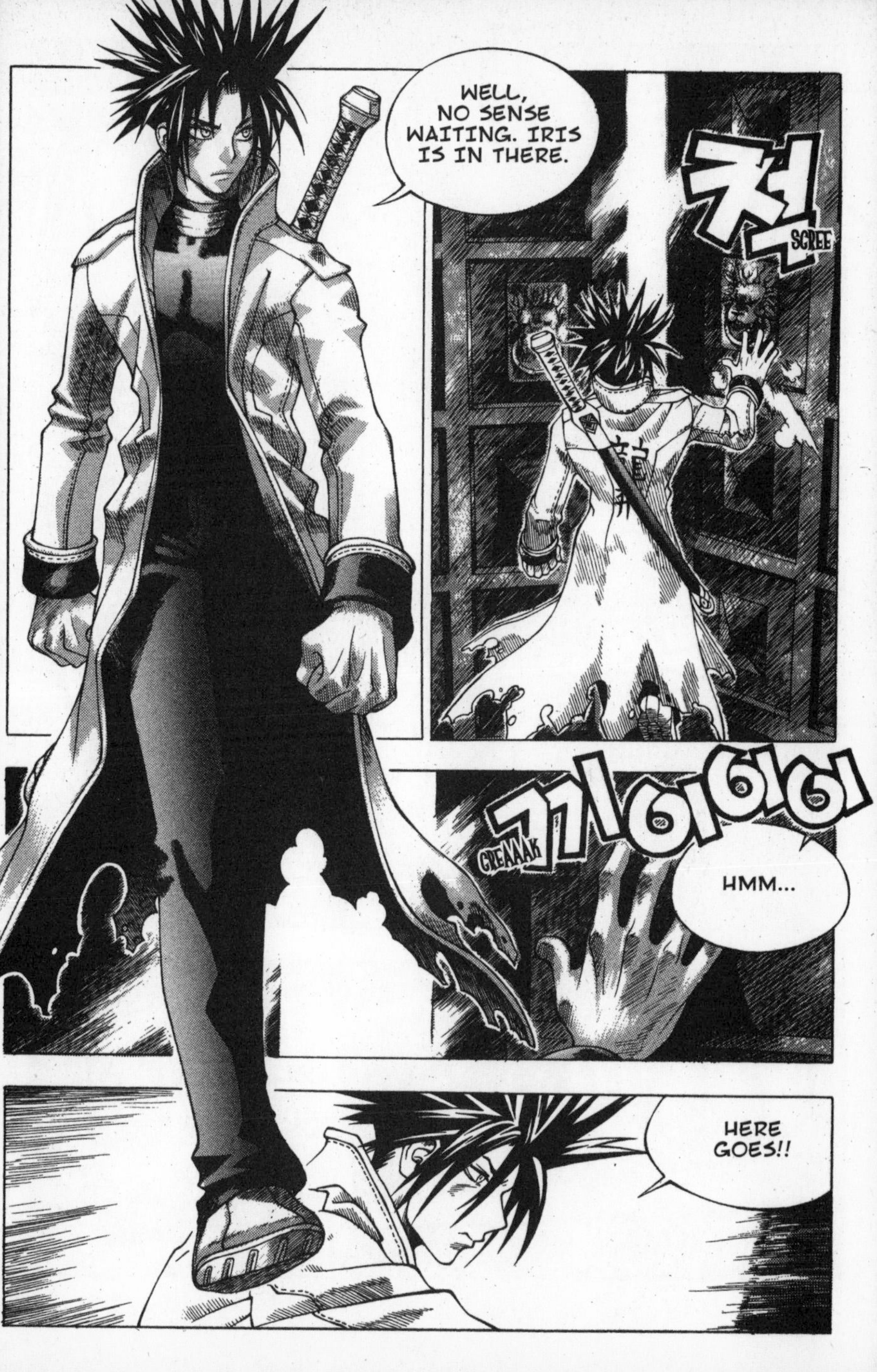
WELL, NO SENSE WAITING. IRIS IS IN THERE.
SCREE
CREAAAK
HMM...
HERE GOES!!

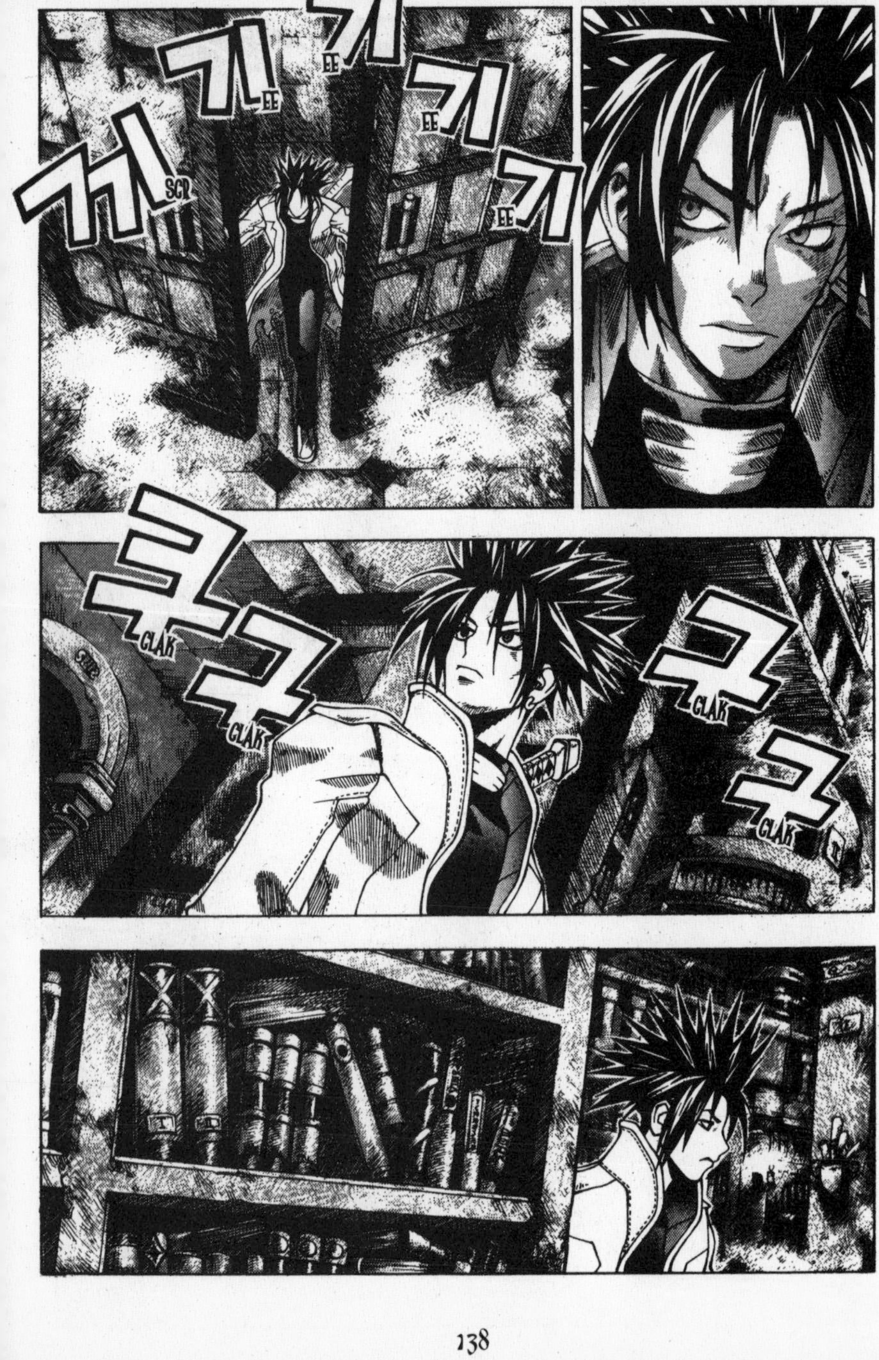
SCR
EE
EE
EE
EE
CLAK
CLAK
CLAK
CLAK

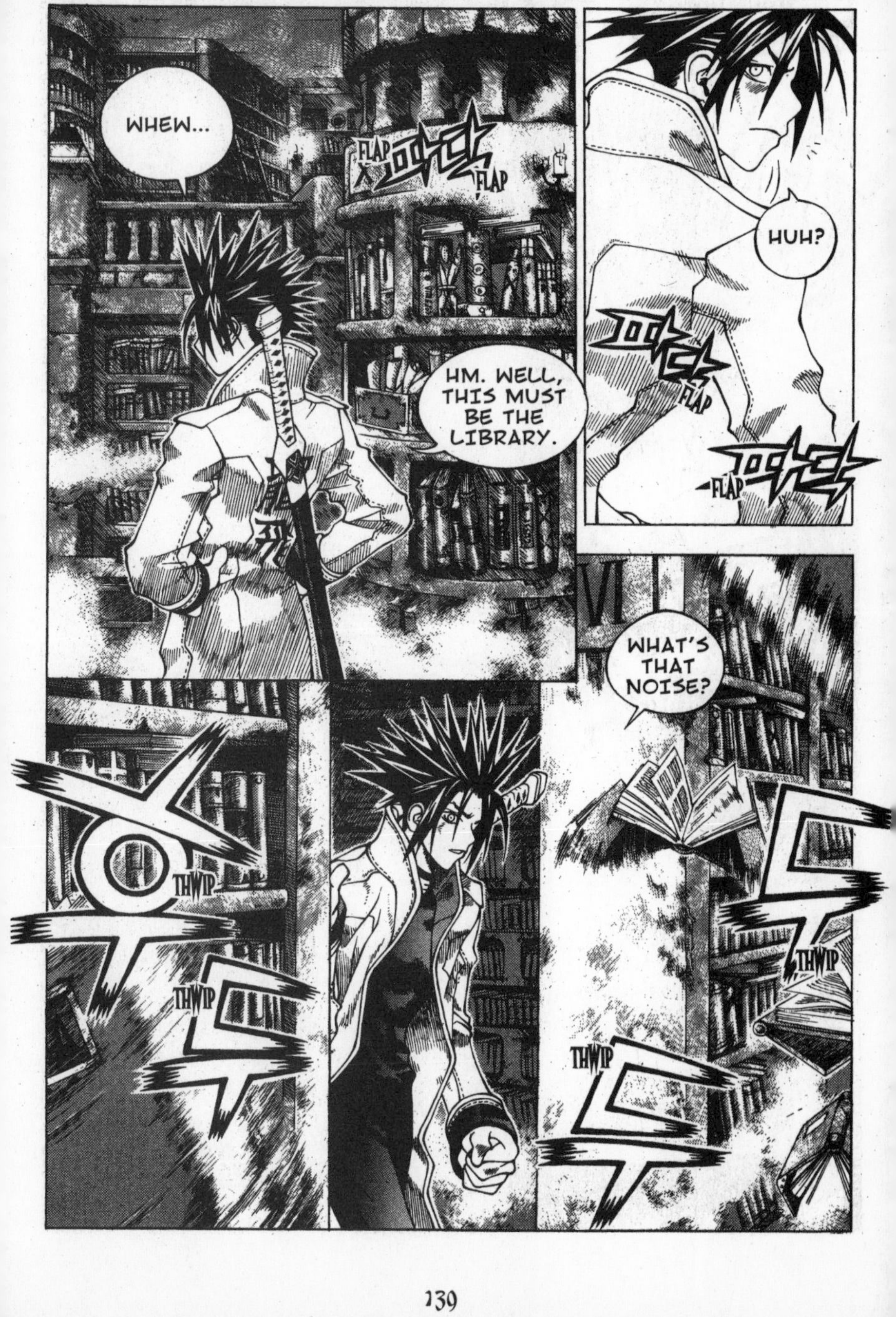
WHEW...
FLAP
FLAP
HM. WELL, THIS MUST BE THE LIBRARY.
HUH?
FLAP
FLAP
THWIP
THWIP
WHAT'S THAT NOISE?
THWIP
THWIP

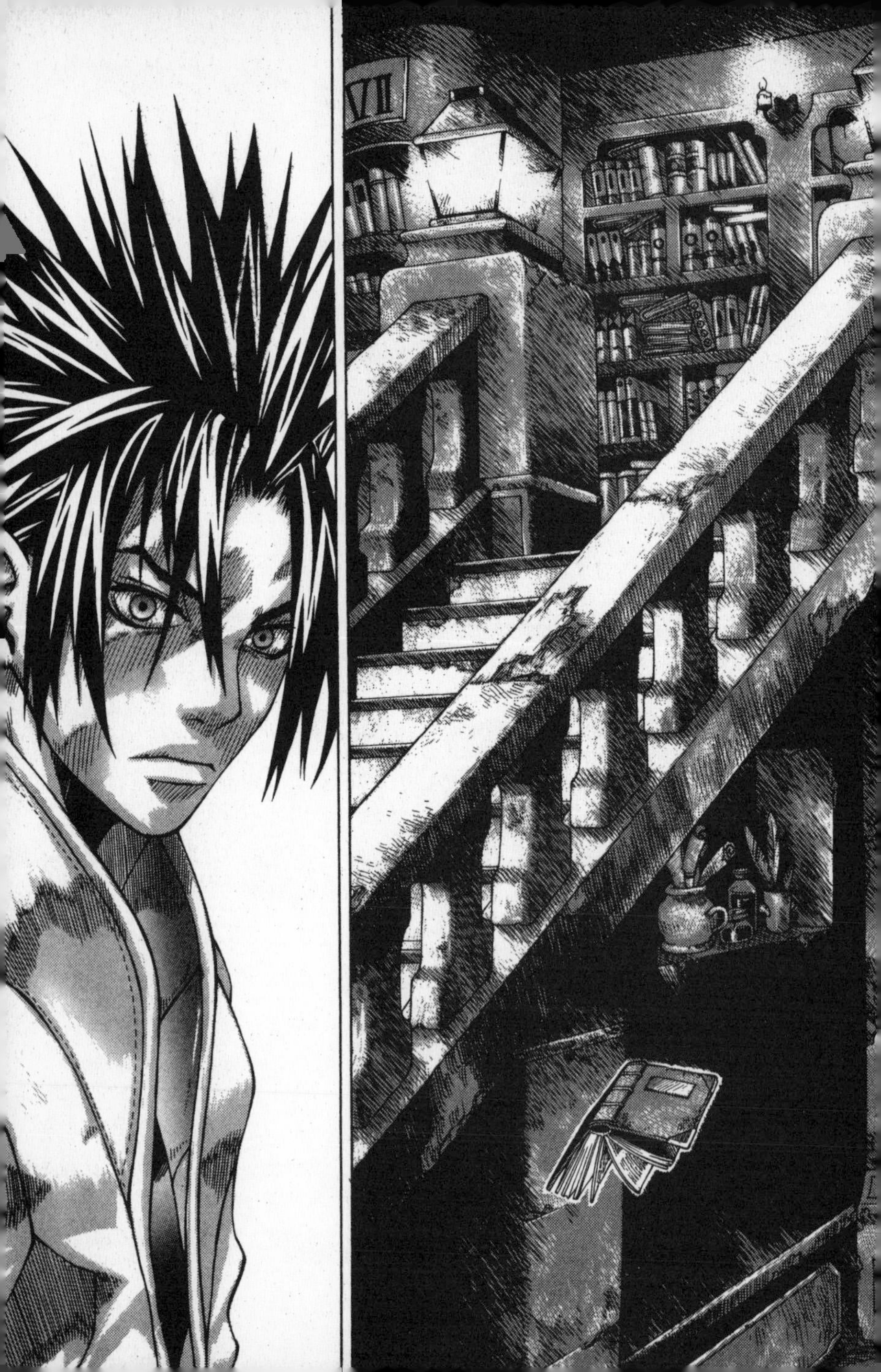
VII

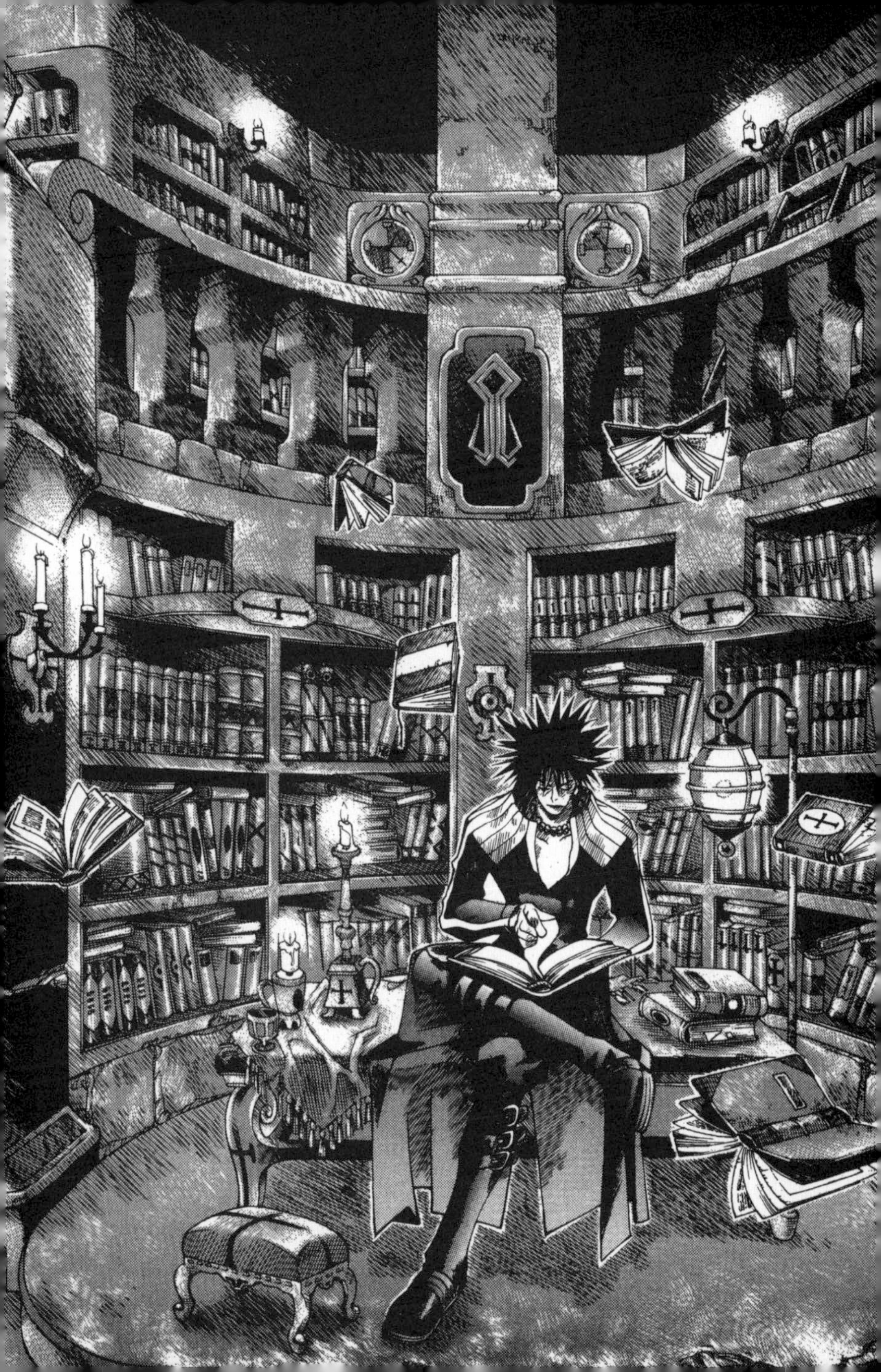

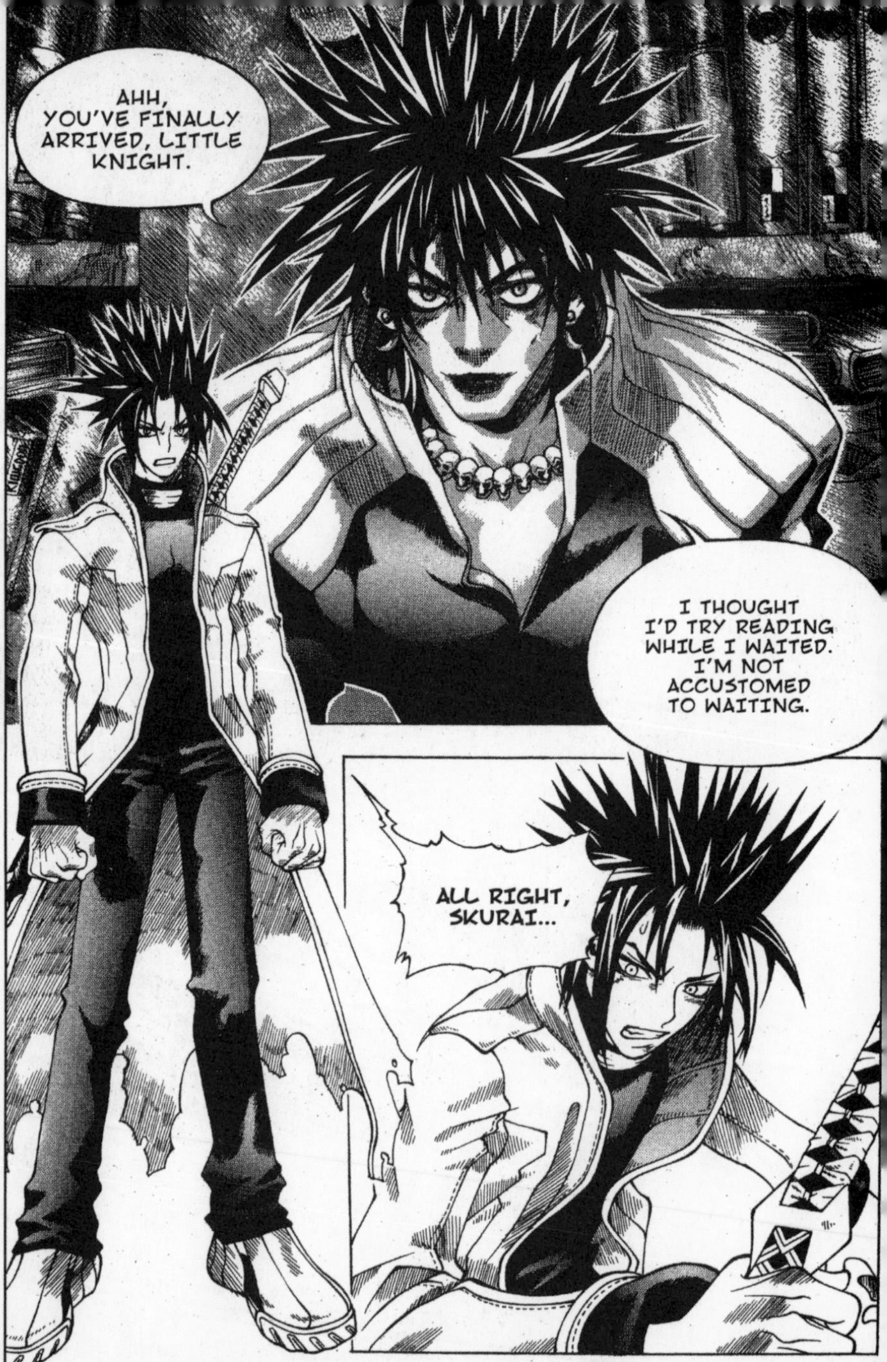
AHH, YOU'VE FINALLY ARRIVED, LITTLE KNIGHT.
I THOUGHT I'D TRY READING WHILE I WAITED. I'M NOT ACCUSTOMED TO WAITING.
ALL RIGHT, SKURAI...

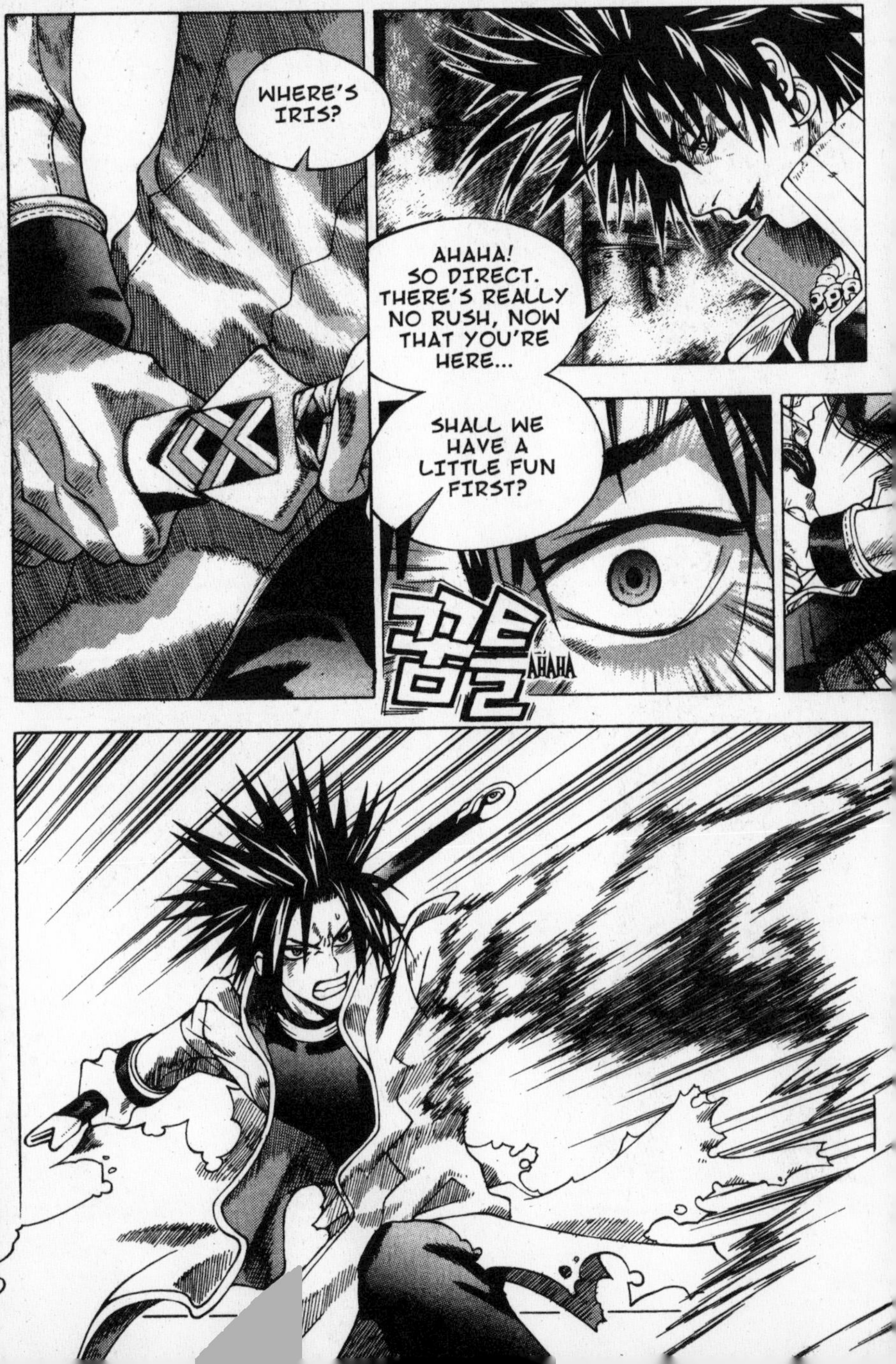
WHERE'S IRIS?
AHAHA! SO DIRECT. THERE'S REALLY NO RUSH, NOW THAT YOU'RE HERE...
SHALL WE HAVE A LITTLE FUN FIRST?
AHAHA

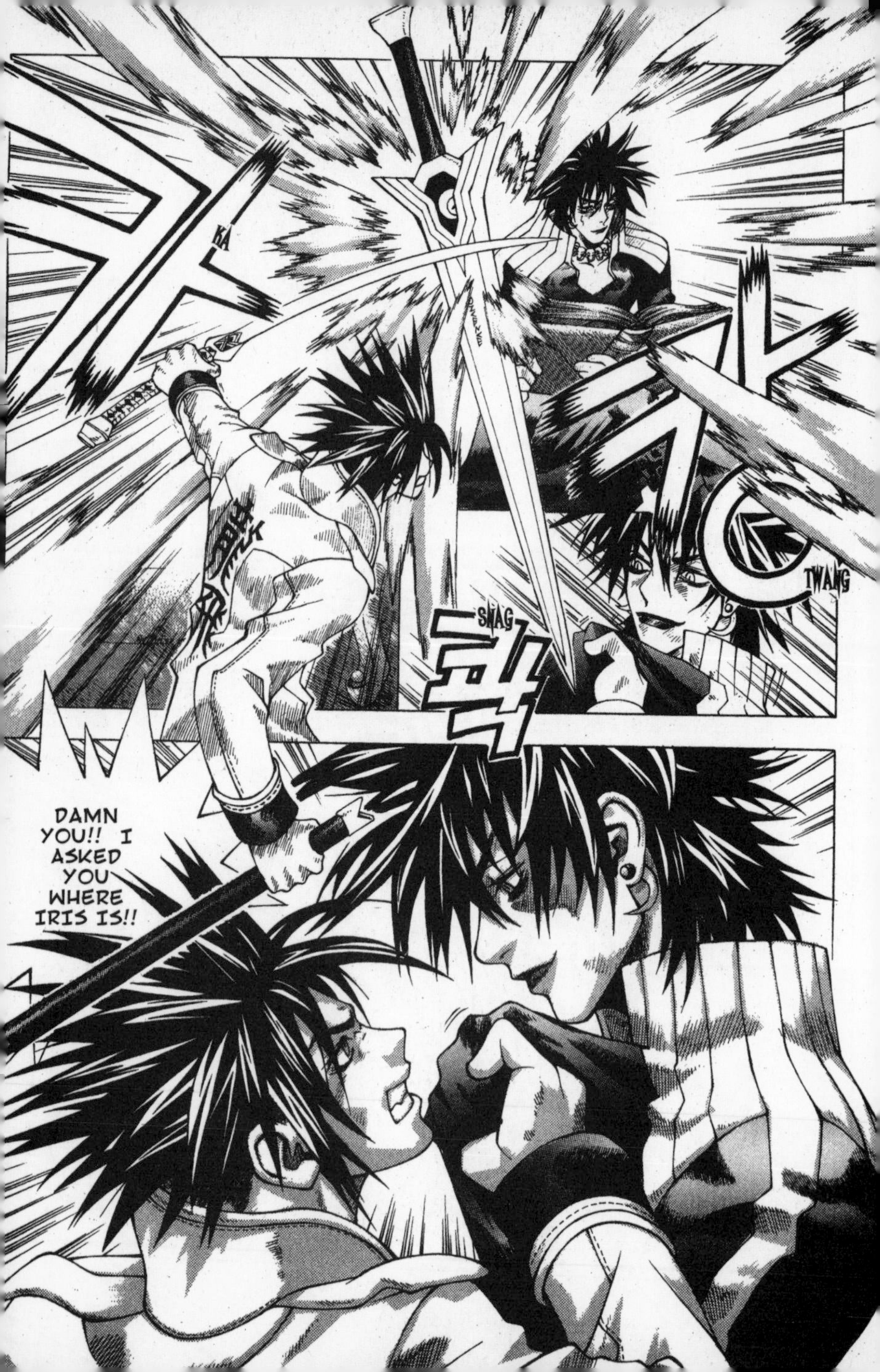
KA
TWANG
SNAG
DAMN YOU!! I ASKED YOU WHERE IRIS IS!!

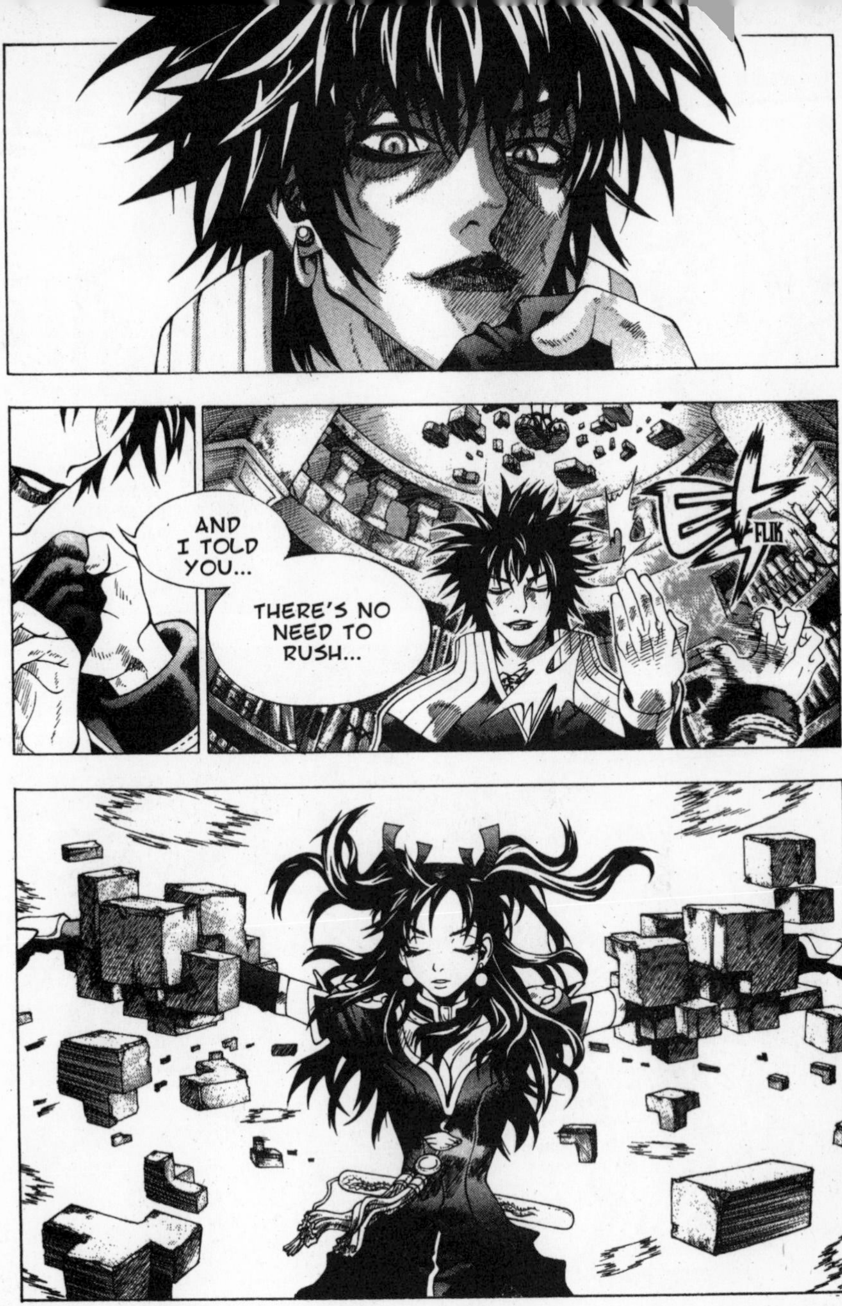
AND I TOLD YOU...
THERE'S NO NEED TO RUSH...
FLIK

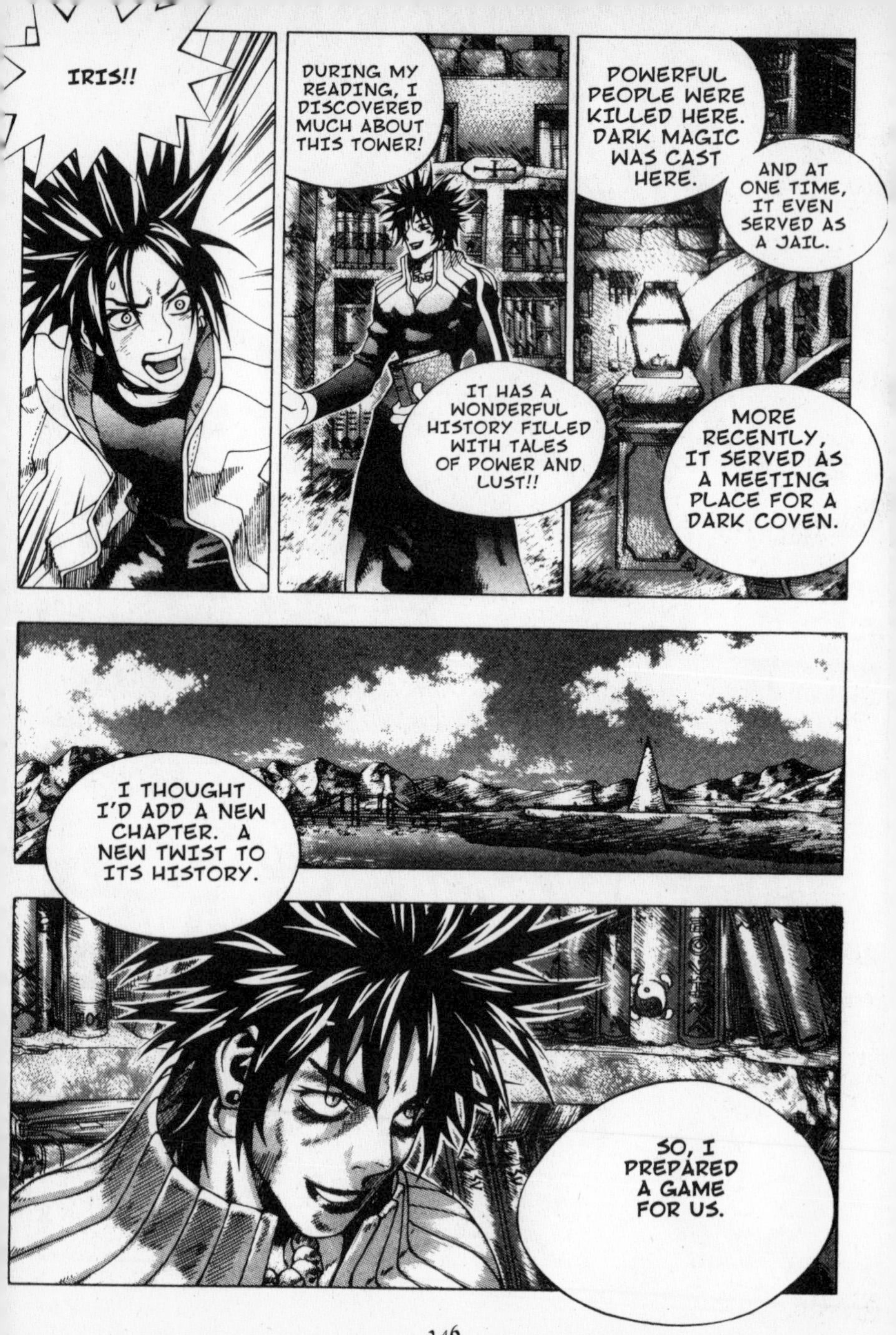
IRIS!!
DURING MY READING, I DISCOVERED MUCH ABOUT THIS TOWER!
IT HAS A WONDERFUL HISTORY FILLED WITH TALES OF POWER AND LUST!!
POWERFUL PEOPLE WERE KILLED HERE. DARK MAGIC WAS CAST HERE.
AND AT ONE TIME, IT EVEN SERVED AS A JAIL.
MORE RECENTLY, IT SERVED AS A MEETING PLACE FOR A DARK COVEN.
I THOUGHT I'D ADD A NEW CHAPTER. A NEW TWIST TO ITS HISTORY.
SO, I PREPARED A GAME FOR US.

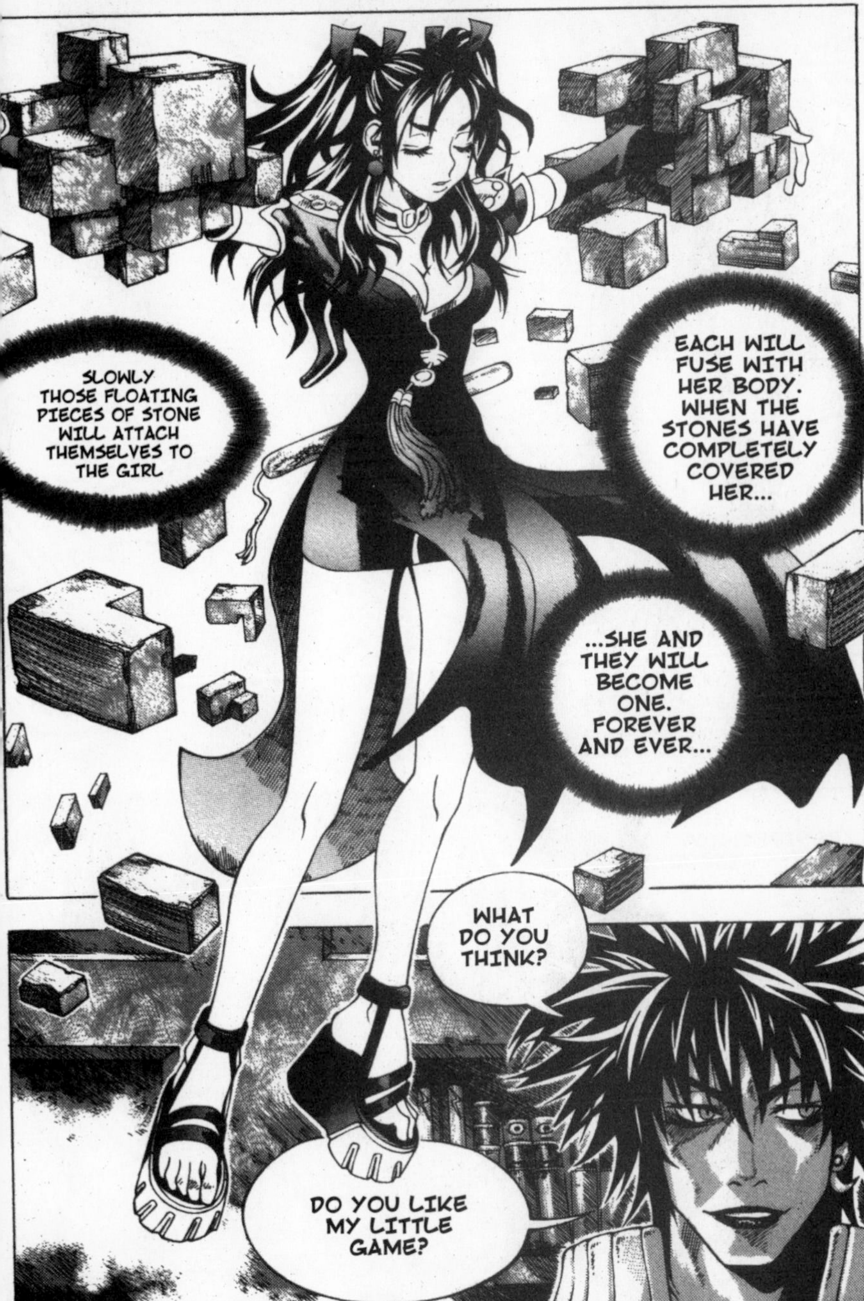
SLOWLY THOSE FLOATING PIECES OF STONE WILL ATTACH THEMSELVES TO THE GIRL
EACH WILL FUSE WITH HER BODY. WHEN THE STONES HAVE COMPLETELY COVERED HER...
...SHE AND THEY WILL BECOME ONE. FOREVER AND EVER...
WHAT DO YOU THINK?
DO YOU LIKE MY LITTLE GAME?

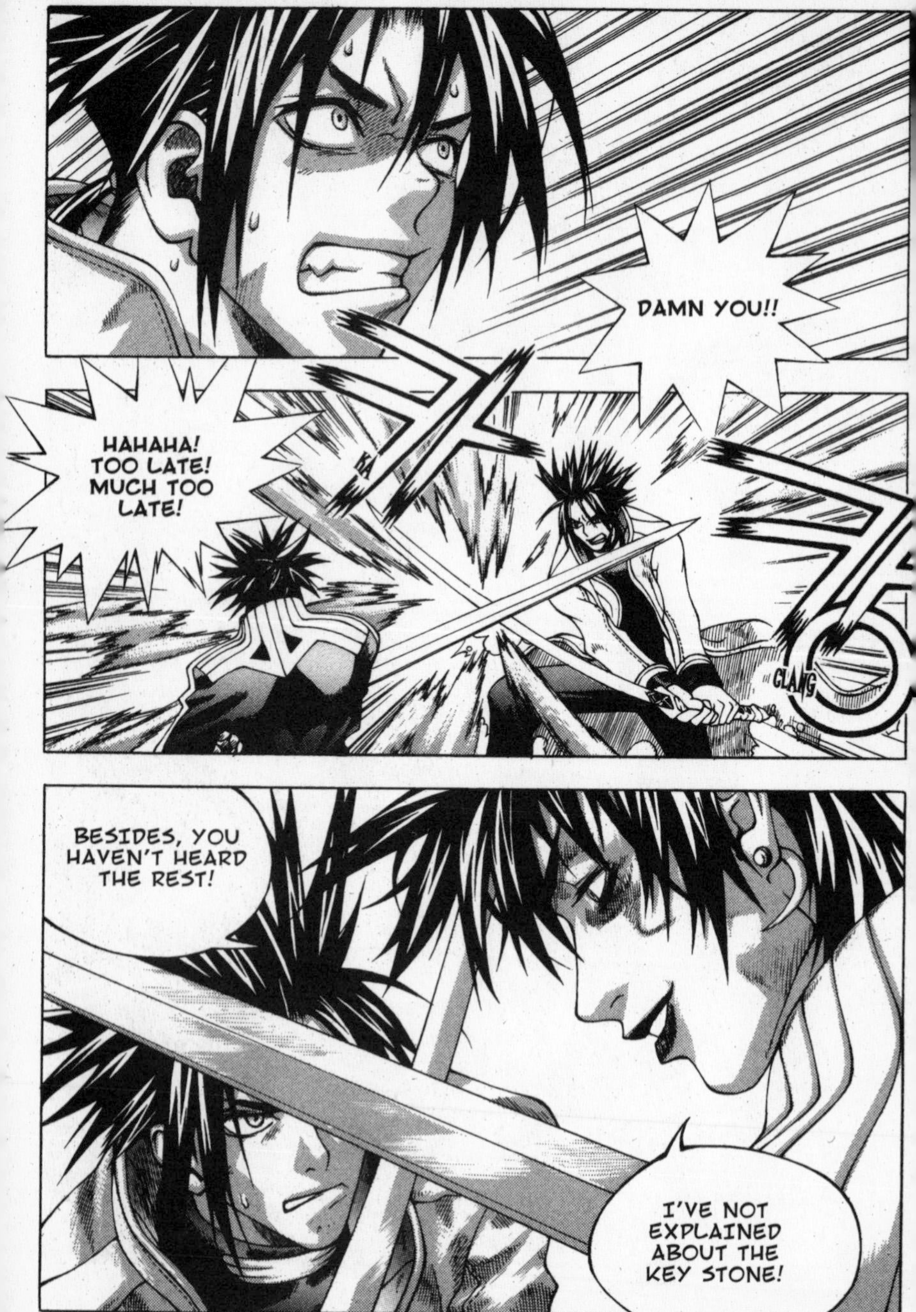
DAMN YOU!!
HAHAHA! TOO LATE! MUCH TOO LATE!
KA
CLANG
BESIDES, YOU HAVEN'T HEARD THE REST!
I'VE NOT EXPLAINED ABOUT THE KEY STONE!

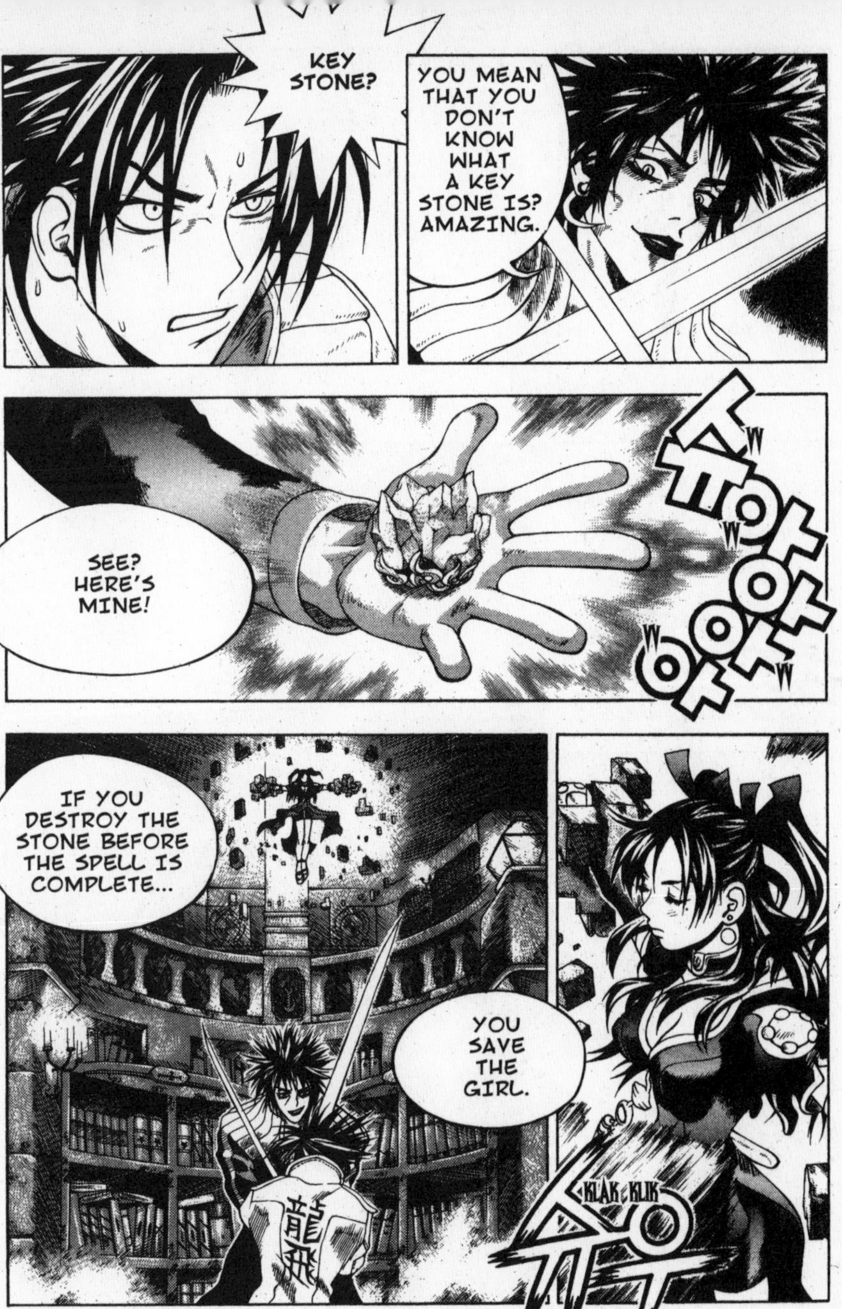
KEY STONE?
YOU MEAN THAT YOU DON'T KNOW WHAT A KEY STONE IS? AMAZING.
SEE? HERE'S MINE!
IF YOU DESTROY THE STONE BEFORE THE SPELL IS COMPLETE...
YOU SAVE THE GIRL.
KLAK KLIK

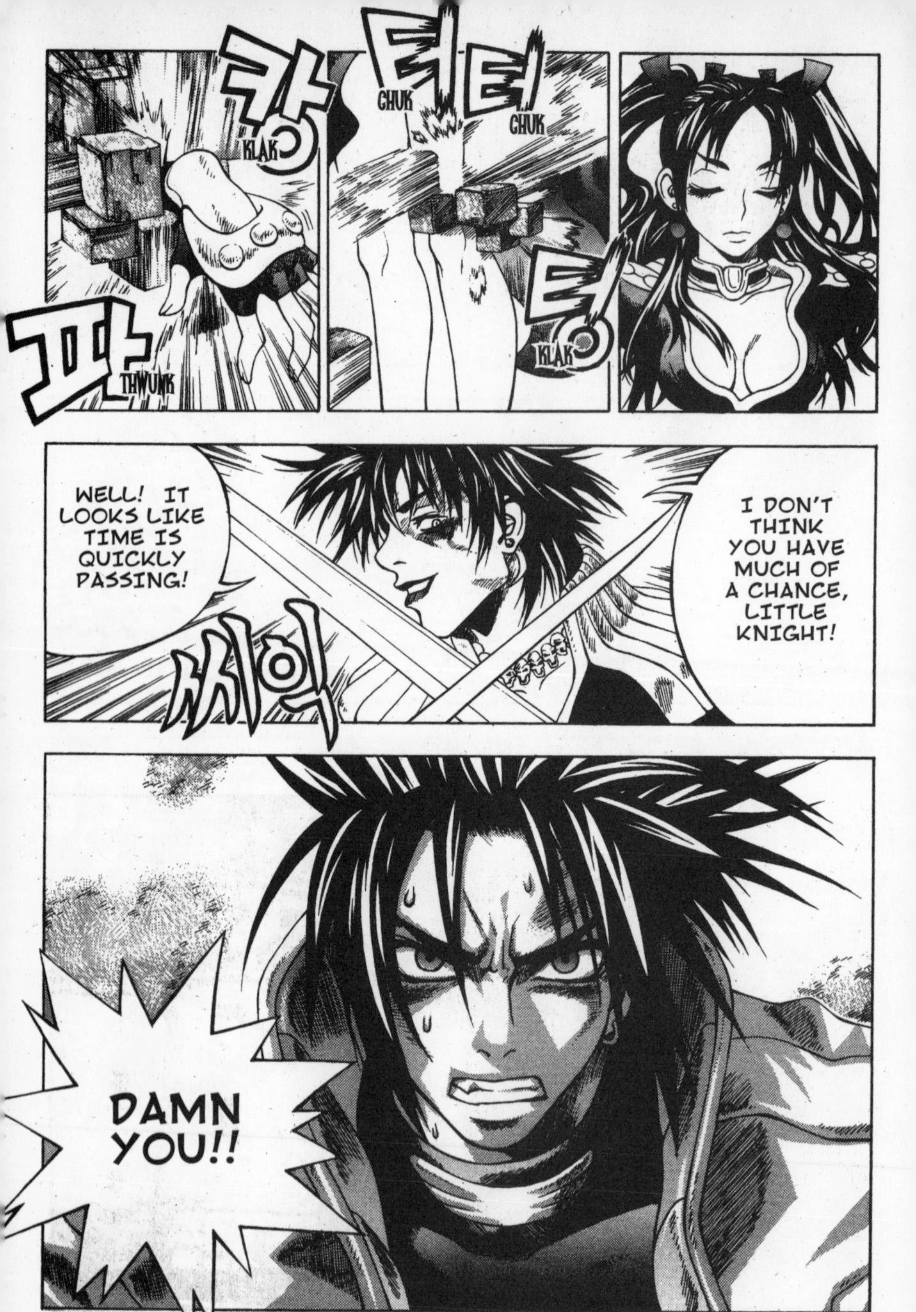
KLAK
THWUNK
CHUK
CHUK
KLAK
WELL! IT LOOKS LIKE TIME IS QUICKLY PASSING!
I DON'T THINK YOU HAVE MUCH OF A CHANCE, LITTLE KNIGHT!
DAMN YOU!!

RAGNAROK
라그나로크
IN TO THE ABYSS

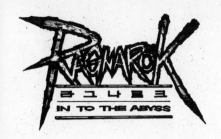

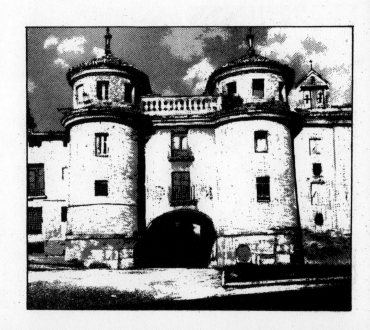

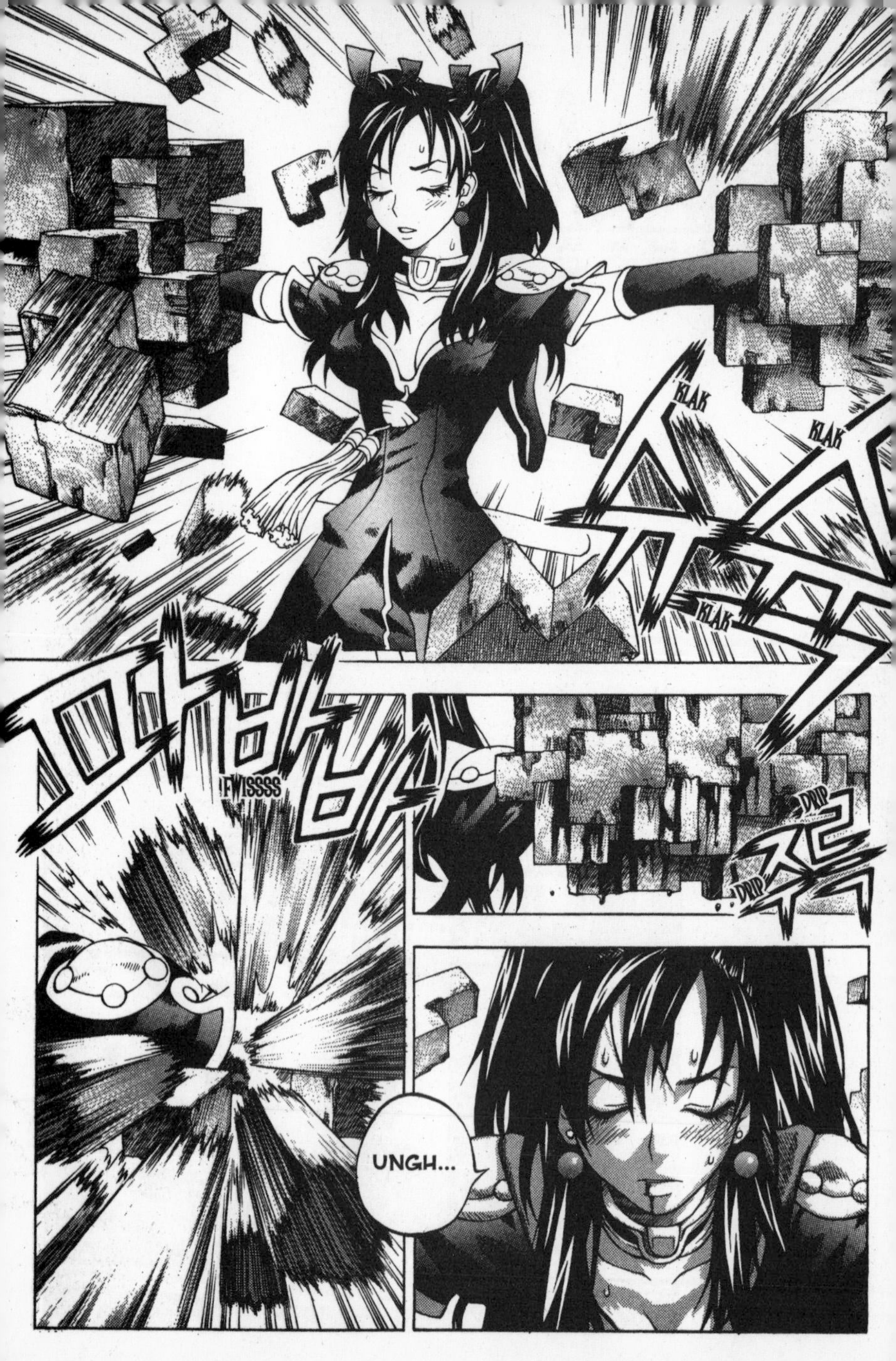
KLAK
KLAK
KLAK
FWISSSS
DRIP
DRIP
UNGH...

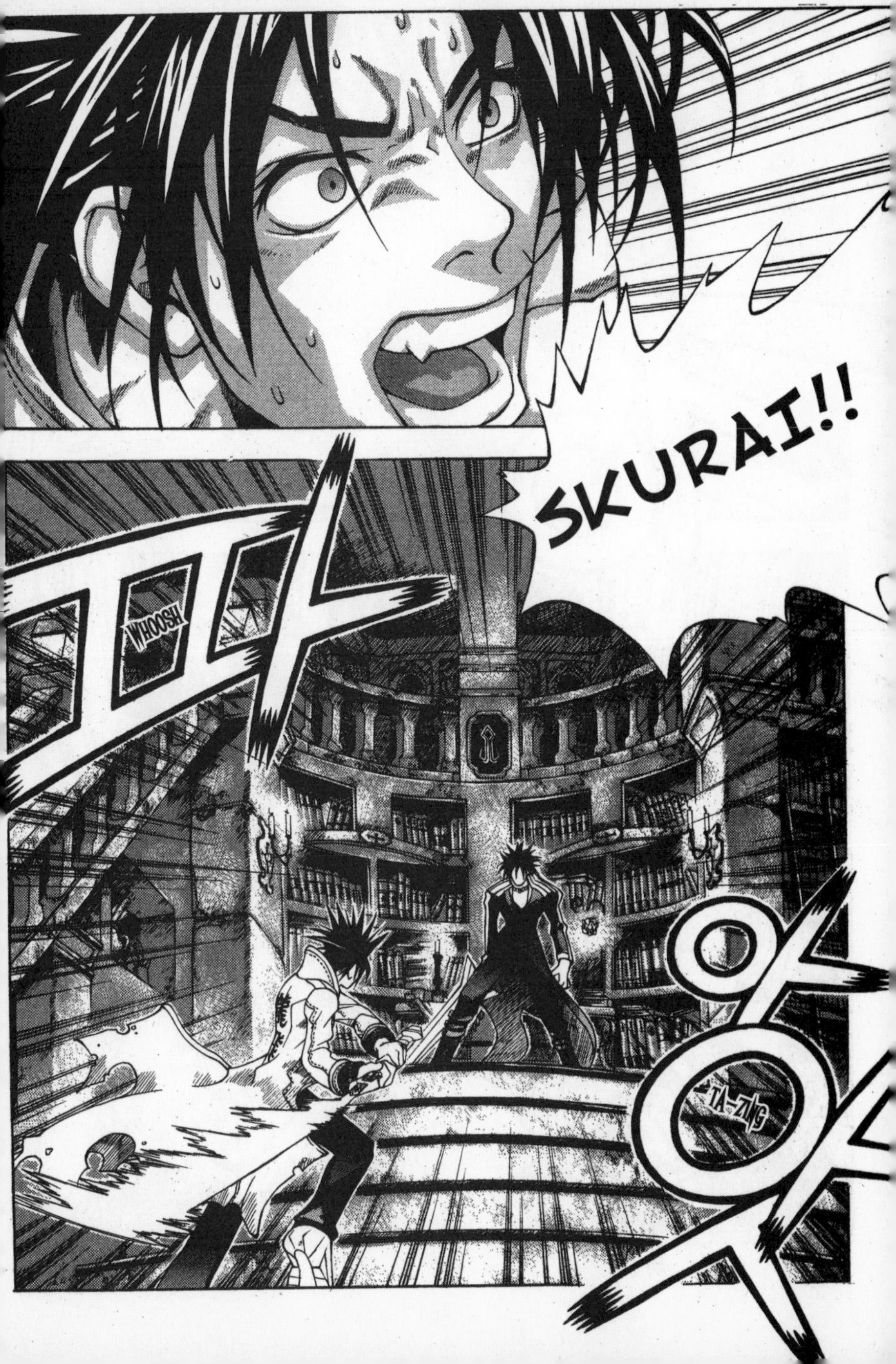
SKURAI!!
WHOOSH
TA-ZING

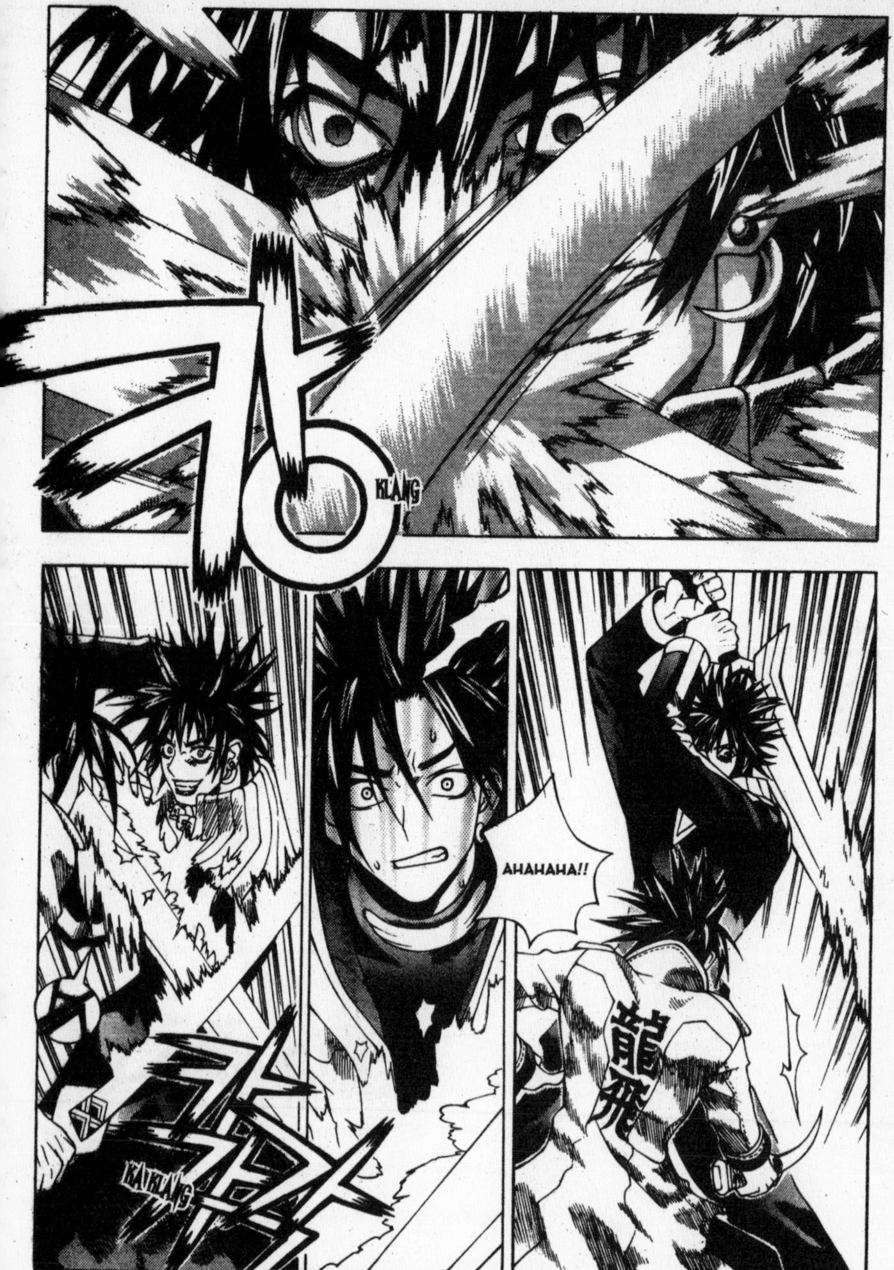
KLANG
KA KLANG
AHAHAHA!!
龍飛

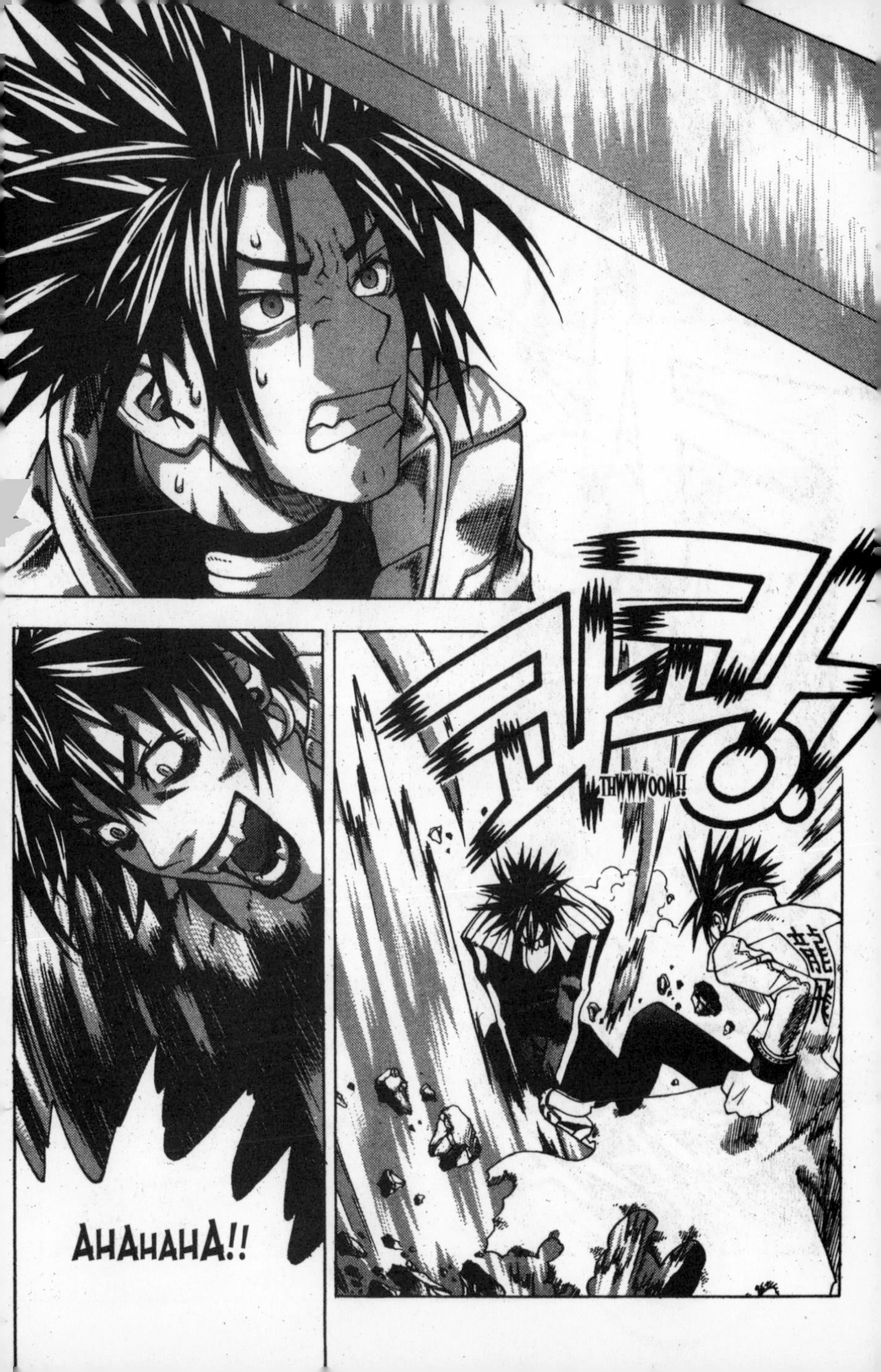
AHAHAHA!!
THWWWOOM!!

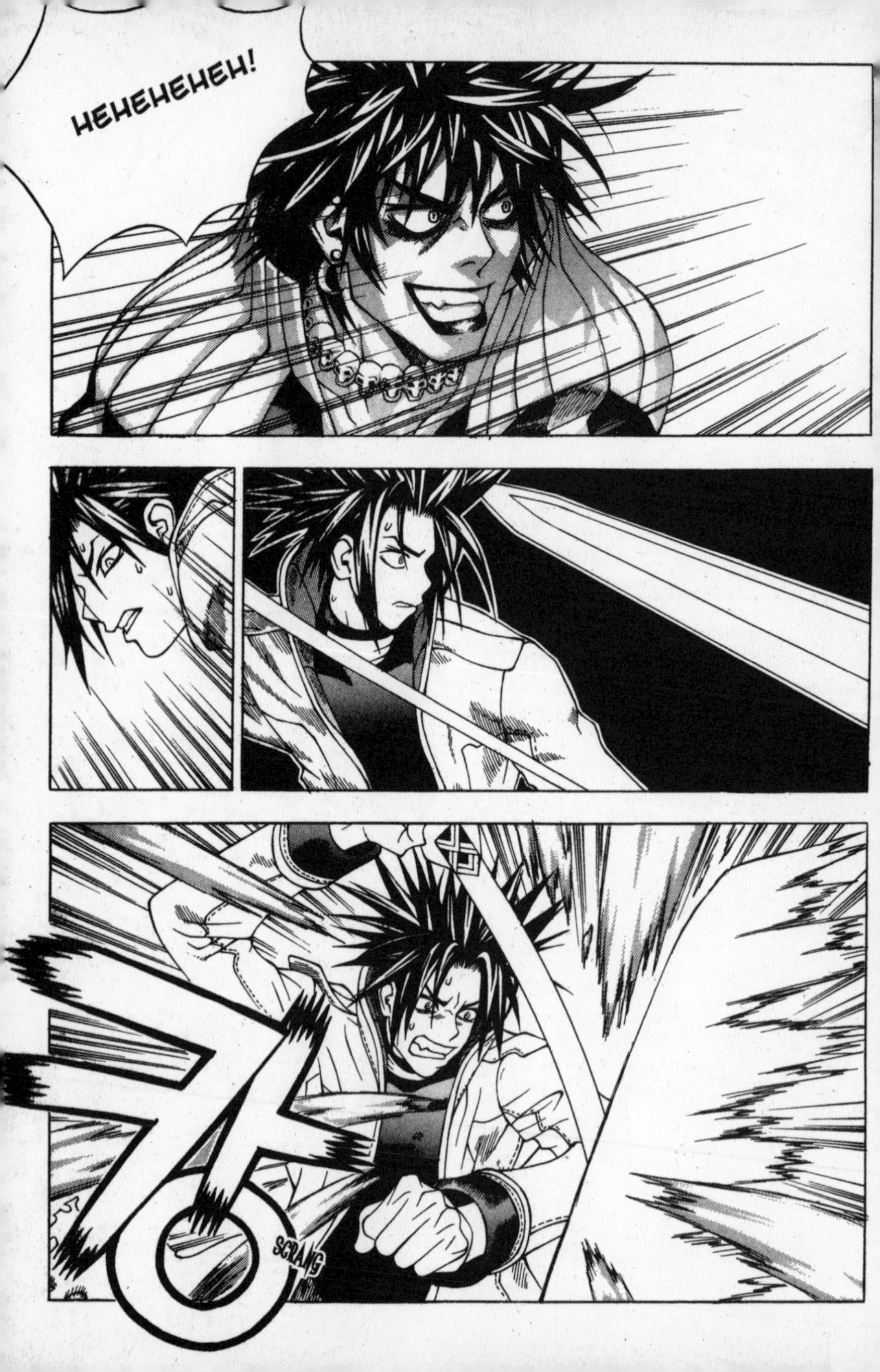
HEHEHEHEH!
SCRANG

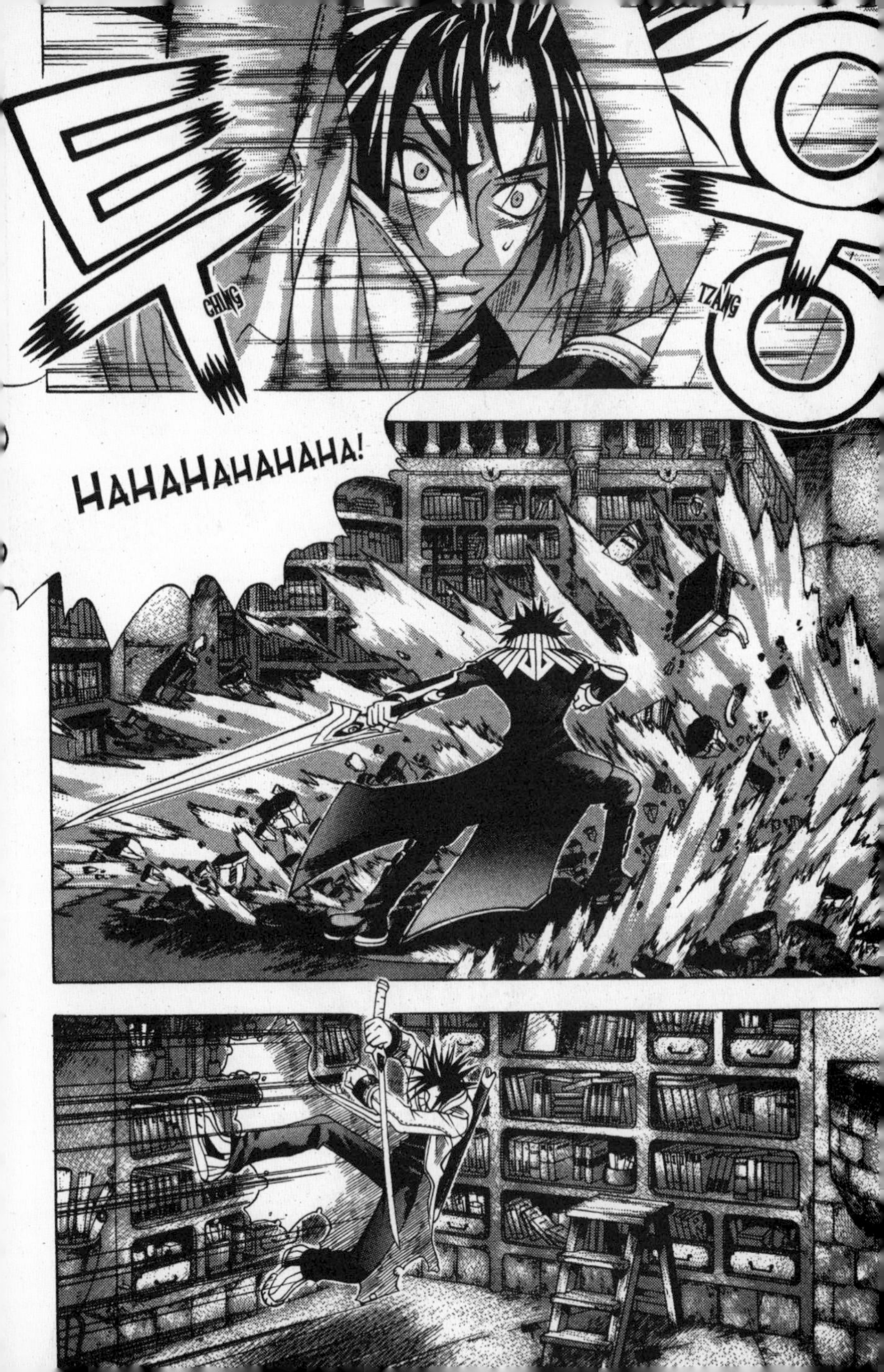
CHING
TZANG
HAHAHAHAHAHA!

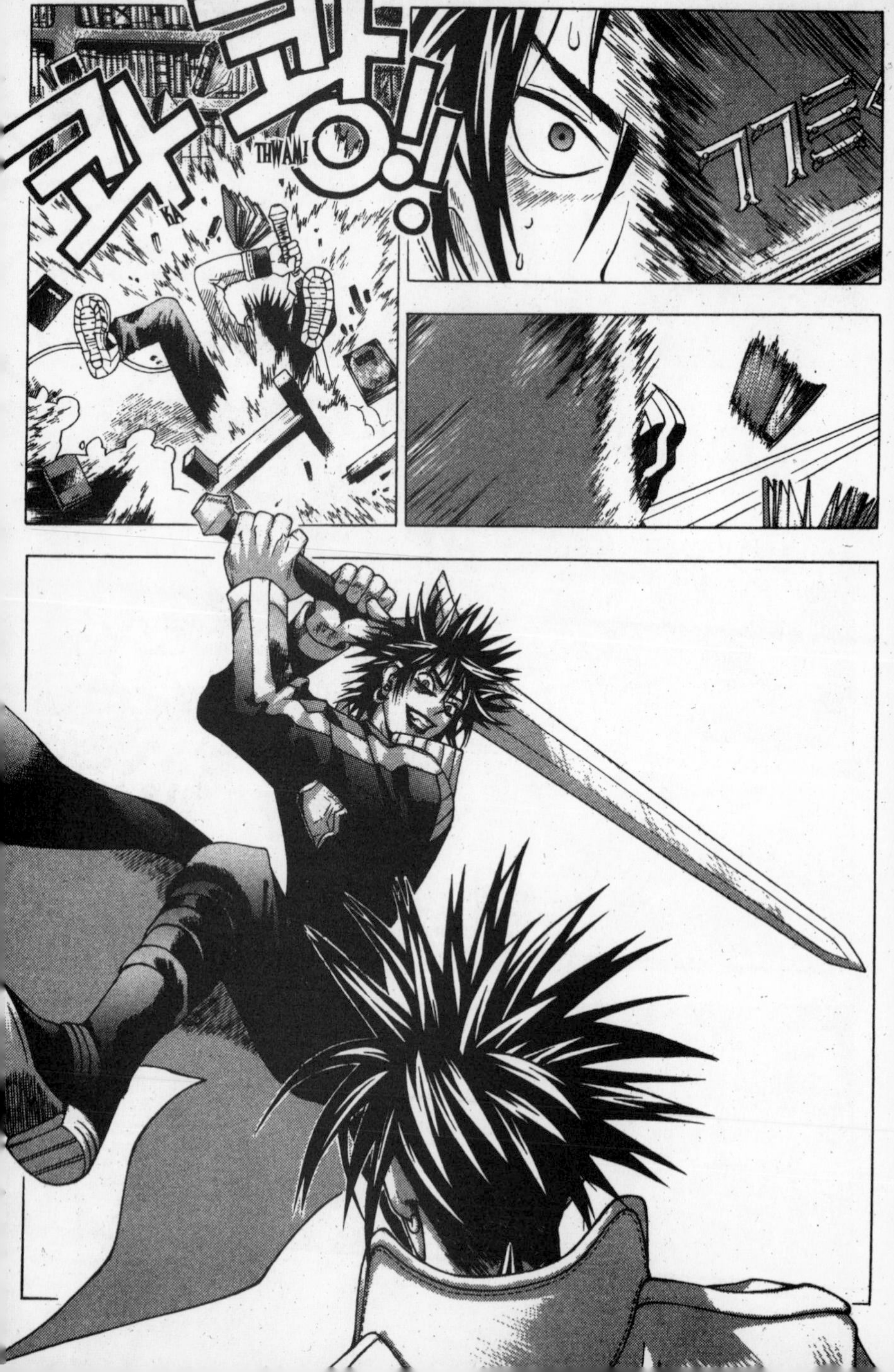
콰콰앙!!
KA
THWAM!

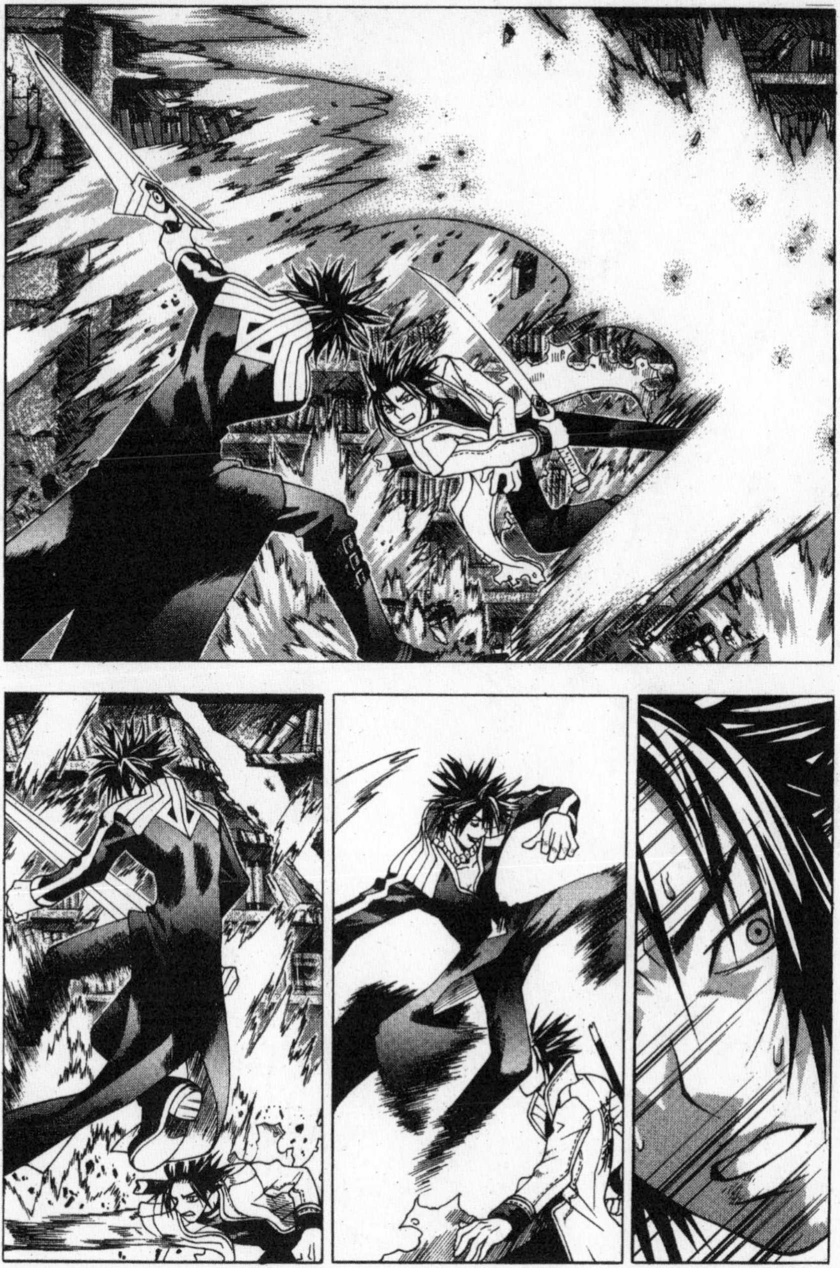

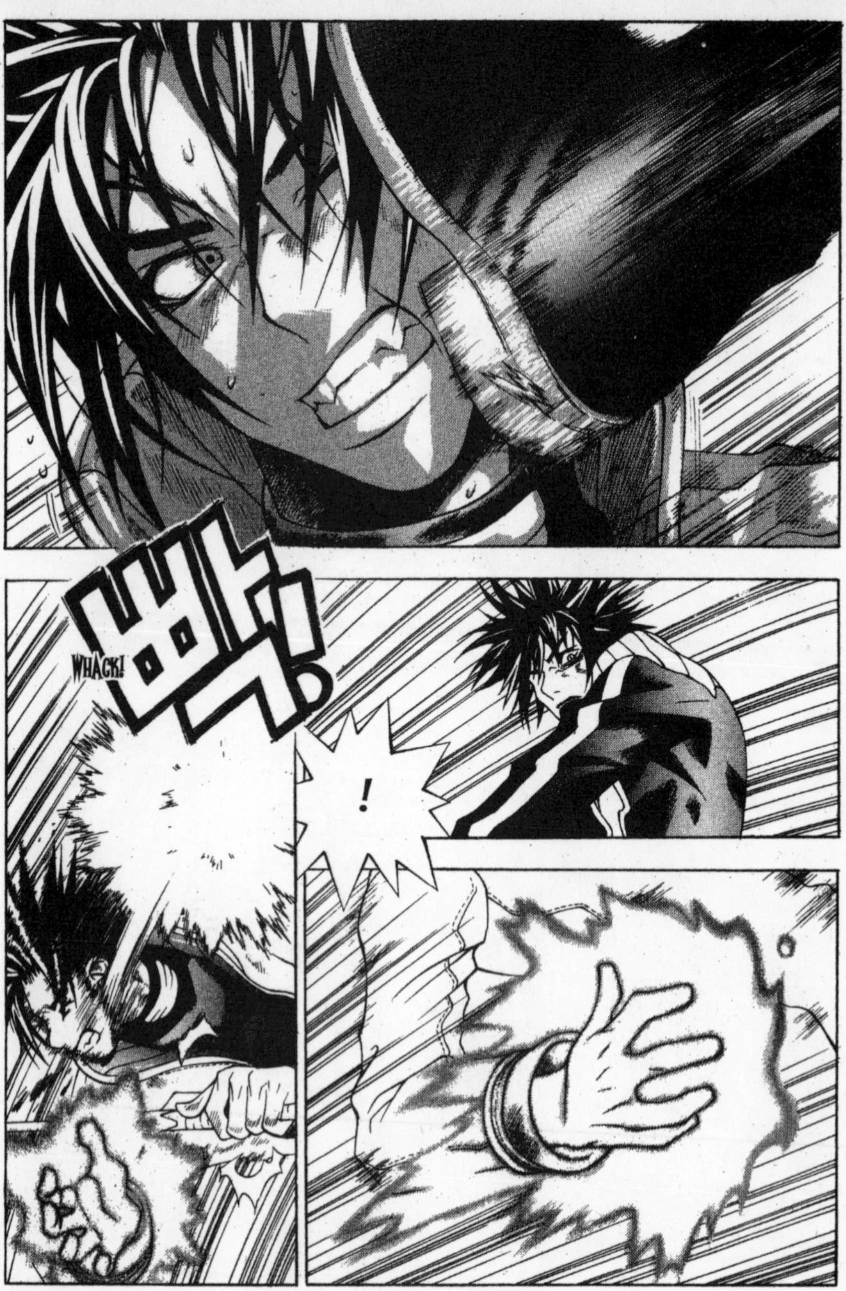
빠!
WHACK!
!

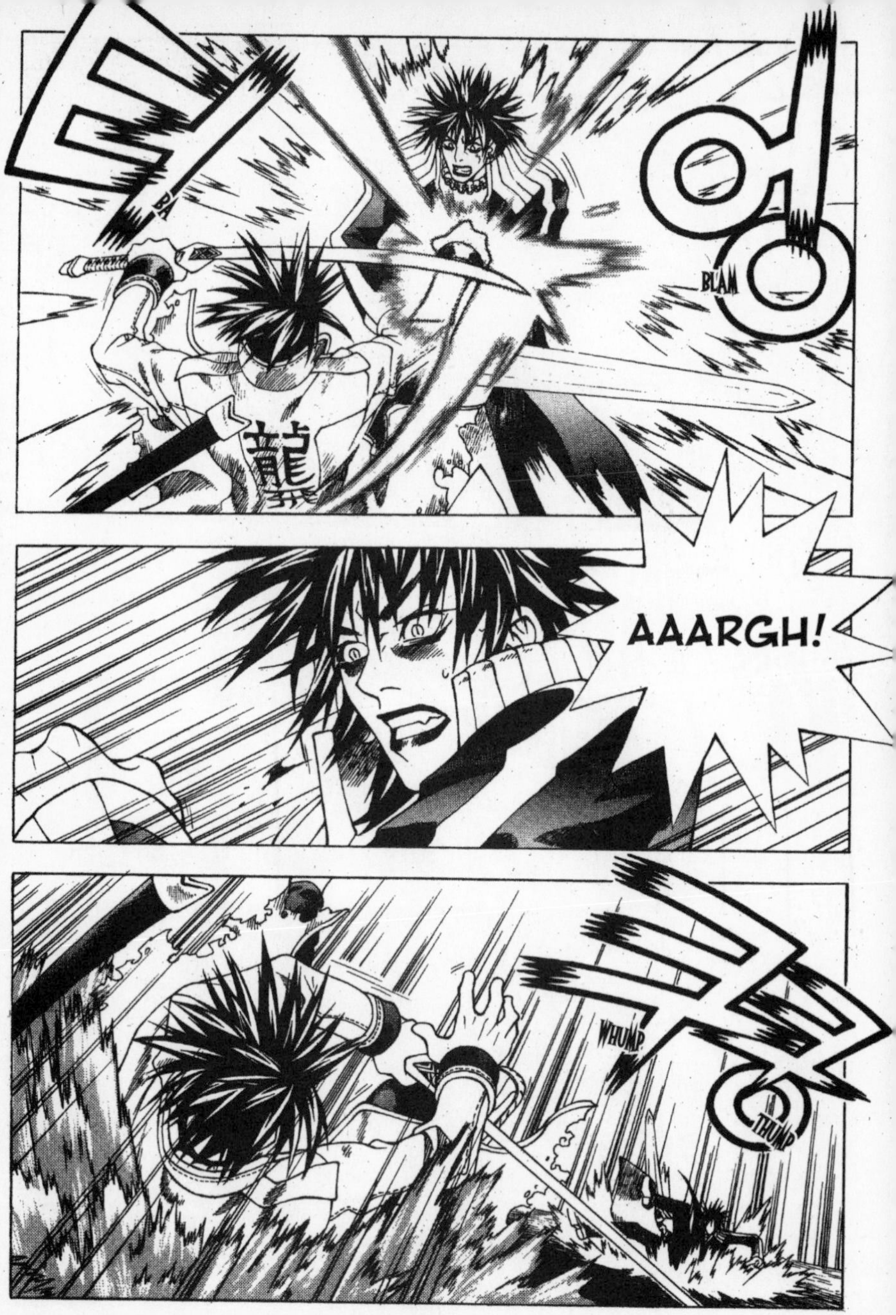
BA
BLAM
AAARGH!
WHUMP
THUMP

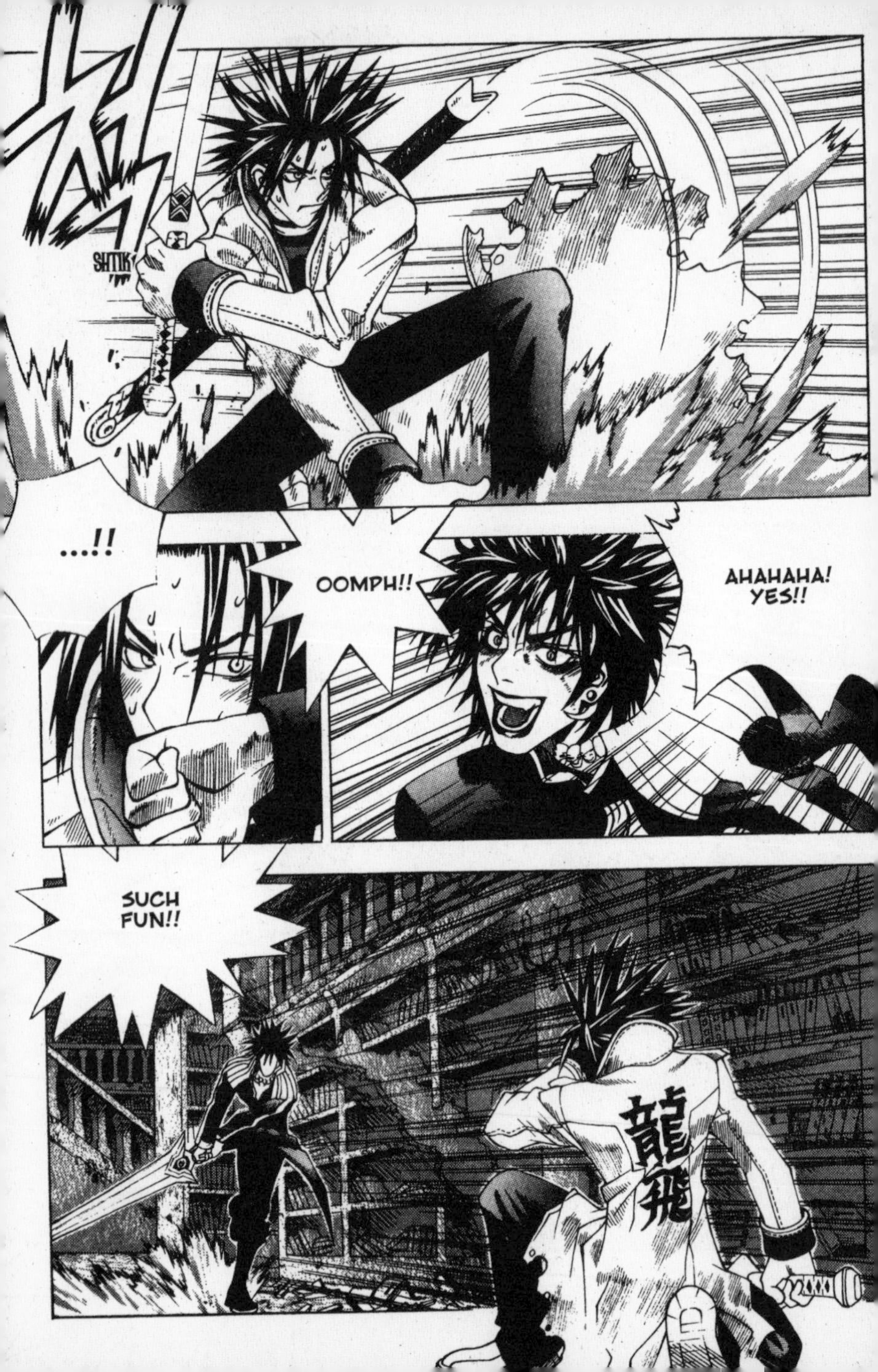
SHTIK
...!!
OOMPH!!
AHAHAHA! YES!!
SUCH FUN!!
龍飛

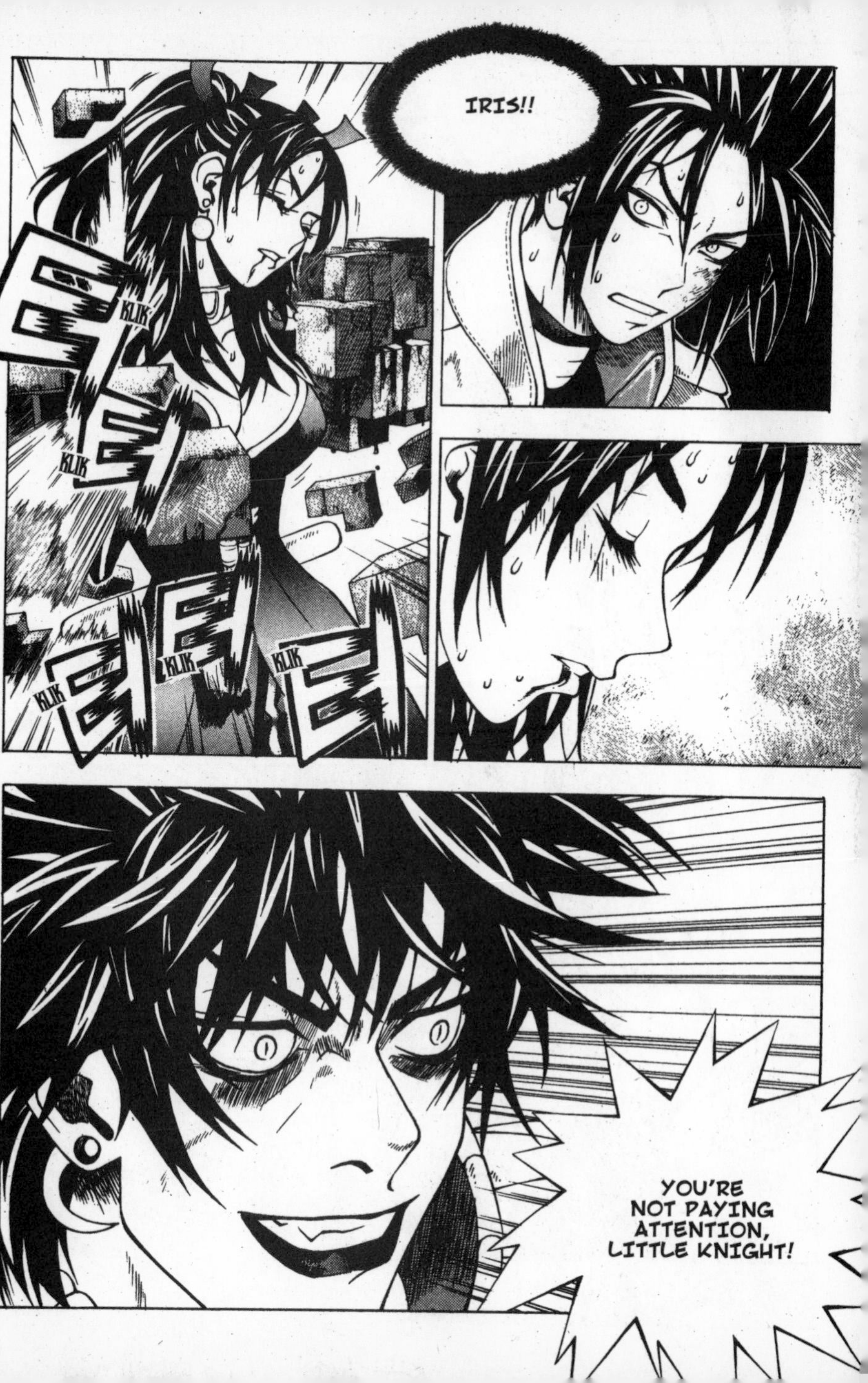
KLIK
KLIK
KLIK
KLIK
KLIK
IRIS!!
YOU'RE NOT PAYING ATTENTION, LITTLE KNIGHT!

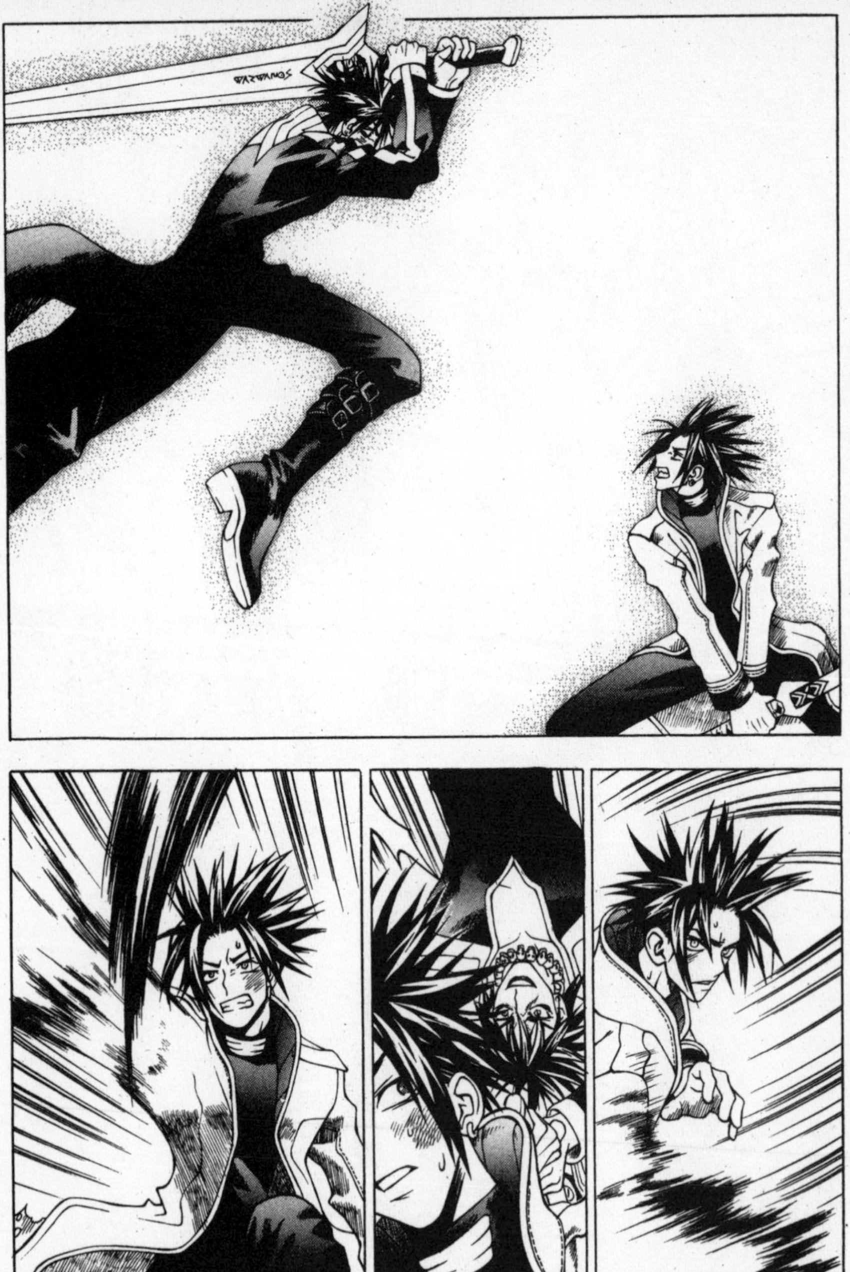

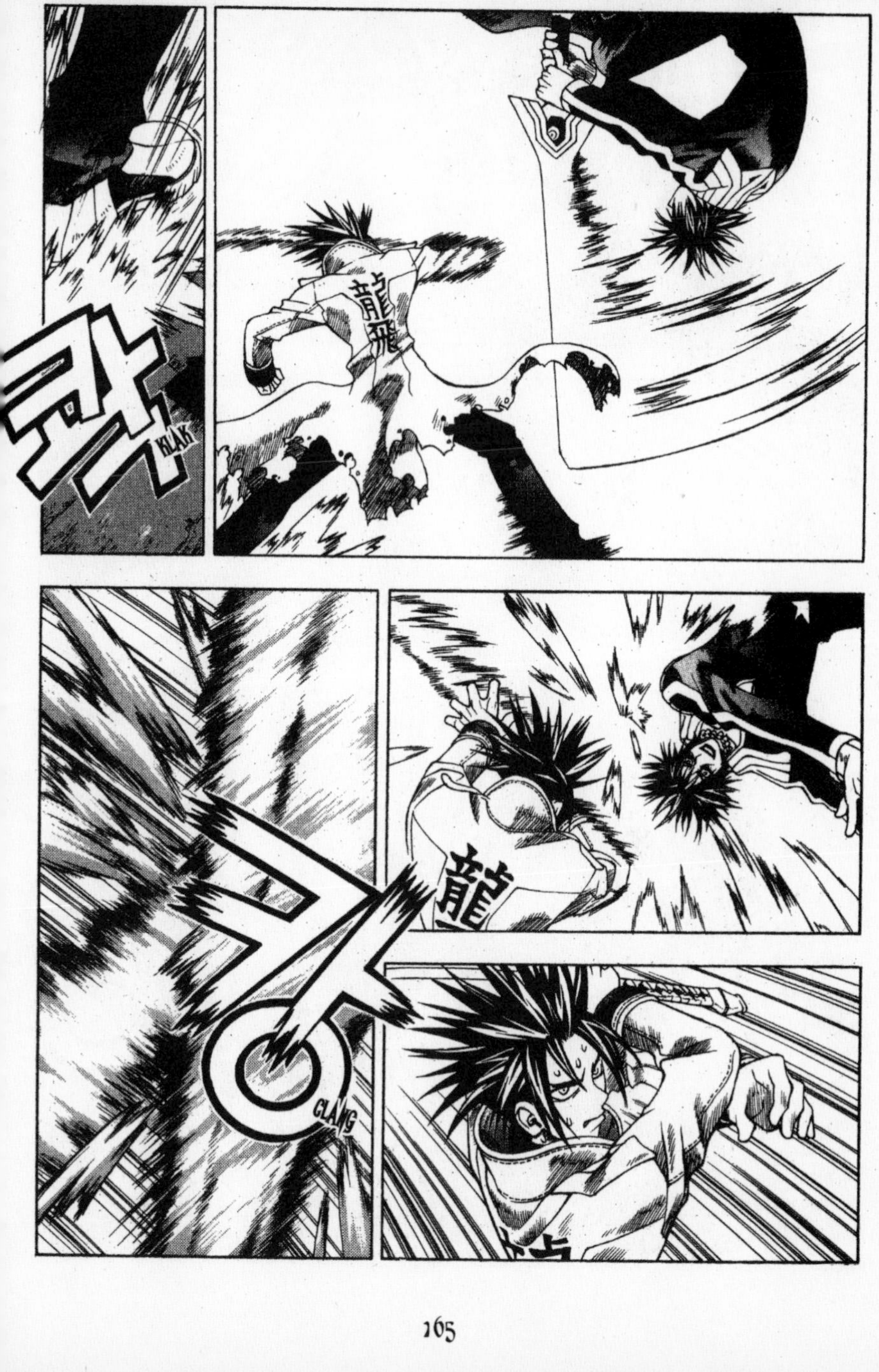
KLAK
CLANG

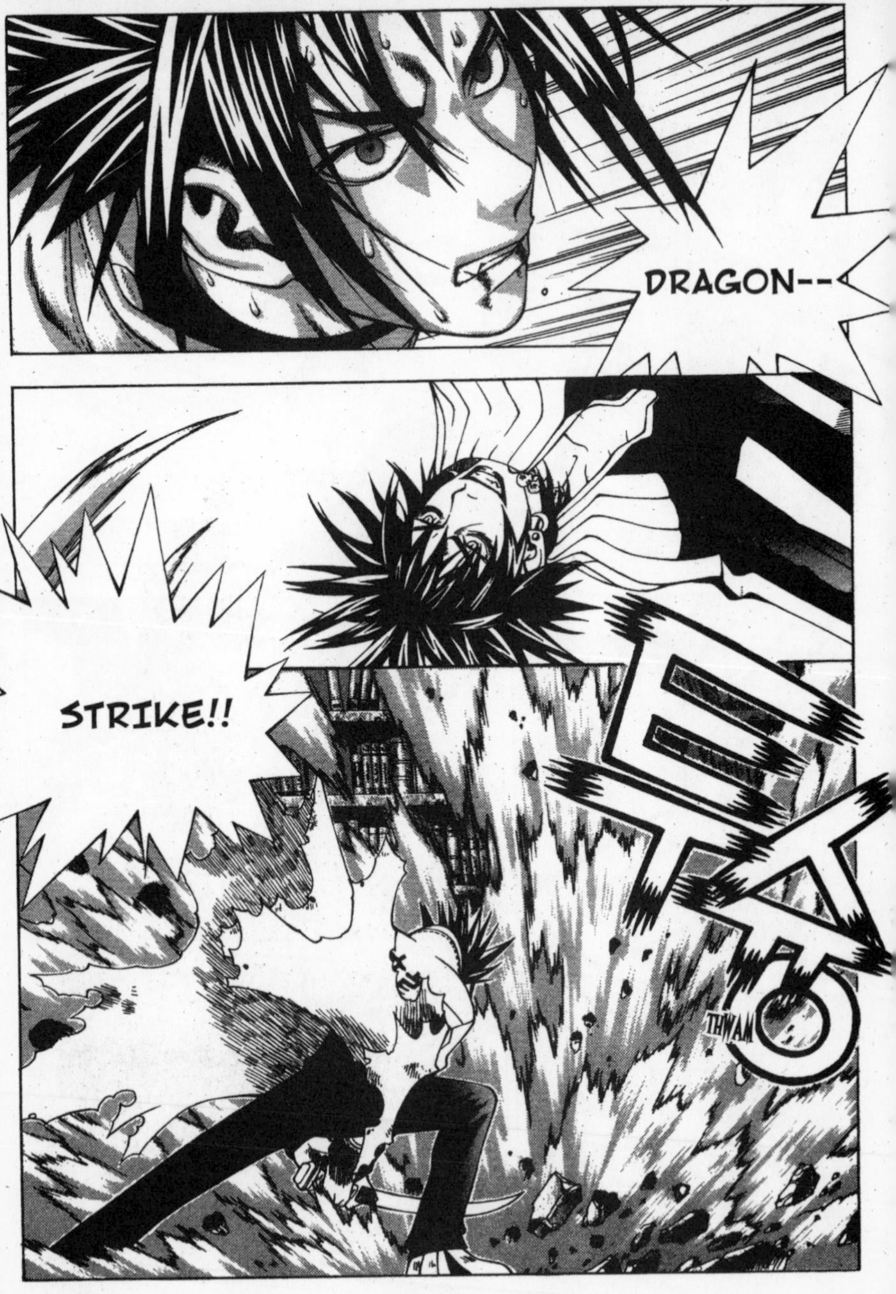
DRAGON--
STRIKE!!
THWAM

RAGNAROK
라그나로크
IN TO THE ABYSS

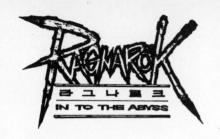

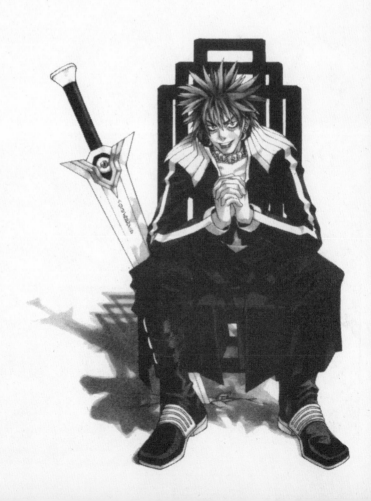

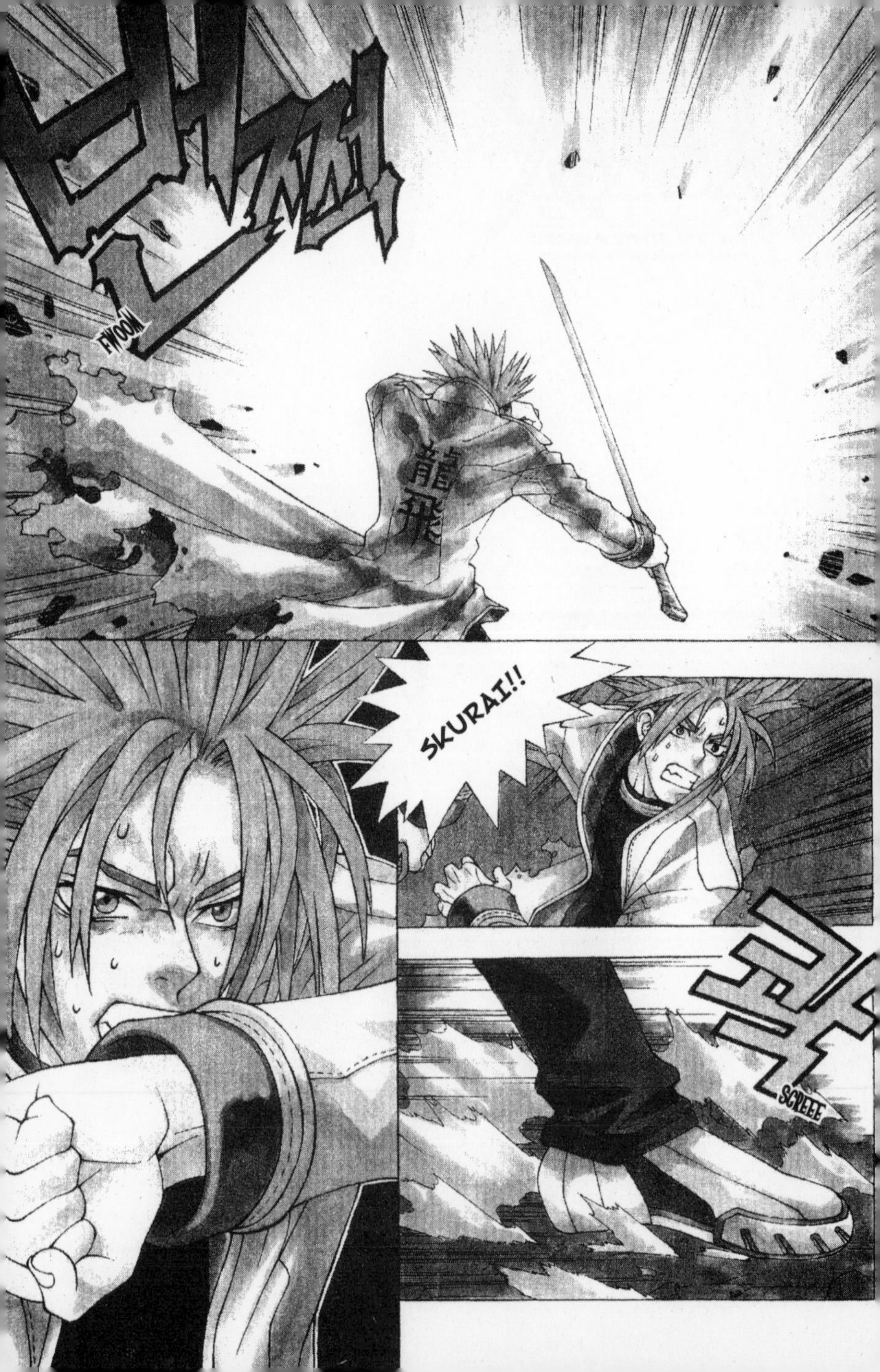
FWOOM
龍飛
SKURAI!!
SCREEE

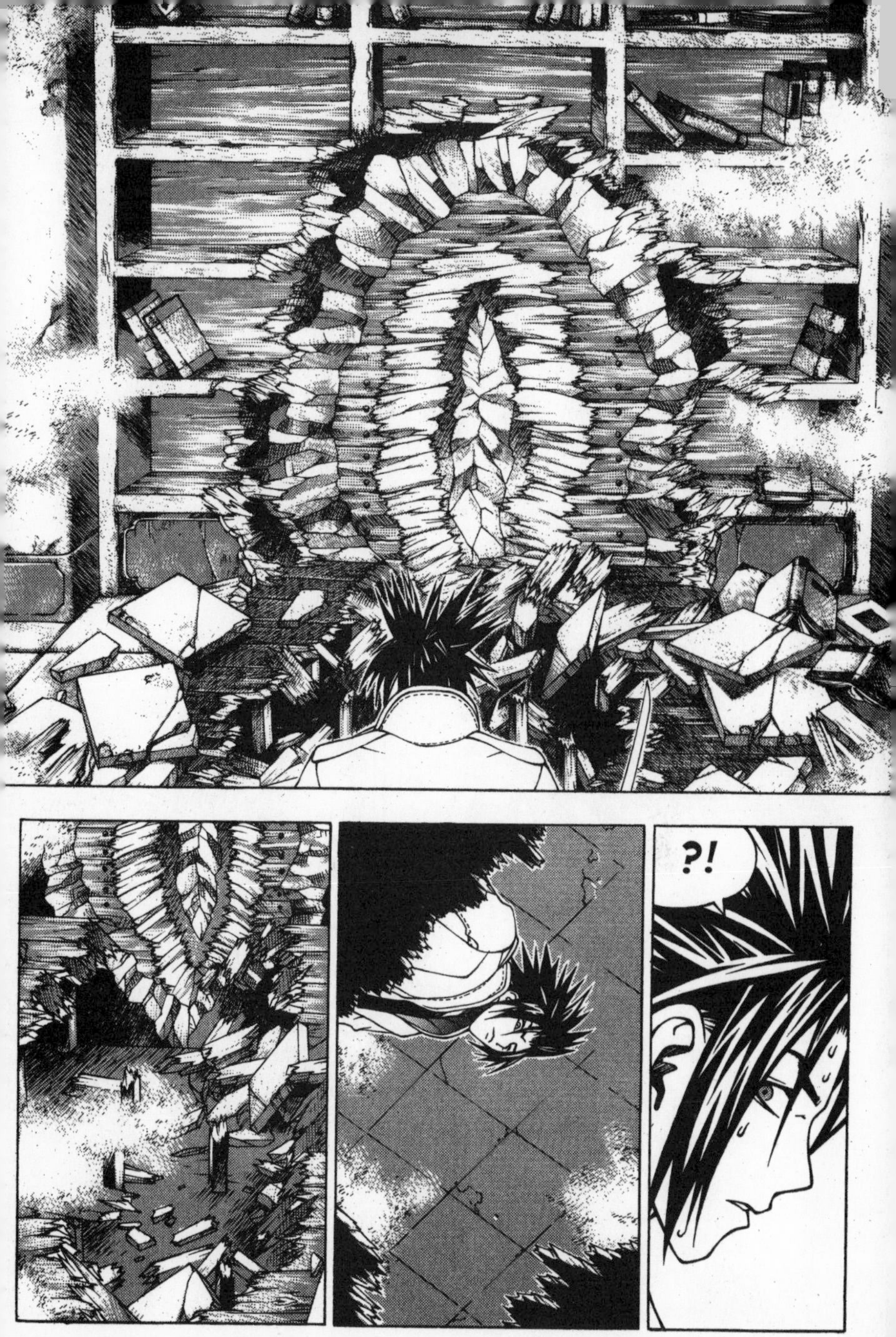
?!

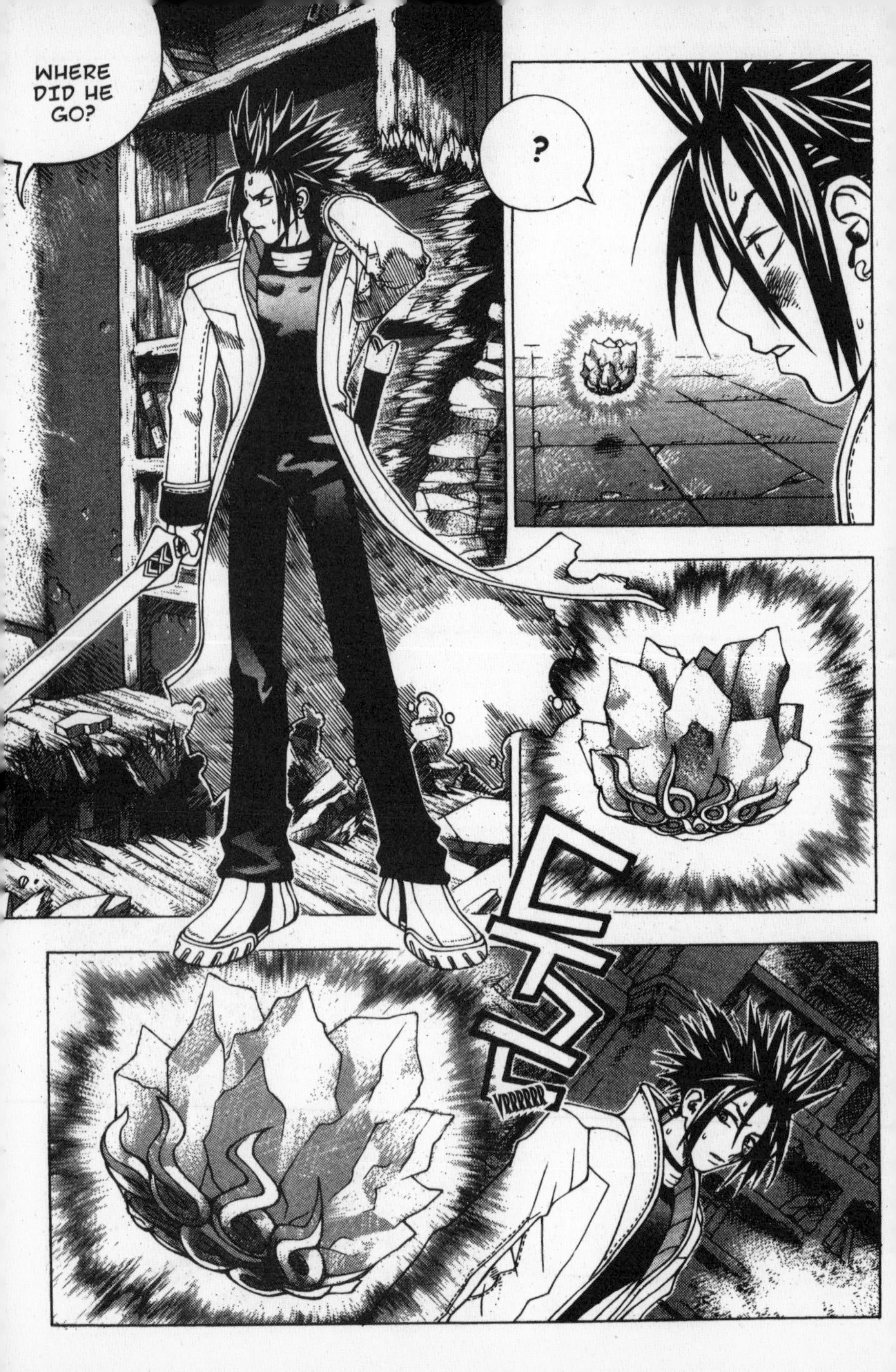
WHERE DID HE GO?
?
VRRRRRR

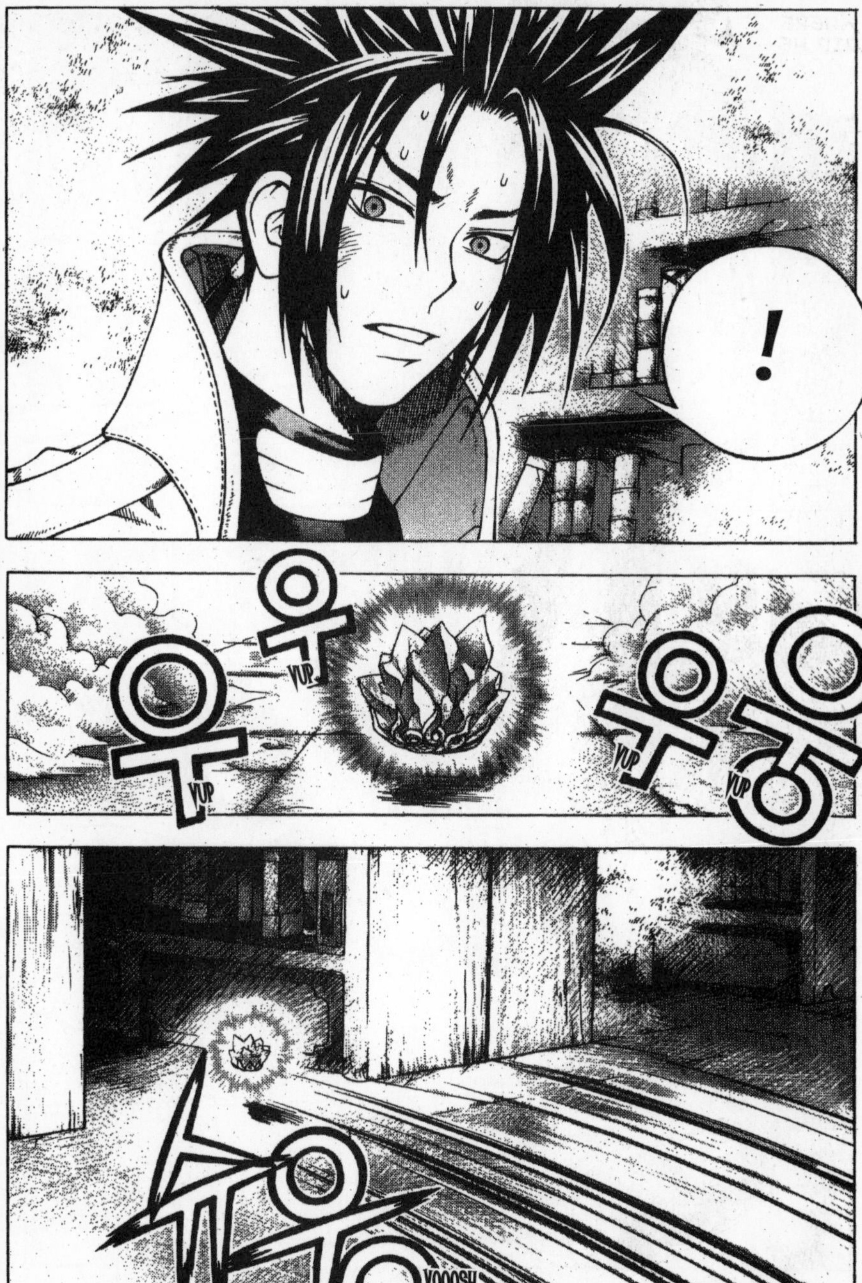
!
우
VUP
우
VUP
우
VUP
웅
VUP
쑤우우
VOOOSH

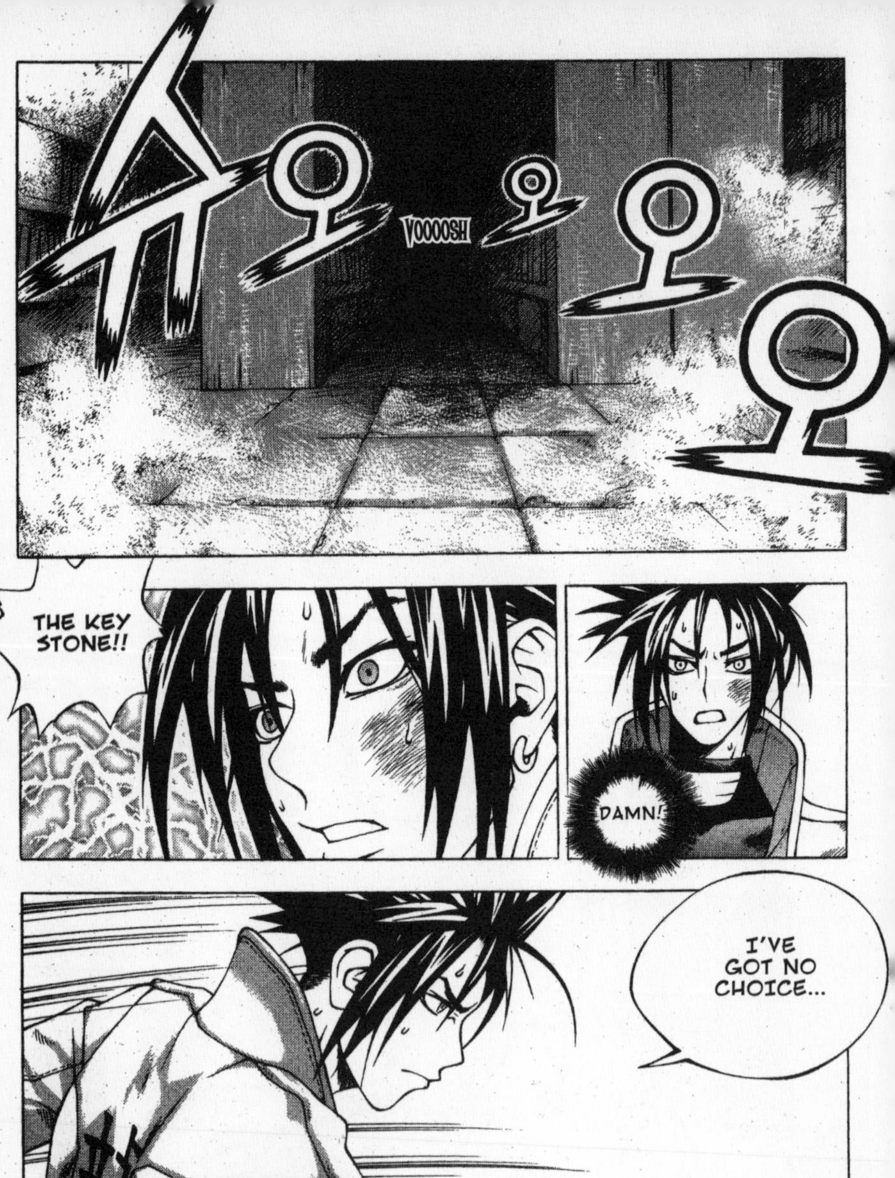
VOOOOSH
THE KEY STONE!!
DAMN!
I'VE GOT NO CHOICE...

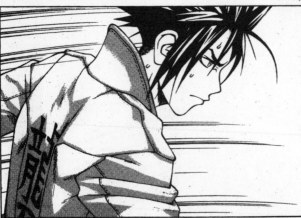

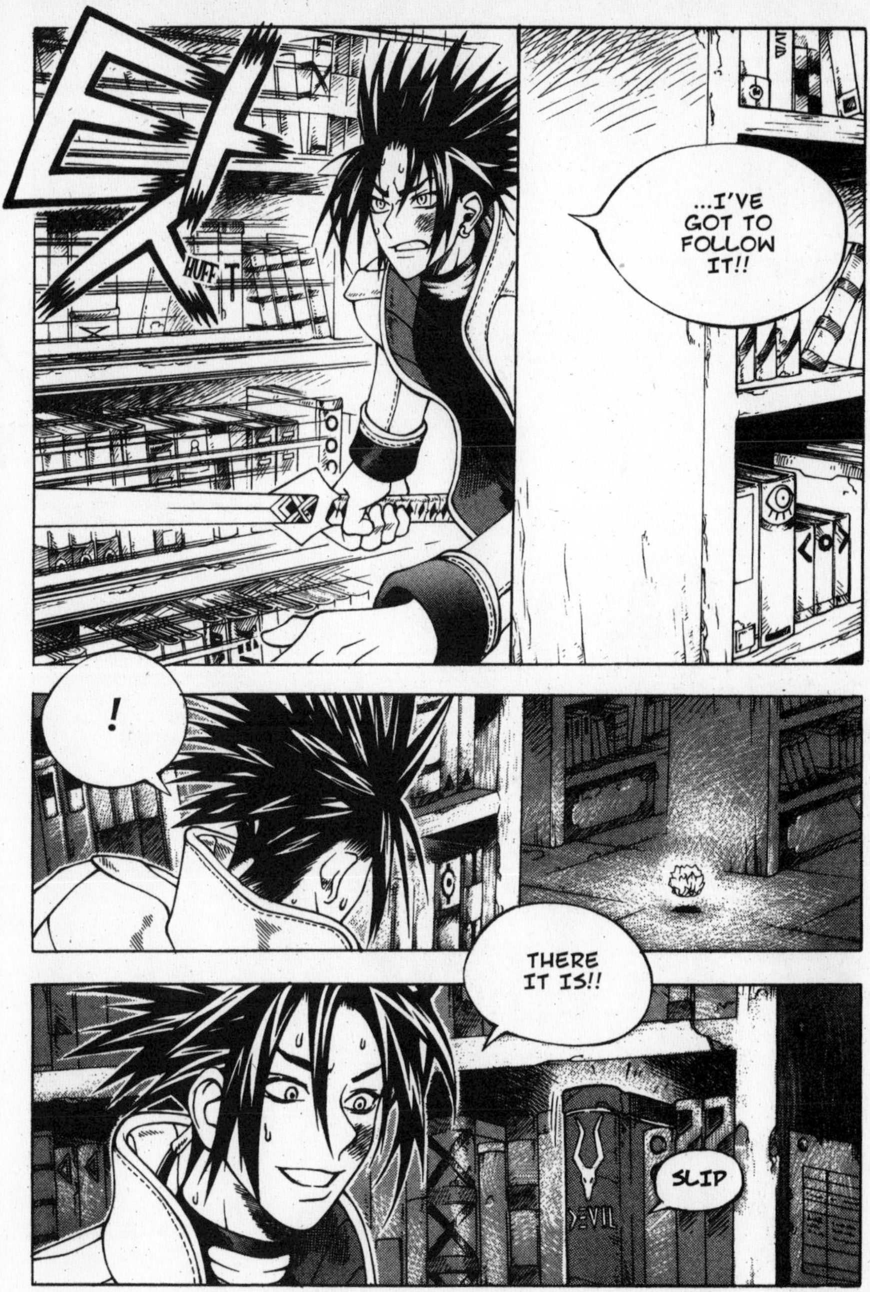
HUFF
...I'VE GOT TO FOLLOW IT!!
!
THERE IT IS!!
SLIP
DEVIL

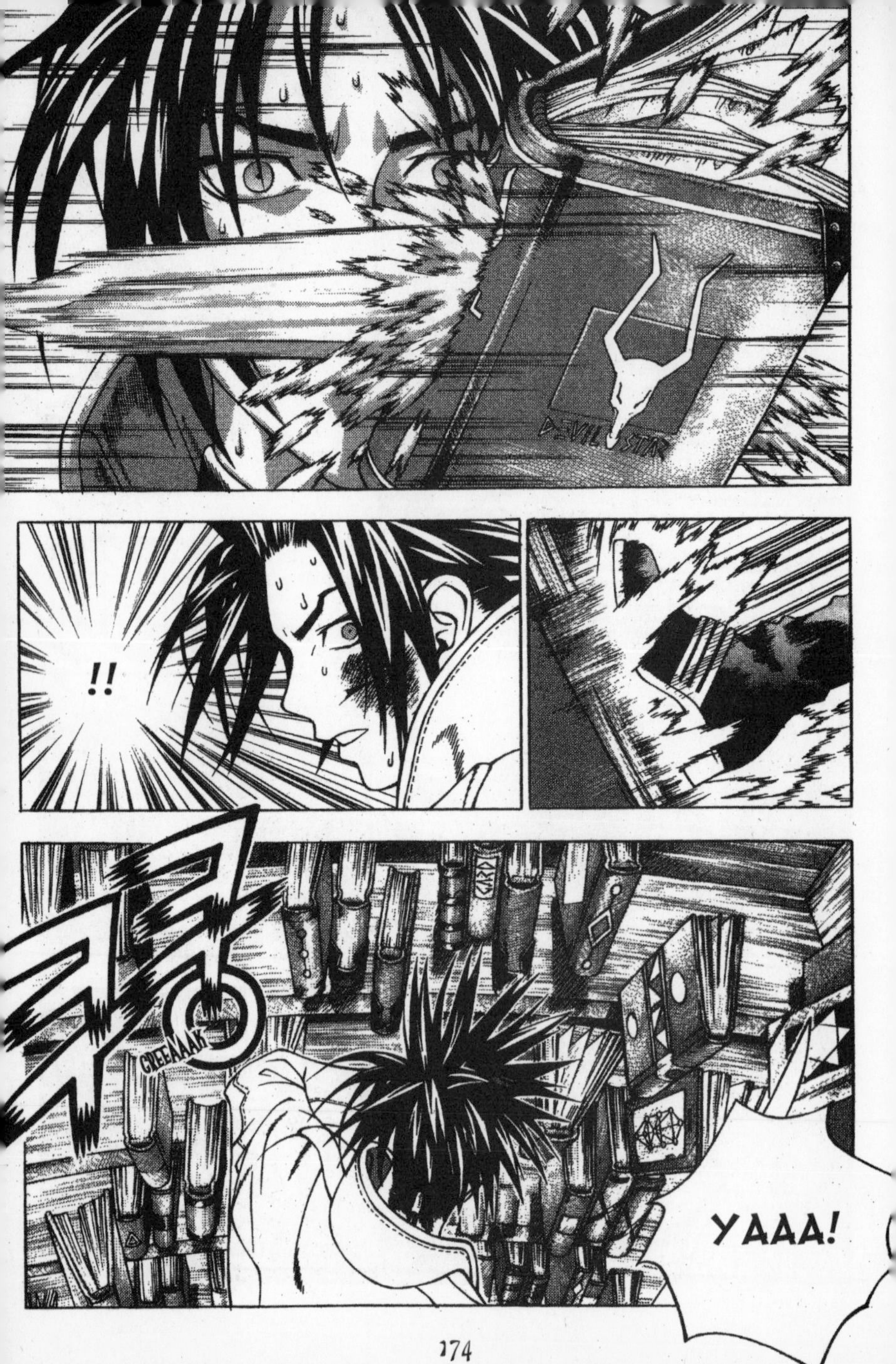
DEVIL STAR
!!
CARD
GREEAAAK
YAAA!

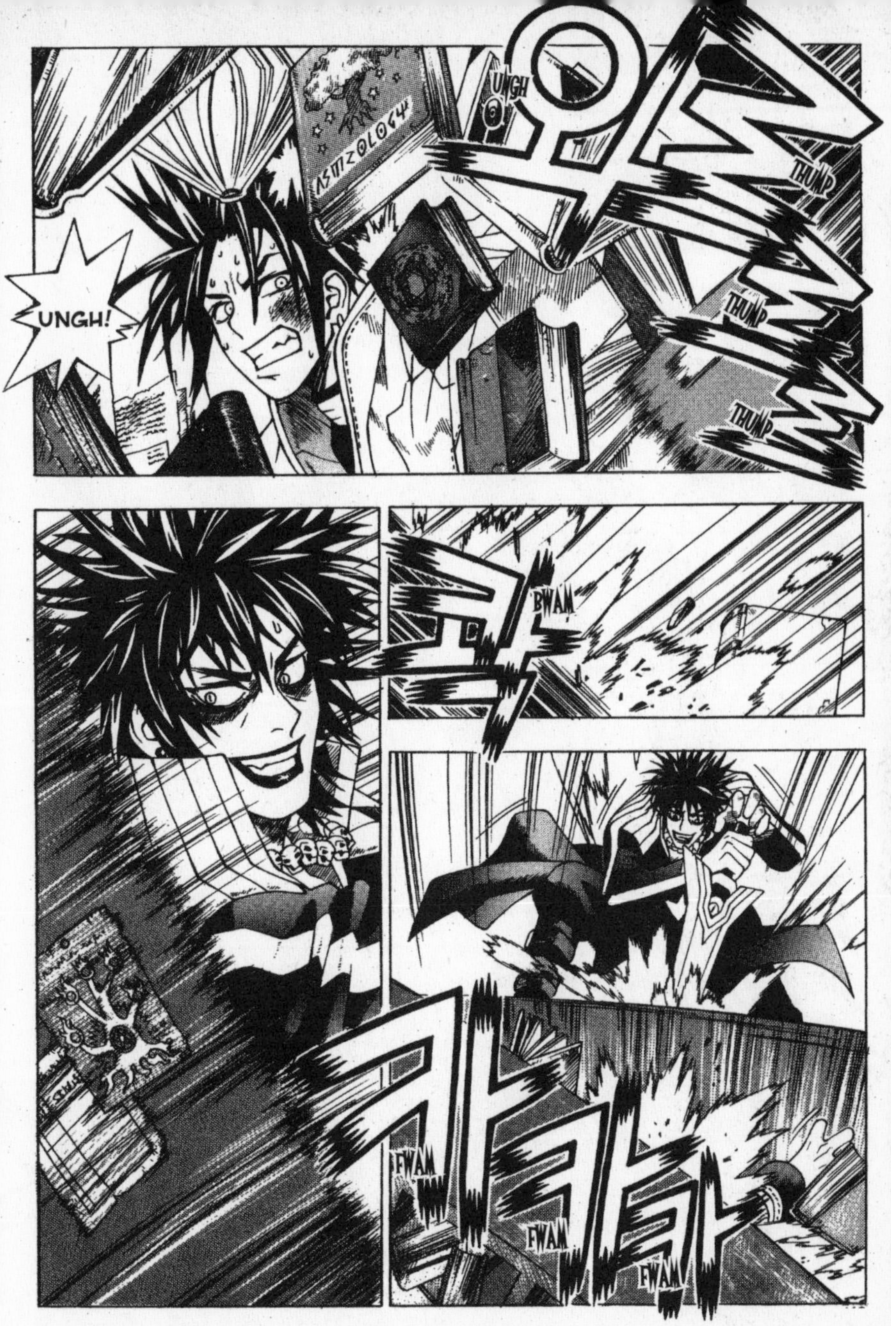
UNGH!
UNGH
THUMP
THUMP
THUMP
BWAM
FWAM
FWAM
FWAM

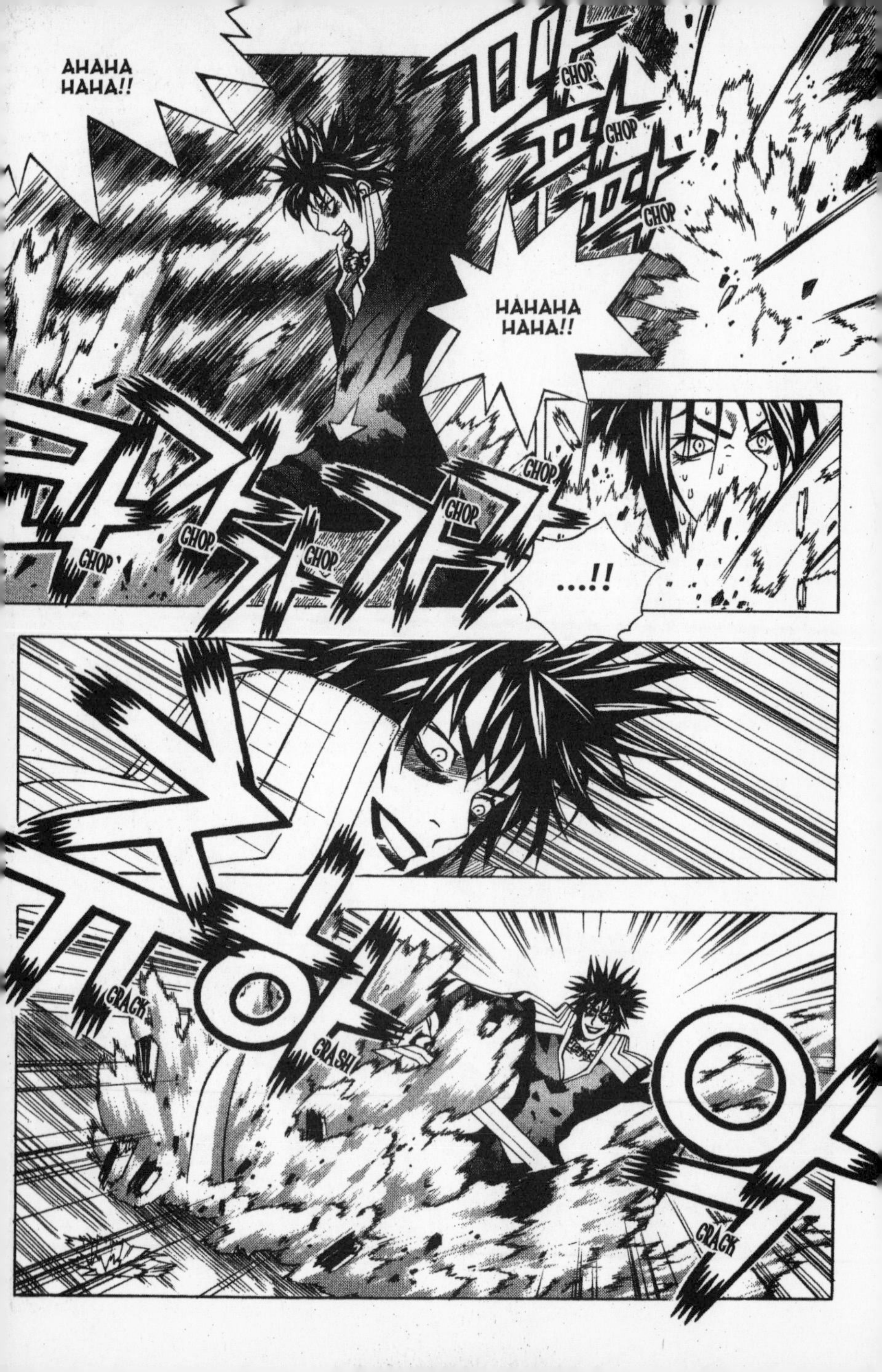
AHAHA HAHA!!
CHOP
CHOP
CHOP
HAHAHA HAHA!!
CHOP
CHOP
CHOP
CHOP
CHOP
...!!
CRACK
CRASH
CRACK

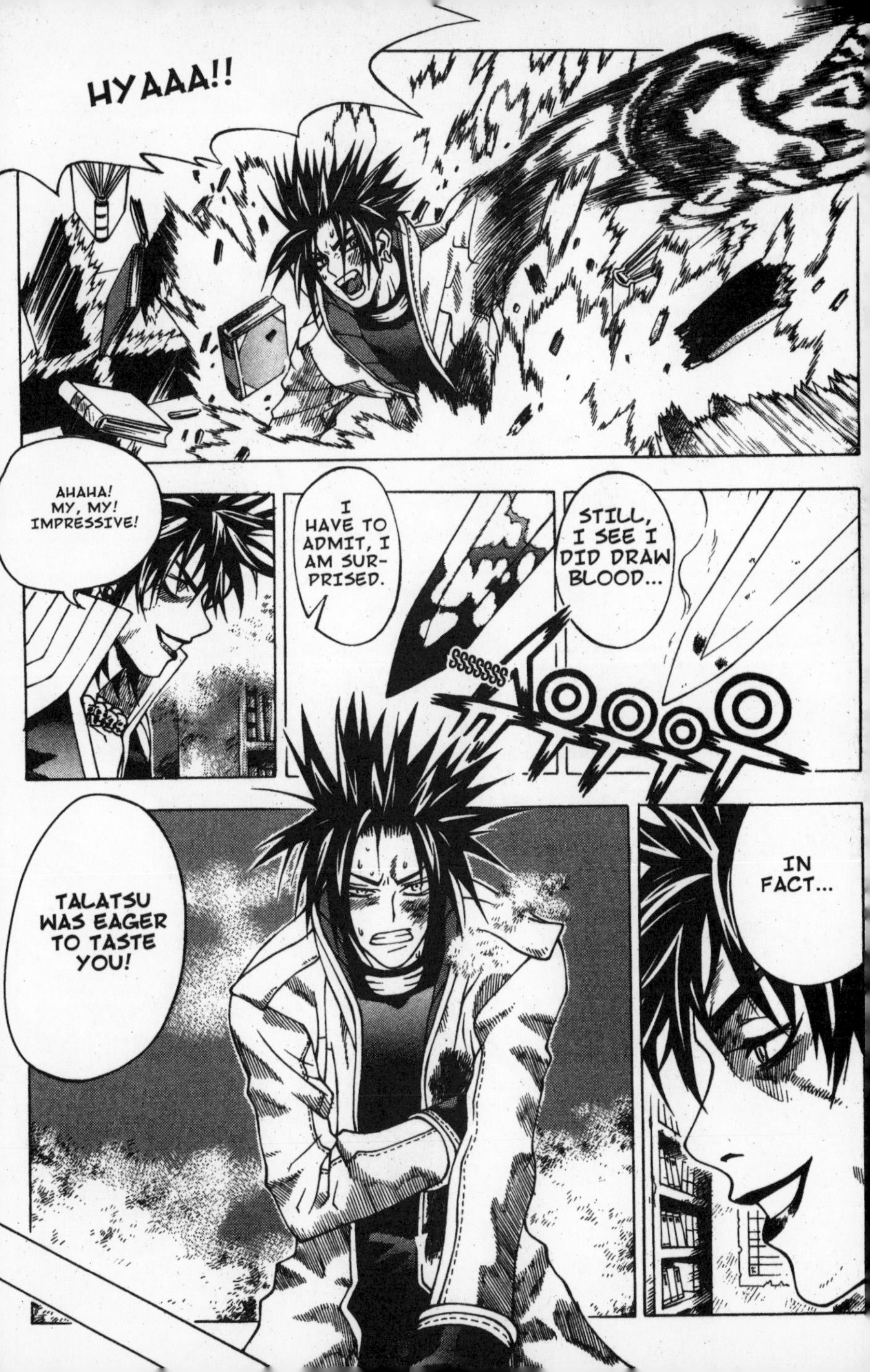
HYAAA!!
AHAHA! MY, MY! IMPRESSIVE!
I HAVE TO ADMIT, I AM SURPRISED.
STILL, I SEE I DID DRAW BLOOD...
SSSSSSS
TALATSU WAS EAGER TO TASTE YOU!
IN FACT...

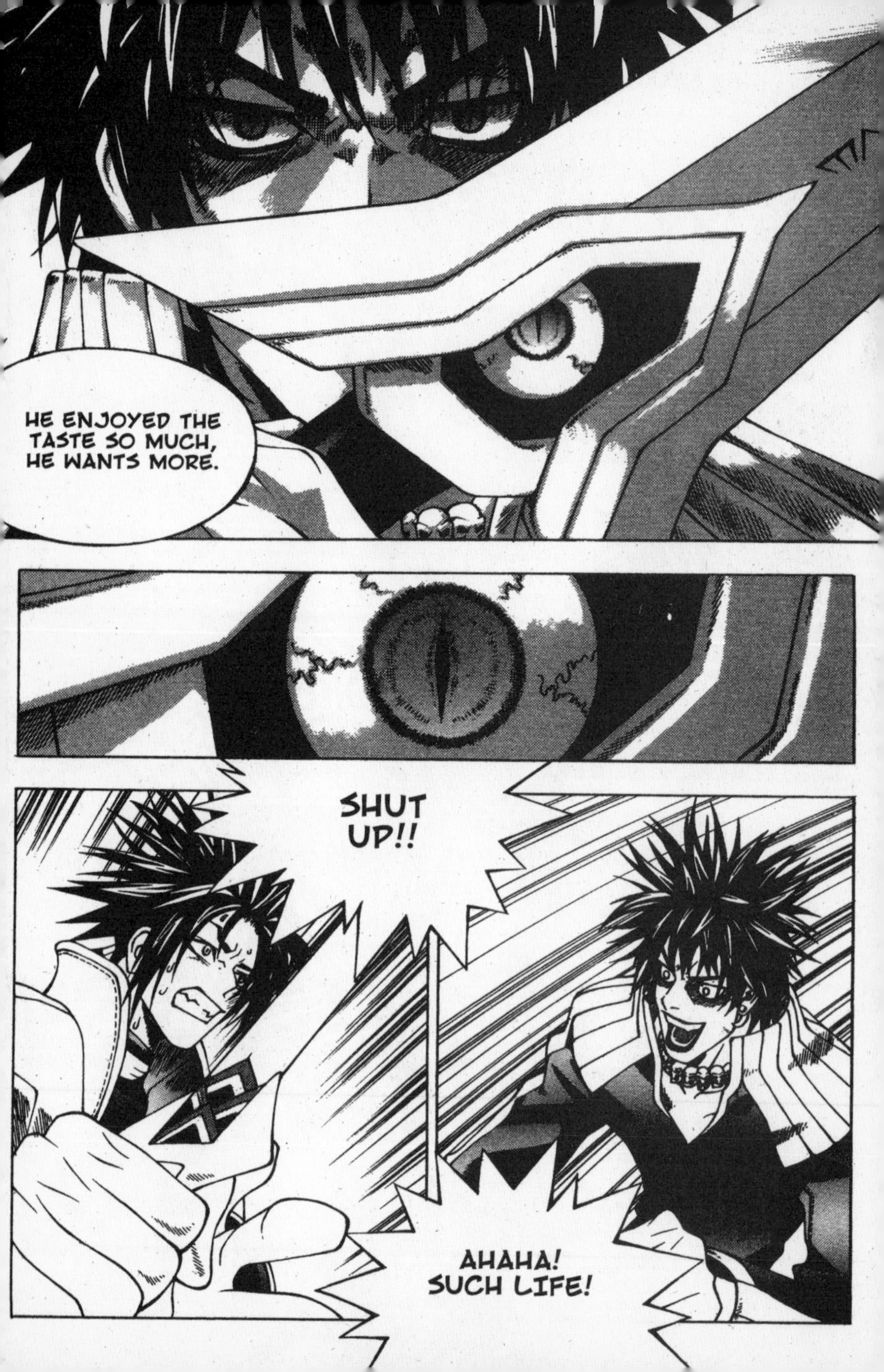
HE ENJOYED THE TASTE SO MUCH, HE WANTS MORE.
SHUT UP!!
AHAHA! SUCH LIFE!

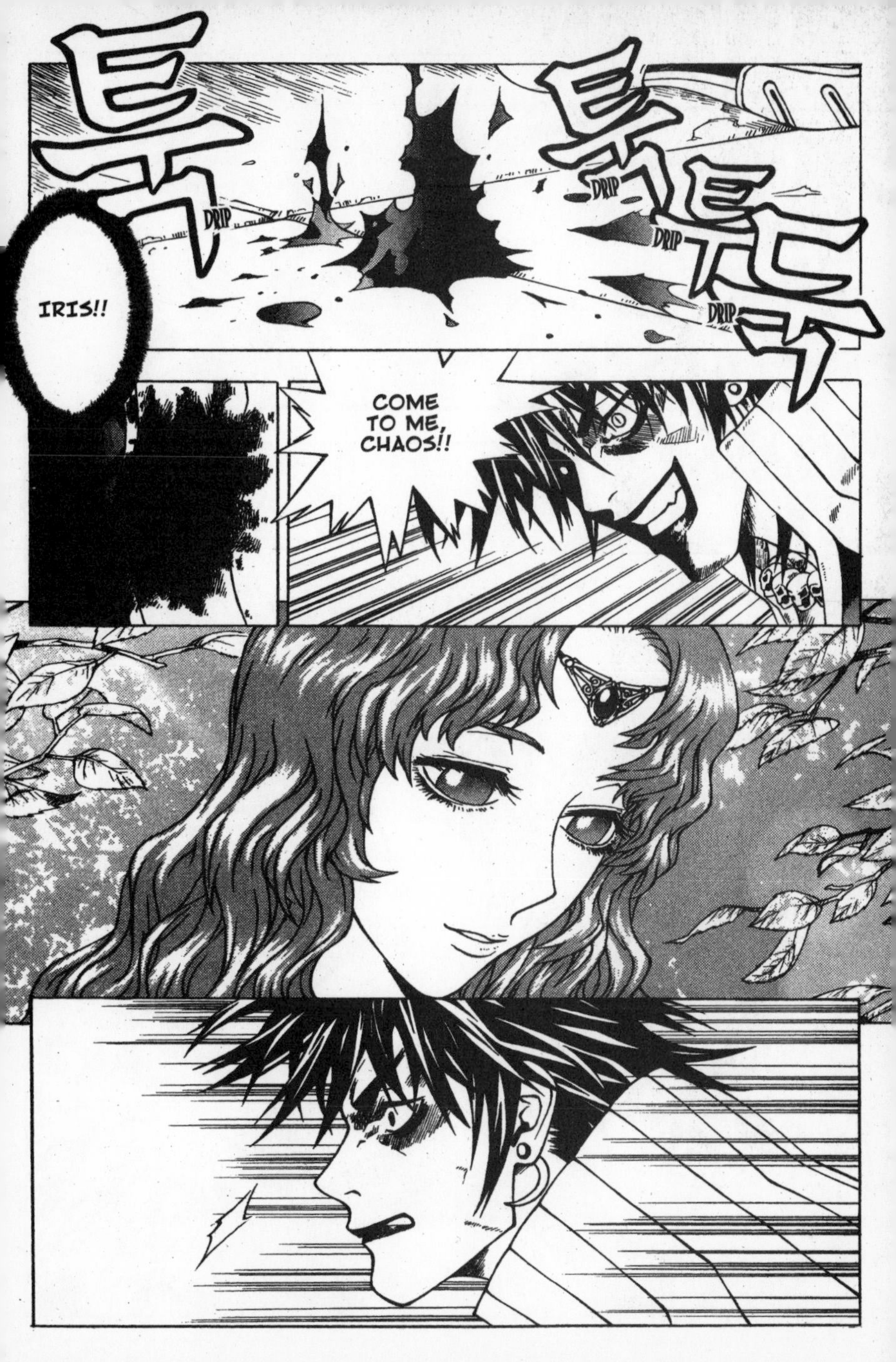

툭
DRIP
툭
DRIP
툭
DRIP
DRIP
IRIS!!
COME TO ME, CHAOS!!

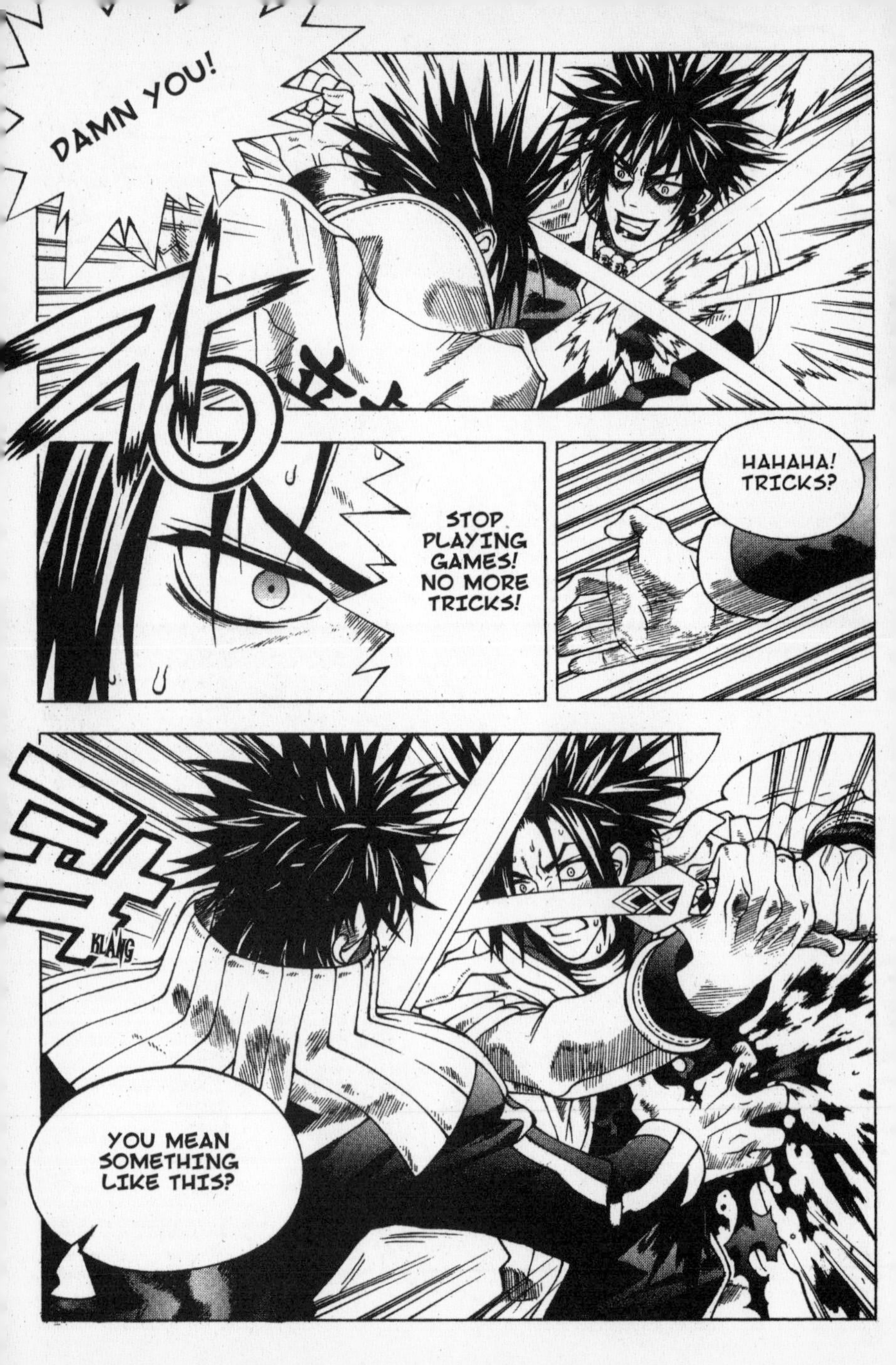
DAMN YOU!
STOP PLAYING GAMES! NO MORE TRICKS!
HAHAHA! TRICKS?
KLANG
YOU MEAN SOMETHING LIKE THIS?

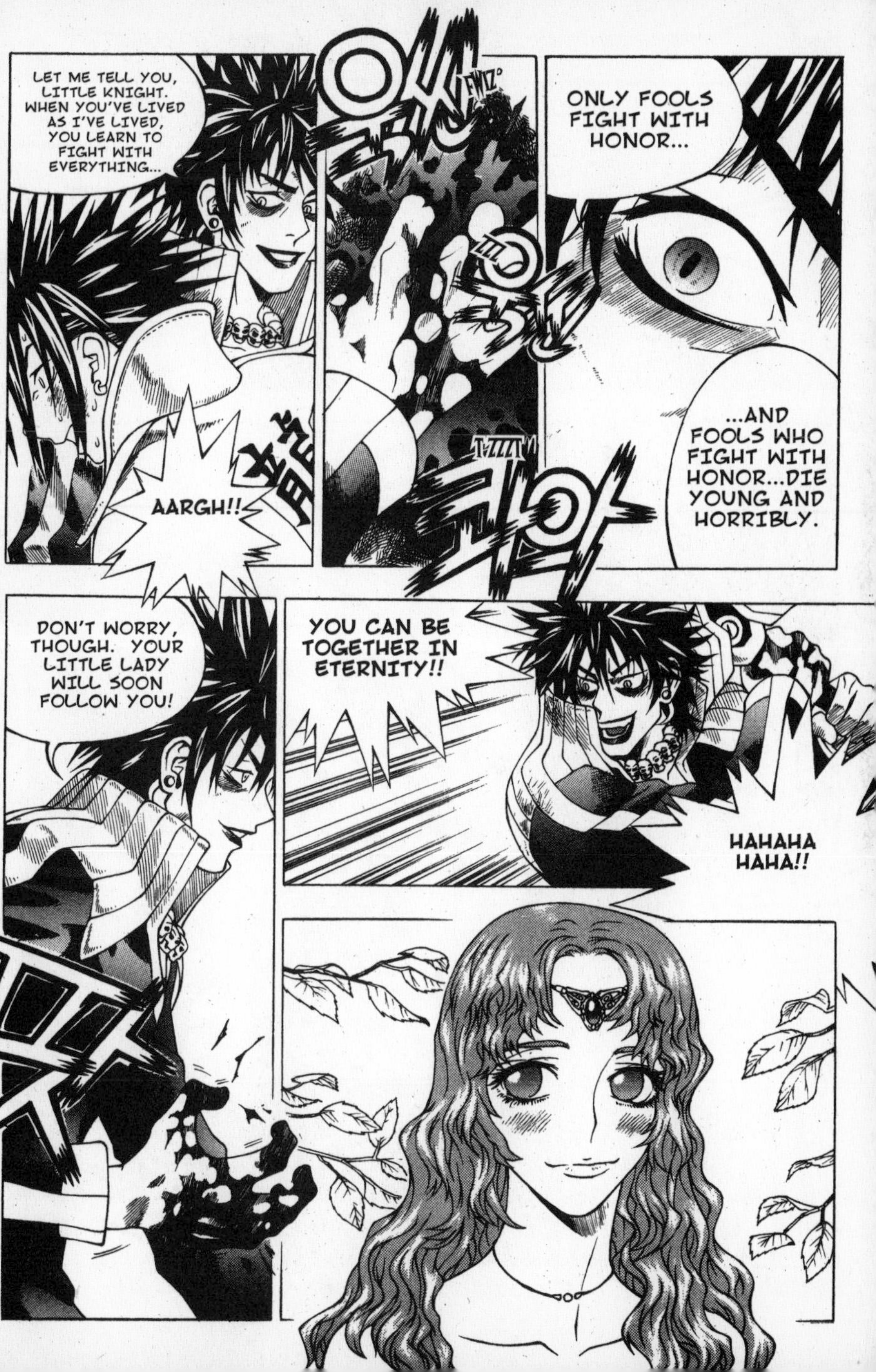
LET ME TELL YOU, LITTLE KNIGHT. WHEN YOU'VE LIVED AS I'VE LIVED, YOU LEARN TO FIGHT WITH EVERYTHING...
AARGH!!
FWIZ
T-ZZZT
ONLY FOOLS FIGHT WITH HONOR...
...AND FOOLS WHO FIGHT WITH HONOR...DIE YOUNG AND HORRIBLY.
DON'T WORRY, THOUGH. YOUR LITTLE LADY WILL SOON FOLLOW YOU!
YOU CAN BE TOGETHER IN ETERNITY!!
HAHAHA HAHA!!

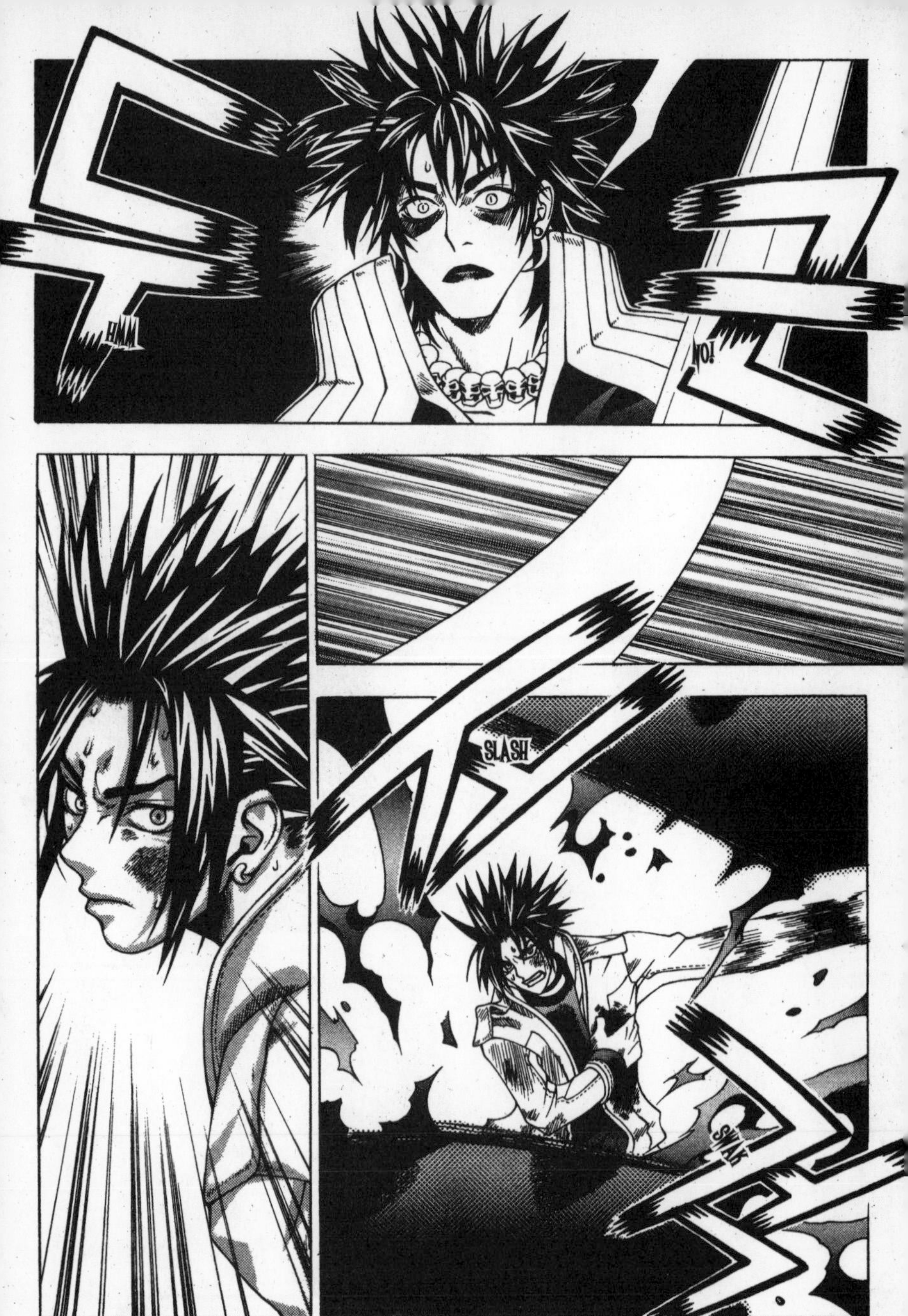
HMM
NO!
SLASH
SWAK

TO BE CONTINUED...

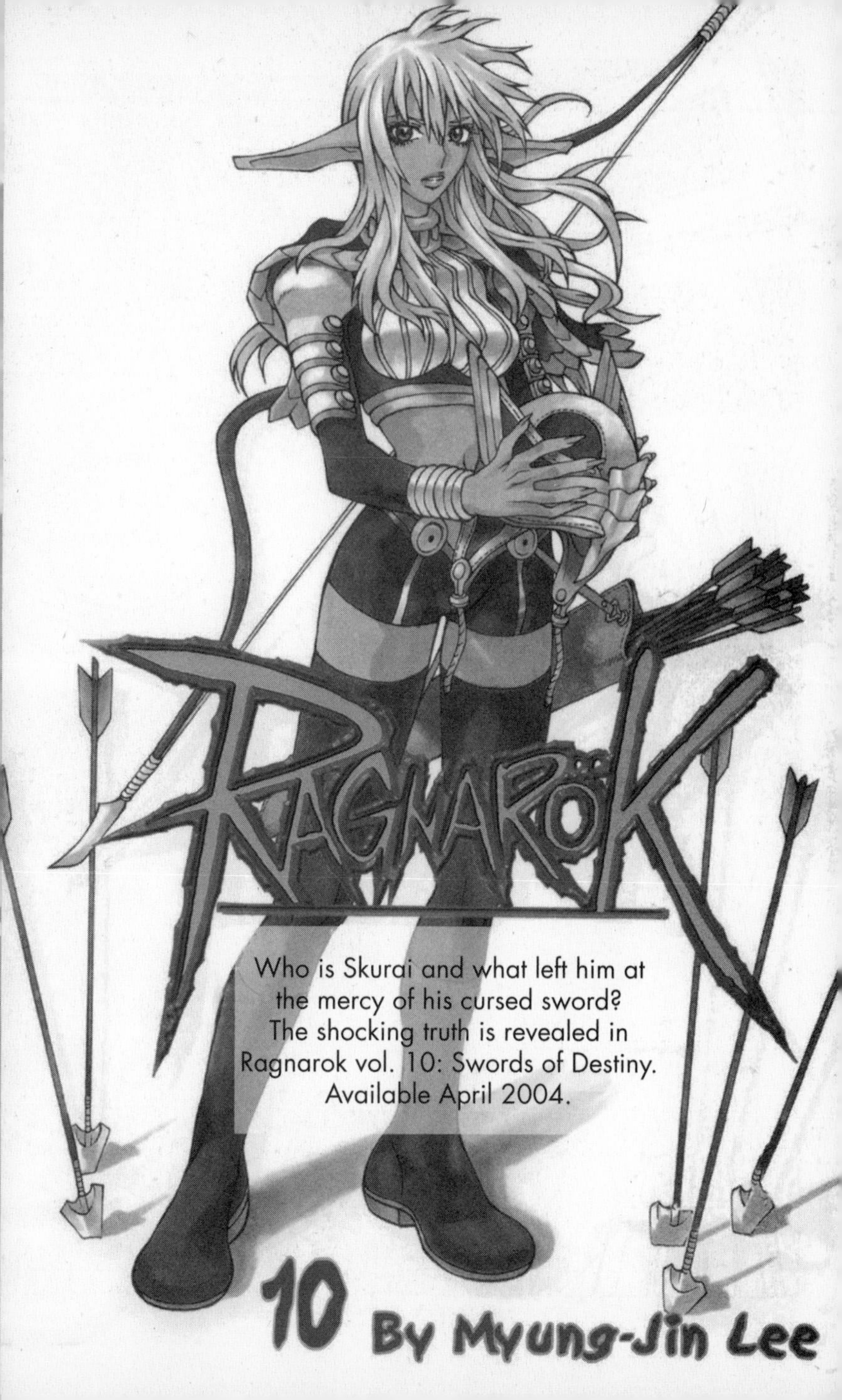
RAGNAROK
Who is Skurai and what left him at the mercy of his cursed sword? The shocking truth is revealed in Ragnarok vol. 10: Swords of Destiny. Available April 2004.
10 By Myung-Jin Lee

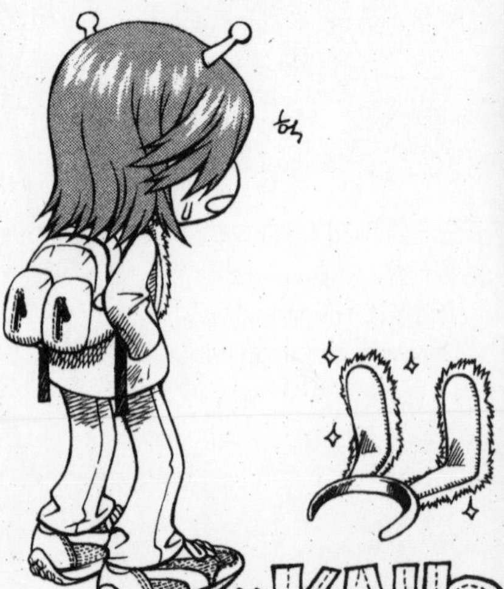
헉

KAHO

HTTP://RAGNAROK.CO.KR
HTTP://theRagnarok.Com

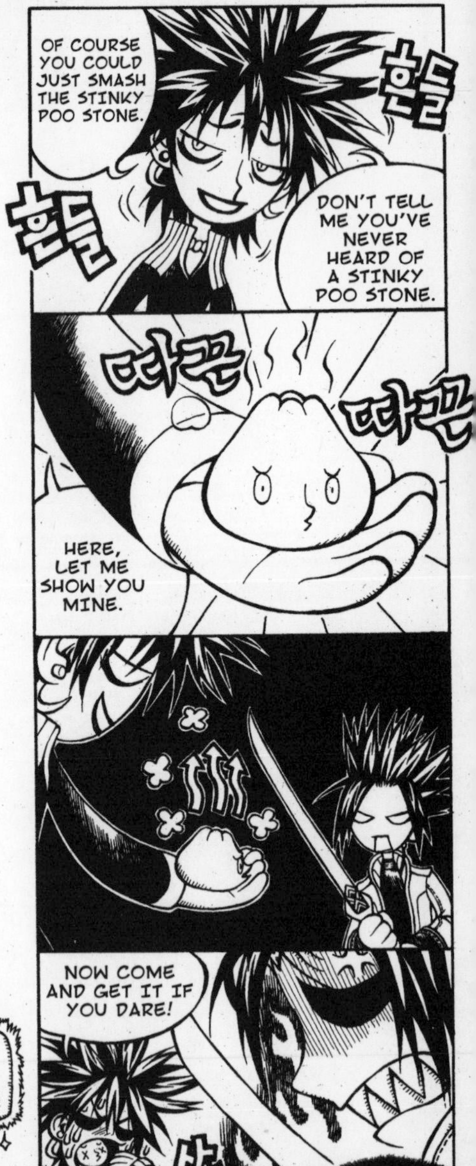
OF COURSE YOU COULD JUST SMASH THE STINKY POO STONE.
흔들
흔들
DON'T TELL ME YOU'VE NEVER HEARD OF A STINKY POO STONE.
따끈
따끈
HERE, LET ME SHOW YOU MINE.
NOW COME AND GET IT IF YOU DARE!
싹
EWWW!

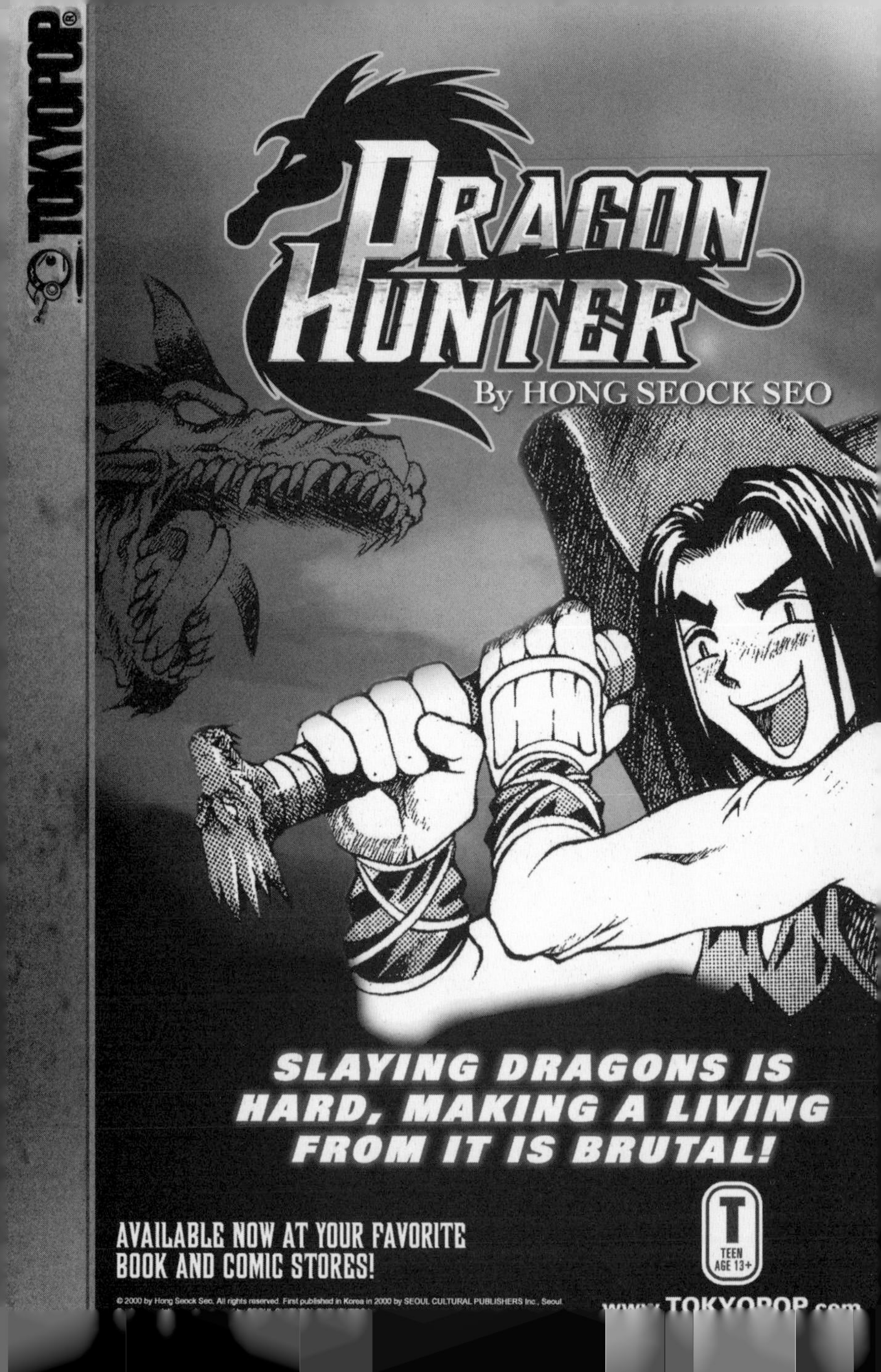
TOKYOPOP
DRAGON HUNTER
By HONG SEOCK SEO
SLAYING DRAGONS IS HARD, MAKING A LIVING FROM IT IS BRUTAL!
AVAILABLE NOW AT YOUR FAVORITE BOOK AND COMIC STORES!
T
TEEN AGE 13+
© 2000 by Hong Seock Seo. All rights reserved. First published in Korea in 2000 by SEOUL CULTURAL PUBLISHERS Inc., Seoul.
www.TOKYOPOP.com

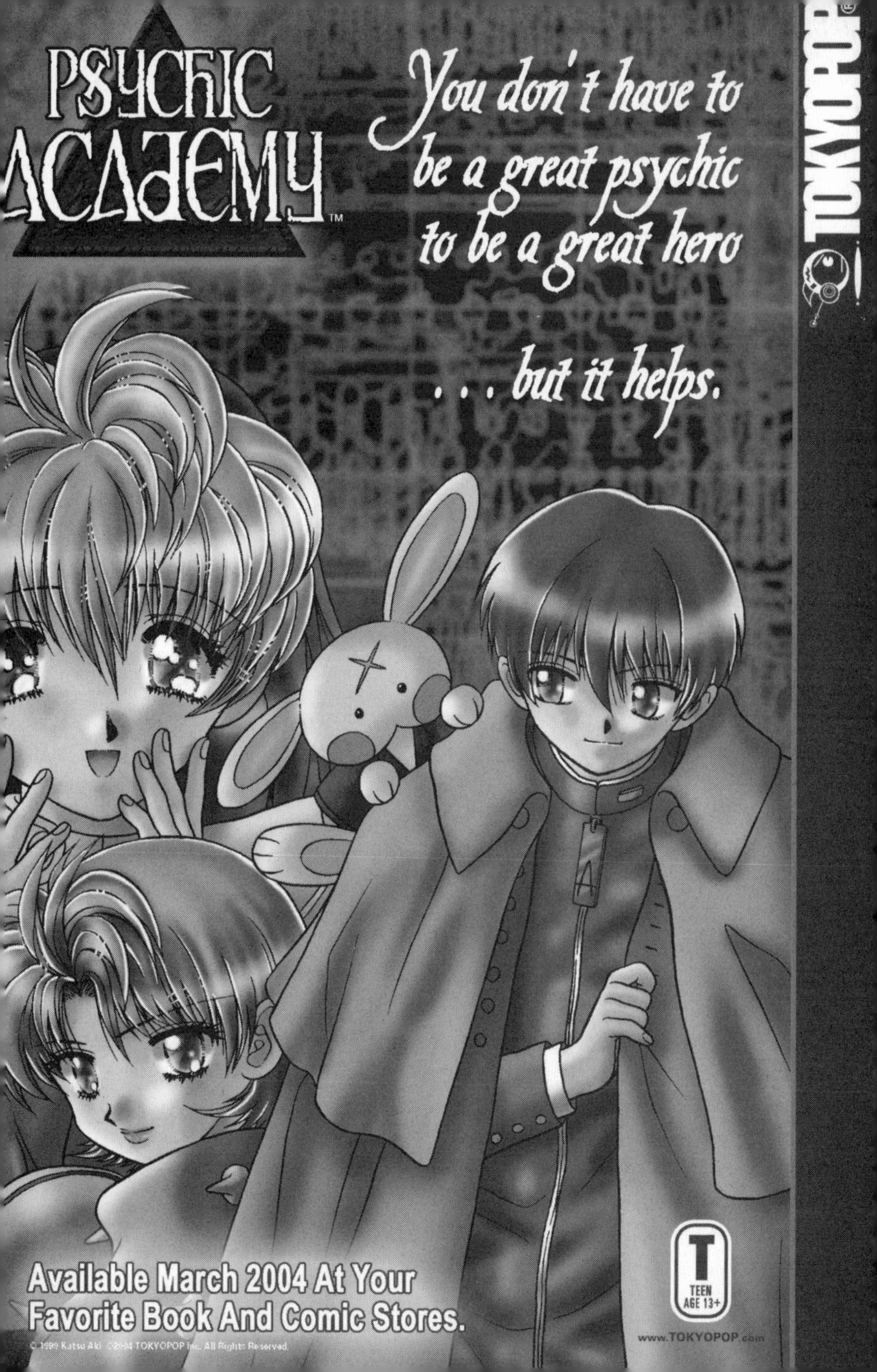
PSYCHIC ACADEMY™
You don't have to be a great psychic to be a great hero
. . . but it helps.
TOKYOPOP®
Available March 2004 At Your Favorite Book And Comic Stores.
T TEEN AGE 13+
www.TOKYOPOP.com
© 1999 Katsu Aki ©2004 TOKYOPOP Inc. All Rights Reserved.

MANGA

.HACK//LEGEND OF THE TWILIGHT
@LARGE
A.I. LOVE YOU February 2004
AI YORI AOSHI
ANGELIC LAYER
BABY BIRTH
BATTLE ROYALE
BATTLE VIXENS April 2004
BIRTH May 2004
BRAIN POWERED
BRIGADOON
B'TX
CARDCAPTOR SAKURA
CARDCAPTOR SAKURA: MASTER OF THE CLOW
CARDCAPTOR SAKURA: BOXED SET COLLECTION 1
CARDCAPTOR SAKURA: BOXED SET COLLECTION 2
   March 2004
CHOBITS
CHRONICLES OF THE CURSED SWORD
CLAMP SCHOOL DETECTIVES
CLOVER
COMIC PARTY June 2004
CONFIDENTIAL CONFESSIONS
CORRECTOR YUI
COWBOY BEBOP: BOXED SET THE COMPLETE
   COLLECTION
CRESCENT MOON May 2004
CREST OF THE STARS June 2004
CYBORG 009
DEMON DIARY
DIGIMON
DIGIMON SERIES 3 April 2004
DIGIMON ZERO TWO February 2004
DNANGEL April 2004
DOLL May 2004
DRAGON HUNTER
DRAGON KNIGHTS
DUKLYON: CLAMP SCHOOL DEFENDERS
DV June 2004
ERICA SAKURAZAWA
FAERIES' LANDING
FAKE
FLCL
FORBIDDEN DANCE
FRUITS BASKET February 2004
G GUNDAM
GATEKEEPERS
GETBACKERS February 2004
GHOST! March 2004
GIRL GOT GAME
GRAVITATION
GTO

GUNDAM WING
GUNDAM WING: BATTLEFIELD OF PACIFISTS
GUNDAM WING: ENDLESS WALTZ
GUNDAM WING: THE LAST OUTPOST
HAPPY MANIA
HARLEM BEAT
I.N.V.U.
INITIAL D
ISLAND
JING: KING OF BANDITS
JULINE
JUROR 13 March 2004
KARE KANO
KILL ME, KISS ME February 2004
KINDAICHI CASE FILES, THE
KING OF HELL
KODOCHA: SANA'S STAGE
LAMENT OF THE LAMB May 2004
LES BIJOUX February 2004
LIZZIE MCGUIRE
LOVE HINA
LUPIN III
LUPIN III SERIES 2
MAGIC KNIGHT RAYEARTH I
MAGIC KNIGHT RAYEARTH II February 2004
MAHOROMATIC: AUTOMATIC MAIDEN May 2004
MAN OF MANY FACES
MARMALADE BOY
MARS
METEOR METHUSELA June 2004
METROID June 2004
MINK April 2004
MIRACLE GIRLS
MIYUKI-CHAN IN WONDERLAND
MODEL May 2004
NELLY MUSIC MANGA April 2004
ONE April 2004
PARADISE KISS
PARASYTE
PEACH GIRL
PEACH GIRL CHANGE OF HEART
PEACH GIRL RELAUNCH BOX SET
PET SHOP OF HORRORS
PITA-TEN
PLANET LADDER February 2004
PLANETES
PRIEST
PRINCESS AI April 2004
PSYCHIC ACADEMY March 2004
RAGNAROK
RAGNAROK: BOXED SET COLLECTION 1
RAVE MASTER
RAVE MASTER: BOXED SET March 2004

ALSO AVAILABLE FROM  TOKYOPOP®

REALITY CHECK
REBIRTH
REBOUND
REMOTE June 2004
RISING STARS OF MANGA December 2003
SABER MARIONETTE J
SAILOR MOON
SAINT TAIL
SAIYUKI
SAMURAI DEEPER KYO
SAMURAI GIRL REAL BOUT HIGH SCHOOL
SCRYED
SGT. FROG March 2004
SHAOLIN SISTERS
SHIRAHIME-SYO: SNOW GODDESS TALES December 2004
SHUTTERBOX
SNOW DROP
SOKORA REFUGEES May 2004
SORCEROR HUNTERS
SUIKODEN May 2004
SUKI February 2004
THE CANDIDATE FOR GODDESS April 2004
THE DEMON ORORON April 2004
THE LEGEND OF CHUN HYANG
THE SKULL MAN
THE VISION OF ESCAFLOWNE
TOKYO MEW MEW
TREASURE CHESS March 2004
UNDER THE GLASS MOON
VAMPIRE GAME
WILD ACT
WISH
WORLD OF HARTZ
X-DAY
ZODIAC P.I.

NOVELS
KARMA CLUB APRIL 2004
SAILOR MOON

ART BOOKS
CARDCAPTOR SAKURA
MAGIC KNIGHT RAYEARTH
PEACH GIRL ART BOOK April 2004

ANIME GUIDES
COWBOY BEBOP ANIME GUIDES
GUNDAM TECHNICAL MANUALS
SAILOR MOON SCOUT GUIDES

CINE-MANGA™
CARDCAPTORS
FAIRLY ODD PARENTS MARCH 2004
FINDING NEMO
G.I. JOE SPY TROOPS
JACKIE CHAN ADVENTURES
KIM POSSIBLE
LIZZIE MCGUIRE
POWER RANGERS: NINJA STORM
SPONGEBOB SQUAREPANTS
SPY KIDS
SPY KIDS 3-D March 2004
THE ADVENTURES OF JIMMY NEUTRON: BOY GENIUS
TRANSFORMERS: ARMADA
TRANSFORMERS: ENERGON May 2004

TOKYOPOP KIDS
STRAY SHEEP

**For more
information visit
www.TOKYOPOP.com**

10103